INTRODUCTION TO SEMANTICS

INTRODUCTION TO SEMANTICS

by

Adam Schaff

Translated from Polish by
OLGIERD WOJTASIEWICZ

A Pergamon Press Book

THE MACMILLAN COMPANY
NEW YORK

PERGAMON PRESS INC.
122 *East 55th Street, New York 22, N.Y.*
1404 New York Avenue, N. W., Washington 5, D. C.

PERGAMON PRESS LTD.
Headington Hill, Oxford.
4 & 5 *Fitzroy Square, London W.* 1.

PERGAMON PRESS S.A.R.L.
24, *Rue des Ecoles, Paris* V^e.

PERGAMON PRESS G. m. b. H.
Kaiserstrasse 75, *Frankfurt am Main.*

Library of Congress Card Number 61–18879

Printed in Poland
by Wrocławska Drukarnia Naukowa

CONTENTS

THE AUTHOR'S FOREWORD

On submitting this book to the readers I wish to thank all those who have helped me to bring it to its present form.

First of all, I wish to thank Professor Tadeusz Kotarbiński, who had been kind enough to read the manuscript. His profound and penetrating criticism helped me to add precision to many passages of this book.

I also thank the translator Dr Olgierd Wojtasiewicz and Mr George Bidwell who checked the translation.

Quotations from non-English-language books are either given in existing English version, if available, or translated into English. In three cases only they are given in the original version. This refers to quotations from Husserl, Jaspers, and Vossler, and is due to the specific character of these texts.

A. S.

PREFACE

Authors' prefaces tend to be mere conventions, tributes paid to usage. In my case, however, I do really feel a need to explain to the reader my intentions before he starts to read this book. Hence I regard this Preface not as an appendix to, but as a component part of, my work.

The point is that the subject matter of my interests is extremely complicated and very vast. I lack, unfortunately, such competence and erudition as would be necessary adequately to treat all aspects of that subject matter; indeed, it is to be feared that no individual can master that subject matter in a completely satisfactory degree. Consequently, here too, as in many other cases, a conscious restriction of research interests should be the token of mastery. I do not know whether I can satisfy that requirement properly, but I should like to explain what tasks I have set myself, and why. It is up to the reader to decide whether, and to what extent, I have achieved them.

First of all, I wish to explain, both to myself and to others, what we mean by semantics. As a discipline, semantics is now so intricate, and its name so ambiguous, that semantic analysis must be applied to the very term "semantics", if deplorable misunderstandings and errors of logic are to be avoided.

Such is the objective aspect, not to mention the attitude towards semantics adopted in Marxist literature. And yet the present author would like to approach and handle the issue of semantics from the Marxist point of view, both in the sense of making Marxist philosophy assimilate as far as possible the real research problems of semantics, and of subjecting to criticism any possible philosophical abuses of such problems.

In its present form of a logical and philosophical theory, semantics is a comparatively young discipline. Setting aside the embryonic form of linguistic semantics, no such discipline existed at the time of Marx and Engels. It was already taking shape in Lenin's time, but its philosophical implications were revealed only towards the end of his life, when he was otherwise absorbed. Even an incurable "quotation maniac" could find no authoritative Marxist statement on this issue except for a paragraph in Stalin's *Marxism and the Problems of Linguistics* which rightly emphasized the importance of linguistic semantics, and no less rightly warned against abusing it. But that is far from adequate in view of the enormous scope of the problems involved.

In recent years Marxist literature has, of course, included critical publications on semantics, but it can be definitely affirmed that they were not creditable performances.

The brief formulations of the problem in Marxist encyclopaedias, philosophical dictionaries, etc., which are available to this day, show that semantics was understood exclusively as the idealistic semantic philosophy, and that the latter was in turn identified with Stuart Chase's somewhat peculiar interpretation offered in his book *The Tyranny of Words* (New York 1938). The credit for having introduced Chase into Marxist literature belongs, it seems, to B. Bykhovsky[1]. Chase has since then stereotypically haunted all Marxist publications in which the term "semantics" has appeared.

It is characteristic that it is not only Marxist publications which have interpreted semantics as a pseudo-science devised to blur class struggle, a theory implying that a mere removal of certain terms (such as "capitalism", "socialism", etc.) would eliminate the corresponding social issues. A similar view is expressed in anti-Communist propaganda. In his *1984*, Orwell has a scene in which Syme, the editor of a dictionary of "Newspeak", explains to Winston that a reduction of the stock of concepts

1 "Маразм современной буржуазной философии" [Marasm in Contemporary Bourgeois Philosophy], in *Большевик*, 1947, №. 16.

can eliminate dangerous social issues which will become inconceivable after an appropriate reform of vocabulary.

I do not mean that there is absolutely no justification for ascribing all these absurd ideas to semantics. Such an attitude is supported by the opinions of circles close to Korzybski, as will be discussed later on in this book. But is that semantics "in general"? Is it fair to identify such opinions integrally with semantics and thereby deny to it all scientific significance?

I see my first task in answering these questions. Both the various fields concerned with semantics, and the various meanings of the term must be reviewed. A *sui generis* semantic analysis will be devoted to explaining the ambiguities of the term itself. Thus an inquiry must be made into what is the significance and the subject matter of semantics as a branch of linguistics; what is the difference between linguistic semantics and semantics connected with logic, semantics born of the specific needs of the latter discipline which has shown that language is not only an instrument but also an object of research; what is semantics as the specific philosophical trend which sees in language treated as a convention *the sole* subject matter of research (so-called semantic philosophy); and finally, what is semantics in the sense of so-called general semantics which – for all its peculiarities – approaches the issue rather from the social and sociological point of view.

Of course, my object is not only to give a passionless semantic analysis, to extricate and to present all the meanings concealed by the single term "semantics". I shall also endeavour to show the actual spheres of interest of semantics and to clarify the real scientific problems it formulates. Such an approach does not, obviously, exclude a critical appraisal. Yet, in my opinion, pride of place should go to a clear understanding as to what are the new and philosophically significant issues raised by semantics.

I believe the emphasis on the *philosophical* significance of these issues to be extremely important in view of the wide diapason of the problems covered by the term "semantics". As already indicated, such problems include both specifically linguistic matters and specifically logical issues, connected with the technique of logical calculus. Such problems will be dealt with in this book only from the point of view of their philosophical implications, since we are concerned with the philosophical aspect of semantics and the philosophical problems of that discipline. Thus, the problems will be treated broadly, and no absolute importance will be ascribed to partial, and consequently one-sided, analyses, as is sometimes done by exponents of formal logic: objections against such a procedure are raised even by people of the same "profession", such as Russell and Wittgenstein. In this connection, the very title of the present work, *Introduction to Semantics*, so fondly used by those semanticists who represent formal logic, takes on a deliberately provocative tone.

Starting from these assumptions, and basing myself on the results of the analysis to be made in the first part of the book, I shall endeavour to expose a number of main problems and to solve them effectively in the light of Marxist philosophy. That is my second task, to be dealt with in the second part of the book.

Such is my programme and such are my intentions. There is a strong impulse to point out changes in the method of presenting and criticizing non-Marxist trends in philosophy, by Marxists, and to analyse the sociological foundations of the distortions revealed in that respect in Marxist literature. Yet perhaps sufficient has been written on that point in Poland, enough postulates have been formulated, maybe, and declarations made. Moreover, to promise too much at the outset involves the risk of disappointing the reader. Consequently, such matters are to be handled in a different way – simply by giving effect, as far as my abilities and competences permit, to the notion of a *scientific* analysis of the various trends and issues.

PART ONE

RESEARCH PROBLEMS OF SEMANTICS

Chapter One

LINGUISTICS

Semantics (semasiology) is a branch of linguistics. The questions which are of particular interest in this connection are – with what is that branch of linguistics concerned, and in what does it see the distinction between itself and the semantic problems found in contemporary logic[1].

To begin with the term itself: it comes from the eminent French linguist Bréal[2] and is genetically connected with linguistics. In the late 19th century Michel Bréal published his *Essai de sémantique. Science des significations*, in which he writes:

"My intention was to give a general outline, to sketch a general division and, as it were, a provisional plan of a domain that has not been studied so far and which should be the result of work for many generations of linguists. The reader is therefore requested to consider this book a simple introduction to the science which I propose to call semantics".

In a footnote, Bréal explains the meaning of the term "semantics": "Σημαντική τὲχνη – the science of meanings, from the word σημαινω – 'denote', as opposed to phonetics, the science of speech sounds"[3].

---

[1] An outline of the history of semasiology and the varying aspects of its interests can be found in such works as: E. Cassirer, *Philosophie der symbolischen Formen*, Pt. I: "Die Sprache" Berlin 1923; H. Kronasser, *Handbuch der Semasiologie*, Heidelberg 1952; S. Ullman, *The Principles of Semantics*, Oxford 1957; В. А. Звегинцев, *Семасиология* [Semasiology], Москва 1957.

[2] Kronasser (op. cit., p. 29), who denies that, comes out against the generally adopted opinion.

[3] M. Bréal, *Essai de sémantique. Science des significations*, Paris 1904 p. 8.

What did Bréal imply by that term, and how in general was the new discipline defined by the linguists?

Bréal defined the subject matter of semantics by detailing appropriate research which ought to be undertaken.

"In that second part we propose to investigate how it happens that words, once created and endowed with a certain meaning, extend that meaning or contract it, transfer it from one group of notions on to another, raise its value or lower it, in a word — bring about changes. It is this second part that constitutes semantics, i.e. science of meaning"[4].

This shows that, for Bréal, semantics was the science the subject matter of which was study of the cause and structure of the processes of *changes in meanings* of words: expansion and contraction of meanings, transfer of meanings, elevation and degradation of their value, etc.

Such a delineation of semantics as a branch of linguistics is maintained to this day, for all the differences between the various schools in linguistics. Such degree of uniformity is not confined to the definition of semantics alone[5]. Not all authors give such a definition; some of them approach the issue from a different point of view as regards general classification (e.g., de Saussure, who develops the concept of semiology as the science which studies the functioning of signs in society, and treats linguistics as a branch of such a general science of signs), but all schools of linguistics engage in the study of the meanings of words and their changes. Thus all of them, in one way or another, engage in semantics as understood by Bréal.

For instance, Darmesteter conceives of the science of the meaning of words, i.e. semantics, as a branch of the history of psychology, but appreciates its responsibilities in the investi-

---

[4] Ibid., p. 99.

[5] Cf. A. W. Read, "An Account of the Word 'Semantics'", in *Word*, 1948, No. 4, pp. 78–97.

gation of the history of meanings and the causes of their changes[6]. Vendryes disagrees with Darmesteter and denies that the general laws of the evolution of meanings of words should be inherent in words themselves[7]. He too, however, engages in the traditional problems of linguistic semantics, and even postulates the foundation of general semantics, to be based on data concerning changes in meanings in all languages[8]. In Polish linguistic literature, similar issues are dealt with by Zenon Klemensiewicz[9]. In fact, the majority of works on general linguistics treat semantic problems as being their focal problems. I shall later endeavour to analyse in greater detail what the general programme of linguistics semantics stands for. But at this point I should like to dwell on certain general formulations.

The fact that the general definition given in a new textbook based on Marxist principles does not in any degree deviate from the old definition as formulated by Bréal, shows that the traditional meaning of semantics has already stabilized. *An Introduction to Linguistics* by L. Bulakhovsky begins with the definition of semantics as one of the important branches of linguistics:

"Semantics (semasiology) as a *branch of linguistics is concerned with the meaning and the changes in meaning of words and expressions*"[10].

All this is not to imply that, within that universal agreement on general definition, there are no differences of opinion, in some cases quite considerable, as to the essence of the problem. Neither does it mean that linguists rest content with such a general definition and direct their controversies and differences of opinion

---

[6] A. Darmesteter, *La vie des mots étudiée dans leurs significations*, Paris (without date).

[7] J. Vendryes, *Le language*, Paris 1950, pp. 228–229.

[8] Ibid., pp. 240–241.

[9] Z. Klemensiewicz, *Język polski* [The Polish Language], Lwów-Warszawa 1937 pp. 10–14, 22–24, et passim.

[10] Л. А. Булаховский, *Введение в языкознание* [An Introduction to Linguistics], Москва 1953, Pt. 2, p. 7.

to the field of special issues concerning the essence of meaning, the causes of changes in meanings, and concrete forms of such changes.

For instance, the attitude of Witold Doroszewski has obvious philosophical implications. For him, at the root of semantic analysis lies the philosophical issue of the relationship between the general and the particular, the starting point being the analysis of the function of the copula "is". Doroszewski analyses the problem of meaning as closely linked with denotation. It is in that question that he sees the focal point of semantics.

"The potential conflict inherent in every word, and finding expression in the fact that the use of every word is an individual embodiment of a general concept, is the focal point of semantics understood as a part of linguistics – that is as a science of the meanings of words and the history of such meanings"[11].

According to Doroszewski, the history of meaning consists in the growth of a "gap" between the sign and its designatum, and the cause of changes in meanings lies in the conflict between the general character of the sign and the need for its being made to rise to the occasion whenever it is concretely embodied.

The attitude of Doroszewski, a representative of linguistic semantics, is of interest not only because he draws concrete conclusions from the general definition of semantics, but also because of his reflections on the relationship between semantics as pursued by linguists, and semantics as pursued by logicians. By touching here upon that issue, I anticipate further analysis. This does not advance the clarity of exposition, but is, unfortunately, often inevitable. In this case, it is justified in so far as it helps us to realize better the specific traits of linguistic semantics and its research objectives.

A colloquium on semantics, attended by logicians and linguists, was held in Warsaw in 1955. The object was to narrow the gap between certain points of view, and to agree on the subject

[11] W. Doroszewski, *Z zagadnień leksykografii polskiej* [Selected Problems of Polish Lexicography], Warszawa 1954, p. 93.

matter of future research. The discussion begot Doroszewski's paper "Comments on Semantics", published in *Myśl Filozoficzna*[12]. There, he defined semantics as "the science of the meanings of words", the central issue of which is "the problem of the relationship between words and designata". Doroszewski declared himself against psychologism in the interpretation of semantics and referred to the objective history of words, as linked with the fact that a given word reflects a fragment of reality. For this reason, the linguist should approach the meanings of words from the social and historical point of view. It is in that issue that Doroszewski sees a distinction between linguistics and logical semantics.

"Not only the tools of manual labour, but also the tools of human thought — words — are subject to the laws of historical development. The history of the meanings of words is outside the area of interest of formal logic, and could not be fruitfully studied by the methods of that discipline.

"The history of language in what is its most essential content is the history of language as a social instrument of thought; it is *historical epistemology* which cannot be studied within the scope of any other discipline.

"The linguist is of necessity only marginally interested in all conventional terminology, whereas certain votaries of formal logic are inclined to investigate domains which are alien to linguistics and even to some extent in contradiction to its basic assumptions"[13].

---

[12] W. Doroszewski, "Uwagi o semantyce" [Comments on Semantics], in *Myśl Filozoficzna*, 1955, No. 3 (17).

[13] Ibid. That thesis is confirmed by the standpoint adopted by the adherents of the logical method in semantics, and expressed by them explicitly; e.g., F. R. Blake in "The Study of Language from Semantic Point of View" in *Indogermanische Forschungen*, 1938, 56, p. 242 (quoted by Звегинцев, op. cit., p. 12), says that as long as semantics engages in the study of changes in meanings of words at the various stages of their existence, it is in fact historical semantics. It is necessary to originate static semantics, which would

Thus the characteristic feature of linguistic semantics is not that it deals with meanings and relationships as between words and their designata, but that it is concerned with the history of meanings, their origins, their changes, and the laws according to which such changes occur. This focuses the specific feature of linguistic semantics.

While laying stress, in its studies, on the *historical* aspect of linguistic entities and their meanings, linguistic semantics (semasiology) does not overlook the other, *systematic*, aspect of the problem. The division into diachronic and synchronic analysis, initiated by de Saussure, is being continued by appropriate research which in its developed form becomes the theory of the semantic domain, to be found in certain linguistic schools (e.g., Jost Trier)[14].

Let us consider now what research problems arise from linguistic semantics so interpreted. Remember that, as indicated in the Preface, we are interested above all in those problems which have philosophical implications and are in one way or another dealt with by the various schools of philosophy.

Linguistics is devoted to the study, in some way or another, of language, linguistic expressions, and their meanings. When approaching relationship between linguistic expressions and the designata they denote, linguistic semantics comes up against the problem of signs. A linguist engaged in the study of semantics may not disregard the theory of signs. That theory has been, to some extent, for a long time within the sphere of linguists' interests. For example, Wilhelm von Humboldt raised the question as early as 1820, when he made a distinction between language as a reflection of reality and language as a system of signs[15].

analyse and systematize the meanings that always exist in the minds of users of language, and would study pure meanings regardless of their form and development.

14 On that point cf. Ullman, op. cit., p. 152 ff.

15 W. v. Humboldt, *Über das vergleichende Sprachstudium*", Taschenausgaben der "Philosophischen Bibliothek", 1, p. 22.

The problem of the sign often appeared subsequently also, especially in works on the philosophy and psychology of language[16]. Pride of place in that respect is held by the work of de Saussure, both in view of its linguistic character and because of its wide theoretical horizon. At the time when semiotics as a general theory of signs has acquired such importance in the literature of the subject, attention ought to be directed to the linguistic aspect of the problem. De Saussure wrote on this matter as follows:

"Thus we may found the science for the study of the life of signs against the background of social life; it would form part of social psychology, and consequently of general psychology; we shall call it semiology (from Greek σεμεῖον – 'sign'). That science would explain to us in what signs consist of and by what laws they are governed. Since it is a science which does not yet exist, we do not know what it will be like; it has, however, a reason for its existence, its place is allocated in advance. Linguistics is only a part of that general science; the laws which semiology will discover, will be applicable also to linguistics, which in turn will be linked with a domain clearly defined throughout the entirety of human affairs"[17].

De Saussure openly protested against the interpretation of his intentions in terms of individual psychology. The sign should be analysed as a social phenomenon, and moreover as such a phenomenon as does not depend on our will, whether indi-

---

[16] The following works may be cited by way of example: K. Bühler, *Sprachtheorie*, Jena 1934; E. Cassirer, *Philosophie der symbolischen Formen*, and *An Essay on Man. An Introduction to a Philosophy of Human Culture*, New York 1954; O. Jespersen, *Language, Its Nature, Development and Origin*, London 1954; A. Marty, *Untersuchungen zur Grundlegung der allgemeinen Grammatik und Sprachphilosophie*, Halle a. S. 1908; A. v. Meinong, *Über Annahmen*, Leipzig 1910; С. Л. Рубинштейн, *Основы общей психологии* [Principles of General Psychology], Chap. XI, Москва 1946; E. Sapir, *Language*, New York 1921; W. Wundt, *Völkerpsychologie*, Vols. 1 & 2, *Die Sprache*, Leipzig 1911–1912.

[17] F. de Saussure, *Cours de linguistique générale*, Paris 1949, p. 33.

vidual or social. In this way a linguist proposed to build a general theory of signs, i.e., semiology (semiotics), a matter which from a different point of view was approached by logicians and philosophers.

Linguistics as such has not developed semiology, but it has indeed developed a theory which is linked directly with linguistic problems – the theory of meaning[18].

The linguists first of all ask themselves what is meaning? Answers to that questions vary. Some of them are quoted below by way of example.

In Polish linguistic literature is found first of all a controversy between two conceptions: associationism and the opponents of associationism.

Stanisław Szober interpreted meaning as the association of a linguistic representation with an extra-linguistic one (i.e., a sound image with an image of an object or attribute).

"The meaning of a word is established by the association of its sound image with an image of some object or attribute ..."[19].

Such an interpretation led Szober to the assertion that the word becomes a *sign* of an extra-linguistic image[20], in such a way that it makes possible to include in the content of the meaning of the word not the full extra-linguistic image, but only some of its details, that is, a simplified image.

A quite different position, opposing associationism, was represented in Polish linguistic literature by Henryk Gaertner, who engaged in direct polemics with Szober[21].

---

18 Cf. G. Stern, *Meaning and Change of Meaning*, Göteborg 1931.

19 S. Szober, *Zarys językoznawstwa ogólnego* [An Outline of General Linguistics], 1., Warszawa 1924, p. 5.

20 Ibid., p. 6.

21 H. Gaertner, *Gramatyka współczesnego języka polskiego* [A Grammar of Contemporary Polish Language], Pt. 2, Lwów 1933, pp. 96 ff. A criticism of Szober's associationism is to be found in an article by M. Ossowska, "Semantyka profesora Szobera" [Professor Szober's Semantics].

I should like now to pay more attention to the interpretations of meaning by de Saussure and by Bulakhovsky. I have chosen these two authors because of the differences in their attitudes towards the issue.

With de Saussure, the concept of meaning is inseparably connected with his concepts of sign and language. The problem can, of course, only be introduced here; it will be analysed in greater detail in the second part of the book.

According to de Saussure, a linguistic sign is a psychic whole with two aspects: sound image and notion[22]. Thus the sign is a specific combination of these two elements. Following from de Saussure's analysis, that two-sided relationship between sound and notion is meaning. This is why de Saussure suggests that the term "sound image" should be replaced by the term "signifiant" (that which means), and the term "notion" by the term "signifié" (that which is the object of meaning). The sign fulfils its function only by virtue of that relationship of meaning, the members of which are connected inseparably. The breaking of that unity would result in the destruction of the sign.

But not of the sign alone. It also refers to language, which is a system of signs. What has been said here concerning the relationship of meaning which conditions the existence of the sign, is fully applicable to the relationship between thought and sound in language.

"Language can be compared to a sheet of paper: thought is its *recto* and sound its *verso*; one cannot cut the *verso* without simultaneously cutting the *recto*. Similarly, in the matter of language, one can separate neither sound from thought nor thought from sound; such separation could be achieved only by abstraction, which would lead either to pure psychology, or to pure phonology"[23].

It is interesting to observe the contrast between the views of Bulakhovsky and of de Saussure on the problem of meaning.

---

[22] F. de Saussure, op. cit., p. 99.

[23] Ibid., p. 157.

It is interesting because it not only enables us to understand what is the subject matter of linguistic semantics, but it also shows us the possibility of approaching the same issue in different ways which depend, among other things, on the individual's philosophical and methodological background. We see here two scholars who are interested in the problem of meaning from the linguistic point of view and in the light of linguistic method. And yet both of them resort to a definite philosophical and methodological background much broader in kind: de Saussure is obviously influenced by the concepts of Durkheim, and Bulakhovsky by those of Marx. Hence the difference of opinion concerning the same research problems.

Bulakhovsky opposes the association theory, which sees the essence of meaning in the association between the representation and the sound aspect of the word. The function of *meaning* is for him inseparably connected with the function of *denotation*[24]. A word above all *denotes* some real fact or phenomenon about which the individual wants to communicate something to others. And meaning is the content of the word, revealed by connections with reality. The proper meaning of a word is shaped by the history of its connections with reality[25].

Let us extract from that statement what is new in relation to the conceptions analysed above. Two points emerge in that respect: emphasis on the connection between sound image and a fragment of *reality* (understood as the world existing objectively), which appears in the function of denotation, and emphasis on the rôle of the *history* of a given word in determining its actual meaning.

To be exact, I must add that this is by no means the dominant attitude among the Soviet linguists. For instance A. I. Smirnitsky rejects the opinion which holds that meaning is connected with the relationship between sound image and the denoted fragment

---

[24] Булаховский, op. cit. pp. 12–13.

[25] Ibid., p. 13.

of reality, and understands by meaning the concept or the representation (reproductive or productive) which reflects the fragment of reality in question. Thus, for him, meaning is the intermediary link between sound and reality[26].

I must explicitly make the reservation that I confine myself here to information; the lack of a critical appraisal is not to be interpreted as indicating that I am in agreement with the opinions I record.

In connection with the problem of meaning, the linguists also deal, within the scope of their semantic pursuits, with certain derivative issues.

What linguistic entities have meaning as their attribute?

That problem is analysed by, for example, Vendryes when he introduces a differentiation as between the word, the semanteme and the morpheme. He understands by semantemes "linguistic elements which express ideas of representations (*les idées des représentations*)", and by morphemes, such linguistic elements as "express the relationships which human mind establishes between semantemes"[27]; he endeavours to define what is to be understood by the word and by the expression[28]. This is a linguistic issue of extreme significance, with a semantic aspect. Vendryes' view has been quoted here just by way of example because the problem is often to be met with in linguistic literature.

The same holds for the differentiation of meanings and attempts to classify them. For instance, Kurylovich distinguishes general meaning, which is an abstraction, and – following his numerous predecessors – principal meaning (independent of the context), and specialized meaning (with elements of the context added). A separate question is that of calque meaning

---

[26] А. И. Смирницкий, "Значение слова" [The Meaning of a Word], in *Вопросы языкознания*, 1955, № 2, pp. 82–84.

[27] Vendryes, op. cit., p. 86.

[28] Ibid., pp. 103–104.

which develops in the actual vocabulary or from neologisms loaded with the content of foreign words[29].

The second great issue of linguistic semantics concerns changes in meanings and the causes of such changes.

Linguistics has since its very inception been concerned, in some form or another, with the history of language and the etymology of linguistic expressions. One might even risk the statement that it is precisely in those problems that the roots of linguistics are to be found. And it is from such roots that linguistic semantics has developed as the science of meanings of words and of causes of changes in meanings.

The specific trait of linguistic semantics, then, consists precisely in the study of the *history* of meanings. The causes of the variability of meanings are seen by semantics either in language itself or in factors – psychological or sociological – external to language. The laws of that variability are accordingly treated either autonomously or heteronomously. Credit, however, must be given to the research realism of the linguists who in principle take both factors into account and interpret them as reacting one upon the other.

Bréal explicitly connected the evolution of linguistic meanings with the evolution of social life in the broad sense of the term.

"In modern society, the meaning of words changes much more quickly than it did in antiquity or even in the recent past. This arises from the intermingling of social classes, the struggle of interests and opinions, the struggle of political parties and the variety of aspirations and tastes ..."[30].

The social and class factor was stressed probably the most strongly by A. Meillet, Bréal's successor in the Collège de France. In particular, in his work *Comment les mots changent de sens*[31],

---

[29] E. P. Курилович "Заметки о значении слова" [Remarks on Meaning of Words], in *Вопросы языкознания*, 1955, № 3, pp. 78–79.

[30] Bréal, op. cit. pp. 105–106.

[31] First published in *Année Sociologique*, 1905–1906, and then reprinted in the book by A. Meillet, *Linguistique historique et linguistique générale* Paris 1948.

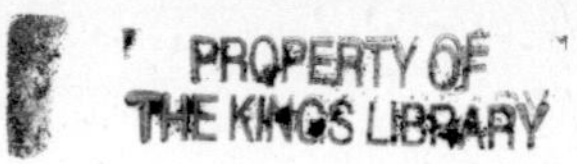

Meillet emphasized the co-operation of three factors in the development of meanings of words: autonomous laws of the language in question, the development of the object denoted, and the class (group) factor. In conclusion he says:

"... Changes in meanings must be treated as phenomena the basic condition of which is differentiation in the component elements of society"[32].

Vendryes, who studied in detail the autonomous laws governing changes in meanings, protested, as we have seen, against these laws being treated as inherent in words themselves[33].

Similarly, Klemensiewicz, who investigates changes in meanings from the point of view of linguistic laws, does not overlook the importance of the extra-linguistic factor in that respect. The factors operating are, above all, changes in human life, reflected in language as the disappearance of certain words (denoting dead institutions and forms of life) and as formation of neologisms (denoting new institutions and forms of life). The same factors also account for changes in meaning of existing words (cf. the common term "pen" for a quill pen and for a fountain pen, or the common term "lamp" for oil, petrol, and electric lamps). Further, the psychological factor is also involved: this concerns the emotional attitude of the speaker, with consequent variations in the emotional shade of meaning of a word. As a result, we avoid certain words by substituting for them euphemisms (which later in turn also deteriorate); in certain other cases, we look for the extraordinary, etc.[34].

Bulakhovsky, who concentrates on the inner problems of language, also clearly sees and emphasizes the significance of the social factor in the development of vocabulary and meanings.

"In connection with changes in the social system, with the development of the various branches of production, with the

---

[32] Meillet, op. cit., p. 271.

[33] Vendryes, op. cit., pp. 229–230.

[34] Klemensiewicz, op. cit., p. 21 ff.

development of material and spiritual culture in general — technology, science, art — with changes in the character of relations with other countries, we notice, on the one hand, the *disappearance* of many words, which lose meanings as the concepts they denote pass out of circulation, and on the other, much more frequently, the *emergence* of word-signs used to denote new ideas and concepts, worked out in practice by the users of the given language"[35].

The understanding of the social and historical character of linguistics, expressed in von Humboldt's lecture quoted above, is also clear in the works of such scholars as de Saussure, Meillet, Vendryes, Marcel Cohen, and others. As regards semantics, it appears with particular force.

Even Bréal, when explaining his theses by way of the example of the etymology of names of Roman magistrates, wrote:

"We must realize the extent to which it is necessary that our knowledge of language be based on history. Only history can impart to words that degree of precision which we need in order to understand them well"[36].

Hence he concluded that semantics belongs to historical disciplines.

"All the more, therefore, should semantics be included among the historical sciences. There are no changes in meanings of words and no peculiarities of syntax which can be regarded as anything other than minor historical events"[37].

From that point of view, the study of languages of primitive peoples must also be viewed as a contribution to a historical

---

[35] Булаховский, op. cit., p. 88.

[36] Bréal, op. cit., p. 112.

[37] Ibid., p. 256.

[38] L. Lévy-Bruhl, *Les fonctions mentales dans les sociétés inférieures*, Paris 1912; F. Boas, *Kultur und Rasse*, Leipzig 1914, and *Race, Language and Culture*, New York 1949; B. Malinowski, *The Problem of Meaning in Primitive Languages* (as an Appendix in C. K. Ogden & I. A. Richards, *The Meaning of Meaning*, London 1953).

interpretation of semantics. I refer here to the works of such scholars as Lévy-Bruhl, Boas, Malinowski and others[38]. I should like to abstract here from such controversial issues as that of the prelogical character of the thinking of primitive people, which at one time evoked a wave of accusations by Soviet authors (accusations which, in my opinion, were largely based on a misunderstanding): Lévy-Bruhl and others were charged with succumbing to the pressure of racialism, imperialism, etc.[39]. Certain results of the relative researches are beyond contention, irrespective of this or that interpretation: I refer to those researches which indicate a greater concreteness in primitive languages, the inability of such languages to express general notions, and the connection between those facts and the mode of life, and the needs, of primitive peoples. It would be difficult to find a more convincing demonstration of the historical character of vocabulary and meaning.

A separate chapter on this subject was provided by the historical semantics of N. I. Marr and his school. It has never reached the linguists in the West, and in the Soviet Union it was annihilated following a discussion in the late 1940's. The manner in which Marr's theory was then rejected must be considered detrimental to science; such methods in scientific discussions must be regarded as inadmissible, in the same way as the previous sanctification of that very theory as the only true and correct one is inadmissible. It is being said at present that Marr's theory, and in particular his analysis based on four elements – in sharp contrast to the historical comparative method – contained many fantastic elements. It is also maintained that Marr's concept of the class character of language, and the development of language by stages, as well as his concept that languages developed only by crossing, constituted a vulgarization of the

[39] Шепякин Ф. Н., "Теория Леви-Брюля на службе империалистической реакции" [Lévy-Bruhl's Theory in the Service of Imperialist Reaction], in *Философские записки*, Вып. 5, АН СССР, Институт Философии, Москва 1950, p. 148–175.

Marxist theory. This is a tenable objection. But Marr's theory, even apart from concrete results in the study of Caucassian languages, included, beyond doubt, many interesting and valuable ideas of general theoretical significance. I refer in particular to the concept of the "manual" language as the proto-language, and the related hypothesis of the development of human speech from the pictorial concrete to the abstract. Further, I refer to the hypothesis connecting the development of language-thinking with the process of production. These are issues of no small importance for a historical interpretation of semantics, and they cannot be rejected without adequate arguments. And such arguments were not always to be found in what Marr's opponents said and wrote, even as regards the criticism of the more detailed theses of his linguistic theory[40].

As already indicated, concern for the historical and social factor in the development of meaning is with all linguists accompanied by the study of the inner linguistic laws of such development.

If we again, by way of example, refer to the textbooks of Vendryes and Bulakhovsky, we find that the course of reasoning is in principle the same in both cases. Since this involves professional analysis, to be met with in all textbooks, and seasoned copiously with examples drawn from many languages, I quote the generalization attempted by Vendryes.

"The various changes in meanings to which words are subject, are sometimes reduced to three basic types: contraction, ex-

---

[40] Cf. В. В. Виноградов — "Свободная дискуссия в 'Правде' по вопросам языкознания и ее значение для дальнейшего развития советской науки о языке" [A Free Discussion in 'Pravda' on Linguistic Problems] in *Вопросы языкознания в свете трудов И. В. Сталина* [Linguistic Problems in the Light of the Works of J. V. Stalin], Москва 1950; Д. И. Рамишвили "Неприемлемость теории первичности языка жестов" [Inacceptability of the Theory of the Priority of a Language of Gestures], in *Известия Академии Педагогических Наук РСФСР, Вопросы психологии Мышления и Речи,* Вып. 81, Москва 1956.

pansion, shifting. Contraction occurs when there is a transition from a general to a specific meaning (for instance, *pondre*, *sevrer* or *traire*); expansion, when, on the contrary, there is a transition from a specific to a general meaning (for instance, *arracher*, *gagner* or *triompher*); shifting, when both meanings either are equal in scope or in that respect indifferent to one another (for instance, *chercher*, *choisir* or *mettre*), and when the shifting from one meaning to another is caused by the neighbourhood of the designata (e.g., when the meaning of a word shifts from what contains to what is contained, from cause to effect, from sign to designatum, etc., or vice versa). It is obvious that contractions and expansions of meanings are in most cases the results of shiftings, and that such shiftings of meanings take on different forms to which the grammarians give special terms (metaphor, synecdoche, metonymy, catachresis, etc.) ..."[41].

These are the problems dealt with by Bréal, Darmesteter, Nyrop[42], and also Klemensiewicz[43], Zvegintsev and Bulakhovsky. The last-named author has a very detailed exposition of the subject, supported by extremely numerous linguistic data[44]. This is why I refer interested readers to his textbook[45].

Finally, I should like to dwell on the linguistic aspect of ambiguity of expressions and on the need to be precise with them. These are matters directly connected with the method of semantic analysis, used in philosophy – a fact which can only add to our interest in them.

Bréal, the father of linguistic semantics, also dealt with the problem of ambiguity and its sources (although the problem itself has a much longer history and can be traced back at least to Aristotle). It was in this context that Bréal saw the proper

---

41 Vendryes, op. cit., p. 235.

42 K. Nyrop. *Das Leben der Wörter*, Leipzig 1903.

43 Klemensiewicz, op. cit., pp. 10–14.

44 Булаховский, op. cit., p. 49 ff.

45 Very interesting and comprehensive data will be found in the work of S. Ullman and H. Kronasser, quoted above.

remedy against the danger of slips in the interpretation of meanings[46]. The attitude of Vendryes was similar[47]. He differentiated between the primary meaning of a word (independent of context) and the secondary meaning (bound up with context). Bulakhovsky, too, is concerned with ambiguity and the ways of eliminating it.

"There are, however, domains of thought – science above all – such as find the psychological shade of the word of minimum importance. In those domains, everything is subordinated to the task a purely intellectual (logical) understanding of reality; that explains why the work of *making speech more precise* is of enormous significance there. That purpose is served by choice of words with a strictly defined scope of application, words which have each only one specified, especially reserved meaning such as in principle evokes no additional associations. It is what are called terms that are such precise ... words, defined so as to become directly conventional"[48].

Thus linguistic semantics appeals for making speech more precise, which is the main methodological postulate of semantic analysis. But the linguists also observe the danger entailed in abuse of that method, and warn against it.

"In the overwhelming majority of cases, the connection between the word and its meaning is purely external, and yet as a result of frequent use that connection becomes so close that we are inclined to take the word for its meaning, and further, following the objectivization of images, to identify words with the objects they denote. We are so easy-going as to accept counters for real values, and symbols of a subjective reflection of reality, for reality itself. Under the overwhelming influence of language ideas, we push into the background the extra-linguistic ideas which link us with the real world, and, having thus broken our

---

46 Bréal, op. cit., p. 143 ff.

47 Vendryes, op. cit., pp. 232–233.

48 Булаховский, op. cit., p. 22.

direct contact with reality, we satisfy the need to feel that contact with sound symbols that lack any intrinsic value. It is just in this that the great danger of language-thinking consists: whoever abuses it and thoughtlessly blurs the clarity of real images associated with it, enters the unsure road of empty verbalism which sooner or later must lead to sterility of mind"[49].

That is the linguist's warning. Let us bear it in mind in our subsequent philosophical considerations.

*

* *

This concludes our general information concerning the subject matter of linguistic semantics.

As we have seen, the subject matter is the meanings of words, changes in meanings, and causes of such changes. The specific trait of linguistic semantics consists in the study of the history of meanings and the historical approach to language.

As regards the detailed spheres of interest of linguistic semantics, we have succeeded in distinguishing the following issues: the nature and the function of the sign; how it is that signs mean something; ambiguity in the form of homonymy and polisemy and the dangers resulting therefrom, etc.

Certainly, these are not all the fields of linguistic semantics. It seems however that they are the principal ones and that to have distinguished them should prove helpful in our further considerations.

---

[49] Szober, op. cit., pp. 20–21.

CHAPTER TWO

LOGIC

IN giving effect to our intention to investigate, by analysis of the various disciplines, what the term "semantics" means and what are its research problems, we pass from linguistics to logic. We thus come to the focus of the problems involved, for it is logic which, since the end of the 19th century, has become the field of semantic pursuits most closely related with philosophy. This is why we encounter here numerous difficulties, especially difficulties methodological in nature.

It is obvious that historical (linguistic) semantics too has significant philosophical implications. It is obvious that the various linguists engaging in semantic research take up quite definite philosophical positions (which they sometimes state plainly and openly) that make them solve semantic problems in specific ways. But in logical semantics the situation is different.

In linguistic semantics, we can easily separate purely linguistic analysis from this or that philosophical interpretation. It is only in exceptional cases, for example in de Saussure's system, that we have to do with a close, organic linking of the linguistic theory with a philosophical conception, so that the two cannot be separated mechanically. But what is involved here is an entire system of the science of language, and not merely studies in the history of meanings.

Now what tends to be an exception in linguistic semantics is a rule in logical semantics. This is so because, first of all, if we disregard the purely technical fields of logical calculi, logic is a philosphical discipline incapable of separation from epistemology and *Weltanschauung*. Secondly, it is so because the logical problems of semantics developed in a close connection with definite philosophical trends – within their framework, as it were – the most vivid example of which is neo-positivism (also called logical positivism) which for the last few decades has been the principal promoter of semantics. Hence the separation of logical semantics from its philosophical background is not only difficult, but also has something artificial about it. And yet it is possible, and even necessary. For it is only thus that we can separate real research problems from their better or worse philosophical shell; those research problems have emerged from the need to develop formal logic and are still important for that process; therefore, if we consider the place and the rôle of formal logic in the system of human knowledge, they are important for the development of science in general.

The doubts which may be expressed about breaking the genetic links between semantics and philosophy and the objection which may be raised that I present ready results of certain mental work – a certain abstraction – instead of an objective exposition of data, will be refuted by the well known argument that the exposition of results of research by no means necessitates reproduction of the entire research procedure. In explaining his method of presenting his economic theory, Marx maintained that the path of the researcher is always empirical and leads through the study of concrete facts in their concrete order, which does not mean that in presenting his theory he must repeat his entire route in detail. The starting point of such a presentation can, and often must, be the result of the abstraction process already performed. Of course, this involves various difficulties and inconveniences, but any other procedure would involve still more of them. In this connection, let me urge that this chapter be read and reflected upon in close association with the next, philosophical, one. A full picture can be obtained only by linking very closely logical problems with their philosophical background – which is historically conditioned – and their philosophical interpretation.

Reverting now, after that brief digression, to the history of the problem, it can be stated that if by semantics we mean, in a most general way, an analysis of the relationships between language expressions and the objects they denote, or else reflections on the meaning of expressions, then elements of such a discipline are to be found even in antiquity, especially in the works of Aristotle. Throughout the whole course of the history of philosophy, we find various philosophers who are interested in these matters. Yet as a separate discipline logical semantics appears only in the late 19th century, arising out of quite specific difficulties and research problems in logic and mathematics. The understanding of the fact that language is not only an instrument but also an *object* of research emerged mainly from the need to overcome difficulties in laying the logical (set theoretical) foundations of arithmetic, difficulties which threatened the entire conceptual structure of arithmetic and logic as well. Far be it from me to claim that that was the only cause of an increased interest in language by logicians. There was another source of that interest, which from experimental disciplines led to conventionalism, and hence to the study of language. But the stimuli due to the discovery of antinomies were specific and particularly strong: they were autogenous, connected with the particular needs of mathematics and logic, and independent of – even if accompanied by – any philosophical interpretations.

It all began with a letter from, young then Bertrand Russell, to the great Gottlob Frege at the time when the latter was just finishing the second volume of his *Grundsätze der Arithmetik*. In his letter, Russell formulated his famous paradox of a class of classes which are not their own elements, and demonstrated that at the very foundation of Frege's *magnum opus* there was contradiction which threatened the entire system. Hence that great mathematician and logician, now believed to have been the greatest innovator in logic since Aristotle, had to write in the "Appendix" to his work these sad words:

"Hardly anything more unfortunate can befall a scientific writer than to have one of the foundations of his edifice shaken after the work is finished.

"This was the position I was placed in by a letter of Mr. Bertrand Russell, just when the printing of this volume was nearing completion ...

"*Solatium* (sic) *miseris socios habuisse dolorum.* I at least have this comfort, if comfort it is; for everybody who has made in his proofs use of extensions of concepts, classes, sets, is in the same position as I. What is in question is not just my particular way of establishing arithmetic, but whether arithmetic can possibly be given a logical foundation at all"[1].

This shows that Frege was far from underestimating the significance of Russell's criticism, which in fact affected Cantor's set theory, with which Frege's system was also related. This was also the issue to which *Principia Mathematica*, the main logical treatise by Russell and Whitehead was devoted.

In what did the criticism contained in Russell's letter to Frege consist? To use Frege's words again:

"... Mr. Russell has discovered a contradiction which may now be stated.

"Nobody will wish to assert of the class of men that it is a man. We have here a class that does not belong to itself. I say that something belongs to a class when it falls under the concept whose extension the class is. Let us now fix our eyes on the concept: *class that does not belong to itself.* The extension of this concept (if we may speak of its extension) is thus the class of classes that do not belong to themselves. For short, we will call it the class *K*. Let us now ask whether this class *K* belongs to itself. First, let us suppose it does. If anything belongs to a class, it falls under the concept whose extension the class is. Thus if our class belongs to itself, it is a class that does not belong to

---

[1] "Frege on Russell's Paradox", in *Translations from the Philosophical Writings of Gottlob Frege*, Oxford 1952, p. 234.

itself. Our first supposition thus leads to self-contradiction. Secondly, let us suppose our class *K* does not belong to itself, then it falls under the concept whose extension it itself is, and thus does belong to itself. Here once more we likewise arrive at a contradiction!"[2]

Russell's paradox achieved special fame, although many others were discovered later. It also came to be formulated in various manners, more or less intuitive, more or less difficult. Not all the paradoxes will be presented here[3], but in view of the exceptional historical importance of Russell's paradox I shall give it once more as formulated by Mostowski. It must be borne in mind that for Mostowski the concepts "set" and "property" are identical.

"Let *normal* properties be called those properties which are not attributes of themselves. Thus the properties: *to be a man*, *to be a function*, *to be a number*, etc., are normal properties (since no man is identical with that property, etc.). The property: *to be a property* is not normal since it is an attribute of itself.

---

2 Frege, op. cit., p. 235.

3 The reader who would be willing to study the problem of paradoxes in greater detail can be referred to the exhaustive literature of the subject.

A general approach to the problem is given by: A. N. Whitehead & B. Russell, *Principia Mathematica,* Vol. 1, Cambridge 1925, pp. 60–65; R. Carnap, *The Logical Syntax of Language,* London 1937, § 60 a. ff.; F. P. Ramsey, *The Foundations of Mathematics*, New York 1931, pp. 20 ff.; D. Hilbert & W. Ackermann, *Grundzüge der theoretischen Logik*, Berlin 1928, p. 92 ff.

In Polish literature these problems are analysed in detail by A. Mostowski in *Logika matematyczna* [Mathematical Logic], Warszawa-Wrocław 1948, pp. 204–222 and 308–324. See also T. Kotarbiński, *Elementy teorii poznania, logiki formalnej i metodologii nauk* [Elements of Epistemology, Formal Logic and the Methodology of Sciences], Lwów 1929, pp. 138–139; L. Chwistek, *Granice nauki* [The Limits of Science], Lwów-Warszawa [1935], pp. 125–136; T. Czeżowski, *Logika* [Logic], Warszawa 1949, pp. 13–19.

More specialist works by S. Leśniewski, L. Chwistek and A. Tarski are given in the Bibliography at the end of this book.

"If we use the term *set* instead of *property* we shall say that *normal* sets are those sets which are not their own elements. Thus the sets of men, functions, numbers, are normal; the set of all sets is not normal.

"Let us now examine the following property W_o:

to be a normal property

(In another formulation: W_o is the set of all normal sets.) Thus, for any property W there is the equivalence:

(1) (*W has the property* W_o) $\equiv$ (*W is a normal property*), from which by the law of transposition we obtain the second equivalence:

(2) (*W has not the property* W_o) $\equiv$ (*W is not a normal property*)

"Let us now ask whether W_o is, or is not, a normal property.

"If W_o is a normal property, then (by definition of the normal properties) the property W_o is not an attribute of itself, so that W_o has not the property W_o. Hence by (2) we infer that W_o is not a normal property, contrary to the assumption that it is.

"If W_o is not a normal property, then (by definition of the normal properties) the property W_o is an attribute of itself. Hence by (1) we infer that W_o is a normal property, contrary to the assumption that it is not.

"Thus both the assumption that W_o is a normal property and the assumption that W_o is not a normal property, lead to a contradiction; in other words, W_o neither is nor is not a normal property although, by the law of the excluded middle, one of these cases should occur"[4].

This reasoning can be still more simply presented by means of formula:

"The definition of the property W_o is

$$W_o \underset{df}{=} (X) \quad (X \in X)'.$$

From that definition we obtain

$$\vdash X \in W_o \equiv (X \in X)',$$

[4] Mostowski, op. cit., p. 209.

whence, by substitution of the constant W_o for the letter X, and on the strength of the tautology $\vdash (p \equiv p') \equiv p.p'$, it follows that

$$\vdash (W_o \in W_o) \cdot (W_o \in W_o)'$$[5].

I have dwelt at some length on Russell's paradox because it is typical as least of the group of paradoxes connected with set theory and with the unrestricted use of the words "every" and "all". In *Principia Mathematica*, Russell still did not differentiate between the various types of paradoxes, but the publication of *The Foundations of Mathematics* ... by F. P. Ramsey initiated the division into mathematical and linguistic (semantic) paradoxes; that division was accepted by Russell in the introduction to the second edition of *The Principles of Mathematics* (1937).

What is the issue at stake in the case of this paradox which, like the semantic paradoxes of "the liar" type (Eubulides' paradox), appears to be a sophistic quibble? The problem involved is no trifling one, since the demonstration that contradictions can be constructed within a deductive theory is tantamount to cancelling such a theory. Russell's and similar paradoxes thus gave rise to the necessity of either abandoning the law of the excluded middle and the logical principle of contradiction, that is from the system of formal logic as we know it, or else seeking ways of eliminating contradictions by correcting the system of formulating one's thoughts. This has directed the attention of scientists to language not only as an instrument, but also as an *object* of research, the more so since one type of the paradoxes, e.g., the classical antinomy of the liar or the later antinomies of Berry and Richard[6], showed clearly that the issue was one of language.

Linguistic interests in logic thus resulted from the natural needs of that discipline and were dictated by the necessity to elim-

---

[5] Ibid., p. 210.

[6] Ibid., pp. 315–320.

inate contradictions threatening the very foundations of logic. It has been found that, in the case of the mathematical paradoxes, the point lay in an illegitimate use of the word "every", which inevitably exposed set theory and related logical theories to the danger of contradictions; in the case of linguistic paradoxes the point lay in the confusion of the language being studied with the language used as concerning the language under investigation. "In both cases," says Mostowski, "we observe the same phenomenon: *a system that is too universal, a system in which 'too much can be said', must be contradictory*"[7].

In any case, linguistic problems have since become an inseparable part of logical research (more strictly, research into the foundations of mathematics and logic), creating a stimulus to the various philosophical interpretations and speculations, which thus intertwine with logical investigations *sensu stricto*. That philosophical trend rests on logic and the results of logical research, but it in turn influences the further course and direction of investigations. That is why it is so difficult, as mentioned above, to separate philosophy and logic in these matters. Although strictly philosophical problems will be dealt with in the next chapter, I should like to anticipate my further remarks by stating my negative attitude towards the various forms of semantic philosophy as a new variation of subjective idealism. But the more so, in my opinion, is it necessary to bring out the real scientific achievements of contemporary mathematical logic, which consist in making us realize that language also is an *object* of logical research. This discovery is brilliant in its very simplicity. True, elements of a knowledge of that fact can be found much earlier in the history of science, but they were brilliant intuitions rather than scientific conclusions. As a developed theory, the matter was raised at the very end of the 19th century and is in fact a product of the 20th century. As a statement it is now so simple and self-evident that it seems almost trivial. But such is the fate of

---

[7] Ibid., p. 320.

all great discoveries, once they are absorbed by the organism of science. To be exact, it must be added that the latter opinion has many violent opponents as far as regards conclusions from a general statement.

The logical study of language followed various courses and took various forms in different periods. They began with an analysis of language from the point of view of its different layers (some scientists distinguished hierarchical types; others, semantic categories). Then the logical syntax of language was the subject of investigation. Finally, came the study of the relationship between linguistic expressions and the objects they denote, and also between linguistic expressions and the subject using the language. These researches and theories bore different names: type theory; the theory of metalanguage, metascience and metalogic; the logical syntax of language; semantics; semiotics (divided into syntax, semantics and pragmatics). Thus, the term "semantics" seems to be reserved here for a special field of research. But let us not fall into error: the overwhelming majority of linguistic analysis and research belongs to semantics in the broad sense of the word, since it deals, in some form or another, with the relationship between linguistic expressions and the objects they denote. We are thus in full agreement with linguistic intuition when we speak of *semantic analysis* as of semantics applied in every case of investigating linguistic ambiguity. In such analysis, we avail ourselves not only of data from historical (linguistic) semantics, but also from the theory of metalanguage, logical syntax and semantics in the narrower sense of the word. This is why it is correct to distinguish between semantics *in a broad sense of the term*, which covers all linguistic interests of logic, from semantics *in a narrower sense of the term*, confined to special studies of the relationship between expressions and the objects they denote. This view is in full accord with that of Alfred Tarski. He understands semantics as the whole of the analysis concerned with concepts which refer to certain relationships between expressions and the objects they denote (as example of such concepts he gives those of denoting, satisfying and defining), and thinks that such an interpretation of the term "semantics" is narrower than the usual sense of the word[8]. Kotarbiński *expressis verbis* refers to the whole of semiotics (i.e., syntax semantics and pragmatics) as to semantics in the broader sense of the term[9].

But let us revert to Russell's paradox and its consequences.

As early as in 1892, Gottlob Frege in his paper "Über Sinn und Bedeutung"[10], raised the theoretical problem of meaning and denotation, that is the focal issue of semantics (Frege undoubtedly based himself on the tradition of differentiating between denotation and connotation), but that idea, like other ideas of that great thinker, remained unnoticed for a long time. As we know, linguistic problems came to the forefront in logic following the discovery of Russell's paradox. The possibilities of overcoming that and similar paradoxes were analysed by Russell in his *The Principles of Mathematics*, and the full-fledged idea on that issue was presented in *Principia Mathematica*, which he wrote together with A. N. Whitehead. This was called the *theory of types*.

The operation he recommends is very simple, though by no means intuitive. As in other similar theories, it consists in so restricting the "universal" character of language as to avoid contradictions. Thus, it was at first a purely negative operation[11]. It

[8] A. Tarski, "O ugruntowaniu naukowej semantyki" [On Laying the Foundations for Scientific Semantics], in *Przegląd Filozoficzny*, Vol. 39, pt. 1, p. 50.

[9] T. Kotarbiński, *Przegląd problematyki logiczno-semantycznej* [A Review of Problems of Logical Semantics], reprinted from *Sprawozdania z czynności i posiedzeń Łódzkiego Towarzystwa Naukowego za I półrocze 1947*, Vol. 2, No. 1. (3), Łódź 1947, p. 1.

[10] *Zeitschrift für Philosophie und philosophische Kritik*, 1892.

[11] In the introduction to the second edition of *Principia Mathematica* we read: "It should be observed that the whole effect of the doctrine of types is negative: it forbids certain inferences which would otherwise be valid, but does not permit any which would otherwise be invalid" (A. N. Whitehead & B. Russell, op. cit., Vol. I, p. VII).

was the further development of type theory, and in particular transition from what is called the *ramified theory of types* (Russell) to what is called the *simplified theory of types*[12] (Chwistek, Ramsey), that made it more natural and intuitive and brought it closer to distinctions of grammatical categories, as especially manifested in Stanisław Leśniewski's *theory of semantic categories*, a concept related to the simplified theory of types[13].

Russells's idea is that language cannot be so universal as to admit of statements about all the elements of a set, if that set has not been previously strictly defined and closed. Or, in other words: a statement about *all* the elements of a set cannot be one of the elements of that set, a statement about a totality can be made validly only "from the outside" of that totality. To fail to observe that restriction, is to obtain statements that are not wrong, but simply meaningless. Such meaningless statements lie at the root of a vicious circle in reasoning, leading to paradoxes. This is, put briefly, the fundamental idea of the theory of types.

But let Russell speak for himself:

"An analysis of the paradoxes to be avoided shows that they all result from certain kind of vicious circle. The vicious circles in question arise from supposing that a collection of objects may contain members which can only be defined by means of the collection as a whole. Thus, for example, the collection of propositions will be supposed to contain a proposition stating that 'all propositions are either true or false'. It would seem, however, that such a statement could not be legitimate unless 'all propositions' referred to some already definite collection,

---

12 L. Chwistek, "Antynomie logiki formalnej" [Antinomies in Formal Logic], in *Przegląd Filozoficzny*, Vol. 24, 1921, pts. 3 and 4, and *Granice nauki* [The Limits of Science], Chap. V; F. P. Ramsey, *The Foundations of Mathematics*.

13 S. Leśniewski, "Grundzüge eines neuen Systems der Grundlagen der Mathematik", in *Fundamenta Mathematicae*, 1929, vol. 14, and "O podstawach ontologii" [The Foundations of Ontology], in *Sprawozdania z posiedzeń Towarzystwa Naukowego Warszawskiego*, Section 3, Vol. 23, 1930, pts. 4–6.

which it cannot do if new propositions are created by statements about 'all propositions'. We shall, therefore, have to say that statements about 'all propositions' are meaningless. More generally, given any set of objects such that, if we suppose the set to have a total, it will contain members which presuppose this total, then such a set cannot have a total. By saying that a set has 'no total', we mean, primarily, that no significant statement can be made about 'all its members'. Propositions, as the above illustration shows, must be a set having no total. The same is true, as we shall shortly see, of propositional functions, even when these are restricted to such as can significantly have as argument a given object *a*. In such cases, it is necessary to break up our set into smaller sets, each of which is capable of a total. This is what the theory of types aims at effecting.

"The principle which enables us to avoid illegitimate totalities may be stated as follows: 'Whatever involves all of a collection must not be one of the collection'; or, conversely: 'If, provided a certain collection had a total, it would have members only definable in terms of that total, then the said collection has no total'. We shall call this the 'vicious-circle principle', because it enables us to avoid the vicious-circles involved in the assumption of illegitimate totalities ... 'All propositions' must be in some way limited before it becomes a legitimate totality, and any limitation which makes it legitimate must make any statement about the totality fall outside the totality"[14].

Russell applies the analysis of paradoxes to propositional functions and demonstrates that there, too, without the help of a hierarchy of types, paradoxes arise which are based on a vicious circle in reasoning.

"... We shall find that it is possible to incur a vicious-circle fallacy at the very outset, by admitting as possible arguments to a propositional function terms which presuppose the function.

---

[14] Whitehead & Russell, op. cit., pp. 37–38.

This form of the fallacy is very instructive, and its avoidance leads, as we shall see, to the hierarchy of types.

"... When we say that 'φx' ambiguously denotes φa, φb, φc etc., we mean that 'φx' means one of the objects φa, φb, φc, etc., though not a definite one, but an undetermined one. It follows that 'φx' only has a well-defined meaning (well-defined, that is to say, except in so far as it is of its essence to be ambiguous) if the objects φa, φb, φc, etc., are well-defined. That is to say, a function is not a well-defined function unless all its values are already well-defined. It follows from this that no function can have among its values anything which presupposes the function, for if it had, we could not regard the objects ambiguously denoted by the function as definite until the function was definite, while conversely, as we have just seen, the function cannot be definite until its values are definite. This is a particular case, but perhaps the most fundamental case, of the vicious-circle principle. A function is what ambiguously denotes some one of a certain totality, namely the values of the functions, hence this totality cannot contain any members which involve the function, since, if it did, it would contain members involving the totality, which, by the vicious-circle principle, no totality can do"[15].

In order to avoid such dangers Russell suggests a division of the universe of discourse into "types": individuals, sets of individuals, relations between individuals, relations between sets of individuals, etc. The "types" are correspondingly symbolized, which makes it possible to distinguish them and thus restricts the possibility of using them in an improper way, leading to contradictions and paradoxes. As we already know, in the case of an improper substitution, a function changes into a nonsense, that is, certain substitutions are meaningless by virtue of the linguistic prohibitions formulated by the theory of types.

---

[15] Ibid., pp. 38–39.

Thus, the theory of types is a result of studies in the language of logical statements and of determination on that basis of a certain definite hierarchy of objects and their names. That theory, however, was not intuitive enough and moreover had for technical reasons to introduce such additional elements as the axiom of reducibility. It is the so-called simplified theory of types of Leon Chwistek which makes it possible to avoid antinomies and at the same time is natural and intuitive. Its fundamental idea is that in logic it is possible to speak only about objects of a strictly defined type, so that it is not permissible to speak of a class "in general", but only of a class of strictly defined objects. In conformity with *the principle of purity of types*, connected with that theory, propositional functions (which are equivalents of classes) in which there is at least one variable ranging over objects of different types, are meaningless[16].

That idea appears to be still more natural in Stanisław Leśniewski's theory of semantic categories[17], which comes close

---

[16] "In order to eliminate Russell's antinomy it suffices to adopt the simplified theory of logical types. The theory of types has been formulated by Bertrand Russell. It is a complicated theory and cannot be formulated clearly in a few words. But it can be simplified so that it really can be expressed in a couple of simple sentences.

"I adopt the so-called universe of discourse consisting of objects which I call *individuals*. No properties or concrete examples of individuals are given.

"Apart from the individuals I adopt *classes of individuals*, *classes of classes of individuals*, etc.

"That is all. It is obvious that here a concept of class as such has no sense. One may speak only of classes of certain definite objects. Consequently the problem whether a class is its own element must be rejected as devoid of sense.

"That simplified theory of types has been for the first time formulated by me in my work *Antynomie logiki formalnej*, published in 1921" (L. Chwistek, *Granice nauki*, p. 129).

[17] "In 1922 I outlined a certain conception of 'semantic categories' which was to replace for me such or another 'hierarchy of types' – deprived, in my opinion, of any intuitive substantiation – and which, in my desire to speak meaningfully, I would have to adopt even if there had been no

to distinctions in grammatical categories. Here too, as in type theory, stress is laid on *the principle of purity of semantic categories*, a confusion of which leads to meaninglessness.

Since Leśniewski expounded his ideas mainly by word of mouth, in lectures and conversations, and his works are very technical and full of short cuts in the course of reasoning, we refer to the excellent presentation of the problem of *semantic category* by Alfred Tarski, formulated with his usual classical lucidity:

"For reasons mentioned at the beginning of this section, we cannot offer here a precise structural definition of semantical category and will content ourselves with the following approximate formulation: two expressions *belong to the same semantical category* if (1) there is a sentential function which contains one of these expressions, and if (2) no sentential function which contains one of these expressions ceases to be a sentential function if this expression is replaced in it by the other. It follows from this that the relation of belonging to the same category is reflective, symmetrical and transitive. By applying the principle of abstraction, all the expressions of the language which are parts of sentential functions can be divided into mutually exclusive classes, for two expressions are put into one and the same class if and only if they belong to the same semantical category, and each of these classes is called a semantical category. Among the simplest examples of semantical categories it suffices to mention the category of the sentential functions, together with the categories which include respectively the names of individuals, of classes of individuals, of two-termed relations between individuals, and so on. Variables (or expressions with variables)

'antinomies' whatever. My conception of 'semantic categories', while being in a close formal connection with the known 'theories of logical types' as far as its theoretical consequences are concerned, referred, as for its intuitive aspect, rather to the tradition of Aristotle's 'categories', to 'the parts of speech' of the traditional grammar, and to the 'semantic categories' of Herr Edmund Husserl" (S. Leśniewski, "Grundzüge eines neuen Systems"..., p. 14).

which represent names of the given categories likewise belong to the same category"[18].

For technical purposes, to every category is assigned a particular natural number called *the order of the category*. The same order is assigned to all expressions which belong to the given category. It is said of two functions that they are of the same semantical type, if the number of free variables of every semantical category in the two functions is the same.

Here too, as in the ramified and the simplified theory of types, antinomies are avoided by observing certain linguistic prohibitions: variables in functions cannot range over different types of expressions or expressions belonging to different semantical categories. The operation is practically identical with that seen above, the difference consisting, apart from the technical aspect, in a greater comprehensibility and naturality of the theory of semantical categories[19].

---

[18] A. Tarski, "The Concept of Truth in Formalized Languages", in: A. Tarski *Logic, Semantics, Mathematics*, Oxford 1956 p. 216.

[19] Under the impact of those theories, and especially the simplified theory of types, Russell later changed his argumentation and actually came close to the standpoint characteristic of the simplified theory of types and the theory of semantic categories. The introduction to the second edition of *The Principles of Mathematics* (London 1937, p. XIV) reads:

"The technical essence of the theory of types is merely this: Given a propositional function 'φx' of which all values are true, there are expressions which it is not legitimate to substitute for 'x'. For example: All values of 'if x is a man, x is mortal' are true, and we can infer 'if Socrates is a man, Socrates is a mortal'; but we cannot infer 'if the law of contradiction is a man, the law of contradiction is a mortal'. The theory of types declares this latter set of words to be nonsense, and gives rules as to permissible values of 'x' in 'φ'. In the detail there are difficulties, and complications, but the general principle is merely a more precise form of one that has always been recognized. In the older conventional logic, it was customary to point out that such a form of words as 'virtue is triangular' is neither true nor false, but no attempt was made to arrive at a definite set of rules for deciding whether a given series of words was or was not significant. This theory of types achieves. Thus, for example, I stated above that 'classes of things are not things'. This will mean: 'If «x is a member of the class α»

In any case, it may be said that the interest in the theory of language (semantics in the broad sense of the term) was inseminated in logic by the analysis of antinomies, and that the antinomies connected with the use of the word "every" (set theoretical antinomies) can be removed by means of this or that form of the theory of types. This is also admitted by Ramsey who was the first to differentiate between the two groups of antinomies – set theoretical antinomies and semantical antinomies.

"It is not sufficiently remarked, and the fact is entirely neglected in *Principia Mathematica*, that these contradictions fall into two fundamentally distinct groups, which we will call A and B. The best known ones are divided as follows:

A. (1) The class of all classes which are not members of themselves.
   (2) The relation between two relations when one does not have itself to the other.
   (3) Burali-Forti's contradiction of the greatest ordinal.

B. (4) 'I am lying'.
   (5) The greatest integer not nameable in fewer than nineteen syllables.
   (6) The last indefinable ordinal.
   (7) Richard's contradiction.
   (8) Weyl's contradiction about the word 'heterologisch'.

The principle according to which I have divided them is of fundamental importance. Group A consists of contradictions which, were no provision made against them, would occur in a logical or mathematical system itself. They involve only logical or mathematical terms such as class and number, and show that there must be something wrong with our logic or mathematics. But the contradictions of Group B are not purely logical, and cannot be stated in logical terms alone; for they all contain some reference to thought, language, or symbolism, which are not

is a proposition, and «φx» is a proposition, then «φa» is not a proposition, but a meaningless collection of symbols".

formal but empirical terms. So they may be due not to faulty logic or mathematics, but to faulty ideas concerning thought and language"[20].

The second group requires more particular concentration of attention on linguistic aspects and different operations than did the antinomies of the first group. Hence the additional stimuli which intensified the theoretical interest of logicians in the hierarchy of languages and the problems of metalanguage and metascience. The concept of metalanguage and the hierarchy of languages is closely connected with the theory of types and in a sense results from the latter, a fact already realized by Russell[21]. For if expressions of a language belong to different logical types (or to semantical categories of different orders), this necessarily makes us think of differences in the hierarchy of languages as depending on the logical types (or on the order of semantical categories) of the expressions they contain. The more so since this conception is connected with certain practical needs relating to the elimination of logical antinomies.

In order to understand this issue better, let us take a look at the difficulties which appeared in deductive disciplines in connection with antinomies of the type of the classical antinomy of Eubulides (the antinomy of the liar). For the sake of maximum clarity, I quote the Jan Łukasiewicz's version, in Tarski's formulation, which will enable us to separate the real linguistic problem from its sophistic shell.

"For the sake of greater perspicuity we shall use the symbol '*c*' as a typographical abbreviation of the expression 'the sentence printed on this page, line 5 from the top'. Consider now the following sentence:

c is not a true sentence[22].

---

[20] Ramsey, op. cit., pp. 20–21.

[21] This is stated explicitly in *An Inquiry into Meaning and Truth*, London 1951, p. 62.

[22] That sentence precisely appears in line 17th from top.

"Having regard to the meaning of the symbol '*c*', we can establish empirically:

(α) '*c is not a true sentence' is identical with c.*

"For the quotation-mark name of the sentence *c* (or for any other of its names) we set up an explanation of type (2)[23]:

(β) '*c is not a true sentence' is a true sentence if, and only if, c is not a true sentence.*

"The premises (α) and (β) together at once give a contradiction:

c is a true sentence if, and only if, c is not a true sentence"[24]. Commenting on that antinomy Tarski remarks:

"The source of this contradiction is easily revealed: in order to construct the assertion (β) we have substituted for the symbol '*p*' in the scheme (2) an expression which itself contains the term 'true sentence' (...) Nevertheless, no rational ground can be given why such substitutions should be forbidden in principle"[25].

All this stands out in still greater relief in connection with Weyl's antinomy: is the word "heterological" heterological? This antinomy – consisting in the fact that when we say that it is heterological, then it is not heterological, and *vice versa* – is also clearly linguistic in nature.

"For the way," says Ramsey, "in which this distinction of functions into orders of which no totality is possible is used to escape the contradictions of Group B, which are shown to result from the ambiguities of language which disregard this distinction, reference may be made to *Principia Mathematica* (Vol. I, 1st ed., 1910, p. 117). Here it may be sufficient to apply the method to a contradiction not given in that work which is particularly free from irrelevant elements: I mean Weyl's contradiction concerning

---

[23] This refers to an explanation of the statement of the type "*x* is a true sentence", which is: "*x* is a true sentence if and only if *p*".

[24] A. Tarski, "The Concept of Truth in Formalized Languages", in A. Tarski, *Logic, Semantics, Mathematics*, Oxford 1956 p. 158.

[25] Ibid. p. 158.

the word 'heterologisch' (Weyl, *Das Kontinuum*, p. 2), which must now be explained. Some adjectives have meanings which are predicates of the adjective word itself; thus the word 'short' is short, but the word 'long' is not long. Let us call adjectives whose meanings are predicates of them, like 'short', autological; others heterological. Now, is the word 'heterological' heterological? If it is, its meaning is not a predicate of it; that is, it is not heterological. But if it is not heterological, its meaning is a predicate of it, and therefore it is heterological. So we have a complete contradiction"[26].

At first, attempts were made to avoid antinomies of that kind by resorting to the operation already described above and based on the theory of types (or semantical categories). It was only later that they came to be separated into a distinct group, and attention was focused on the hierarchy of languages and the consequences of disregarding that hierarchy.

The starting point of reasoning is very simple: one has to bear is mind the difference between the language *which* is being analysed (*object language*) and the language *in which* that analysis is made (*metalanguage*). A classic example here is the discussion in Polish of grammatical rules of e.g. the English language. Such a situation may, however, occur within one and the same language, if some of its expressions are discussed in the language to which they belong. This applies, e.g., to analysis of meaning, denotation, truth, etc. We have then to do, so to speak, with different layers of that language, the hierarchy of such layers being fixed by their lesser or greater "richness". Of course, that can, in a pure form, appear only in formalized languages, which are consciously and purposefully made to serve the needs of deductive sciences. In the ordinary language, which is universal in character (i.e., includes all possible expressions), confusion covers not only expressions belonging to different logical types, but also linguistic layers belonging to different levels of the

---

[26] Ramsey, op. cit., pp. 26–27.

hierarchy of languages. This is precisely the source of difficulties, and gives rise to the danger of antinomies resulting from the confusion of expressions of different types, and of languages of different hierarchies. Yet, if a correct distinction is made as between object language and metalanguage, the latter will be "richer", and object language will form a part of it: metalanguage will include, apart from the signs and expressions of object language, also their individual names (structural-descriptive, or other), the names of relations between them and general logical expressions[27].

If such a distinction between languages of various levels is made, we may no longer confuse them. If we say that "*c is not a true sentence*" and then ask whether that sentence is true or not, then the error consists in the original statement which is impossible if object language and metalanguage are kept strictly separate. This is so because that statement includes the term "true", which belongs to metalanguage: we have thus subjoined a metalanguage category to object language. The same holds when it comes to the antinomy connected with the word "heterological". Here, too, the contradiction arises when we use a too comprehensive language. That contradiction can be avoided if we observe the prohibition on using too "rich" language, that is, language which in its system includes expressions belonging to metalanguage (names of expressions and such categories as "to denote", "to be true", etc.).

It is obvious that none of this applies to the normal use of ordinary language. It is universal and includes all possible expressions. But for that very reason it is exposed to all sorts of dangers, which have been exploited since the time of the Sophists. Yet what in ordinary language is a curiosity and a linguistic

---

[27] Cf. A. Tarski, "The Concept of Truth in Formalized Languages", in A. Tarski, *Logic, Semantic, Mathematics*, pp. 166, 170–171, 173–174, 212–214, et passim; R. Carnap, *The Logical Syntax of Language*, pp. 153 ff; and *Introduction to Semantics*, Cambridge (Mass.), 1948, pp. 3–4.

trick without any practical significance, becomes a real problem when it comes to formalized theories. But it is precisely in those theories that the problem can be solved, and adequate means to solve it are found there. These means are connected with language analysis, and with the discovery that language, too, is an *object* of study.

The distinction between object language and metalanguage presses for more advanced analysis with a view to providing criteria for such a distinction, and in particular for the study of such metalanguage expressions as refer to the relationship between object language expressions and the objects they denote. All this has given rise in logic to interest in the *description* of a given language, in its *syntax* and in *semantics* in the narrower sense of the term.

Let us now try to characterize these fields of research and the problems with which they are concerned.

Before, however, giving a general characteristic of logical syntax and the issues it deals with, it seems advisable to remove the danger of misunderstandings that might arise from our exposition of the subject. It might seem that only the concept of metalanguage, which was a result of grasping the fact that ordinary language is a multi-layer structure, stimulated interest in syntax and semantics. Such is the *logical* order of things, which can be established *ex post facto*. Actual chronology was different: all these problems and interests were intertwined and helped one another to develop, rather than to appear *successively*. A clear sequence in time can only be observed in the case of syntactical and semantical studies. The true development of semantics *sensu stricto* began only when it was shown that logical syntax does not include a number of notions indispensable for the development of logic, and when Tarski had demonstrated that it is possible to introduce the concept of truth into the theory of deduction without falling into contradiction.

What then is so-called logical syntax and what is its subject matter?

According to Carnap, it is such a field of linguistic research in which we abstract from the users of language and from the designata of linguistic expressions, and analyse exclusively the relations between expressions[28]. Elsewhere, Carnap defines logical syntax as a formal theory of linguistic forms, that is such a theory as is interested not in the meaning of expression, but only in the kinds and the order of symbols of which those expressions are built[29]. In such an interpretation, logical syntax determines the rules according to which such linguistic entities as sentences are built of such elements as words. Thus, in such an interpretation, syntax in the narrower sense of the term lays down *formation rules* for linguistic entities, and formal logic establishes *transformation rules* for them. Since both can be formulated in terms of syntax, Carnap combines them into a single system as *the logical syntax of language* (in such a case formal logic becomes a part of syntax and acquires a purely formal character).

Conceived in this way, logical syntax treats language as a specific calculus. Exponents of that conception do not claim that such a calculus exhausts the analysis of language, and do not fail to appreciate the importance of semasiological, psychological, and sociological analysis (latterly, the last two have come to be replaced by the term "pragmatics"). They divide the syntactical study of language into *descriptive* syntax, which deals with the empirical study of the syntactical properties of given languages, and *pure* syntax, which includes analytical sentences of metalanguage obtained from the adopted definitions of such syntactical concepts as, e.g., "sentence in [the system] *K*", "provable in *K*", "derivable in *K*", etc.[30].

If we now ask, which concrete problems are the subject matter of logical syntax, we find ourselves in an embarrassing position, because in the period of euphoria, especially at the time

---

28 R. Carnap, *Introduction to Semantics*, p. 9.

29 R. Carnap, *The Logical Syntax of Language*, p. 1.

30 R. Carnap, *Introduction to Semantics*, p. 12.

when the so-called Vienna Circle saw in logical syntax a specific panacaea and philosophers' stone, logical syntax was made to include not only all the logical problems, but also all that was considered meaningful in philosophy.

This fact gives rise to the difficulty already mentioned at the beginning of this chapter, namely the difficulty of separating logical problems from philosophical ones. In this concrete case, they intertwine so as to form a single indivisible whole. The issue of philosophical interpretation will be treated again in the following chapter. Yet here I shall also point to two philosophical tendencies closely connected with the problems of syntax now being discussed.

First of all, there is the conventionalist tendency linked with the problems of logical syntax. When investigating the syntactical aspect of language, Carnap and others assumed that the adoption of this or that language and the laws by which it is governed – that is, consequently, the adoption of this or that logic – is an arbitrary matter, a matter of convention. That idea was explicitly formulated by Carnap in the form of the so-called principle of tolerance[31] and the principle of a free choice of rules[32]. He held the same opinion also in a later period when from recognizing syntax alone, he passed to a broader theory of semantics. At that period, the basing of syntax and semantics on the conventionalist principles is to be found in his *Introduction to Semantics*[33]. The same attitude is no less sharply marked in Carnap's article of 1950, "Empiricism, Semantics and Ontology"[34], in which he to a large extent pursues his idea concerning the freedom of choice of the so-called *Weltperspektive*, an idea that is an element of Kazimierz Ajdukiewicz's

---

[31] R. Carnap, *The Logical Syntax of Language*, pp. XV and 29.

[32] Ibid., p. 52.

[33] Cf. pp. 13 and 24.

[34] *Revue Internationale de Philosophie*, 1950, No. 11 (reprinted in: L. Linsky (ed.), *Semantics and the Philosophy of Language*, Urbana 1952, pp. 210–212, 223–224, et passim).

radical conventionalism[35]. It must, however, be stated explicitly in this connection that there is no necessary junction between these issues: the problems of syntax do not inevitably lead to conventionalism, nor do they lose their meaning if separated from that philosophical background.

The same also applies to the clearly philosophical tendency to impart to logical syntax a universal character: endeavours are made to contain within it not only all the problems of the theory of deduction, constructive in the field of syntax, but all logical and even all philosophical problems in general. Such a tendency to let logical syntax embrace all the philosophical problems, freed from the so-called pseudo-problems (*Scheinprobleme*), was at that time represented by neo-positivism. Whatever of philosophy was left coincided with the logical analysis of language, i.e., with logical syntax[36]. Here, too, it must be emphasized that there is no necessary junction between the study of the syntax and such maximalist tendencies. Further, there is also no such junction between syntactical analysis and neo-positivist philosophy.

While rejecting these tendencies, arising out of quite definite, idealistic trends in philosophy, it must be said that all those researches which are connected with the *description* of linguistic signs and expressions, with the study of the *rules of formation* of such expressions from more elementary signs, with the analysis of *relationships* between those signs, and of the *rules of transformation* of expressions do deal with real problems of logical syntax. Thus research problems of logical syntax come close to the problems of syntax in its grammatical interpretation. This holds, above all, for the issue of what is called descriptive (de-

---

35 Cf. K. Ajdukiewicz, "Sprache und Sinn", in *Erkenntnis*, 1934, Vol. 4; "Das Weltbild und die Begriffsapparatur", in *Erkenntnis*, 1934, Vol. 4; "Naukowa perspektywa świata" [A Scientific Perspective of the World], in *Przegląd Filozoficzny*, Vol. 37, 1934, pt. 4.

36 Cf. e.g. R. Carnap, *The Logical Syntax of Language*, pp. XIII, 321-323.

tailed) syntax, concerned with the study of individual languages. The issues of pure (general) syntax are quite formal in nature. They involve abstraction from the relations between signs and expressions on the one hand and their designata on the other, and the exclusive study of the form of expressions, i.e., their types and the order in which they appear (which makes it possible to formulate the rules of building sentences and the rules of deduction). Pure syntax belongs, of course, to the domain of metalanguage which must include names of expressions of the object language, names of relations between them (in particular structural relations), as well as general logical expressions. The practical importance of pure (general) syntax can now be seen in connection with the work on the translatability of concrete languages into an abstract language of digital computers (a language which would enable such computers to make calculations in the binary system), and with the construction of machines for the mechanical translation of languages, etc.

Thus, despite philosophical contaminations and distortions, these are real research problems, needed, as we can now see, not only in formal logic. True, a reading of treatises on the subject (e.g., the now classical work of Carnap on the logical syntax of language) may give rise to doubt as to whether the issues raised there are of any practical significance, and in particular, whether the symbolism there used, so very intricate and carefully developed, does not occasionally contribute to obscurity. I express here my doubts and mixed feelings experienced when watching magnificent logical cranes so ingeniously built to lift pebbles which can much more easily be moved with the hand. But I dare not grudge, and *a fortiori* protest. Recent history has taught us modesty and restraint in that respect. Now that sentential calculus, once seemingly useless and purely speculative, has proved to have practical applications in the theory of electric circuits, now that mathematical logic and cybernetics have proved indispensable in the construction of digital computers which are gradually covering semantics by way of their practical needs and applications, it would be difficult to declare with conviction that research of any kind is useless just because we fail, for the time being, to see its practical significance and applicability. In that respect I fully agree with the interesting and correct formulation of the problem by Tarski.

"... I do not wish to deny that the value of a man's work may be increased by its implications for the research of others and for practice. But I believe, nevertheless, that it is inimical to the progress of science to measure the importance of any research exclusively or chiefly in terms of its usefulness and applicability. We know from the history of science that many important results and discoveries have had to wait centuries before they were applied in any field. And, in my opinion, there are also other important factors which cannot be disregarded in determining the value of scientific work ... Hence, I believe, the question of the value of any research cannot be adequately answered without taking into account the intellectual satisfaction which the results of that research bring to those who understand it and care for it"[37].

I think that we should endorse that opinion when passing to an analysis of research problems of semantics *sensu stricto*.

The period of syntactic euphoria passed under the influence of two factors.

First, it soon became apparent that logical syntax alone is not sufficient, that it does not include a number of notions that are indispensable for logical, and the more so for philosophical, pursuits. Such scientifically important semantic concepts as truth, denotation etc. cannot be formulated in terms of syntax alone[38]. This explains why at least a certain branch of neo-positivists tried to do away with them.

---

[37] A. Tarski, *The Semantic Conception of Truth ...*, quoted after L. Linsky (ed.), *Semantics and the Philosophy of Language*, pp. 41–42.

[38] M. Kokoszyńska, "Logiczna składnia języka, semantyka i logika wiedzy" [The Logical Syntax of Language, Semantics and the Logic of Knowledge], in: *Przegląd Filozoficzny*, Vol. 39, 1936, pt. 1.

Secondly, Tarski has shown that one can use the concept of truth (in accordance with its classical definition) without being involved in contradictions; this has broken the resistance of the propounders of logical syntax to semantic concepts. Tarski distinguished in metatheoretical research the *morphology* of language, over which he has then placed other parts of syntax and semantics *sensu stricto* (i.e., the problems of truth, meaning, denoting, satisfying, etc.)

That opened the period of *semantics* which drove logical syntax from its monopoly position. Semantics also took over the responsibility for constructing the theory of deduction in a formalized way. The introduction of that theory has greatly widened the scope of interest in logic, formerly confined to syntax, and has removed from many issues the brand of "pseudo-problems". In any case, there came a full development of the study of problems of truth, denotation and meaning. Carnap introduced corrections to his former ideas expressed in *The Logical Syntax of Language*: in an annex to *Introduction to Semantics* he renounced his claim that "*a logic of meaning is superfluous*"[39]. This led to a change in his attitude towards the extensional character of logic and to endeavours to formulate a modal logic[40], and further to a certain modification of the nominalist thesis propounded by him and his followers[41].

More detailed analysis of these issues will constitute the subject matter of the second part of this book, which will discuss such problems as those of communication, sign, meaning and denotation, and permissibility of general terms in view of their ambiguity and the danger of hypostases. As regards the technical aspect of the problem, i.e., the building of the various calculi and a deductive system in semantics, this is neither the task of this book nor the subjects matter of our analysis. The reader

---

[39] R. Carnap, *Introduction to Semantics*, p. 249.

[40] R. Carnap, *Meaning and Necessity*, Chicago 1947.

[41] Cf. *Empiricism, Semantics and Ontology*.

who is interested in such matters is referred to the literature of the subject, above all to the two works by Carnap already quoted above: *Introduction to Semantics* and *Meaning and Necessity*.

The *theory of models*, very interesting from the philosophical point of view, has developed in semantics. As compared with logical syntax, confined to the domain of purely linguistic entities and to the study of formal relations between them, semantics has made a step forward towards recognizing the legitimate character of research on the relation between linguistic expression and that which is expressed by them. The neo-positivist "decree" on the elimination of apparent problems (*Scheinprobleme*) tended to disqualify research of that kind by adopting Wittgenstein's view that the limits of one's language are the limits of one's world. The turn towards semantics constituted a breach in that linguistic monism and brought to the fore the question of the object spoken about in a given language, the question of something which exists outside language. The theory of models is a further step in the same direction, a step that is philosophically important since it raises the problem of the object spoken about, the object which exists not only *outside* language, but also *independently* of language. The conceptual apparatus of language is, as it were, "added" to the model. This is so at least in certain formulations of the theory of models.

The theory of models is a product of mathematical research. As indicated above, I shall not deal with the technical aspect of the problem, but, as in other similar cases, shall only refer the reader to the literature[42]. The philosophical aspect will be

[42] J. G. Kemeny, "Models of Logical Systems", in *The Journal of Symbolic Logic*, March 1948, Vol. 13, No. 1; J. Łoś, "The Algebraic Treatment of the Methodology of Elementary Deductive Systems", in *Studia Logica*, 1955, Vol. 2; by the same author, "On the Extending of Models" (I), in *Fundamenta Mathematicae*, 1955, Vol. 42; A. Mostowski, "On Models of Axiomatic Systems", in *Fundamenta Mathematicae*, 1952, Vol. 39; H. Rasiowa, "Algebraic Models of Axiomatic Theories", in *Fundamenta Mahtematicae*, 1955,

discussed in the next chapter; here, I shall confine myself to a few remarks intended to provide general information. In diong so I base myself on Roman Suszko's "Logika formalna a niektóre zagadnienia teorii poznania" (Formal Logic and Some Problems of Epistemology), availing myself of his attempt to popularize problems of the theory of models, problems which are difficult in their mathematical formulation and not in the least intuitive.

The starting point is the following statement by Suszko: "The opposition of a formalized language to its models is an extremely abstract formulation of the cognitive relation between the subject and the object, the relation between thinking and that which is the subject matter of thinking."

The concept of a model of language is meaningful with reference to formalized languages. Every entity about which one may speak in a given language, is a model of that language. In the case of simpler languages, every model consists ot two parts: the *universe* of the model, i.e., a set of individuals which may be objects of an arbitrary type, and the *characteristic* of the model, i.e., a set the elements of which are properties, relations and other aspects of the individuals of the model. The relation between a language and its model is such that an element of the characteristic of the model corresponds to every constant expression of that language as the value of that expression, and every element of the characteristic is represented by a constant expression belonging to that language.

A language has a number of models which belong to the same type and about which one can speak in the given language. But, as Suszko points out, the problem should be viewed from another angle as well: there is a family of languages of a given

Vol. 41; R. Suszko, "Syntactic Structure and Semantical Reference", in *Studia Logica*, 1958, Vol. 8; by the same author, "Logika formalna a niektóre zagadnienia teorii poznania" [Formal Logic and Some Problems of Epistemology], in *Myśl Filozoficzna*, 1957, No. 2 & 3; A. Tarski, "O pojęciu wynikania logicznego" [On the Concept of Logical Consequence], in *Przegląd Filozoficzny*, Vol. 39, 1936, pt. 1.

model, connected with that model; these languages can be used to speak about that model and all have the same syntactic structure. Among them we distinguish *meaningful* languages, that is such which under given circumstances (reference to a social group and its activity) perform the function of *communication*. Such languages are obtained by "joining" appropriate conceptual apparatus to the given model. That "joining" of a language is a definite *social* action.

"We shall say that the language J, meaningful under circumstances t, is a *conceptual apparatus joined* to models belonging to the family $RMA_t(J)$ (i.e., to a non-empty subfamily of the family of models of a language that is meaningful under the given circumstances – A. S.). We assume that every language J (meaningful under certain circumstances t) has come into being as a result of the operation, performed in a human group, of joining conceptual apparatus to certain models of the language J, which include the proper model $M_t(J)$".

Suszko says further that the "joining" of conceptual apparatus to a model can take place in a social group only through its direct contact with that "model", that is through sensory perception and practical action. As the model becomes better understood, the language in question becomes further developed.

This is a popular exposition of the intuitive ideas connected with the theory of models. These ideas are closely connected with the philosophical interpretation of semantics, to be discussed in the following chapter.

CHAPTER THREE

SEMANTIC PHILOSOPHY

> " 'In the beginning was the Word', says our version of St. John's Gospel, and in reading some logical positivists I am tempted to think that their view is represented by this mistranslated text".
>
> (Bertrand Russell: *Human Knowledge*)

THIS pithy, trenchant and excellent characteristic was applied by Russell to neo-positivism, but in fact it was addressed in principle to the entire philosophical trend which, on the basis of the cognitive importance of language, as confirmed by the various specialized disciplines, raises language problems to the rank of the only or at least the focal issue of philosophy. Thus Russell's remark applies to most trends and schools in contemporary semantics in the broad sense of the term.

As stated earlier, the discovery that language is not only an instrument but also an object of research has been a great achievement in the development of science, in particular logic and mathematics. But if the merits of semantics (in the broad sense of the word) are connected with definite problems of specialized disciplines and their needs, its demerits are most closely linked with philosophy. Not for the first time in the history of science does poor philosophy prey on great scientific discoveries. Such was the fate of Einstein's theory of relativity, such has also been the fate of semantics. The idealistic interpretation suggested by so-called semantic philosophy preyed on the discovery of the rôle of language in research. The essence of that interpretation consists of making an extremely important, though apparently small, step from the assertion that language also is an object of philosophical study to the assertion that language *alone* is the object of such study.

In discussions with representatives of the Lwów-Warsaw School, the assertion was often heard that such an objection is a wrong one, since no one has ever formulated such a thesis. I shall do my best to demonstrate that not only has such a thesis been formulated by various propounders of semantics, but more-over, that it constitutes *the* sense of semantic philosophy in its various shades. I admit that I derived considerable satisfaction in opening the present chapter with Russell's words which were so much in agreement with my own appraisal of semantic philosophy. My thesis is thus supported not by just a somebody, but by Russell, not only an eminent philosopher but one of the spiritual fathers of that trend in research which has given rise to contemporary semantics. His understanding of such matters is thus exceptionally keen, and his appraisal, exceptionally significant.

The forebears of that variation of idealistic philosophy which, in recognizing language to be the sole object of research wants to eliminate the issue of reality and to regard the conflict between materialism and idealism as a pseudo-problem, had appeared in science long before Russell. The same applies to the interpretation of the rôle of language in the process of cognition. It is necessary to go back to the nominalist tradition, above all to its English version in the 17th and 18th centuries. I shall not, however, enter into those matters, since it is not my intention to write a study of the history of philosophy. In this book we may spare ourselves historical analysis, but must dwell on those elements in the philosophical interpretation of semantics which are connected with modern philosophical trends, first of all with conventionalism and neo-positivism.

But even that I do not want to discuss in too much detail, the more so as I have already had an opportunity to present at once facts and my opinions about them[1]. In our stormy times,

[1] I principally mean the chapters dealing with a criticism of conventionalism and neo-positivism in my work *Z zagadnień marksistowskiej teorii prawdy* [Some Problems of the Marxist Theory of Truth], Warszawa 1951,

so full of political and ideological upheavals, five or six years may sometimes amount to an epoch. That is why I affirm that in the *essential* points I support *in toto* my criticism of the trends now under discussion, published several years ago, and I consider them to be a supplement to what is here written. I should like however, to avail myself of this opportunity and to raise a number of points which I believe to have been at fault in the manner of that criticism.

First of all, in my present opinion the very style of that criticism was wrong.

It is often said of Marxist criticism that it should not be empty-worded and should not confine itself to attaching labels, but that it should be documented and based on a profound knowledge and honest presentation of opinions under discussion. This is basic to all scientific ideological criticism, although it is, unfortunately, not always observed in Marxist literature.

There are, however, other, more subtle, requirements as regards the style of criticism. First of all, such criticism should not consist of pure negation. Let me explain that more fully.

There was a prevalent opinion in Marxist literature that if criticism is to be ideologically engaged it must disarm and annihilate the opponent; to recognize that some of the views of that opponent might be correct was tantamount to "objectivism", which distorted analysis, and to succumbing to academic vices. The fear of being accused of academic objectivism weighed heavily on Marxist science especially after Zhdanov's well-known 1947 speech in the discussion on philosophy. People used to avoid that objection in a very simple way: they sought in the opponent's views only what was false, passing over in silence what was true, not to mention what, being new, was problematic and controversial. Obviously, any opponent so processed could easily be

---

as well as the criticism of radical conventionalism in *Poglądy filozoficzne Kazimierza Ajdukiewicza* [The Philosophical Views of Kazimierz Ajdukiewicz], Warszawa 1952.

overhelmed. It is equally obvious that, especially in philosophy, there is no difficulty in thus processing an opponent: for a materialist the principles of idealism are as absurd as for an idealist are the principles of materialism. Thus, if the opponent's position is reduced to such absurd (from our point of view) principles – and this can always be done – then we can score an easy triumph. It is doubtful, of course, whether *such* criticism will convince anybody except those who are already convinced and share the critic's view. Then, the question arises as to how long such a game can continue, if it is remembered that the opponent can in the same manner and with equal ease overwhelm his critic. All this has very little in common with science and scientific philosophy, but assists an understanding of the duration, hopelessness, and sterility of many philosophical disputes.

The issue would be clear enough, and a remedy for the disease of criticism by denial not difficult to find, were it not based on a misunderstanding, which goes much deeper and is much more of the essence. The conviction that the falsity of some opinions expounded in a work cancels the correctness of all other theses of its author arises from a specific interpretation of the development of science as following a straight-line course in which some theoretical systems represent pure truth, whereas others represent pure untruth. This is nonsense, and can be refuted by any confrontation with facts. Thus, myths can play a certain rôle even in the history of science.

In the history of science, progress is not a matter simply of white against black. The notion that certain trends have a monopoly of truth, and others a monopoly of untruth is simply not acceptable. It would be only too easy to be a sage and to hold only true opinions in a world where the interpretation of the progress of science was thus utopian. But in reality, matters are much more complicated. Truths, even those of great significance, can be found in systems that are otherwise in error and even anti-scientific (an example near and dear to the heart of every Marxist: the dialectic method and the Hegelian system).

Falsehoods, even very serious ones, can appear in systems that are otherwise highly correct.

All this holds *a fortiori* if we consider not only the results of research, but also new ideas and research problems posed to science. It is well known that in science the placing a finger on the problem itself is often no less important than its positive solution. And in that field there can be no monopoly at all, especially in philosophy, where conflicting trends thrive on the errors of opponents. This is how new problems, stimulating the progress of thought, are born. In that respect, idealism certainly has a great deal to its credit.

Does it follow that the criticism of idealism is to be weakened, and that the ideological engagement of philosophy is to be abandoned? Not in the least. The point is that that postulate should be understood properly: adherence to ideological principles should not be identified with clamorous words, and ideological engagement with criticism by annihilation, merely in the interest of the ideological engagement and, above all, the effectiveness of criticism. If criticism is not to be a rite for the initiated, but is to perform its proper task, i.e., to convince those who are not yet convinced, then it may not be confined to denial. To say "no", especially in philosophical matters where a direct and final verification of theses is usually impossible, means very little, since the opponent can reply with an analogous "no" and stick to his own views. Effective criticism should consist, above all, in *taking up the given issue*, explaining its sense and its place in the system of our knowledge, and when rejecting a certain solution as in error it should suggest another, true, one. Such an attitude has nothing to do with "objectivism" and "academism" – it is simply *scientific criticism* properly understood. The inability to adopt such an attitude with respect to bourgeois ideology has been, in my opinion, the greatest defect of Marxist criticism, and therefore also of my own interpretation of conventionalism and neo-positivism.

But let us come back to the point.

I have stressed many a time that when we speak about semantics we cannot separate its linguistic or logical aspect from the underlying philosophy which in this case is not only a shell or a connective tissue of given research problems, but often the very blood and bone. Yet efforts can be made, as in the preceding chapters, to bring out those special research problems of semantics and take them up regardless of philosophical attitude. We might also try to proclaim and appraise critically those elements of philosophical interpretation which have manifested themselves thus far in the development of semantics. I shall attempt to do that now.

What I call semantic philosophy, that is, all those philosophical views which see in language the only, or at least the principal and the most important, object of cognition and philosophical analysis, includes ideas linked with the various trends of contemporary philosophy, from which semantic philosophy drew its inspiration and stimuli. Conventionalism accounts for the thesis that language and its morphology, the system of logic, and ultimately this or that perspective of the world, may be chosen in an arbitrary fashion. This is consistently complemented in the idea, arising from neo-positivism, that language is the only object of philosophical analysis. Finally, the marriage of neo-positivism with pragmatism gave birth to the belief that semantics can be a specific panacea in social matters.

In analysing these three points which, in my opinion, are the most important in semantic philosophy I do not intend, as I have already said, to give a full analysis and a complete evaluation of conventionalism, neo-positivism and pragmatism (which are made up of different, although interconnected, ideas and research problems). I am interested here in the concept of the rôle of language in the cognitive system, and I shall confine my analysis to that issue. Attention will be focused on neo-positivism, since its influence, especially that of the Vienna Circle, was the greatest as regards the problems in which we are interested. I will also concentrate on the period more or less before 1936, when, under the influence of Tarski and pragmatism, Carnap and others began to modify their views and at least to discard the "pure" form of logical empiricism, so characteristic of the Vienna Circle.

1. THE ALLEGED "TURNING POINT" IN PHILOSOPHY. LANGUAGE AS THE ONLY SUBJECT MATTER OF RESEARCH

Moritz Schlick, at one time the recognized philosophical leader of the Vienna Circle, wrote in the first issue of the neo-positivist periodical *Erkenntnis*, in the leading article under the significant title "The Turning Point in Philosophy":

"What, then, is philosophy? Well, it is not a science, but it is something very important and great, so that even now it can be considered the queen of sciences, although it is not itself a science. It is not anywhere laid down that the queen of sciences must itself be a science. Nowadays we see in it — and that is the characteristic trait of the great turn in contemporary philosophy — not a system of results of cognition, but a system of acts. Philosophy is an activity through which the meaning of statements is asserted or explained. Philosophy explains sentences, and sciences verify them"[2].

In the same issue of that periodical Rudolf Carnap accompanied Schlick:

"The new trend of this periodical, initiated with this issue, sets out to support a *new scientific method of philosophical thinking*, a method which can be characterized most briefly as consisting of a *logical analysis of theorems and concepts of empirical science* ..."[3]

---

[2] M. Schlick, "Die Wende der Philosophie", in *Erkenntnis*, 1930–1931, Vol. 1.

[3] R. Carnap, "Die alte und die neue Logik", in *Erkenntnis*, 1930–1931, Vol. 1.

Carnap, as well as other followers of neo-positivism, was consistent in carrying out that programme. A few years after the philosophical manifesto of the *Erkenntnis* group, mentioned above, Carnap wrote in his fundamental work on the logical syntax of language:

"Philosophy is to be replaced by the logic of science – that is to say, by the logical analysis of the concepts and sentences of the sciences, for *the logic of science is nothing other than the logical syntax of the language of science*"[4].

Let us examine that "turning point in philosophy" more closely.

I shall begin with a couple of trivial remarks, which are however necessary for future considerations.

There are two basic types of idealism: objective and subjective. The former recognizes the existence of objective reality, which is ideal by nature (the understanding of the term "ideal" varies according to the various systems of objective idealism). The latter sees in so-called reality only a construction of the mind. According to one of its variations, reality is tantamount to combinations of inner experience (the various versions of immanent empiricism, the classical representative of which was Berkeley). That attitude leads, in its logical consequences, to solipsism. According to the other variation, what is given in cognition is a construction of the mind, and the problem of reality is disregarded as transcending experience (Hume's version of agnosticism).

So much for the sake of recollection.

Now, there is no doubt that a theory which limits one's "world" to language, to linguistic entities that are an external expression of one's inner experience, must be classed as a form of subjective idealism. It is not important which of the two variations of that trend comes in question in this case. The point

---

[4] R. Carnap, *The Logical Syntax of Language*, London 1937, p. XIII.

of consequence is that this form of subjective idealism, also, leads to solipsism, and that a man was found who had enough courage to draw such a conclusion and to formulate it in an explicit way. That man was Ludwig Wittgenstein, one of the spiritual fathers of neo-positivism.

Abrogating my undertaking, I must now for the time being set aside the purely linguistic issues of semantic philosophy and deal, in a few words at least, with its other aspect which was particularly marked in the Vienna Circle and which accounts for the whole trend being called *logical empiricism.* I mean here the *empiricism* of semantic philosophy, strictly speaking the character of its empiricism. A most general explanation of that issue is indispensable for a proper understanding of the concept of language in semantic philosophy.

Empiricism, in particular in its radical form, appears in a close connection with subjective idealism from the moment when, adopting the form of immanent philosophy, it interprets experience as inner experience. The classical representatives of that interpretation of empiricism were Hume and Berkeley. It is obvious that contemporary immanent empiricism claims to continue their ideas. The latter trend includes not only "pure" immanentists, who often end in plain solipsism (e.g., Schuppe, Rehmke, Schubert-Soldern, and others), but also the "shy" forms of immanentism, such as empiriocriticism and, lately, neo-positivism. The last named directly refers to empiriocriticism, in particular to Mach's doctrine of elements, i.e., impressions supposed to be philosophically neutral, the subjective or objective character of which depends on the "co-ordination order" (Koordinationsreihe) (Avenarius). The programme of the Vienna Circle[5], the subtitle of the periodical *Erkenntnis*, the retrospective views of the origin of neo-positivism as held by its founders and outstanding representatives — all

[5] *Wissenschaftliche Weltauffassung. Der Wiener Kreis,* Vienna 1929.

these indicate connections with Machism[6]. Neo-positivism also looked still further back, to Hume and Berkeley, although Russell criticized its exponents for doing so insufficiently. Be that as it may, the neo-positivist doctrine of *protocol sentences*, to which all our knowledge is reducible, a doctrine basing the edifice of knowledge on protocols of certain elementary experiences and impressions of the subject as the *only* content of cognition, is a new, although very radical, form of immanent empiricism.

From the psychological point of view, it might by interesting to analyse the strange fact that people who for the most part represented exact and natural sciences, people who wanted to eliminate all metaphysics in favour of exact and reliable knowledge, finally ended in what is, in my opinion, radical metaphysics bordering on solipsism.

Empiricism, which refers to the positions of clock hands and recordings of measuring instruments, to controllability and verifiability of human perception and the knowledge that is based on it, must be attractive and alluring to representatvies of the natural science. The more so if it makes it possible to be rid of the mysticism of the various irrationalisms that haunted the philosophy of the 1920s and which, beginning with phenomenology and neo-Hegelianism and ending in existentialism, made all philosophy — by their concepts of "Wesenschau", "essence and existence", "das Nichts", etc. — repulsive to every man who thinks in a sober and precise manner. And yet Engels at one time warned the naturalists that contempt for philosophy most often leads to the worst philosophy possible. It turns out that even the boundless confidence in clock hands and scales of measuring instruments can lead to mysticism and metaphysics

[6] See for instance: Ph. Frank, *Modern Science and Its Philosophy*, Cambridge 1950 (in particular "Introduction: Historical Background"); R. von Mises, *Positivism. A Study in Human Understanding*, Cambridge 1951; H. Reichenbach, *The Rise of Scientific Philosophy*, University of California Press, 1956.

when it leads to the belief that the world is our product, our construction. This is precisely what happened to the neo-positivists, for all their anti-metaphysical declarations.

Little would have to be added to the criticism of Mach's elements or Avenarius's *Koordinationsreihe*, contained in Lenin's *Materialism and Empiriocriticism*, in order to obtain a critical treatise directed against the radically subjective, neo-positivist doctrine of *protocol sentences* of the 1930s. For it was rather the form of the doctrine than its essential content that was changed.

Neo-positivism was born in a new period, and was founded by new people. Especially were the natural scientists and the representatives of the exact sciences, who gave birth to the Vienna Circle, subjectively concerned with the precision and reliability of science, with the elimination of all that which in traditional philosophy shocked them by indefiniteness and vagueness, by indecision arising from questions wrongly formulated, with the removal beyond the limits of science of all that they often quite correctly called philosophical flapdoodle and pseudo-problems. For such people, and in such an intellectual situation, the traditional, philosophical vulgar forms of idealism, with all their phraseology, were quite unacceptable. After all, it was precisely that against which they had rebelled. Since they did not understand contemporary materialism[7], they chose that version of

[7] I think that it is a duty of the Marxists to correct certain inexact or just erroneous opinions which were formed with reference to neo-positivism and neo-positivists in the past; they have worked to the detriment of the cause by weakening the force of otherwise correct argumentation, and they have done undeserved injustice to various people.

It cannot be doubted that there is an essential contradiction between the materialist philosophy of Marxism and the subjective and idealist philosophy of neo-positivism. But there is a *non sequitur* between the statement that a given thinker represents a wrong philosophy and the accusation that he is a political obscurantist and a political enemy. It is a fact that the majority of the members of the Vienna Circle were politically progressive people, friendly to the workers' cause. Carnap was known as "the red professor" ("der rote Professor"), and Neurath was a communist by conviction.

idealism which offered them the appearances of precision and reliable knowledge. Since he saw salvation in the replacement of philosophy by the logical syntax of language, that is in fact by an analysis of the syntax of the language of science, Carnap wrote: "The step from the morass of subjectivist philosophical problems on to the firm ground of exact syntactical problems must be taken"[8]. Yet, in fact, this was again an offer of subjective idealism disguised as language analysis, a new version of idealism prepared by conventionalism (the rôle of language in scientific conventions) and by *logistic* (in particular the discovery of the rôle of language as an object of study and Russell's doctrine of atomic and molecular propositions). Thus the combination of immanent empiricism with a new concept of language and of its rôle in philosophical research gave rise to semantic philosophy. That marriage was also reflected in the original name of the new trend: logical empiricism.

Thus semantic philosophy is not a philosophy that overestimates the rôle of language and its place in the process of cognition, is not just *a* philosophy of language, but is such a philosophy of language which is genetically and organically connected with immanent empiricism. As such it has developed as a variation of subjective idealism.

As mentioned above, the neo-positivist concept of language and its rôle and place in the process of cognition had been prepared by conventionalism, and also by the development of linguistic research of a special type, connected with logistic.

In their *Principia Mathematica*, Russell and Whitehead dealt not only with the problem of antinomies and the related problem of levels of language, but also with the analysis of the structure of language in which they distinguished *elementary* (atomic and molecular) propositions as the category of propositions of particular import, propositions that are the foundation of

---

[8] R. Carnap, *The Logical Syntax of Language*, p. 332.

all our knowledge[9]. Ludwig Wittgenstein, Russell's disciple, pursued the ideas of logical atomism and, by imparting to them, as already mentioned, a clear form of epistemological solipsism (we might speak here of linguistic solipsism), bridged the gap between English *logistic* and continental neo-positivism of which he was the spiritual father[10].

By coming thus to Wittgenstein, we have reached the essential point of our remarks on semantic philosophy. His *Tractatus* is certainly one of the strangest philosophical books, both in view of the style and in view of the metaphorical and intuitive manner of exposition, accompanied by claims to precision. It is indeed a paradox that the work which represents the trend whose intention is to eliminate all metaphysics is in fact the twin brother of Bergsonian intuitionism and his metaphysical conceptions. In Wittgenstein's *Tractatus* we find the fundamental ideas of semantic philosophy: that language is the only object of study; that the task of philosophy reduces to explaining the meaning of the language of science; and that everything which exceeds that task is meaningless metaphysics. Many years later, Carnap, in his fundamental work, confirmed that dependence of neo-positivists on Wittgenstein and expressed full solidarity with his basic ideas except for two: that it is not possible to formulate sentences about syntax, and that it is not possible to formulate sentences about the logic of science[11].

Wittgenstein wrote in his *Tractatus*:

"5.5561 Empirical reality is limited by the totality of objects. The boundary appears again in the totality of elementary propositions.

5.6 *The limits of my language* mean the limits of my world.

---

[9] A. N. Whitehead & B. Russell. *Principia Mathematica*, Vol. 1, Cambridge 1925, pp. XVI ff.

[10] Compare the reminiscences of Ph. Frank in his *Modern Science and Its Philosophy*, pp. 31 ff.

[11] R. Carnap, *The Logical Syntax of Language*, pp. 282–284.

5.61 Logic fills the world: the limits of the world are also its limits ...

What we cannot think, that we cannot think: we cannot therefore *say* what we cannot think"[12].

Wittgenstein's position is in no way univocal. I have deliberately begun with his statements on empirical reality as the totality of objects. But it is well known that such a statement acquires a definite meaning only when what is meant by an "object" is explained. But further paragraphs tell us that *my* language is the limit of *my world*, since we can say only that which we can think (in paragraph 4 Wittgenstein says that the thought is a meaningful sentence, and in paragraph 3.5 that the thought is an applied sign of a sentence, about which we have thought). In order to disperse any doubts as to his interpretation of the enigmatic statement about language and the limits of *my* world, Wittgenstein exposes his view on solipsism.

"5.62 This remark provides a key to the question, to what extent solipsism is a truth.

In fact what solipsism *means*, is quite correct, only it cannot be *said*, but it shows itself.

That the world is *my* world, shows itself in the fact that the limits of the language (*the* language which I understand) mean the limits of *my* world.

5.621 The world and life are one.

5.63 I am my world (The Microcosm) ...

5.64 Here we see that solipsism strictly carried out coincides with pure realism. The *I* in solipsism shrinks to an extensionless point and there remains the reality co-ordinated with it.

5.641 There is therefore really a sense in which in philosophy we can talk of a non-psychological *I*.

The *I* occurs in philosophy through the fact that the 'world is my world'.

The philosophical *I* is not the man, not the human body

---

[12] L. Wittgenstein, *Tractatus Logico-Philosophicus*, London 1933.

or the human soul of which psychology treats, but the metaphysical subject, the limit – not a part of the world"[13].

Is that not a classical illustration of Engel's statement about the fate of those who dare to treat philosophy lightly? Is there a worse and more self-annihilating philosophy than solipsism? It is both amusing and piquant to see an author who in the name of combating metaphysics and vagueness (Wittgenstein says in p. 4.116 that everything that can be expressed can be expressed clearly) introduces in a very obscure manner certain metaphysical objects which moreover are not elements but limits of the world.

On the other hand, Wittgenstein cannot be denied moral courage: few people in the history of philosophy have not been frightened by the spectre of solipsism. Even Berkeley sought refuge in objective idealism. For to arrive at solipsism means to reach philosophical self-annihilation, especially now, in the epoch of brilliant development in natural science. True, the neo-positivists did not repeat Wittgenstein's thesis (Carnap was the only one to speak of methodological solipsism in his *Der logische Aufbau der Welt*), but that part of Wittgenstein's heritage which they continued to develop was most closely linked with solipsism.

In continuing Russell's theory of elementary propositions Wittgenstein arrived at linguistic solipsism. The essential sense of that solipsism is formulated in the sentence saying that "the limits of my language are the limits of my world". The conclusions drawn by Wittgenstein from that formulation came to play a significant rôle in the further development of neo-positivism.

First of all, Wittgenstein assigned to philosophy the task of logically explaining (logically analysing) thought, which in his eyes is tantamount to a "criticism of language".

"4.112 The object of philosophy is the logical clarification of thoughts.

Philosophy is not a theory but an activity.

---

[13] Ibid.

A philosophical work consists essentially of elucidations.

The result of philosophy is not a number of 'philosophical propositions', but to make propositions clear.

Philosophy should make clear and delimit sharply the thoughts which otherwise are, as it were, opaque and blurred"[14].

He also says:

"4.0031 All philosophy is 'critique of language' (but not at all in Mauthner's sense). Russell's merit is to have shown that the apparent logical form of the proposition need not be its real form"[15].

Next, Wittgenstein reduced that explanation to the formal syntactical aspect of language, completely dissociating it from the semantic aspect.

"3.33 In logical syntax the meaning of a sign ought never to play a rôle; it must admit of being established without mention being thereby made of the *meaning* of a sign; it ought to presuppose *only* the description of the expressions"[16].

Finally, everything what transcends those limits was considered by him to be unsense, and consequently a pseudo-problem.

"4.003 Most propositions and questions, that have been written about philosophical matters, are not false, but senseless. We cannot, therefore, answer questions of this kind at all, but only state their senselessness. Most questions and propositions of the philosophers result from the fact that we do not understand the logic of our language.

(They are of the same kind as the question whether the Good is more or less identical with the Beautiful.)

And so it is not to be wondered at that the deepest problems are really *no* problems"[17].

In the conclusion of the *Treatise* Wittgenstein writes:

[14] Ibid.

[15] Ibid.

[16] Ibid.

[17] Ibid.

"6.522 There is indeed the inexpressible. This *shows* itself; it is the mystical.

6.53 The right method of philosophy would be this. To say nothing except what can be said, i.e., the propositions of natural science, i.e., something that has nothing to do with philosophy: and then always, when someone else wished to say something metaphysical, to demonstrate to him that he had given no meaning to certain signs in his propositions. This method would be unsatisfying to the other — he would not have the feeling that we were teaching him philosophy — but it would be the only strictly correct method"[18].

So much for Wittgenstein's philosophy. The numerous quotations given above correspond to the importance of his philosophy in the development of neo-positivism.

Now let us see how his ideas have been taken over, adapted and developed by neo-positivists. I shall confine myself to authoritative illustrations given by way of example, without delving into erudite details[19].

In continuing the ideas of Russell and Wittgenstein, neo-positivists brought to a radical formulation the principle that language is the sole subject matter of philosophy. And in explicitly combining that concept of language with immanent (logical) empiricism they brought semantic philosophy to perfection.

What are the arguments in favour of such an interpretation of neo-positivism? Most varied — both direct and indirect. They can be drawn from works of *all* representatives of that

[18] Ibid.

[19] Apart from the reminiscences referred to above — those of Frank and von Mises — and the work of Reichenbach, the following books pertain to the issue now under discussion: J. Jörgensen. "The Development of Logical Empiricism", in *International Encyclopedia of Unified Science*, Vol. 2, No. 9, University of Chicago Press, 1951; V. Kraft, *Der Wiener Kreis. Der Ursprung des Neopositivismus*, Vienna 1950; J. R. Weinberg, *An Examination of Logical Positivism*, London 1936.

trend. Scanty exemplification is necessitated only by the consideration explained above.

Even in the early period of the Vienna Circle, Carnap formulated, in *Der logische Aufbau der Welt*, the theory of *constitution* and the theory of *methodological solipsism*. Basing himself on Russell's theory of atomic propositions and his theory of the world as a logical construction consisting of many aspects, and on Wittgenstein's radical formulation of Russell's theory, Carnap in fact took the stand of a specific linguistic solipsism. The theory of constitution which lay at the foundation of Carnap's ideas at that time, affirms that compound ideas are deducible from basic ideas. The latter (and in this point the logical and linguistic conception is joined by immanent empiricism) are identical with "that which is given". Carnap postulates "a reduction of 'reality' to 'that which is given' (*das Gegebene*), and what has been postulated, and partly carried out by Avenarius, Mach, Poincaré, Külpe, and above all Ziehen and Driesch"[20]. Carnap maintains that his conception is neutral in the "materialism versus idealism" controversy, that that controversy is purely linguistic in nature and depends on the choice of fundamental concepts, that is, on the choice of language; but at the same time he urges the following:

"The theory of constitution and subjective idealism agree that all statements about the objects of cognition can in principle be transformed into statements about structural relationships ... The view that which is given, is my experience, is common to solipsism and the theory of constitution. The theories of constitution and transcendental idealism agree in defending the view that all the objects of cognition are constructed (in the idealist language: 'created in thinking'); that is, the constituted objects are an object of conceptual cognition only as logical forms built in a definite manner. In the last analysis, the same applies to the basic elements of the constitution system"[21].

---

[20] R. Carnap, *Der logische Aufbau der Welt*, Berlin 1928, p. 3.

[21] Ibid., p. 249.

That conception was called "methodological solipsism" by Carnap. In this interpretation, Wittgenstein's thesis that 'the limits of my language are the limits of my world' acquires particular significance.

Wittgenstein took over from Russell the idea that all statements are reducible to atomic propositions, of which we build molecular propositions; higher-level propositions are built only of those elementary ones. But neither Russell nor Wittgenstein stated anything definitive about the nature of those propositions (it was only under the influence of the neo-positivists, especially Ayer, that Russell along with the concept of "atomic propositions" introduced the concept of "basic propositions"). Now the first step on the part of the neo-positivists to make Wittgenstein's conception more radical was the replacement of atomic propositions by protocol sentences which, in the neo-positivist interpretation, base the whole conception on the subjective experience of the subject[22]. By making a further step in the same direction, the neo-positivists linked that conception with conventionalism. They rejected the idea that the protocol sentences are a distinguished class, their choice left to convention.

In such an interpretation of the rôle of language in cognition, Wittgenstein's thesis that the task of philosophy is to explain sentences, to make "a criticism of language", and to reduce such a "criticism" to an analysis of logical syntax, must have been simply salutary to the conception of semantic philosophy. These ideas consequently came to dominate neo-positivism and to be repeated in various forms and shades.

In taking up Wittgenstein's ideas, Schlick and then Carnap and others (as shown at the beginning of the present section) saw, as the turning point in the development of philosophy, the replacement of all philosophical problems by the logical syntax of the language of science. I shall not illustrate that with

---

[22] C. G. Hempel, "On the Logical Positivists' Theory of Truth", in *Analysis*, 1935, Vol. 2, No. 4.

quotations since the most characteristic formulations have already been cited above. These ideas have been repeated hundreds of times in neo-positivist literature, as has also the related concept that what in philosophy cannot be formulated in the language of logical syntax, is mere metaphysics, and consequently a pseudo-problem, and unsense.

The latter view was stressed in particular by Carnap. He divided all theoretical problems into *objective* and *logical*. The former pertain to the objects of the field under investigation and are the exclusive domain of empirical disciplines. The latter pertain to the form of expressions (their syntax) and are the proper content of scientific philosophy. The objective problems traditionally covered by philosophy either are pseudo-objective problems, and as such are translatable into the language of syntax, or are just pseudo-problems, that is a metaphysical unsense (Carnap also worked out a complete theory of the translatability of sentences from a material into a formal mode, i.e., a theory which makes it possible to use sentences about sentences in order to eliminate sentences about things, and which consequently provokes the impression that language, in fact, is the only object of human study).

"The material mode of speech is a transposed mode of speech. In using it, in order to say something about a word (or a sentence) we say instead something parallel about the object designated by the word (or the fact described by the sentence, respectively)"[23].

No wonder, then, that Carnap drew the following conclusion with respect to philosophy:

"*Translatability into the formal mode of speech constitutes the touchstone for all philosophical sentences*, or more generally, for all sentences which do not belong to the language of any one of the empirical sciences"[24].

Everything else is meaningless.

---

[23] R. Carnap, *The Logical Syntax of Language*, p. 309.

[24] Ibid., p. 313.

"In the field of *metaphysics* (including the philosophy of value and the normative science) logical analysis leads to a negative result, namely that *the alleged theorems in that field are completely devoid of meaning*"[25].

It will be clearly seen how the circle closes: we began with the thesis that language is the only subject matter of study in the field of philosophy, and we end with the thesis that everything which transcends that scope of research is simply meaningless. The negative method has thus confirmed the assertion that nothing *beyond* language can be studied in philosophy.

I do not engage here in the appraisal and refutation of idealistic theses, since it is not worth while repeating trivial statements resulting obviously from the opposition between materialism and idealism (and arguments pertaining to certain selected issues will be found in the second part of this book). I deliberately confine myself to stating certain *facts*. The essential fact bears out the idealistic character of the philosophy which reduces the object of cognition to inner experience in the case of empirical sciences (the theory of protocol sentences; the meaningfulness of statements is to depend on their reducibility to such sentences), and to the analysis of the language of those statements in the case of philosophy. It is on the establishment of that fact that the appraisal of the scientific significance of semantic philosophy depends.

It is obvious that the demonstration of the idealistic character of a certain view does not in the least disqualify that view in the eyes of an idealist. On the contrary, it is at that point that the conflict between the materialist and the idealist begins. But when it comes to a situation in which acknowledgment is denied to idealist views, such a statement concludes the initial stage of the conflict. Such precisely is the situation in the case of semantic philosophy, and in particular in the case of neo-positivism (logical empiricism). That trend, like Machism before it, pro-

[25] R. Carnap, "Überwindung der Metaphysik durch logische Analyse der Sprache," in *Erkenntnis*, 1931, Vol. 1, p. 220.

claims its neutrality in the conflict between materialism and idealism, and attempts to demonstrate its alleged scientific superiority by writing off that conflict as a pseudo-problem and metaphysical unsense. Now these claims are completely groundless. So-called semantic philosophy, while anathematizing metaphysics which is to include the whole of classical philosophical problems, itself sinks into traditional metaphysics, and of a very mediocre sort at that. Why make wry faces at Berkeley's subjective idealism (Russell was much more consistent in that respect since he was not ashamed of the relationship), while copying its ideas via the concept of protocol sentences? Why thunder against metaphysics, when one's own philosophical attitude is based on the completely metaphysical (in the traditional sense of the word) thesis that language is the only object of philosophical analysis? No less metaphysical than the thesis about the exclusive existence of the products of the individual mind is the thesis about the exclusive existence of linguistic entities which are products of the individual mind. And such is the thesis to which, in the last analysis, immanent empiricism leads, combined with a specific philosophy of language and with agnosticism. Linguistic solipsism is as metaphysical as all other variations of solipsism.

As indicated above, the demonstration of the idealistic character of the basic theses of semantic philosophy does not mean that the holders of such theses will be convinced of error. I do not think that that could be achieved at once, even should we bring into play the entire arsenal of materialistic argumentation. These matters are much too complicated and include too many elements of various kinds to allow the controversy to be solved so easily and simply. But the refutation of the myth about the anti-metaphysical character of semantic philosophy and the bringing to light of its openly metaphysical and idealistic assumptions is much easier and at the same time decisive in our case. The testimony of such a thinker as Bertrand Russell will be for us of exceptional importance in that respect. The same reasons which urged me to choose Russell's words as the text for this chapter, prompt my quoting him at the end of the present section.

In his *An Inquiry into Meaning and Truth* Russell gave a detailed analysis of the neo-positivist theory of protocol sentences. He appraised negatively both the empiricist and the linguistic aspect of that theory, and wrote in conclusion, in the chapter entitled "Basic Propositions":

"When I say 'the sun is shining', I do not mean that this is one of a number of sentences between which there is no contradiction; I mean something which is not verbal, and for the sake of which such words as 'sun' and 'shining' were invented. The purpose of words, though philosophers seem to forget this simple fact, is to deal with matters other than words. If I go into a restaurant and order my dinner, I do not want my words to fit into a system with other words, but to bring about the presence of food. I could have managed without words, by taking what I want, but this would have been less convenient. The verbalist theories of some modern philosophers forget the homely practical purposes of everyday words, and lose themselves in a neo-neo-Platonic mysticism. I seem to hear them saying 'in the beginning was the Word', not 'in the beginning was what the word means'. *It is remarkable that this reversion to ancient metaphysics should have occurred in the attempt to be ultra-empirical*"[26].

I have nothing to add to this appraisal.

*

* *

We have so far been taking for granted that there exists a language which we analyse. But the problem of the origin of that language and of its relation to reality has been rather left in the dark. Yet precisely in the system of semantic philosophy that problem is of extreme importance. The lack of a clear answer

[26] B. Russell, *An Inquiry into Meaning and Truth*, London 1951, pp. 148–149 (italics – A. S.).

to that question always leaves room for a realistic interpretation which might be as follows: language ought to be analysed because *through* that analysis we may learn something about actual reality that is mapped by that language. I have said explicitly that the interpretation *might* be such had we not dotted the *i*'s and crossed the *t*'s in explaining the origin of language and its possible connections with reality in the light of semantic philosophy. I therefore hasten to add that all the *i*'s have been dotted and all the *t*'s crossed by the founders of that philosophy in a manner that frees us from all doubts. Moreover, only the introduction of that issue enables us fully to understand the nature of semantic philosophy. For whoever proclaims not only that language is *the only* object of philosophical analysis, but also that that language is chosen or created by us *in an arbitrary manner*, that it is a result of an arbitrary *convention* with the change of which the picture of the only reality that is accessible to us is also changed, in fact proclaims a radical variation of idealistic philosophy. As we shall see, such reasoning leads directly to epistemological solipsism (stating that every individual can become aware only of his own ideas), which simply borders on ontological solipsism.

2. LANGUAGE AS A PRODUCT OF ARBITRARY CONVENTION

One of the fundamental assertions of semantic philosophy is that language is a product of arbitrary convention and that, consequently, when choosing this or that language, we may arbitrarily change our image of the world. This sounds strange (to say the least), especially when accompanied by its sequel, formulated by so-called radical conventionalism and affirming that those languages, formed in an arbitrary manner, are closed with respect to one another and mutually untranslatable. The resulting conclusion is not only that we can change our image of the world, and not only that there are different images of the world, but also that there can be different and closed images of the world between which there is no connection whatever.

Before proceeding to a philosophical appraisal of such affirmations, let us examine what is their origin, what are the sources of that strange form of linguistic idealism. For the claim that what is concerned here, is a conscious camouflage of idealism, is naive and trivial, and does not bear investigation. Without having recourse to other arguments, it is refuted by what we know about the authors of those views.

As has been said above, the authors of those conceptions were mostly (especially as far as regards the neo-positivists) people connected with the exact sciences, people for whom the theory of deduction was the symbol of perfection. And it is very well known what, in the theory of deduction, is meant by "to build a language" or "to choose a language"; it is well known what is meant by the statement that different languages can exist and that the choice of language is decisive for "perspectives of the world" in the sense of the formulation and resolution of certain problems. It is also well known what is meant by the statement that there are "richer" and "poorer" languages, etc. Was the temptation to treat natural languages and their problems in a similar way not due to the theory of deduction? In my opinion such was the case precisely.

Moreover, the temptation to consider natural languages to be arbitrary products of convention might also have had other sources. There exist "languages" which in fact are products of more or less arbitrary convention, such as certain signal codes (the "language" of flags used by ships), ciphers, the gesture language of deaf-mutes, the lovers' "language of flowers", etc. If we disregard the subtle distinction between language and speech, we can define language as a system of signs used in human communication. In this sense, each of the examples quoted above represents a "language" which is a product of an arbitrary convention. Does that not increase the temptation to treat the natural languages in a similar way, the more so since natural languages have much in common with artificial ones?

It is not my intention to offer here an analysis of the analogies and differences between natural and artificial languages. Such an analysis would imply an investigation of the relationship between language on the one hand and thought and reality on the other. This is an immense problem in itself, some aspects of which will be dealt with in the second part of this book. There is, however, one point to which I must draw attention here and now, since in my opinion it puts a spot-light on the entire issue.

In all the comparisons and analogies between artificial and natural languages, one essential point must not be lost sight of: artificial languages are always built on the basis of natural ones, and it is only on such a basis that they are possible and comprehensible. This also refers to their arbitrarily conventional nature: the conventions used in building the various languages (the languages alike of deductive theories, of codes, ciphers, etc.) are based on *existing* natural languages and would not be possible without them. This is why, for all the analogies and similarities between the various systems of signs used in human communication, the attempt to extend to natural languages the conclusions drawn from the analysis of artificial languages is basically in error, precisely because natural languages can perfectly well exist without artificial ones, whereas the latter must be based on the former and as such shine with reflected light only. We need not, therefore, study the relation to reality of e.g., the language of deductive theories or the language of the flag code (although they too refer to the real world) because these languages are somehow or other translated into natural languages. We may agree that in those cases we have to do with products of conventions and leave it at that. We may not, however, conclude that in the case of the natural languages also we may abstract from the issue of their relation to thought and reality. Such a conclusion, however, is suggested by neo-positivists (Wittgenstein, Carnap, and others) and radical conventionalists. By reasoning in such a way one simply commits a logical error, which in my opinion, lies at the root of the conventionalist conception of language.

The starting point of conventionalism is the assertion that scientific cognition is based on a convention, and that building up a science we in fact produce conventions which are chosen from the point of view of their suitability. Yet Le Roy only was the first to develop conventionalism consistently by stating that theory depends on *the choice of language*[27]. This choice is free, there is no necessity to choose precisely *that* language, although the actual choice made by a given individual is conditioned psychologically[28].

That conventionalist thesis was transferred to neo-positivism, the more so as the neo-positivist conception of language as the only object of philosophical analysis requires such thesis. All non-conventionalist solutions of the problem of the choice of language raise the issue of reality and of the relation "language-reality".

Conventionalist conclusions from the conception of language as adopted by the neo-positivists were in their most radical form (within the Vienna Circle) drawn by Rudolf Carnap. In Poland, Ajdukiewicz's radical conventionalism took a similar direction (although independently from the neo-positivists).

Carnap formulated his idea in the form of *the principle of tolerance* which states a full freedom of the choice of language (both the formation rules and the transformation rules applying to sentences) and of logic.

"In logic, there are no morals. Everyone is at liberty to build up his own logic, i.e., his own form of language, as he wishes. All that is required of him is that, if he wishes to discuss it, he

[27] E. Le Roy, "Science et Philosophie", in *Revue de Métaphysique et de Morale*, 1899, pp. 529–530, 533.

[28] E. Le Roy, "Un positivisme nouveau", in *Revue de Métaphysique et de Morale*, 1901, p. 144.

must state his methods clearly, and give syntactical rules instead of philosophical arguments"[29].

That principle of arbitrarily selecting one's language (with all the consequences for the *creation* by the subject of his own image of the world – the perspective of the world) was brought to its most sweeping conclusion in Ajdukiewicz's radical conventionalism. His conception is related to that held by neo-positivists, but without their theory of protocol sentences, and carries the theses of semantic philosophy to the extreme. I mean here the theory of closed and untranslatable languages, chosen in an arbitrary manner on the strength of a convention. In radical conventionalism, such a theory transforms the subject into a monad without windows, which not only is in a sense the maker of reality, but also is inaccessible to any argument beyond the scope of its own language.

As Ajdukiewicz says:

"The fundamental thesis of ordinary conventionalism, represented for instance by Poincaré, states that there are problems which cannot be solved by appeal to experience unless one introduces a certain convention, since only such a convention, together with experimental data, makes it possible to solve the problem in question. The judgements which combine to make up such a solution are thus not forced on us by empirical data alone, but their adoption depends partly on our recognition, since the said convention which co-determines the solution of the problem can be arbitrarily changed by us so that as a result we obtain different judgements.

"In the present paper it is my intention to make that thesis of ordinary conventionalism more general and more radical. Namely, we want to formulate and to prove the theorem that not only some, but *all the judgements which we accept and which combine to make up our image of the world are not univocally determined by empirical data, but depend on the choice of the*

[29] R. Carnap, *The Logical Syntax of Language*, p. 52; see also pp. XV and 29.

conceptual apparatus by means of which we make mappings of those empirical data. We can, however, choose this or that conceptual apparatus, which will change our whole image of the world"[30].

Ajdukiewicz's view, published in the *Erkenntnis*, certainly did not fail to influence the opinions held by the neo-positivist supporters of semantic philosophy. But Ajdukiewicz was not alone in his opinions which fitted Carnap's principle of tolerance and, e.g., the theories of C. G. Hempel[31].

Additional light on the issue of the choice of language is shed by the neo-positivist theory of physicalism[32].

This is how Carnap describes that theory:

"The thesis of *physicalism* maintains that the physical language is a universal language of science — that is to say, that every language of any sub-domain of science can be equipollently translated into the physical language. From this it follows that science is a unitary system within which there are no fundamentally diverse object-domains, and consequently no gulf, for example, between natural and psychological sciences. This is the thesis of the *unity of sciences*"[33].

As I have already mentioned, neo-positivist circles included many people connected with the natural and the exact sciences.

---

[30] K. Ajdukiewicz, "Das Weltbild und die Begriffsapparatur", in *Erkenntnis*, 1934, Vol. 4, p. 259; by the same author: "Naukowa perspektywa świata", in *Przegląd Filozoficzny,* Vol. 37, 1934, pt. 4; "Sprache und Sinn", in *Erkenntnis*, 1934, Vol. 4; "Die wissenschaftliche Weltperspektive", in *Erkenntnis*, 1935, Vol. 5; "W sprawie artykułu prof. A. Schaffa o moich poglądach filozoficznych" [Concerning the Paper by Prof. A. Schaff On My Philosophical Views], in *Myśl Filozoficzna,* 1953, No. 2 (8).

[31] C. G. Hempel, "Le problème de la vérité", in *Theoria*, 1937, Vol. 3.

[32] See e.g., R. Carnap, "Die physikalische Sprache als Universalsprache der Wissenschaft", in *Erkenntnis*, 1931, Vol. 2; by the same author, "Psychologie in physikalischer Sprache", in *Erkenntnis*, 1932–3, Vol. 3; and *The Logical Syntax of Language* (§ 82: "The Physical Language"); O. Neurath, "Soziologie im Physikalismus", in *Erkenntnis*, 1931, Vol. 2.

[33] R. Carnap, *The Logical Syntax of Language*, p. 320.

Hence their tendency to transform philosophy after the pattern of the exact sciences, hence, too, their liking for physics and its language, a liking that often took a vulgarized form of *behaviourism*[34] (cf. Carnap's view on psychology, or Neurath's views on sociology as a branch of physics). There is no doubt that physicalism was a manifestation of the yearnings of naturalists. But this cannot change the obvious and irrefutable fact that the very idea of physicalism is conventionalist from its inception, that it was born from the concept of language as an arbitrary convention, and that it is conceived as a convenient way of making science unified – and not as a concession to some form of epistemological realism.

Conventionalism can clearly be found in many statements of the founders of physicalism. My proof of that statement will be confined to a minimum of examples.

---

[34] For instance, in his article "Psychologie in physikalischer Sprache" Carnap says that "The thesis will be explained and substantiated below, stating that *every theorem of psychology can be formulated in the language of physics ... that all the theorems of psychology speak of physical events, namely of a physical behaviour of man and other animals.* This is a partial thesis of the general thesis of *physicalism* that *the language of physics is a universal language*, i.e., a language into which every theorem can be translated".

In another of his articles ("Die physikalische Sprache als Universalsprache der Wissenschaft") Carnap generalized his thesis: "Our formulation of the problem has often been called 'positivist': should any one be willing to do so, he might also call it 'materialist'. No objections may be raised against such a term, if one does not lose sight of the difference between early materialism and methodological materialism as a purified form of the former".

But somewhat earlier he explains the meaning of his "methodological materialism" in a clearly conventionalist spirit: "In an analogous manner one may define the thesis on the universal character of the language of physics as 'methodological materialism'. The apposition 'methodological' emphasizes that we have here to do with theses which exclusively refer to a logical possibility of performing certain linguistic transformations and of deducing derivative theses, and not to some 'reality' or 'non-reality' ('existence' or 'non-existence') of what is 'given', what is 'psychic', what is 'physical'".

Moritz Schlick, who was a much more moderate supporter of neo-positivist philosophy than were Carnap or Neurath (see, e.g., his arguments against the theory of coherence), had, long before the birth of physicalism, laid its epistemological foundations.

"'The physical' does not mean any particular kind of reality, but a particular kind of denoting reality, namely a system of concepts in the natural sciences which is necessary for the cognition of reality. 'The physical' should not be interpreted wrongly as an attribute of one part of reality, but not of the other; it is rather a word denoting a kind of conceptual construction, as, e.g., the markers 'geographical' or 'mathematical', which denote not any distinct properties of real things, but always merely a manner of presenting them by means of ideas"[35].

The founders of physicalism took precisely that direction by making their theory a sort of linguistic trick, and transforming in into a purely linguistic problem.

Carnap wrote:

"It is easy to see that both (i.e., both the physicalist thesis, and the thesis on the unity of science — A. S.) are theses of the syntax of the language of science"[36].

And the principle of tolerance states that language and its syntax may be chosen in an arbitrary manner.

The *i* was dotted and *t* crossed by Neurath, the chief promoter of physicalism and of other radical neo-positivist theories. He combined physicalism with the theory of coherence and thereby imparted to the latter a purely linguistic form.

In his paper "Soziologie im Physikalismus" Neurath defended the thesis concerning the unity of science and the unity of the language of that science. For instance, he interpreted sociology as social behaviourism, comprising a component part of physics in a broad sense of the term. And in what was the truth of the

---

[35] M. Schlick, *Allgemeine Erkenntnislehre*, Berlin 1925, p. 271.

[36] R. Carnap, *The Logical Syntax of Language*, p. 320.

theses of that science to consist? In the *coherence* of its sentences as *between themselves.*

"Science as a system of statements is always an object of discussion. *Statements are to be compared with statements,* and not with 'experience', or with 'the world', or with something else. All that meaningless *doubling* belongs to more or less subtle metaphysics and as such must be rejected. Every new statement is to be confronted with existing ones, already brought to a state of harmony between themselves. *A statement will be considered correct if it can be joined to them*"[37].

In the light of the principle of tolerance, radical conventionalism and physicalism, the conventionalist character of so-called semantic philosophy stands beyond all doubt. Philosophical analysis is confined to the analysis of language, and language is chosen on the strength of arbitrary convention – these are its main theses. As I have indicated already, I do not intend to discuss those theses here since that would above all require the solution of the problem of the relation: language-thinking-reality. It serves our purpose here to demonstrate the idealistic character of semantic philosophy, which is in no wise anti-metaphysical. Every objective reader must admit that this has been done.

A word by way of conclusion. My sharp opposition to the conventionalist thesis on the arbitrary character of natural languages, treated in abstraction from reality and from thinking that reflects that reality, does not in the least mean that I negate all the formulations of the idea of the *active rôle* of language in the process of cognition, to be found in those theses (especially in the case of K. Ajdukiewicz). Comparative linguistic and anthropological studies (Sapir, Whorf, and others) leave no doubt in that respect, and a moderate formulation of that idea evokes no philosophical reservations. But these are different matters, to be discussed again in the second part of this book (Chapter IV. 2).

---

[37] Neurath, op. cit., p. 403.

*

* *

A few more remarks, as a postscript, on the present development of semantic philosophy.

One of the weak points to this day in Marxist criticism is the neglect of analysis of changes and transformations of the opinions under discussion. If such neo-positivists as Carnap or Ayer at one time expounded certain views – e.g., the theory of protocol sentences or the reducibility of philosophy to the logical syntax of language – such views are considered as petrified opinions either of *all* neo-positivists or of some of them. And yet people are free to modify their views and willingly make use of that right. As a result it often happens that we criticize the one-time views of Carnap or Ayer, but do not know their present-day opinions.

It is obvious that a critic may take into consideration and analyse a certain period or stage in the development of a given doctrine of theory. *Scripta manent*, and hence even those trends and views which have long since been abandoned retain their historical significance. The logical empiricism of the Vienna Circle is an objective ideological phenomenon to be dealt with by every one who studies neo-positivism, notwithstanding that, as far as I know, none of the former expounders of the theory of protocol sentences (already much differentiated at that time) holds it to-day, at least in its original form. The researcher who investigates a phenomenon that belongs to the past is under obligation to point out that he is interested only in a definite *stage* in the development of the given theory, and not in that theory in general. It is also desirable, in such a connection, to mention what was the further evolution of the theory in question. This is just what I intend to do now.

In the case of semantic philosophy I should, in a most general way, describe the changes as a transition from subjectivism to more realist views.

A certain duality and vacillation was inherent in the theory of physicalism, although Carnap's philosophical position in the period of *Der logische Aufbau der Welt* or of his later work *Die logische Syntax der Sprache* was quite univocal. It was a position typical of semantic philosophy, as I have described it above. But if we compare it with Carnap's views in the period of *Testability and Meaning*, and even more so the period of *Introduction to Semantics* or *Empiricism, Semantics and Ontology*, then, while noticing all the similarities and the continuity of certain concepts of semantic philosophy, we shall not fail to see that his position has undergone a considerable modification.

The same applies to the English expounder of neo-positivism, A. J. Ayer, if we compare his early works, such as *Language, Truth and Logic* (1936) and *The Foundations of Empirical Knowledge* (1940) with *The Problem of Knowledge* (1956).

Among the many changes taking place in the views of the expounders of semantic philosophy, we are here interested above all in the changes connected with the concept of language and its analysis. Externally, this is manifested as a transition from an exclusive recognition of logical syntax to the recognition of semantics *sensu stricto* as well. The causes of that process were explained in the preceding chapter. From the philosophical point of view that transition means the introduction of the problem of the relation of expressions to the *objects* denoted by them and therefore to the problem of *meaning*. In spite of lack of consistency in the adoption of the classical definition of truth and the point of view of semantics *sensu stricto*, the problem of an *objective* counterpart of language has nevertheless penetrated semantic philosophy. Of course, the issue can be made obscure and tangled if one does not take a consistently realist, that is materialistic, stand in epistemology. This is precisely the case of those semanticists. But the most important point is that these issues have entered the field of vision of semantic philosophy, that semantic philosophy has withdrawn from the magic circle of formal linguistic operations seen as the only object of philosophical investigations.

It is obvious that such a step entails further consequences. In semantics, they have been drawn by the so-called theory of models which, as already mentioned, gives a theoretical generalization to the thesis that language *is a mapping* of some of its models, i.e., of some reality which may find various linguistic expressions. The theory of models has developed as part of the theory of deduction and is one of its instruments, but it is also of considerable philosophical significance as an expression of *realist* tendencies in semantic philosophy.

It would be difficult to say now how that philosophy will continue to develop, the more so since the rejection of idealist theses in one field may be accompanied by the adoption or expansion of such theses in another. My duty is to draw attention to the changes now taking place and to show their trend.

*

* *

A separate mention is due here to *semiotic*, a product of cross-breeding of neo-positivism and pragmatism.

Semiotic as a general theory of signs has, as demonstrated by Charles Morris[38], a long history leading from the Stoics, through Hellenistic philosophy, Occam (*scientia sermocinalis*), Leibniz (*characteristica universalis*), and Locke (σεμειοτική), to contemporary mathematical logic. The roots of semiotics in the form given to it by Morris go through neo-positivist influence precisely to that logical tradition, and also to American pragmatism and its analysis of the influence of signs on human behaviour. I mean here above all the works of Ch. Peirce on semiotic, and those by James, Dewey and G. Mead.

There can be no doubt that the need of a *general theory of signs* arose from the interest shown in syntax and semantics

[38] Ch. W. Morris, *Signs, Language and Behavior*, New York 1946, pp. 285 ff.

by exponents of mathematical logic and neo-positivism. The trends of reasoning which started from semantic philosophy and consequently considered language to be the only, or at least the principal, object of philosophical analysis, had to engage in an all-round analysis of signs in view of their rôle in the problems of language.

Such a general theory of signs necessitated taking into consideration the relationship between signs and the human beings who produce and perceive them. That aspect of the issue, in principle alien to logical research, was analysed by pragmatism and behaviouristic psychology, that is by typically American trends in philosophy. It is, therefore, not astonishing that a new version of semiotic came to be represented by a man who in his university studies was influenced at home by pragmatism, and during his post-graduate research in Europe, by neo-positivist ideas. Charles Morris is now the best known representative of semiotic which, by distinguishing between the syntactic, the semantic and the pragmatic aspect of semiosis (that is, the process in which the semantic function of signs is revealed) has in fact absorbed logical syntax and semantics as its component parts. As a result, semiotic aspired to the rôle of Philosophy with a capital *P*. Morris wrote:

"Semiotic provides a basis for understanding the main forms of human activity and their interrelationship, since all these activities and relations are reflected in the signs which mediate the activities ... In giving such understanding, semiotic promises to fulfil one of the tasks which traditionally has been called philosophical. Philosophy has often sinned in confusing in its own language the various functions which signs perform. But it is an old tradition that philosophy should aim to give insight into the characteristic forms of human activity and to strive for the most general and the most systematic knowledge possible. This tradition appears in a modern form in the identification of philosophy with the theory of signs and the unification of science, that is, with the more general and systematic aspects of pure and descriptive semiotic"[39].

It must be mentioned here that the representatives of semiotic proclaim its philosophical neutrality:

"Semiotic itself neither rests on nor necessarily implies a particular philosophy. A science of signs no more decides between an 'empirical' and a 'non-empirical' philosophy than it decides between a 'naturalistic' and a 'supernaturalistic' religion. In itself it cannot force one to believe only scientifically verified statements, nor to use only scientific discourse, nor to form one's appraisals and prescriptions in the light of science. It will nevertheless have a profound influence on the course of philosophy, since it deals with topics peculiarly relevant to philosophic systematization ... In this sense, the philosophy of the future will be semiotically oriented. But the nature of this influence will not always be the same, and will depend upon the rôle which given individuals and societies assign to scientific knowledge"[40].

This is true in so far as formal, classificatory and terminological considerations (and that is the principal subject matter of semiotic) can be combined with different systems of *Weltanschauung*. Another point is that Morris often adopts a much more realist attitude, coming close to materialism, than do his colleagues engaged in the neo-positivist analysis of language. Reference might be made in this connection to the paragraphs devoted to the issue of meaning and of the universals in Morris's article in *The International Encyclopedia*. His attitude is still clearer when it comes to his analysis of the social aspect of the process of semiosis.

The last-named issue is of especial interest. Yet Morris's views on the essence of signs and on semiosis will not be presented here, since they are discussed in greater detail in the second part of this book, where the process of human communication and the rôle of signs in that process come to the forefront.

---

[39] Ch. W. Morris, "Foundations of the Theory of Signs", in *International Encyclopedia of Unified Science*, Vol. 1, No. 2, pp. 58-59.

[40] Ch. W. Morris, *Signs, Language and Behavior*, p. 238.

CHAPTER FOUR

GENERAL SEMANTICS

IN his splendid exposition of the foundation of semantics in the article "The Semantic Conception of Truth and the Foundations of Semantics" Alfred Tarski wrote:

"It is perhaps worth while saying that semantics as conceived in this paper (and in former papers of the author) is a sober and modest discipline which has no pretensions to being a universal patent-medicine for all the ills and diseases of mankind, whether imaginary or real. You will not find in semantics any remedy for decayed teeth or illusions of grandeur or class conflicts. Nor is semantics a device for establishing that everyone except the speaker and his friends is speaking nonsense"[1].

It is not difficult to guess who is the addressee of that piquant remark in the spirit of the newspaper announcement: "I repudiate responsibility for the debts and actions of my husband"; it is necessary only to read, for instance, the following passage from a book by Alfred Korzybski, much quoted in literature abroad, but practically unknown in Poland:

"The new methods eliminate or alleviate different semantogenic blockages; many 'emotional disturbances', including even some neuroses and psychoses; various learning, reading, or speech difficulties, etc.; and general maladjustments in professional and/or personal lives. These difficulties result to a large extent from the failure to use 'intelligence' adequately so as to bring about proper evaluation.

[1] A. Tarski, "The Semantic Conception of Truth ..."; reprinted in L. Linsky (ed.), *Semantics and the Philosophy of Language*, Urbana 1952, p. 17.

"It is well known that many psychosomatic symptoms such as some heart, digestive, respiratory, and 'sex' disorders, some chronic joint diseases, arthritis, dental caries, migraines, skin diseases, alcoholism, etc., to mention a few, have a semantogenic, and therefore neuro-semantic and neuro-linguistic origin. In general semantic training we do not go into the medical angle as such. We eliminate the harmful semantogenic factors, and in most cases the corresponding symptoms disappear provided the student is willing to work at himself seriously"[2].

Knowing the opinions and the attitude of Polish representatives of semantics, I can easily imagine Alfred Tarski's horror – I use the word advisedly – on reading that "bill of fare" of problems covered by the respectable term of "semantics".

In fairness, it must be said that Alfred Korzybski also emphasized the difference between former semantics and what he himself called semantics.

"There is a fundamental confusion between the notion of the older 'semantics' as connected with a theory of *verbal* 'meaning' and words defined by words, and the present theory of 'general semantics' where we deal only with *neuro*-semantic and *neuro*-linguistic living reactions of $Smith_1$, $Smith_2$, etc., as their reactions to neuro-semantic and neuro-linguistic *environments as environments*"[3].

One cannot fail to agree, also, with the opinion of Anatol Rapoport – in his excellent informative article "What Is Semantics?"[4] – that there is a justified resistance both in academic

---

[2] A. Korzybski, *Science and Sanity*, Lancaster (Penn.) 1941, p. VII.

[3] Ibid., p. X.

[4] A. Korzybski's book is quite useless as a source of information about general semantics. It is embarrassingly vague and dilettantish, and greatly oversized at that (nearly 800 pages). I can, however, recommend three excellent articles from the collection *Language, Meaning and Maturity*, New York 1954, which includes selected papers chosen first of all from the periodical *ETC* for the period 1943–53. I mean the above mentioned work by Anatol Rapoport, "What Is Semantics?" and two works by S. I. Hayakawa: "Se-

circles and among the followers of Korzybski against classing semantics and Korzybski's so-called general semantics in the same intellectual current. In any case, we cannot identify semantics, which is connected with logic and epistemology, with general semantics which in the interpretation of its most radical representatives is a psychotherapeutic technique.

In certain matters there are genetic connections between semantics and general semantics, but they are superficial and confined rather to points of formal influence. In fact, we have to do with trends and opinions that are not only different one from another but often opposing one another, especially if the attitudes of their exponents are taken into consideration. That is why the confusion of ideas on that point, prevailing so far in Marxist literature, a confusion to which even so reliable an author as Maurice Cornforth has fallen a victim (in his *Science Versus Idealism*), is extremely embarrassing.

There is no doubt that this state of affairs is due to the search for easy triumphs in the criticism of bourgeois ideology; this in turn results in the tendency to stress whatever in the works under review is in error, ridiculous and weak, and to disregard what is correct and intellectually stimulating, since that does not fit into the "black-and-white" pattern. That way, one can pickle any opponent, not to mention those whose views are such a combination of strange and often contradictory statements as is the case of general semanticists. But what is gained from such an easy triumph over so mishandled an opponent? In my opinion, nothing whatever. For in such cases the strengthening of our negative attitude towards the views which we criticize is only apparent. Ignorance is not a good adviser on ideological issues, and as a preventive measure against the influence of alien ideology, it fails completely at critical moments. On the other hand, the losses we suffer as a result of such manipulations are obvious

---

mantics. General Semantics and Related Disciplines" and "What Is Meant by Aristotelian Structure of Language?"

and painful: we lose a certain amount of knowledge acquired by mankind and, sometimes still more important, valuable stimuli to creative analyses. Books can be read in two ways. First – in search of what is wrong and stupid in them, "prey" for criticism – this is the manner of reading typical of those who do not know how to avail themselves of the achievements of science. But one can also read them in a quite different manner, looking for what is new, stimulating and calculated to promote science, despite all the errors and falsehoods, which may be quite numerous in given cases. This way of reading books is characteristic of people who know how to make use of science. If a scientific work includes even a single new and creative thought to stimulate scientific inventiveness, then it must not be lost, it must not be allowed to be drowned in the ocean of errors.

That postulate must cause us firmly to reject our practices, of many years standing, in the matter of criticism of non-Marxist views in philosophy. I have referred to that matter above, but those reflections return with redoubled force when we discuss general semantics, precisely because in this connection we see with particular clarity all our mistakes and shortcomings in criticism, and sometimes cannot overcome an embarrassing suspicion that in many cases that criticism has been marked by ordinary *ignorance*. After all, only ignorance can explain the identification, over many years, of semantics with *general* semantics, the identification of the views of Stuart Chase (who is only a popularizer of Korzybski's ideas) with the opinions of Carnap or Tarski. Further, only ignorance can explain the failure to notice the *real* problems that after all underlie general semantics. It is difficult to escape the impression that probably none of those who in our literature have written about Korzybski has read his book thoroughly. This is not said in defence of that book which, on the contrary, I hold to be, apart from all its other defects, morbid and marked by monomania. But the criticism of it in our literature has been at fault: it has not pursued its essential errors and has failed to discern the real problems it discusses. It is easy to demonstrate that Korzybski's *Science and Sanity* is an obscure work of a dilettante, eclectically amassing vastly different concepts and unceremoniously assimilating other people's ideas: that it is a book about which it has been said justly that what is correct in it is old, and what is new in it is in error. Yet at the same time it might be shown how the book takes up Pavlov's ideas, and that in some of its concepts it comes close to epistemological realism and to the dialectics of the cognitive process. To say that it comes close to Marxism would prove ignorance, but what has thus far been said about that book in our literature proves ignorance in no less degree. And what shall be said about works by some authors belonging to the school of general semantics, such as A. Rapoport and S. I. Hayakawa, already quoted above, or Irving J. Lee, Wendell Johnson and others?

There is no doubt that general semantics is very remote from the usual scientific standards. When studying that strange mixture of *Dichtung und Wahrheit*, it should be borne in mind that that is a specifically American product, a sect rather than a school. This is clearly realized by sober observers and even by the more sober among those who themselves are followers and celebrants of general semantics. In his article already cited, A. Rapoport writes on that subject:

"The accusations of cultism leveled against Korzybski's followers are not altogether unfounded. In the United States there is a large floating population of 'truthseekers'. Many of them lack the capacity of strenuous intellectual effort required in a fruitful pursuit of knowledge and wisdom; others lack the power of critical evaluation, which would enable them to tell the genuine from the false. Still others cannot be comfortable until they find a panacea to believe in. These people support 'movements' and cults. They are as likely to 'go for' Christian Science as for technocracy, for psychoanalysis as for theosophy, for the Great Books programme as for dianetics. And so inevitably one finds some of them among the adherents of general semantics ... Whether they were actually helped by general semantics or by other factors cannot be determined without sufficient controls. But they went about spreading the faith, thus giving a cultist flavour to the 'movement'"[5].

General semantics therefore has all the characteristics of a sectarian movement with its own cult. This is confirmed by the author quoted above, an apparently sober and realistic critic of that "sect". Rapoport states that Korzybski's book is an obscure work of a dilettante and that, contrary to declarations, it is in no way a result of empirical research. And then he concludes:

"If Korzybski cannot be said to have established an empirical science, what then has he done? He has pointed a way toward the establishment of such a science. *He was a precursor of an intellectual revolution which is just now begining and which promises to match that of the Renaissance.* If Korzybski is seen in this rôle, then the question of his originality or erudition is not important. He might have something of a dilettante in him. He might have pretended to have more specialized knowledge than he actually had. Great portions of his outlook might be found in the works of more modest and more meticulous workers. That is not important. *He was a man of vision and an apostle.* Such men are all too rare in our age of specialization"[6].

In this way a member of the sect replaces a rationally thinking man! A very instructive phenomenon for an understanding of what is general semantics, and for ascertaining the secret of its social successes in the 1930s, when the birth of Nazism was accompanied by growing interest in the influence of propaganda upon public opinion, and the influence of human communication on the attitudes and behaviour of men. These circumstances account for the rapid and violent career made in America by Korzybski's conception. I deliberately refer here to *Korzybski's* ideas, since I distinguish clearly between the attitude of the master

---

[5] A. Rapoport, "What Is Semantics?", p. 6.

[6] Ibid., p. 17 (italics – A. S.).

and that of at least some of his continuators. The latter I not only value more, but also appraise them in quite different terms. Their opinions and activity account for the fact that general semantics may not be treated as mere bluff and shamanism: while criticizing in with full force, one has yet to see and examine the real problems which it has raised.

I shall now try to inform the reader very briefly about the fundamental concepts of Korzybski.

He himself defined general semantics as the science of neuro-semantic and neuro-linguistic reactions of human individuals to semantic "environment" (see above). Rapoport defined it in a more comprehensible manner as the science of "how people use words and how words affect those who use them"[7]. In this can clearly be seen that part of semantics which Morris calls pragmatics.

For Korzybski, general semiotics is above all a *psychotherapeutic technique* covering, as we have seen above, almost everything, from stomach ache and dental caries to social conflicts. In his aspirations, Korzybski was guided by Freudian patterns.

The theoretical assumptions on which he based his ideas were as follows.

The starting point of Korzybski's interest and analysis was a general theory of man and culture, the subject matter of his first book[8]. From that point of view he approached the rôle of symbols in man's social life, or, strictly, the issue of the pathology of signs.

Unfortunately, to recount these matters in abbreviated form makes them look much more rational and serious than they were in fact. Korzybski's conception is a strange conglomeration of various theories drawn from the most diverse disciplines. And the main idea, to be observed in all his explanations, is quite striking: all organic and social pathology is semantogenic. "Listen to me and you will be saved!"

---

[7] Ibid., p. 4.

[8] A. Korzybski, *Manhood of Humanity*, New York 1921.

The recipe to be used is only too simple: one must reject the obsolete Aristotelian (two-valued) system of language in favour of a non-Aristotelian system – i.e., a system which rejects the two-value principle of traditional logic – and the semantic blockage, the cause of all evil, will disappear at once. Of course, his idea, as formulated here, is somewhat exaggerated.

The problem of the rôle of symbol in social life was drawn by Korzybski from many sources, above all from behaviourism and the Pavlovian theory (Korzybski considered his theory to be a development of the theory of conditioned responses). Freudianism served him as inspiration for a specific conception of the pathology of symbols. This was the point where the theory of a non-Aristotelian language and the related psychotherapeutic technique set in.

That conception is Korzybski's theoretical contribution. But is must be asserted that it is in no way original. Birth certificates of all its elements can easily be produced, although the original ideas are often completely mystified.

Let us begin with the general concept of a non-Aristotelian language system. The existing system of language which Korzybski calls Aristotelian (his more reasonable followers, e.g., S. I. Hayakawa, speak of an Indo-European system of language) is alleged to impose a two-valued system of appraisals (e.g., "You either are a communist, or you are not"), which is said to evoke certain neurotic ailments. On the contrary, a non-Aristotelian system, supposedly connected with contemporary science (in his arguments Korzybski often flings about such terms as "colloidal", "quantum", without making them fit into any system whatever), is said to have an infinite scale of appraisals. The ideas taken from Łukasiewicz and his theory of many-valued logic can clearly be traced (Łukasiewicz is mentioned in the bibliography), but these ideas are used in a manner that has nothing in common with the original concept and without any justification for their new applications.

But this is only the beginning of the issue, since here we learn new details about that non-Aristotelian system of language.

First of all, the use of the copula *is* for identification is prohibited. "The word is not the thing it denotes", says Korzybski. On the "non-verbal level" we can only indicate things, and when we say "This *is* a table" we are said to *identify* the word with the object, which gives rise to serious semantogenic pathology. Here again we recognize the source from which "the non-verbal level" was borrowed: credit for that concept belongs to the neopositivists. But with Korzybski it becomes a caricature. No normal man identifies the word with the thing in the manner he suggests, and the cure, consisting in repeating: "This *is not* a table" or the appropriate mechanical operations of the "structural differential" invented by Korzybski, savours of shamanism[9].

The second principle affirms that "a map is not a territory", which implies that a sign cannot aspire to be fully representative. The Aristotelian system of language is said to be "elementalistic", to break cognition into elements which pretend to be complete and absolute. And the non-Aristotelian system is "non-elementalistic", recognizing the necessity for grasping the whole of the process of cognition. This obviously goes back to *Gestalt-psychologie.*

Finally, the third principle affirms the "multi-ordinality" of symbols. Not only is a map not a territory, but also the map of the map_l is not the map_l. In other words, the language in which we speak about another language is not that object language. Consequently, we must take note of the hierarchy of languages and avoid ambiguity by placing words in clear contexts so that we may know on what level of abstraction we are. We find no difficulty in identifying here the idea suggested by Russell's theory of types and the related concept of the hierarchy of languages.

---

9 A penetrating criticism of those views is given by Max Black in the article "Korzybski's General Semantics", included in his book *Language and Philosophy,* New York 1949.

Starting from these theoretical assumptions, Korzybski undertakes, in his book, an analysis of the structure of language, by passing from the language of a person who is mentally deranged to the language of higher mathematics. His purpose is to discover a psychotherapeutic technique which would enable him to consolidate the new structure of language and to establish its relation to human behaviour. This is supposed to increase the sum of social health; hence the title of the book – *Science and Sanity.*

Korzybski also made a number of concrete proposals intended to modify language by imparting to it a "non-Aristotelian" structure.

First of all, he maintains, indices should be added to general nouns in order to remove the mystifying conceptualization of classes of objects, and to emphasize the specific and unique character of the individuals. According to Korzybski, if we say not "Negro" in general, but concretely "Negro_1", "Negro_2", etc., we shall remove the causes of such a social phenomenon as racial hatred.

Secondly, dates are to be added in order to distinguish the various phases of the phenomena and thus to eliminate incorrect generalizations. Thus, we should not say e.g., "William Shakespeare" in general, but "William Shakespeare January 1600", "William Shakespeare January 1601", etc.

Thirdly, all sorts of characteristics should he supplemented with the word "etc.", in order to remind us that the "map" does not represent the whole of the "territory", or, in other words, that we never achieve full cognition (this explains the strange-looking title of the principal periodical of the school of general semantics: *ETC*).

Finally, Korzybski recommends the use of quotation marks to indicate that we dissociate ourselves from the actual meaning of certain words.

As a remedy, Korzybski recommends exercises with an instrument he has designed and called a "structural differential";

these exercises are supposed to make the patient realize, first, that the word is not the thing to which it refers, and, secondly, that words occupy different levels of abstraction.

Does this brief summary confirm the thesis that whatever in Korzybski's theory is correct, is old and well known; and what is new, is in error?

I do not comment on the therapeutic aspect of the "semantic" measures. Psychogenic ailments undoubtedly are an extremely important domain of medicine and it may be that in some cases putting rods into the appropriate holes of the "structural differential" may help. But that is a separate issue.

Is Korzybski's general semantics, then, just monstrous nonsense to be thrown in the dustbin? Is it *only* a deliberate idealistic mystification dictated by class considerations, as would appear from many Marxist publications? I am not at all sure.

For all its oddity and its simply maniacal traits, Korzybski's conception includes something which cannot be dimissed lightly. It may be that that comes from the borrowings which in Korzybski's case are innumerable. But precisely that "something" has made it possible to establish an influential school of general semantics, which, apart from sectarians, includes people who are voices in science, especially in linguistics. That "something", too, induced certain outstanding scientists, among them Bronisław Malinowski, P. W. Bridgman, Bertrand Russell and others, to endorse Korzybski's book with their approval of his ideas and with a favourable appraisal of what he had done. Let me also point it out to those with a liking for easy triumphs, that from the *philosophical* point of view Korzybski is sometimes a hard nut to crack precisely for a Marxist critic.

There is no doubt that all his ideas are marked by ascribing an absolute value to the function of language. This in particular stands out in relief when it comes to social issues which Korzybski would also like to reduce to semantogenic perturbances. For instance, he quite seriously tried to treat the problems of Communism and Fascism in terms of neuro-semantic reactions to definite signals[10]. That notion, which for obvious reasons was attacked with particular force by Marxist critics, was very seriously continued by Stuart Chase in his *The Tyranny of Words*[11]. But also in Korzybski's works we find understanding of the fact that language can perform its function correctly only it if reflects reality. That idea is the guiding principle of Korzybski's campaign in favour of modifying the structure of language, and that very idea was taken up by his continuators (e.g., Stuart Chase, Irving J. Lee, S. I. Hayakawa, Wendell Johnson). This is what Korzybski himself says on the subject:

"As words *are not* the objects which they represent, *structure and structure alone* becomes the only link which connects our verbal processes with the empirical data. To achieve adjustment and sanity and the conditions which follow from them, we must study structural characteristics of the word *first*, and, then only, build languages of similar structure, instead of habitually ascribing to the word the primitive structure of our language... Moreover, every language, having a structure, by the very nature of language reflects in its own structure that of the word as assumed by those who evolved the language. In other words, we read unconsciously into the word the structure of the language we use. The guessing and ascribing a fanciful, mostly primitive assumed structure to the word is precisely what 'philosophy' and 'metaphysics' do. The empirical search for word structure and the building of new languages (theories), of necessary, or similar, structure, is, on the contrary, what science does. Any one who will reflect upon these structural peculiarities of language cannot miss the semantic point that the scientific method uses the only correct language-method. It develops in the *natural order*, while metaphysics of every description uses the reversed, and ultimately a pathological, order"[12].

---

[10] A. Korzybski, *Science and Sanity*, pp. XXIII–XXIV.

[11] New York 1938. Stuart Chase repeats that idea in his later work, *The Power of Words*, New York 1954.

[12] A. Korzybski, *Science and Sanity*, pp. 59–60.

Are these ideas correct or not? Personally I think they are not only correct (their formulation here is of secondary importance), but even of great significance for a criticism of idealism and of semantic philosophy. Consequently, they are something which does not fit well into traditional patterns and hackneyed formulations. The more so since with Korzybski these are not certain accidental ideas, but the ideas to which he devoted many dozens of pages and which he placed at the very root of his conception. The more so, further, since these ideas have been taken up by his continuators of the school of general semantics. Says Wendell Johnson:

"The crucial point to be considered in a study of language behaviour is the relationship between language and reality, between words and not-words. Except as we understand this relationship, we run the grave risk of straining the delicate connection between words and facts, of permitting our words to go wild, and so of creating for ourselves fabrications of fantasy and delusion"[13].

Why, even Stuart Chase, clearly bent on producing a "best-seller", says the same:

"What the semantic discipline does is to blow ghosts out of the picture and create a new picture as close to reality as one can get. One is no longer dogmatic, emotional, bursting with the rights and wrongs of it, but humble, careful, aware of the very considerable number of things he does not know. His new map may be wrong; his judgments may err. But the probability of better judgments is greatly improved, for he is now swayed more by happenings in the outside world than by reverberations in his skull"[14].

"Good language alone will not save mankind. But seeing the things behind the names will help us to understand the structure of the world we live in. Good language will help us to communi-

---

[13] W. Johnson, *People in Quandaries*, New York 1946, p. 113.

[14] S. Chase, *The Tyranny of Words*, p. 206.

cate with one another about the realities of our environment, where now we speak darkly, in alien tongues"[15].

But, ye Gods!, that *is* reasonable! Contrary to all expectations, these people do understand certain things which neo-positivists and radical conventionalists could not understand. That cannot be simply erased; that accurately smashes all evaluations made to conform to the "black-and-white" pattern.

And what is to be done about the fact that Korzybski, by declaring himself in favour of a mobile, against a static, interpretation of reality, occasionally comes close to the well-known argumentation of at least some adherents of dialectics? This, too, is not coincidence. In rejecting the "Aristotelian" structure of language, Korzybski is at the same time opposed to the traditional formulation of the so-called laws of thought and says:

"It is impossible, short of a volume, to revise this 'logic' and to formulate an $\bar{A}$ (i.e., non-Aristotelian – A. S.) ∞-valued, *non-elementalistic* semantics which would be structurally similar to the world and our nervous system; but it must be mentioned, even here, that the 'law of identity' is never applicable to processes. The 'law of excluded middle' or 'excluded third' as it is sometimes called, which gives the two-valued character to $\bar{A}$ 'logic', establishes, as a general principle, what represents only a limiting case and so, *as a general principle*, must be unsatisfactory"[16].

But "the worst" is still ahead of us. Now Korzybski refers *expressis verbis* to the intellectual kinship between his ideas and the Pavlovian theory, and in my opinion he is to a certain extent justified in his claim. I am even inclined to believe that Korzybski formulated his ideas under Pavlov's influence. Korzybski himself speaks of congeniality, and asserts that he became acquainted with Pavlov's ideas only after he had formulated his own non-Aristotelian system[17].

[15] Ibid., p. 361.

[16] A. Korzybski, *Science and Sanity*, p. 405.

[17] Ibid., pp. 315–316.

"My linguistic, structural, *non-el.*, *theoretical revision* leads to a new and important enlargement of the application to man of the Pavlov *experimental* theory of 'conditioned' reflexes. The fact that these independent discoveries reinforce and support each other is a striking instance of the usefulness of theoretical researches"[18].

I do not know whether Korzybski knew the Pavlovian theory of the second system of signals, but what he writes on the subject (e.g., on pp. 331–2) resembles that theory even by the terminology he uses. If that is really congeniality, then the fact is striking in itself. But even if Korzybski wrote under Pavlov's influence, the problem remains intricate. The point is that the concept of semantogenic blockages in human behaviour perfectly well fits into the theory of conditioned responses, and the more so into the theory of the second system of signals. The explanation of neuroses by the mechanism of the conflict between stimulation and inhibition comes precisely from Pavlov. What is at stake there, is not only the signals which cause conditioned responses, but also the signals of signals, that is words. If we reject the odd form of the pathology of signs in Korzybski's work the real problem of semantogenic disturbances remains. Moreover, that problem applies not only to the psychiatric level; there is the issue formulated, as mentioned above, by Rapoport in the following way: "How people use words and how words affect those who use them" (S. I. Hayakawa, on the outer of his book, put it in slogan form: "How men use words and words use men".). Thus, Korzybski's idea is concerned with many real research issues.

This is still more true with reference to some of Korzybski's followers in the school of general semantics.

Their undoubtedly rational idea is the programme of a *pragmatic* study of language, that is the study of language from the point of view of the *producers* of language signs. Rapoport formu-

---

[18] Ibid., p. 326.

lates the question in the following manner: grammar investigates relations between words; logic studies relations between propositions; semantics studies the relation between words and propositions and their referents, and on that basis establishes their meaning and truth; and general semantics goes furthest of all since it also investigates the influence of words and propositions on human behaviour:

"For a general semanticist, communication is not merely words in proper order properly inflected (as for the grammarian) or assertions in proper relation to each other (as for the logician) or assertions in proper relation to referents (as for the semanticist), but all these together, with the chain of 'fact to nervous system to language to nervous system to action'"[19].

This clearly reveals the influence of pragmatism, working principally through semiotic. Certainly, but it is no coincidence that general semantics has developed in the home of pragmatism. This is the same trend of influence as in the case of Morris's semiotic, although here the research programme is different, much broader, and going beyond the general theory of signs.

In its rational form, general semantics refers to increased interest revealed by such disciplines as psychology, psychiatry, and above all cultural anthropology, in "neuro-linguistic" factors of human behaviour. Adherents of general semantics claim that precisely these disciplines provide proof of the fact that human experience consists in selecting among the stimuli coming from the environment, and human behaviour, in organizing experience in conformity with definite patterns. Both these functions depend in a definite way on language, on its structure, and on linguistic habits. Hence the importance of concrete research on language and the programme of such research.

It would be impossible to deny the importance of this research, regardless of our attitude toward this or that justification of its programme. And here is a brief specification of problems.

---

[19] A. Rapoport, "What Is Semantics?", p. 14.

First come the issues connected with human communication. As we already know, the original success of general semantics was due to its interest in the rapid progress of Nazism in the 1930s. This gave rise to an interpretation of social conflicts in terms of semantic perturbations. That trend was initiated by Korzybski, who was followed by Stuart Chase, S. I. Hayakawa, Wendell Johnson, and others. It must be said that as early as 1949 S. I. Hayakawa, in the preface to the new edition of his *Language in Thought and Action*, confirmed the failure of such efforts, which were correctly treated by Marxists as enemy Number One. But there remained other questions, more moderate in their claims but very important in practice: the conditions of success in discussion; blockages and facilities in human communication; etc. These issues have given rise to a rich literature, based on the principles of general semantics and connected with the influence of language on correct thinking and on human behaviour, both social and individual. A special field is constituted by problems of education and psychiatry, where Korzybski's original interest in the pathology of language signs comes to the fore.

This somewhat practical problem is connected with the more theoretical issues of general semantics, namely the rôle of sign and symbol, the relation between language and thought, and the various questions which I should call applied semantics, concerned with vagueness and ambiguity of expressions.

Finally, general semantics deals with the influence of language on the shaping of culture in the sense of cultural anthropology. This covers comparative studies in culture as related to the development of language, for instance B. Malinowski's *The Problem of Meaning in Primitive Languages* and B. L. Whorf's *The Relation of Habitual Thought and Behavior to Language* (a study of the Hopi language).

The aspirations of general semantics go much further. I do not mean here such extravagant formulations as "semantics and dental surgery", but more moderate claims – to influence upon literature and art, to genetic connections with cybernetics, etc. These are, to say the least, controversial issues. This is why I have stopped at these problems which are in fact investigated by the school of general semantics, include *real* research issues, and have a literature of their own[20]. There are many of such problems, and their importance is not secondary. Be that as it may, it must be stressed once more that these issues should not be dismissed lightly. I agree with Max Black, who in his work on Korzybski's semantics concludes that the theoretical foundations of general semantics are logically wrong, but adds: "...The history of science provides a number of examples of how confused theoretical systems evoked useful and interesting effects"[21]. Let it be added further that it was so when they raised *real* scientific problems.

Do the problems of general semantics belong to philosophy? That is a separate question. Its adherents certainly do not admit that they are philosophers. In fact, they are above all social technicians, and their theoretical research is much more remote

---

[20] I offer here some information which may be of help to those who would like to continue the study of the subject.

Many works, differing in the subject matter and varying in scientific value, can be found in the yearly volumes of the periodical *ETC*, which has been appearing since August 1943. As mentioned above, selected articles from *ETC* for 1943-53 have been published in book form as *Language, Meaning and Maturity*.

A series of monographs has appeared under the auspices of the International Non-Aristotelian Library. I should like to mention the following items, whether included in that series, or not: S. Chase, *The Tyranny of Words* and *The Power of Words*; R. Weil, *The Art of Practical Thinking*, New York 1940; H. Walpole, *Semantics*, New York 1941; S. I. Hayakawa, *Language in Thought and Action*, New York 1949; I. J. Lee, *Language Habits in Human Affairs*, New York 1941, and *How to Talk With People*, New York 1952; W. Johnson, *People in Quandaries*; A. Rapoport, *Science and the Goals of Man. A Study in Semantic Orientation*, New York 1950, and *Operational Philosophy*, New York 1953; K. S. Keyes Jr., *How to Develop Your Thinking Ability*, New York 1950.

[21] Black, op. cit., p. 246.

from philosophy *sensu stricto* than the semantic problems connected with logic and epistemology. Nevertheless, general semantics has certain philosophical implications. There are certainly idealistic implications, loudly bandied about in Marxist criticism. But there are also other implications passed over in silence by that criticism, since they spoil the schematic pattern and blur the picture of "pure" idealism. The passing over in silence is, since everything that distorts the truth is harmful, useless and harmful. The more so since that objection can be raised not only against former publications, such as Bykhovsky's article on Cornforth's book, but also against more recent publications[22].

Such criticism is harmful also because, contrary to the intentions of the authors, it undermines the prestige of Marxism. The notorious article by B. Bykhovsky on semantics (published in the *Bolshevik* in August 1947) was reprinted without any comment in the *ETC* (in the Autumn of 1948), and the item "Semantic Philosophy" from the *Concise Philosophical Dictionary* (in Russian, ed. Rozental and Yudin, Moscow, 1951) was also reprinted without comment as an annex to *Language, Meaning and Maturity*. In this way, the critical discussions of semantics came to share the fate of many other items from the *Concise Philosophical Dictionary* which were reprinted without comment as a separate publication and circulated by the anti-communist periodical *Preuves*. Thus our ideological opponents consider statements which were intended as "annihilating" criticism of bourgeois idealistic ideology, to be the best counter-propaganda, the best weapon against Marxism and Communism. Can there be a sharper condemnation of such forms of ideological criticism?

*

* *

---

[22] I mean here the work of Г. А. Брутян "Идеалистическая сущность семантической философии" [The Idealist Essence of Semantic Philosophy], in the collection *Современный субъективный идеализм* [Contemporary Subjective Idealism], Москва 1957,

This concludes the first part of my book. It not only provides information about semantics and the subject matter of its investigations in the various fields, but has also enabled us to remove a number of misunderstandings and erroneous appraisals accumulated in Marxist literature, mostly as a result of an insufficient knowledge of the subject. It has further given a review of a wide range of problems, often quite untouched by Marxist analysis and criticism. Certain issues belonging to semantics, mainly those related to the theory of communication, signs and meaning, will be taken up in the subsequent chapters.

Part Two

SELECTED PROBLEMS OF SEMANTICS

CHAPTER ONE

THE PHILOSOPHICAL ASPECT OF THE COMMUNICATION PROCESS

"And the whole earth was of one language, and of one speech.

And it came to pass, as they journeyed from the east, that they found a plain in the land of Shinar; and they dwelt there.

And they said one to another, Go to, let us make brick, and burn them thoroughly. And they had brick for stone, and slime had they for mortar.

And they said, Go to, let us build us a city and a tower, whose top may reach unto heaven; and let us make us a name, lest we be scattered abroad upon the face of the whole earth.

And the Lord came down to see the city and the tower, which the children of men builded.

And the Lord said, Behold, the people is one, and they have all one language; and this they begin to do: and now nothing will be restrained from them, which they have imagined to do.

Go to, let us go down, and there confound their language, that they may not understand one another's speech.

So the Lord scattered them abroad from thence upon the face of all the earth: and they left off to build the city".

(*Genesis*, XI, 1-8)

"Error is never so difficult to be destroyed as when it has its roots in Language".

(Bentham)

EVEN in their pre-scientific reflections on reality, people came to realize, to a certain extent, the social function and the social power of language. Lucian of Samosata relates that the Gauls represented Hercules, the symbol of strength, as a patriarch, drawing men after him, their ears fastened to his tongue with golden chains. Those people, says Lucian, follow their subjugator willingly and joyfully, although they might easily free themselves. From that extraordinary picture it seems that to the Gauls that physical strength was nothing as compared with the power of the word. And the chains which tied people to Hercules' tongue were but the words which flowed from his lips to their minds[1].

These problems have many a time been taken up in literature, principally philosophical, both ancient (chiefly Greek) and modern (chiefly English). But for a profound, truly scientific, and at the same time many–sided and broad analysis of the problem of the social rôle of language, and in particular the problem of the *philosophical* significance of language, we had to wait until the most recent times. In the 20th century, the problem of language has become the dominant philosophical issue.

Hence an embarrassing situation for one who has resolved to give a Marxist analysis of the problem. Embarrassing for various reasons.

First of all, the wealth of literature. In the latest period alone, an ocean of ink has been poured out in discussions on the subject.

Next, the immensity of the problem itself. The issue of the social rôle and the social significance of language (the question of the rôle of language in science and philosophy is but a small part of the wider problem) is so broad that it is absolutely impossible to exhaust it in a single book. Thus, the necessity to be selective — but to select what?

Finally, there is an additional difficulty arising from the fact that, while Marxist literature has for many years neglected those matters, the frequent analysis made of them has often been from clearly idealistic positions. A Marxist author who takes up the discussion of these issues — and automatically also a discussion involving the solutions suggested thus far — is in some sense a pioneer. The choice of problems, therefore, must be extremely cautious and somewhat restricted, especially at first.

Such being the situation I think that choice should cover focal issues, the solution of which is the starting point for further,

---

1 Described by Stefan Czarnowski in his work "Herkules Galijski" [Gallic Hercules], included in Vol. III of his *Dziela* [Collected Works], Warszawa 1956; reference is made there to Lucian's *Heracles*.

detailed considerations and analysis. It also seems advisable to begin by indicating the problems selected and by outlining a *programme* of research rather than by trying to offer a definitive solution, since a full solution of such problems again presupposes specialized research. Such precisely is the dialectics of all fully developed research: it is necessary to raise, and to solve in outline, the general issues in order to be able to work fruitfully on detailed problems without the risk of being lost, as to theory and method, in a jungle of detail; but at the same time, the understanding of detail is an indispensable condition to a proper solution of the general problems which otherwise are overshadowed by generalities and verbalism.

What problems, then, are to be classified as focal? What is to be the starting point of an attempt at a Marxist analysis of them?

The great merit of logical semantics consisted in its revealing the philosophical significance of the problems of language. A number of mistakes were made: the problem of language, which is *one* of the focal problems of contemporary philosophy, was made into the principal, and even the *only* issue; moreover, that problem was reduced to its formal aspects, chiefly those of syntax; analysis was confined to artificial languages, to suit the needs of the theory of deduction. All this, of course, refers to the situation in the 1930s.

Certainly, every discipline is entitled to analyse the object of its research from a particular point of view. This is even necessary, in view of the advancing specialization in science, and entails no unfavourable consequences, provided that it means a *conscious* restriction of the field of vision. The error of logical semantics consisted in making a virtue of necessity and, moreover, in presenting its limited point of view as the absolute. Logical semanticists denied nearly all sociological and gnoseological issues of language, precisely those which for philosophy are of decisive importance. This is connected with the fact that such a limited approach is quite valueless in the analysis of natural languages. This is by no means incidental. The limitations of logical semantics were a result of the *philosophically* limited point of view of its founders, both adherents of analytical philosophy, and those of logical empiricism. Attempts to remove those limitations were made even before 1939, although they got into full swing only after 1945. The development has occurred of the general theory of signs, i.e. semiotics, which, although born of the marriage of neo-positivism with pragmatism, goes beyond the narrow formal treatment of language by the neo-positivists. The tendencies of general semantics to analyse the social influence and the social power of language go still further. At the same time, a critical situation affecting the foundations of analytical philosophy has been revealed[2] and certain formal analyses which are of no use in the study of the natural language have been subjected to criticism[3]. Logical semantics, and the method of such, have also been criticized severely by the linguists, who attack its purely formal and consequently ahistorical and asocial analysis of linguistic phenomena.

For all the achievements and successes of logical semantics, its restricted character is obvious. Obvious, too, is the need of new researches: narrow formalism must be abandoned; the *social* aspect of the problem must be taken into account; idealistic metaphysics must be rejected (this was connected with logical atomism and logical empiricism, and included elements of Platonism on the one hand and those of epistemological solipsism on the other); and such philosophical positions must be adopted as would make possible a profound analysis of the relation of language to thought and reality (Tarski's semantics, adopted by the neo-positivists, does not solve the problem, if only because of the philosophical "neutrality" of his conception, declared by Tarski himself, i.e., neutrality in the face of the issue as to what is the nature of referents of signs).

---

[2] Cf. J. O. Urmson, *Philosophical Analysis*, Oxford 1956.

[3] Cf. Max Black's critical essays, extremely important in this respect, included in his *Language and Philosophy*.

It is by no means accidental that the difficulties have been felt for a fairly long time, that their being resolved is still a matter of the future, that criticism is growing even among the semanticists themselves, and that new tendencies are clearly gaining in strength. This is because at the root of the crisis lie erroneous philosophical assumptions typical of the traditional semanticist trend. It is precisely this which offers great opportunities to the theoretical rôle of Marxist philosophy. By organically combining gnoseological and sociological problems, materialism in theoretical interpretations with historicism in methodology, Marxist philosophy is as it were predestined to removing those difficulties and symptoms of crisis which are now observed in semantics (in the broad sense of the term).

If we now ask – What is the focal theoretical problem which from that point of view should be investigated first ?, the answer must be, beyond all doubt – *the theory of communication*[4].

Semantics certainly includes certain detailed questions which are in no way connected with philosophical issues – for instance certain specific problems of logical syntax. Far be it from me to deny the scientific importance of such problems, but when we leave the purely technical ground, we immediately face the paramount question, a question on the solution of which depends this or that solution of a number of problems that are usually termed semantic. That question is – what is the process of human communication (the process the most important part of which is human communication by means of a phonic language) and what are the conditions of that process?

Let us not shirk the issue, but begin by analysing that problem first.

---

[4] Reference is made here to the philosophical aspect of the theory of communication, which also has other aspects: psychological, linguistic, and technical, the last-named being now extensively developed.

1. THE ESSENCE OF THE PROBLEM OF COMMUNICATION

In the 1920s, Ogden and Richards, authors who have rendered great service to the development of semantics, thus outlined the programme of that discipline in the study of the theory of communication:

"In yet another respect all these specialists fail to realize the deficiencies of current linguistic theory. Preoccupied as they are – ethnologist with recording the details of fast vanishing languages; philologist with an elaborate technique of phonetic laws and principles of derivation; philosophers with 'philosophy' – all have overlooked the pressing need for a better understanding of what actually occurs in discussion. The analysis of the process of communication is partly psychological, and psychology has now reached a stage at which this part may be succesfully undertaken. Until this had happened the science of Symbolism necessarily remained in abeyance, but there is no longer any excuse for vague talk about Meaning, and ignorance of the ways in which words deceive us"[5].

In what however, does the problem of interhuman communication consist?

It often happens that a philosophical problem begins at the point where common sense stops short. Just at that point where common sense seems satisfied, stating plainly that people speak to one another and in this way convey mutually all kinds of information, and in this sense communicate with one another, the philosopher starts asking questions: but how do they do that? and why? and what does it all mean? He often questions in a way involving risk to his reputation, a way which leads laymen to impart to the term "philosopher" a derogatory shade. So it must also be conceded that the poet may be right in ridiculing philosophical speculation and raising his voice in defence of common sense. The honesty of a professional philosopher im-

[5] C. K. Ogden & I. A. Richards, *The Meaning of Meaning*, London 1953, p. 8.

pels me to quote the witty and profound, though little known, poem by Erich Weinert, entitled *Der Philosophenkongress*:

Die Philosophen veranstalteten einen Kongress
Auf Beschluss des Philosophenbundes
Zwecks Eindringung in das Innre des
Noch unerschlossenen Daseinsgrundes.

Da trafen sich die delegierten Weisen
Mit Dietrichen, Schlüsseln und anderen Eisen
An der Tür mit dem grossen Fragezeichen
Und bestellten da unverdrossen.

Aber die Tür wollte nicht weichen;
Sie blieb verschlossen.
Und schliesslich kamen sie überein,
Es müsse eine ganz komplizierte Mechanik sein.

Soeben begannen sie einen tiefen Disput
Über: als ob, an sich und dergleichen,
Da trat ein Mann ohne Doktorhut
Aus der Tür mit dem Fragezeichen.

Die Philosophen rümpfen ihre Rüssel:
Woher haben dann Sie den richtigen Schlüssel?
Der Bestaunte aber sagte gelassen:
Man braucht nur an die Klinke zu fassen:

Ich dachte beileibe noch nie daran,
Dass man die Tür auch verschliessen kann.
Die Philosophen lächelten ob dieses Manns:
Ja, ja, die heilige Ignoranz:

Wollte man ein so wichtiges Problem
In so einfältiger Weise lösen,
Brauchte man doch kein wissenschaftliches System,
Und auserdem
Wäre ja auch der Kongress dann nicht nötig gewesen.

Do such things happen? Yes, of course they do! That will be demonstrated before long by way of an example which interests us.

But can such common-sense argumentation suffice for our analysis? Certainly not. It was Engels who said that what is termed common sense fares well enough in every-day matters, but strange things begin to happen to it when it seeks to become involved in the wider arena of scientific, philosophical, etc., investigations.

Human communication embraces a far from negligible philosophical problem, strange as that may seen from the common-sense point of view.

Is there anything simpler in every-day life than the fact when we say to a person we are working with, "hand me the axe, please" or "steady that beam, please", that person, on hearing what we say, behaves as we have asked him to. It is all so simple and self-evident that should the behaviour expected in reply to our words *not* occur, we should see it as something extraordinary and seek the causes of such a state of things. Just the fact what we are stimulated to reflect on the communication process only when it becomes disturbed shows how natural that process seems to us. Nevertheless *here* lies a philosophical and sociological problem of enormous significance: how does it happen that people do communicate with one another? It is only against the background of that problem that we see in a proper light and in a proper context the traditional, almost classical issues of semantics, such as the questions of sign, of symbol, of meaning, of language and speech, and the related philosophical (strictly: gnoseological) issues. Of course, it is possible to engage in the study of logical antinomies, of the theory of types, and of logical calculus, without paying heed to their wider theoretical aspects. But only to a certain point. So it is not a practical possibility to deal only with the narrow technical aspects of these problems without crossing the frontier beyond which the philosophical issue looms large. Neither a logician nor a linguist can avoid that eventuality, if he sets out to study the theoretical aspect of language as the subject matter of his investigations. He has to do so sooner or later and thereby become, willy-nilly, a philosopher.-

To understand that, it suffices to take a look at the controversy concerning the promises and conditions of the communication process, a controversy between the two principal conceptions in that respect: *transcendental* and *naturalist*. That controversy will be discussed below and, in order to show the arguments in full relief, I shall follow Urban[6] in choosing as the principal opponents Jaspers[7] as the representative of the transcendental conception, and Dewey[8] as the representative of the naturalist conception. But as background to their arguments certain general remarks are necessary.

*

* *

The problem of communication is certainly one of the fundamental problems of philosophy. Suffice it to point out that communicability is one of the essential properties belonging to the definition of knowledge, of *scientific* cognition: this is so because intersubjective verifiability would be impossible without communicability. Moreover, communication seems to be an element inseparable from all processes connected with cognition: even speechless thinking in monologue is a specific act of communication (in the extended sense of the term). Consequently, it is no matter for wonder that philosophy cannot disregard that problem, if epistemology is to be pursued in any reasonable manner.

Further, the statement that communication is one of the essential phenomena of social life is not only obvious, but trivial. Without human communication, without a *possibility* of such communication, social life would be impossible; this refers

6 The controversy is very lucidly presented by Wilbur Marshall Urban in *Language and Reality*, London 1951, Chap. VI: "Intelligible Communication". Urban declares himself in favour of the transcendental conception, in which he evidently follows Kant.

7 Cf. K. Jaspers, *Philosophie*, Vol. 2: *Existenzerhellung*, Berlin 1932. Chap. III: "Kommunikation", is devoted to the explanation of the existentialist theory of communication.

8 Cf. J. Dewey, *Experience and Nature*, London 1929, Chap. V.

in particular to the process of labour, which lies at the root of social life. It is self-evident that the problem of communication is also one of the focal issues of sociology.

No wonder, then, that philosophers are now paying particular attention to the question. I should say much more: efforts must be made to extract the kernel of the problem from the mystifying shell of this or that philosophical speculation. Moreover, one should not even allow oneself to be discouraged *a priori* in the case of the controversy around "true" communication, a controversy between the two conceptions mentioned above.

First of all, however, the concept of communication must be explained in greater detail and the object of controversy must thus be made more precise.

I follow Urban in dividing acts of communication into two principal categories: acts communicating a certain behaviour or emotional state (behavioural communication), and acts communicating a certain knowledge or mental state (intelligible communication).

Various attempts have been made to give a definition of man, to bring out his *differentia specifica.* Marx said after Franklin that man is an animal which produces tools; contemporary semanticists see that *differentia* in the ability to use signs and symbols. In fact, in both cases we have to do with different aspects of the same process of *human* social life. The process of labour and the process of using signs, i.e., human communication – are interconnected genetically and functionally. If that connection is understood, one can well introduce communication as an element in the definition of man and human society. But *what* communication?

In a certain sense of the term, communication can be observed in the animal world as well. The bee, with its "dance" and flicks of the antennae, induces its hive-mates to fly to rich finds, and thus "communicates" something to them. The same applies to the ants, which with touches of the antennae warn their "community" against threatening danger. Birds' love songs, and the rutting of the deer, are also specific forms of communication. "Communication" of a similar kind with others; expressing fear, exultation, etc., occurs between men as well; in extraordinary situations, the very utterance of some sound or even the very expression of the face or gestures of the body "communicate" to us something concerning the experiences of those impelled to such actions. But is this communication? In so far as it transfers knowledge of *emotional states* from one individual to another, or provides information about a certain situation *hic et nunc*, yes. But that is a specific communication, resulting from the very behaviour of the individuals concerned, communication working by emotional "contagion". The latter formulation probably corresponds best to the state which follows those specific acts of "communication" – of the bees leaving for meadows that abound in flowers, of a herd in stampede, etc. That communication differs essentially from the typically human communication which transfers certain knowledge and certain *mental* states. It is that human form of communication with which we are concerned in our analysis.

But is it? Are we in fact concerned above all with that form of communication, with communication in *that* sense of the term?

Men communicate to one another their experiences, emotional states, knowledge and mental states in various ways, and by various means. Hence the controversy as to what form of communication is the "true", i.e., the proper form of communication.

As mentioned above, communication working by "contagion", i.e., transmitting above all the emotional state from one individual to another, is also to be observed in men. It forms to a large extent the basis of mob psychology, and becomes a tremendous force in moments of panic, outbreaks of hatred, loosening of the social bonds that hold instinctive actions in check, etc.

But that does not exhaust the issue. Are not music, to a certain extent the visual arts, and to a large extent poetry, particular manifestations of that specific form of communication? Those connoisseurs of music do well who warn against its "programmized" perception, that is against "translating" music into a "language" of thinking in terms of notions or images. They maintain that music should be perceived as a stream of emotional states of a specific kind. I agree with that; consequently, I agree with the assertion that if music "reflects" anything at all, then it reflects only emotional states, and that if it transmits, communicates something to others, then it communicates just such states only. I mean, of course, good, great music. But I do not agree with the assertion that that is the "true" communication, communication *par excellence*, although I admit that it is a *different*, *special* form of communication.

Is not, e.g., the escape sought by the visual arts in abstractionism connected with the existence of that form of communication? The abstractionist thesis is that the intellectual content of visual experience should be rejected and only the "true" transmission of certain emotional states should be left. The promoters of "dadaism" and other similar trends in poetry were also concerned, they claimed, with a "true communication", with some direct transmission to others of their own emotional states and experiences.

Let us sidetrack the appraisal of all those artistic trends, and try to find out what is common to them from the point of view in which we are interested: in all those cases we have to do with human communication, but a communication of a special type, namely of an *emotional*, and *not* an *intellectual*, nature. And yet we imply intellectual communication when we speak of human communication *tout court*.

Why? Because it is most common in the social lives of men and plays in their life a special rôle, is a necessary condition of all social bonds, and especially of the bonds resulting from productive work.

What that type of communication really consists of — after all known to us perfectly well from every-day life — can best be seen if we compare it with communication by means, for instance, of music.

Now the composer experiences an ecstasy of love and expresses it in the language of music in the form of a *Nocturne*, or he experiences patriotic *élan* due to a national uprising in his country and gives expression to his feelings in the form of the *Revolutionary Etude*, or else he transmits emotionally the dreariness of a rainy day in the form of a *Rain Prelude*. After many years, someone else listens to those works without knowing the accompanying circumstances of their birth, without knowing their titles, and without any programmed deciphering of their meaning in intellectual terms. Nonetheless he does experience the longing of the *Nocturne*, the excitement of the *Revolutionary Etude*, and the dreariness of the *Rain Prelude*; provided, however, and this is no trifling proviso, that he belongs to a definite cultural tradition, in particular as regards music. For a Hindu who has not established contacts with European culture, Chopin's music is as non-communicative as is old Hindu music for a European. One point more: since we have to do with an emotional "contagion" by non-intellectual means here, no one can know whether he experiences *the same feeling* as did the composer, or as do other people listening to the same composition. The fact that even the same person differs at various periods in his reaction to the same piece of music, depending on his own emotional "context", forces us to the conclusion that different people perhaps experience different feelings in reaction to specific pieces of music. Some people say that it should be so, and that the "language" of music is the best just because it is flexible. I shall not decide that point here. I should like only to add, in parentheses, that there is some great misunderstanding which arises out of transfering *par force*, in spite of all declarations, the categories of intellectual communication to the field of music.

All in all we can say that in the case of "communicating" one's experiences to others by means of music there is an emotional "contagion": those who transmit the communiqué, and those who receive it, experience definite emotional states; the similarity as between these states cannot be ascertained; the perceptive reaction to what is communicated largely depends on the emotional context in which the comuniqué is placed by the person who receives it.

What about communication combined with intellectual understanding, that is, the case of the communication of certain intellectual states?

No detailed analysis of that type of communication will be undertaken here. I shall confine myself to taking note only of such of its general traits as make it possible to distinguish it from the communication of emotional states.

Suppose Peter is felling trees together with John, and at a certain moment he says: "Hand me the axe, please". John hears what Peter says and, comprehending the content, passes him the axe. A necessary condition for this act of comprehension is that John should know the language used by Peter, since otherwise he would be unable to understand him (just as God correctly concluded in the case of the Tower of Babel). Should John, without understanding the language used by Peter, guess, from the situational context and Peter's gestures, what it is that Peter wants, and pass him the axe, that would not alter the essence of the case: John, guided by the situational context, would tell himself what Peter obviously wanted to communicate to him. *The understanding* of Peter by John would be replaced by John's *guessing* Peter's intentions. But without understanding the partner there is no communication.

In what, then, does the act of communication consist?

A person makes a statement, and another person, who hears that statement, *understands* it, i.e., experiences mental states *analogous* (*not the same*, since that depends on the individual context, which changes) to those of the author of the statement. And that is all.

Without entering into details of that very complicated process, one can at once grasp the difference between the two types of communication discussed.

In communication by means of music, images, and to a certain extent by means of poetry as well, the point is to transmit *emotions* to others; in the other case, to transmit intellectual content, to transmit certain *mental* states. This does not imply that such a communication has no emotional aspect. On the contrary, its *purpose* may be precisely to evoke a certain emotional state: love, hatred, readiness for self-sacrifice, etc. But the emotional aspect is here always secondary in relation to intellectual content, and is transmitted through the intermediary of the latter. Hence we should agree that the "language" of music or images is more suitable for a direct transmission of emotions than is the language of words. As the poet says, "*Spricht* die Seele, spricht die *Seele* nicht mehr".

The intellectual tasks of communication can be performed only by a *language of words*, a *phonic language* (or the written form of such). All other forms of transmitting intellectual content in a civilized society (I exclude here the at least controversial issue of the language of gestures as the hypothetical earliest form of human language) must, in the last analysis, be translated into the language of words; this applies both to the language of gestures and the language of mathematics, or such conventional "languages" as the "language" of flowers, smells, etc. This does not apply to the case of a *spontaneous* language of gestures of deaf-mutes. As mentioned in Part I above, the essential error of all speculations concerning artificial languages consists above all in forgetting that those languages are, in the last analysis, based on a natural language, a language of words, and are interpretable in it.

In contrast with emotional communication, intellectual communication presupposes the *understanding* of what is being communicated. In that type of communication, there is no communication without an understanding of definite intellectual content, which is not only unnecessary, but even contra-indicated, in the case of emotional communication (cf. the prohibition of a "programmatic" interpretation of musical perception, as mentioned above). That is to say – in contrast with emotional communication – intellectual communication is conditioned by the experience of the communicating parties of *analogous* mental states, and the ideal sought in this field is the most precise communication possible of one's own mental states (we imply a full precision and adequacy of communication), with a shifting of the margin of individualization in experiencing *analogous* mental states into the sphere of the context provided by the various intellectual, emotional, etc., associations.

The term "context" has been several times used above in a metaphorical and therefore vague sense; so it must be defined with more precision. This will now be done provisionally, because the problem itself belongs to the issue of *meaning*, to be dealt with later. It will only be outlined here to give a general indication of what I mean when I say that something is understood "in a context".

The matter is quite clear when a literary metaphor is resorted to. If someone says of someone else: "He is a butterfly flitting from flower to flower", then to understand that statement requires a change in the *univers du discours* from natural to social science, since otherwise a complete misunderstanding will arise. Similar, though less self-evident, is the case of changes in the meanings of certain statements according to whether we speak in terms of poetry, or science, or some specialized disciplines; in other words, the sense of an expression changes according to the *univers du discours* in which it is placed. This is due to the fact that linguistic expressions are extremely ambiguous and admit of different interpretations. I do not agree with Urban when he says that the communication of emotional states through behaviour (so called behavioural communication) does not require the consideration of any context, at least in the simplest cases; but I fully agree with him on the point that intellectual communication presupposes a reference not just to an object, but to an object located in a definite *univers du discours*, in other words, that the content of a communiqué can be understood only in a definite context. "All linguistic meaning is referential, but it is also systemic"[9]. If the *univers du discours* is interpreted not only as a changing system of *knowledge* to which a given statement is referred, but also as an individually changing system of accumulated experience, we achieve what I have in a most general way called the intellectual and emotional *context* of a changing understanding of the same expression by different individual recipients. Let us be satisfied, for the time being, with that preliminary explanation.

Thus we come to the following conclusions concerning a more precise formulation of the term "communication":

The specifically human manner of communication refers to the entire domain of man's spiritual life: both to emotional and to intellectual experience. Although these two spheres cannot be separated in an absolute way, they represent *different* fields of spiritual life and thus they are connected with *different* forms of communication (which themselves cannot be separated in any rigid and absolute way).

Communication in the emotional sphere often takes place through the intermediary of extra-linguistic means, and one can accept the thesis that as far as the transmission of certain emotional moods (emotional "contagion") is concerned, the expressive means of music and of the visual arts certainly do achieve something (although it must be borne in mind that the realization of one's emotional state, achieved as a result of extra-linguistic communication, requires linguistic means).

Intellectual communication, i.e., communication intended to transmit to others certain mental states, is a linguistic communication *par excellence* (since the systems of signs always represent some fragments of a phonic language), and the focal problem here is an *analogous understanding* by the communicating parties, which presupposes not only a common reference to the same object, but also a common reference to the same *univers du discours*.

[9] Urban, op. cit., p. 232.

The problem of adequate understanding as between the persons participating in the process of communication is connected with the controversy between the transcendentalist and the naturalist conception, a controversy we are now going to submit to critical analysis.

2. THE CONTROVERSY BETWEEN THE TRANSCENDENTALIST AND THE NATURALIST CONCEPTION

The transcendentalist conception of the communication process — certainly one of the strangest concepts from the point of view of common sense and of a scientific reflection on reality — cannot be understood without due consideration of its philosophical background. Historically, it reaches back to the doctrine of Plato who above empirical cognition placed direct cognition, that is an insight of the soul into the essence of things, into their ideas, an insight that can be neither rendered in words nor communicated. The continuation of that view can be seen in neo-Platonic mysticism; it has also been revived in most recent times in the various versions of irrationalism, above all in Bergson's intuitionism[10] and in Husserl's phenomenology[11]. The conception that belittles or even plainly denies the rôle of verbal communication has its roots in those metaphysical ideas. "*Spricht* die Seele, spricht die *Seele* nicht mehr." And Maeterlinck says: "Does anyone believe that by means of language any *real* communication can pass from man to man?"[12]

Yet the direct philosophical roots of the transcendentalist conception of communication must be sought elsewhere: in Kantianism, or rather in neo-Kantianism. The splitting of the world

---

[10] See his *La pénsée et le mouvant*, Chap. VI: "Introduction à la métaphysique".

[11] Cf. *Ideen zu einer reinen Phänomenologie und phänomenologischen Philosophie.*

[12] Quoted after Urban, op. cit., p. 242.

into *phenomena* and *noumena* (the very terminology indicates a relationship between that conception and Platonism), and at the same time the endowing of human mind with inborn forms of *a priori* perception by means of which what is given in cognition is the construction of the cognitive mind – such was the philosophical soil provided by transcendentalism, especially in its Fichtean version, typical of neo-Kantianism, for the growth of all speculations concerning a "trans-subjective 'I'". That type of speculation obviously lies at the root of the so-called transcendentalist theory of communication.

According to that theory, the problem of communication can be reduced to the following question: supposing that communication takes place between two individuals who are *absolutely separated* from one another – and such, according to transcendentalism, is the position of those individuals not immersed in some mystic ether of "transcendental 'I'" which unites them spiritually (please, take note of that assumption, since it plays the essential rôle in argumentation – we ask, how is it possible for them to communicate by transmitting from one individual to another certain *mental* states, by understanding one another's statements and not only by perceiving certain situations *hic et nunc*, as in the case of behavioural communication? The transcendentalist conception explains this in two ways: (1) true communication is direct (the Platonic motif), and (2) at its root lies a specific metaphysical community formed by the "transcendental 'I'" or by a "universal mind", in which the individual minds participate in some way or another, or of which they are parts (the Thomistic and Kantian motif).

The concept of "true communication" appears most clearly in Jaspers's formulation of "existential communication". Here is a quotation from the chapter several dozen pages long, devoted to the communication process, in Volume II of the author's *Philosophy*:

"Wenn durch alles Äusserliche hindurch der Mensch als er selbst zum anderen Selbst tritt, die Täuschungen fallen, das

Eigentliche offenbar wird, so könnte es Ziel werden, dass Seele mit Seele schleierlos ohne alle Bindung in der Äusserlichkeit des Weltdaseins in Eines schlage.

"Jedoch kann *in der Welt* Existenz mit Existenz sich nicht unmittelbar, sondern nur durch die Medien der Inhalte treffen. Das Ineinsschlagen der Seelen bedarf der Wirklichkeit des Handelns und des Ausdrucks. Denn Kommunikation ist nicht wirklich als die widerstandslose bestehende Helligkeit eines seeligen Seins ohne Raum und Zeit, sondern die Bewegung des Selbstseins im Stoff der Wirklichkeit. Wohl ist es in Augenblicken, als ob die Berührung unmittelbar sei; sie kann im Transzendieren über alles Weltdasein sich erfüllen. Aber auch dann ist Weite und Klarheit des objektiv gewordenen und nun transzendierten Inhalts das Mass für die Entschiedenheit des Augenblicks der eigentlichen Kommunikation. Diese gewinnt ihren Aufschwung durch Teilnahme an Ideen in der Welt, an Aufgaben und Zwecken"[13].

But it is the concept of "transcendental 'I'", introduced in some form or another into the theory of communication, which is here of decisive significance.

That concept was very clearly formulated by Karl Vossler, who in order to explain the essence of communication introduced the notion of "metaphysical language-community" alongside that of "empirical language-community"[14].

According to Vossler, it is always *one* person who is the carrier and author of the conversation in which communication takes place, although his functions and rôles may be distributed over a number of persons. Conversation is something like a drama which is played within each of the participants in that conversation. This looks as if the monologue were said to be the origin of the dialogue. But Vossler goes much further. His explanations show what metaphysical objectives he has in view.

---

[13] Jaspers, op. cit., p. 67.

[14] Vossler, *Geist und Kultur in der Sprache*, Heidelberg 1925.

"In der metaphysischen Ansicht stellt sich die Sache so dar, dass in der menschlichen Persönlichkeit als solcher, die eine Einheit von beliebiger Vielheit ist, sämtliche hienieden stattfindenden Gespräche sich abspielen. All das, was im Laufe der Zeit auf dem Erdball gesprochen wird, muss sonach als ein riesiges Selbstgespräch gedacht werden, in dem der menschliche Geist, in Milliarden von personenhaften Rollen sich entfaltend und aus all diesen Vereinzelungen sich wieder zusammensuchend, begriffen ist.

"Daraus folgt nun freilich, dass der menschliche Geist als solcher eine *einzige* Person sein oder werden müsste; und es fragt sich, ob der Begriff der Person diese Steigerung ins Absolute aushält. Dass der Anspruch auf etwas absolut Geistiges und Einheitliches in ihm enthalten ist, kann nicht mehr zweifelhaft sein; aber die äusserste Formel mit ihrem Verlagen nach unendlich vielen Rollen in *einer* Person ist damit noch lange nicht verwirklicht"[15].

Be that as it may, these metaphysical speculations of a philologist have been used as an argument in the construction of a transcendentalist theory of communication. This is what Urban, one of the exponents of that theory, says in this connection: "Few transcendentalists – certainly not Kant himself – would be disposed to think of the notion of the transcendental Self as more than a symbol for this underlying unity. But the unity thus symbolized is itself not a myth. It is a necessary condition of that universality, that mutuality of mind however small, without which knowledge and its communication are impossible. Whether for the unity thus symbolized we use the 'myth' of an over-individual self or of an over-individual community is, from the present point of view, a matter of relative indifference. I do not much care in the present context whether one thinks of an all-embracing mind in which finite minds live and move and have their being, or as an over-individual society of minds. Important

[15] Ibid., p. 13.

as these issues are in other contexts, they are not the significant thing here. What is significant in the *transcendental minimum* or the minimum of 'transcendental considerations', necessary for the understanding of intelligible communication"[16].

Such an assumption is made because the process of human communication cannot, it is claimed, be explained in any other way. And this is why one has to believe in some transcendental, supraindividual "I". What does it mean? Does it mean anything at all? That is inessential. One has to believe. And, strange as it may seem, there are people who in the name of "philosophy" openly proclaim that. This is no exaggeration: the reader is invited to study carefully the answer offered by Urban to the question about the proof of the existence of something like that "transcendental, supra-individual 'I'": "The supra-empirical unity implied in intelligible communication *is* supra-empirical and, therefore, by definition, not verifiable as an empirical fact by a direct application of the 'empirical criterion'"[17].

The arguments adduced by the transcendentalists in favour of their conception are such a philosophical titbit that I cannot deny myself the pleasure of quoting Urban once more: "The argument of the transcendentalist may be of a peculiar kind, but if so it is only because the facts upon which the argument is based are of a special order. Mind, conceived as *wholly isolated separate selves,* it finds, with Dewey, wholly inadequate to carry the burden of communication and all its works, both science and human institutions. But equally inadequate is mind when conceived in *purely naturalistic terms of history and sociology*. It is upon these considerations that the evidence rests. Such evidence is, to be sure, largely negative, but not wholly so. The force of the transcendental argument rests, in the last analysis, on certain positive considerations, namely the actual character of intelligible communication as we have seen it to be, more especially of understanding which is involved in such com-

[16] Urban, op. cit., 255–256.

[17] Ibid., p. 259.

munication. If the character of these facts is acknowledged – if *real communication as contrasted with merely apparent communication* is recognized, then the 'transcendental considerations' are necessitated for the understanding of these facts. This is evidence in any proper sense of the word"[18].

But let us now leave in peace that curiosity which constitutes the argumentation of the transcendentalists, and let us pay attention to the opposing conception, namely that of the behaviourists, also called the naturalist conception.

Their thesis is that people can communicate, i.e., can mutually understand their statements, because they have analogous physical and intellectual structure and have to do with reality that is common to all. Hence communication is a very prosaic matter, unnecessarily mystified by the transcendentalists. Its essence is: someone experiences something and acts on his milieu so that other minds have similar experiences. There is nothing mysterious in that process: under definite conditions, the various minds have similar experiences. Such is more or less the position of the naturalists, as expounded by I. A. Richards in his *Principles of Literary Criticism*[19].

A similar formulation is offered by John Dewey whom, if only in view of his position in the history of behaviourism, I consider the chief representative of the naturalist conception.

Dewey admits that the transcendentalists have paid more attention than others to the rôle of language in human society. But at the same time it is they who are responsible for the mystification of the issue, since they explain it by having recourse to certain supernatural principles. Yet it can be explained quite naturally, if we take as the starting point social life and its needs, in the satisfaction of which language plays a particular rôle as the means of communication. To understand the function of language and the essence of communication one has to study human *behaviour* and human co-operation: "The heart of language

[18] Ibid., p. 260 (italics – A. S.).

[19] London 1955, Chap. XXI: "A Theory of Communication".

is not 'expression' of something antecedent, much less expression of antecedent thought. It is communication; the establishment of co-operation in an activity in which there are partners, and in which the activity of each is modified and regulated by partnership. To fail to understand is to fail to come into agreement in action; to misunderstand is to set up action at cross purposes"[20].

And here is further explanation of the communicative function of language:

"Language is specifically a mode of interaction of at least two beings, a speaker and a hearer; it presupposes an organized group to which these creatures belong, and from whom they have acquired their habits of speech. It is therefore a relationship, not a particularity. This consideration alone condemns traditional nominalism. The meaning of signs, moreover, always includes something common as between persons and an object. When we attribute meaning to the speaker as his intent, we take for granted another person who is to share in the execution of the intent, and also something independent of the persons concerned, through which the intent is to be realized. Persons and things must alike serve as means in a commonly shared consequence. This community of partaking is meaning.

"The invention and use of tools have played a large part in consolidating meanings, because a tool is a thing used as means to consequences, instead of being taken directly and physically. It is intrinsically relational, anticipatory, predictive. Without reference to the absent, or 'transcendence', nothing is a tool. The most convincing evidence that animals do not 'think' is found in the fact that they have no tools ..."[21].

In many formulations, Dewey comes close to the Marxist viewpoint, but the differences between the two positions also stand in relief. These matters will be discussed at a later stage, when my own opinion on controversial issues will be advanced.

---

20 Dewey, op. cit., p. 179.

21 Ibid., p. 185.

Before passing to the analysis of the critical argumentation of the transcendentalists, let us take note of one other author who stands close to the naturalist conception. I mean here Alan Gardiner, who in his book *The Theory of Speech and Language* formulates Dewey's theses even more sharply.

Gardiner starts by analysing the notions of language and speech. But, like Dewey who, while concentrating his attention on the problem of meaning, had to attack the problem of communication, Gardiner also sheds indirect light upon the issue.

Gardiner, like Dewey, interprets the action of speaking in terms of co-operation between two persons – the speaker and the listener – but at the same time, and very important for the solution of the problem, explicitly introduces as the third element that which is spoken about. True, the naturalists (e.g. Richards) explain the possibility of communication by the similarity of minds and by a reality common to all, but Gardiner, by introducing the category of *things* and the requirement of a realist formulation of the theory of language and speech, thereby admits a new theoretical element which brings him close to materialism.

Gardiner begins with a criticism of the definition of speech as a system of articulated phonic symbols used to express thoughts, and goes on:

"As a first approximation let us define speech as the use, between man and man, of articulate sound-signs for the communication of their wishes and their views about things. Note that I do not attempt to deny the thought-element is speech, but the emphasis of my definition does not lie on that element. The points which I wish to stress are, firstly, the co-operative character of speech, and, secondly, the fact that it is always concerned with things, that is to say with the realities both of the external world and of *man's inner experience*"[22].

Thus, a proper formulation of the notions of language, speech, meaning and understanding (Gardiner draws an explicit

[22] Gardiner, *The Theory of Speech and Language*, Oxford 1951, p. 18.

distinction between the *meaning* of words and the things *denoted* by those words), and consequently a proper formulation of the *process* of communication requires, following Gardiner, that four elements of the situation be taken into account: (1) the speaker, (2) the listener, (3) the thing spoken about, (4) the words spoken.

What is then asserted by the naturalists concerning the essence of the communication process?

They maintain that what is at stake is simple and prosaic, and as such does not require recourse to any supernatural factors. What is involved is simply a mutual transmission of the content of certain personal experiences by linguistic means, which, they hold, can always be reduced to the category of influence. Such a transmission of the content of experience by the speaker to the listener is possible, because (1) the communicating organisms have similar structures, and (2) the reality referred to is common to both parties in the process.

And what do the transcendentalists reply?

They say that the entire reasoning, although it appeals to common sense, can apply only to an "apparent", but not to a "true" communication, and as regards the latter it includes a logical error – it assumes the truth of what in fact needs to be proved.

Their arguments are as follows.

First of all, they question the assumption concerning the "similarity of organisms". A mere external similarity, which would perhaps suffice to explain *behavioural communication*, communication purely situational in character, is not enough. Intellectual communication implies *understanding the content* of statements, and consequently the ability to think analytically, to distinguish elements important and unimportant, significant and non-significant. To ascribe to human minds such a common property goes beyond the recognition of an external similarity of organism and presupposes the existence in them of a common factor or force. Starting from the assumption that there exist *absolutely separated* minds (a thesis imputed by the transcendentalists to the naturalists) the naturalists are unable to explain intellectual communication and must therefore introduce by stealth, in the form of a tacit assumption, the transcendentalist thesis which they claim to oppose, and which argues that there is some transcendental, supra-empirical principle which makes communication possible. And it is of mere secondary importance whether that principle be called the "transcendental 'I'" or "similarity of organism".

Secondly, the transcendentalists also attack the naturalist thesis that communication is made possible by similarity of environment ("common reality"). That thesis applies, they further claim, not to purely situational similarity alone, which would be sufficient in the case of behavioural communication. On the other hand, intellectual communication requires reference to a definite universe of discourse, that is to a reality which is "construed". Thus, they maintain, communication presupposes not only a mind which "construes" a given universe of discourse, but also *the community of the minds* which communicate with one another. The naturalists, they assert, by introducing the concept of "reality common to all" simply presuppose what is to be proved – the community of minds, the possibility of communication.

It cannot be said that transcendentalist criticism, even in its extreme form, finds no fulcrum in the expressed opinions of the naturalists themselves, although certainly it distorts such opinions tendentiously, or is perhaps unable to reach what is rational in them. In naturalists' opinions there are gaps and inconsistencies which expose them to attacks by the transcendentalists. In particular these gaps consist of: (1) the inability to give a *social and historical* explanation of the problem of the human individual, and consequently, of the relationship between the individual and society; and (2) the inability to take a consistently materialistic stand in epistemology, that is to explain the issue of *the common object* of social cognition and of *the individual differences* in its perception by the various individuals.

3. FOUNDATIONS OF A MARXIST FORMULATION OF THE PROBLEM

No Marxist, or any man who thinks in terms of scientific criteria, can accept the transcendentalist position, since it is based on metaphysical speculation incompatible with science. He finds, of course, the naturalist position to be much nearer to his own; this applies in particular to those theses which come close to consistent materialism. But a Marxist cannot be in full solidarity with naturalism: some of its points he must criticize, and he also has to fill many gaps in its argumentation.

Hence the Marxist rejects the notion that there are only two alternative positions in the issue of the possibility of communication: the transcendentalist and the naturalist. Far less can he agree that the bankruptcy of one of the two opposing theories serves to prove the correctness of the other. This is an obvious paralogism. Both parties to the dispute are right, at least to a certain extent, in their criticism of their opponents. No party is right, however, in treating that criticism as adding to its own capital. Transcendentalism is simply counterscientific speculation based on mere metaphysical faith. Naturalism reveals gaps and inconsistencies; the incorrectness of some of its opinions and theses can be demonstrated. The weakness of naturalism consists rather in what it does *not* say than in what it does say. But there must be agreement with many of its theses because they stand for science and common sense. Marxism, consequently, has to treat the two trends differently, although it cannot declare itself in solidarity with either of them. That is why a Marxist attempt to solve the problem of communication must be offered here.

*

*   *

"It is only now, when we have examined the four points, the four aspects of the original historical relations, that we have found that man also has 'consciousness'. But even that is not any *a priori*, 'pure', consciousness. The 'spirit' is from the very beginning ridden with a curse, is 'infected' with matter which comes in as vibrations of the air, as sounds, in a word, as speech. Speech is as old as consciousness, speech *is* a practical, real consciousness which exists both for other people and for myself. And speech comes to being, like consciousness, only from the need, the necessity of contact with other people. Where a relation exists, it exists for me; an animal is in a relation to nothing. For an animal, its relation to others does not exist as a relation. Thus, consciousness is from the very beginning a social product and will remain so as long as men will exist"[23].

These words by Marx on the rôle of speech in the process of human communication date from 1844. More or less at that time, in the spring of 1845, Marx wrote his *Theses on Feuerbach*, three of which are of particular importance for us: Theses VI, VII and VIII pertain to the social character of the human individual and to the conclusions to be drawn for the study of the manifestation of the spiritual life of human individuals. The theses are as follows:

Thesis VI: "Feuerbach resolves the religious essence into the human essence. But the human essence is no abstraction inherent in each single individual. In its reality it is the ensemble of the social relations.

"Feuerbach, who does not enter upon a criticism of this real essence, is consequently compelled:

1. To abstract from the historical process and to fix the religious sentiment as something by itself and to presuppose an abstract — *isolated* — human individual.

2. The human essence, therefore, can with him be comprehended only as 'genus', as an internal, dumb generality which merely *naturally* unites the many individuals."

Thesis VII: "Feuerbach, consequently, does not see that the 'religious sentiment' is itself a *social product*, and that the ab-

[23] K. Marx, F. Engels, *Die deutsche Ideologie*, in *Werke*, Vol. 3, Berlin 1958, p. 30–31.

stract individual whom he analyses belongs in reality to a particular form of society".

Thesis VIII: "Social life is essentially *practical.* All mysteries which mislead theory to mysticism find their rational solution in human practice and in the comprehension of this practice"[24].

I have opened my discussion of the Marxist interpretation of the problem of communication with quotations from Marx since they constitute the foundation for the solution of that problem.

As indicated above, the transcendentalists object that the naturalists commit the error called *circulus in demonstrando*: required to *prove* the possiblity of communication, they instead *assume* such possibility of communication in stating that it is ensured by sufficient "similarity of human organisms". The naturalists are defenceless in the face of this objection, since the assumption of naturalism as the starting point for the explanation of social phenomena involves a fundamental error.

To begin with the issue of the human individual, the naturalists, like Feuerbach before them, conceive the human individual in an abstract manner, only as a specimen of the species "man". That is also materialism, but materialism restricted by abstraction from the social factor. The only "general characteristic" possible in such an analysis of man is the general characteristic of the *species*, and hence the naturalists, like Feuerbach, can conceive the human essence "only as 'genus', as an internal, dumb generality which merely *naturally* unites the many individuals". That weak point in naturalism is correctly attacked by the transcendentalists. Once again it can be seen that idealism feeds above all on the limitations and the resulting restrictions of materialism.

For if the human individual is treated naturalistically, as a specimen only of natural species, if "the similarity of organisms" is understood in just such a way, then what can we say,

[24] K. Marx, *Theses on Feuerbach*, in F. Engels, *Ludwig Feuerbach and the End of Classical German Philosophy*, Moscow 1949, p. 62–63.

what right have we to speak about "the similarity of minds", "the similarity of consciousness", etc., which will not be simply an assumption? The transcendentalists are right. With such an approach nothing reasonable can be said on the matter, and it really does seem that the naturalists assume what they have to prove.

This is so because the issue of "the similarity of minds" cannot be solved in purely naturalistic terms. The issue of the human individual as an individual belonging to human society cannot be solved at all in those terms alone.

In criticizing Feuerbach's naturalistic tendencies Marx objected that he had assumed "an abstract – *isolated* – human individual", and drew attention to the fact that "the abstract individual whom he analyses belongs in reality to a particular form of society". This is a criticism of all "Robinson Crusoe concepts" in the social sciences.

Do the adherents of the naturalistic concept of communication understand these truths? They all analyse the "speaker-listener" relation, but leave the question of the social link between them in the dark. Dewey, as quoted above, says that two such parties belong to a social group from which they have adopted their speech habits, but he draws no further conclusions from that fact. I do not imply that Dewey and other adherents of naturalism are lacking in understanding of the question of social links, or that they really maintain, as is imputed to them by the transcendentalists, that human individuals are "absolutely isolated". But the fact that they do not give voice to such nonsense does not mean that they properly understand the significance of the social conditioning of the communication process, and still less, that their opinions reflect that significance. No, there is nothing like that about them, and it explains why they are exposed to attacks by the transcendentalists. And perhaps they pass over the point in silence because they consider it self-evident, a truism? Such a defence of the naturalists can be answered by pointing out that it is probably a still greater truism to say that a conversation always involves at least two parties — speaker and listener — and yet the naturalists do not pass over that trivial fact in silence (cf. Dewey, and above all Gardiner). If they did see and fully understand the importance of the social conditioning of the position of the individual as an individual in society, should they see and fully understand the importance of the social conditioning of the communication process, surely they would not remain silent, for this is an important issue which would help them to dissociate themselves from the standpoint of their opponents — the standpoint of transcendentalist mysticism. But in science silence, too, is under certain circumstances an eloquent testimony; the lack of certain assertions in definite situation implies approval of assertions to the contrary, or at least denotes inability to oppose, or the impossibility of opposing, such assertions to the contrary.

And yet analysis should begin with the issue of the social status of the individual: that done, then all secrets of "the similarity of minds" and "consciousness common to all", "the mysterious character" of communication, etc., disappear at once.

Marx said that "the human essence is no abstraction inherent in each single individual. In its reality it is the ensemble of the social relations". The crux of the matter lies in understanding that point (though Marx's formulation of the thought is now somewhat obsolete in style). Can a non-Marxist develop a similar idea, or at least can he adopt it? I do not see any absolute obstacles to his doing so. But it is a fact that *the interpretation of man's spiritual life and of the product of his spiritual life from the social, and consequently historical, point of view is the undeniable and immense contribution of Marxism to social research.*

To avoid all misunderstandings, it must be added that Marx's discovery did not take place in a vacuum, but was preceded by reflections on the influence of the milieu on human opinions (French materialists), and on the historical character of human consciousness (German idealists). Marx, however, not only gave a synthesis of those views, but also developed them consistently and, on a new foundation (the attention paid to the rôle of the relations of production in the development of human consciousness), made a true scientific *discovery* which now lies at the root of the modern theories of man's spiritual life and its products.

The human individual – if we consider him not only as the object of study of physics, chemistry, medicine, etc., but precisely as a *human* individual, i.e., as a member of human society – is a *social product*, in the same way as are all the manifestations of his spiritual life: "religious disposition", speech, artistic taste, consciousness in general.

As a "human individual" man is "the whole of social relations" in the sense that this origin and spiritual development can be understood only in the social and historical context, as a specimen of a "species", but this time not only a natural, but also a social species. These are historicism and sociologism in the definite sense of these terms. Thus, historical materialism has introduced a sociological, scientific point of view to the study of man's spiritual life in general, and the study of culture in particular.

All this shows clearly that "consciousness is ... and will be a social product as long ... as men exist". But human speech, also, is such a social product from its very origin, since "the speech *is* the practical, ... real consciousness ... existing also for other people". The origin of both consciousness and speech is to be sought in social life and its needs, "in the necessity to communicate with other people".

But we are not interested here in the origin of language and speech. We are interested in something else: is there any mysterious factor left in the process of communication when the errors arising from the naturalistic interpretation of social phenomena are eliminated, and the study is based on the principles of consistent materialism? Can the transcendentalists reasonably accuse Marxists also of the *circuli in demonstrando*?

Of course, the transcendentalists may say after Urban: "... Equally inadequate is mind when conceived in purely naturalistic terms of history and sociology".

I pass over the fact that history and sociology have nothing to do with naturalism. The latter term has probably been used above to replace the "abhorrent" notion of "materialism". The transcendentalists can say that communication, if analysed in those terms, is not a true communication. But we can, in reply, follow old Joseph Dietzgen, who referred the adherents of the "angelic" manner of communication to heaven, to the angels. We here, on the earth, have at disposal only earthly cognition and an earthly manner of communication. We need not engage in speculation.

But does the argument which was so effective in attacking the naturalists, remain valid? No, because its foundation has been smashed – the thesis concerning "absolutely isolated" beings which the transcendentalists might with impunity ascribe to the naturalists in availing themselves of the gaps and errors in their doctrine. Nothing is left of that thesis, and consequently nothing is left of the critical argumentation of the transcendentalists.

The human individual is a social product both in his physical and his psychical evolution, both from the point of view of his phylogenesis and his ontogenesis. There is nothing mysterious in "the similarity of organisms", as there is nothing mysterious in "the similarity of minds" or "the similarity of consciousness". That similarity (which, by the way, leaves room for individual differences) is most natural and normal, being acquired by *up-bringing* in society, by taking over its historical heritage chiefly through the intermediary of *speech*. Both these factors have the same effect on all members or society, and hence there is nothing extraordinary in the fact that they form a substratum for a "similarity of minds". There is thus nothing extraordinary in the fact that they smash the myths of "absolutely separated" individuals. It becomes quite superfluous to introduce mystical, transcendental factors in order to explain the process of communication. The explanation is quite natural, but not naturalistic. It is *social.*

This is what Marxism contributes to the problem of communication. The Marxist approach makes it possible to solve that problem in a consistently scientific manner, dissociating Marxism both from the metaphysical speculations of transcendentalism, and from the vulgar materialism of the naturalistic interpretation.

No less decisive is the rejection by Marxism of the second transcendentalist objection – that which concerns "the similarity of reality" to which communication pertains. It will be recalled that the transcendentalists refer to the fact that intellectual communication always pertains to some universe of discourse, and consider the reality spoken about in the process of communication to be a mental construction. On this they base their *circulus in demonstrando* objection, for the similarity which had had to be proved is, they argue, adopted as an assumption. What is involved here, they contend, is not an environment independent of human mind, but an environment which is a construction of that mind; these constructions are said to be similar because their similarity is provided by the minds themselves, or, strictly speaking, by "the transcendental 'I'" in which the individual minds somehow participate.

All that is pure mysticism, pure metaphysical speculation. The naturalists are defenceless against such arguments; having once made concession to idealism, they cannot effectively fend off its blows. But for the Marxists, as consistent materialists, that objection is of no consequence.

What is at stake here is the essential controversy between materialism and idealism in the field of ontology and epistemology. The controversy is focused around the issue as to whether the object spoken about by persons who communicate with one another is, or is not, because it exists outside their minds and independently of them, the object of a common discourse.

Of course, in philosophy one can afford the luxury of solipsism. But then not only all *common* objects of communication, but in general *all objects* as such disappear, and what remains is the mystic "I" that creates the world as its own private construction. Here the difference between epistemological and ontological solipsism is blurred. One must realize clearly that we put an end not only to the object of thought, but to communication as well, since nothing remains to be communicated. This is understood even by transcendentalists: e.g., Urban says that "a minimum of realism" is necessary for communication, and states: "No coherent theory of communication can be developed on subjectivist premises, and if idealism involves subjectivism, idealism must be abandoned"[25]. But Urban declares himself against subjective idealism from the standpoint of objective idealism. And he immediately continues: "On the other hand, no coherent theory of communication can be developed without the notion of transcendent mind as well as transcendent objects. Any form of realism that denies this must be abandoned"[26].

Thus the objective character of the object of thought has to be retained (although, according to the transcendentalists, escape can be sought in objective idealism), in order to avoid abandoning all reasonable theory of communication.

But the transcendentalists may urge that they do not mean a denial of the objective character of the object of thought — witness the fact that they recognize the objective character of the object of communication, as is done, e.g., by Urban. Their point is, they might say, that in communicating with other people, we speak about objects; but objects located by us in a definite universe of discourse, according to the "language" we use. Now to construct that *univers du discours*, a "transcendental mind" is necessary.

The argumentation is simply astounding. Yet it suffices to ask: "But why?", and the spell is broken. For, in fact, why is

25 Urban, op. cit., p. 264.

26 Ibid.

a "transcendental mind" necessary for the construction of a *univers du discours*, but not necessary for the existence of the object of knowledge? And what is the meaning of the object of communication being objective, if in communication it always is a subjective product, as a construction? It would be difficult to answer these questions, without reverting to the old concept of inaccessible *noumena*, which have an objective existence, and of apparent *phenomena*, which are our own construction. But that concept was annihilated long ago by the criticism of Kantian phenomenalism. It must be stated clearly: either one accepts an objective existence of the object of communication, or one considers that object to be a subjective product of mind and thereby cancels the possibility of communication. *Tertium non datur*. The transcendentalists entangle themselves desperately in their own subtleties.

But what about that *univers du discours* in the light of the materialistic epistemology?

If we hold that the object of our cognition, and consequently the object of communication, exists objectively — that is, outside all minds and independently of them — then the mind in the process of cognition somehow *reflects* it (in a special sense of the word). But an isolated object is an abstraction: the mind in the process of cognition always reflects the object *in some context*. In that sense, that context must also exist in the communication of cognition. The statement that the object of cognition appears here in a definite *univers du discours* is trivial. Reference to the *univers du discours* in the process of communication does not infer any difficulties, particularly since what is involved here is not objects but *ambiguous words* the meanings of which become concrete only in a definite context. And for that purpose no "transcendental 'I'" is needed; suffice it to indicate clearly and to understand the context, which in turn requires precision of formulations on the part of the speaker and adequate erudition on the part of the listener. No mystic "transcendental 'I'" will help me in understanding the *univers du dis-*

cours of, for instance, quantum mechanics, if I am not familiar with the subject.

One feels compelled to recall Marx's words already quoted: "Social life is essentially *practical.* All mysteries which mislead theory to mysticism find their rational solution in human practice and in the comprehension of this practice".

The standpoint of the Marxists in the controversy between the naturalists and the transcendentalists thus boils down to demonstrating that that controversy focuses on phenomena that are social *par excellence* and in that sense natural.

Is this not a truism; is it not the standpoint commonly adopted in science? Not at all.

That it is not a truism is best proved by the controversy in its entirety as explained above. That it is not a triviality, is best proved by the fact that not only transcendentalists but even naturalists do not fully understand the thesis and are unable to assess it properly.

Certain standpoints, especially that adopted by the transcendentalists in the controversy now under discussion, look strange in the light of common-sense. But the opinions of philosophers are not always in agreement with common sense, and often all their "originality" consists precisely in applying shocks to common sense. Should we then (as was suggested to me in a discussion) consider such opinions as manifestations of imbecility or schizophrenia and consequently reject them as unimportant? May we say – as was said in that discussion – either that, if I ascribe to them such absurd opinions, I do not understand what these authors mean, or that if their opinions are really so absurd then I am absolved from discussion in view of the evidently non-scientific character of the position held by my opponents? I do not agree that we can say either the one or the other. Contrary to all appearances, the holding of such opinions is a manifestation neither of weakness nor of insanity, but is simply part of irrationalist thought, so common in the bourgeois world. Even mysticism is a social phenomenon and a social fact, which must be noticed, understood and properly assessed, if one does not want to come out on the losing side in the ideological strife now proceeding in philosophy. Nor may I say, although I may find it convenient, "I do not understand", and withdraw from the struggle. After all, I *do* understand the meaning of sentences, even if I reject their content as unacceptable (e.g., I understand the meaning of the sentences to the effect that communication is possible owing to some transcendental "I", just as I understand the meaning of the sentence which asserts the existence of an omnipotent God). The words "I do not understand" can only mean here that I do not agree with a given standpoint, that I deny it all meaning from the scientific point of view, etc. But it would be dangerous to abstain, for that reason, from discussion, for then the opponent could claim successfully that he too "does not understand" what we say. Perhaps we should not bother about all that, convinced of being right? But that would mean an end to all intellectual progress, an end to all discussion, a harmful monopolization of the scientific standpoint.

So let us engage in discussion. But if discussion is indispensable, the Marxist standpoint on the issue of communication is neither a truism nor a triviality. Quite the contrary; not only from the point of view of historical priority, but also *at present* it is the only consistent formulation of the issue of communication from the social – both materialistic and historical – point of view.

Certainly, great discoveries, once assimilated by science, assume such apparent simplicity as to seem trivial to those whose opinions have already been shaped by such discoveries. This is the normal course of events. The greatest discoveries, especially in the social sciences, usually concern simple, every-day matters which for various reasons have not been noticed or understood before, or consideration of which has been deliberately put off. That fact by no means detracts from the greatness of the discovery, far less does it preclude one from availing oneself of it in analysis. This holds especially when, as is the case of the theory of communication, the discovery in question is neither universally recognized, nor even understood and taken into consideration by the majority of researchers.

* * *

It has been said that the Marxists treat human consciousness and human speech — consciousness for others — as products of social life. That hypothesis has found expression in Engels's paper *On the Rôle of Labour in Making the Ape Human*, and in the theory of Marx and Engels on the rôle of the division of labour as a factor in social evolution. Labour — thought — language: these are the three elements of fundamental significance in the Marxist conception of the origin of human society. These three elements are inseparable one from another. Man drew a line of distinction between himself and the animal world when he started to produce tools, says Marx. Human labour is inseparably linked with consciousness, that is with thought, which in turn is genetically linked inseparably with speech. Consciousness, and consequently speech as well, are products of labour, products of social life, and at the same time indispensable conditions of a further development of that process, of its higher, more advanced stages. Human labour is based on co-operation, which is impossible without thinking in terms of ideas, and without communication. Such is the dialectics of mutual influence, which makes it possible to explain the process of communication without recourse to miracles and metaphysics.

Thus, the issue turns out to be "prosaic" and natural, though evading a naturalistic interpretation by being an essentially social phenomenon. But is it so simple? Is it enough to state that somebody speaks and somebody else listens to him and the two understand one another?

Here a protest must be registered against a "common-sense" simplification of the problem, since that would threaten to eliminate all deeper analysis and to annihilate the scientific approach.

We say that people talk to one another and that is communication. So far so good. But from the point of view of a scientific analysis the problem only begins here. What problem? Not the metaphysical one, as to whether communication is possible. Of course, it *is* possible, for we witness it everywhere. Not the mystic one. as to what transcendental factor makes communication possible. This can be explained without resorting to miracles and metaphysics. The scientific problem which begins at this point is: *how, in what manner,* does communication take place?

Social psychologists say that communication consists in that the parties concerned mutually interchange their rôles with their opposite numbers, they mentally place themselves in their position and thus come to understand their words[27]. The issue may be formulated so, it may be formulated otherwise. Be that as it may, intellectual communication is always connected with understanding, with *the same* understanding by the two parties of certain definite statements.

Intellectual communication based on understanding is inseparably connected with speech. A stricter definition of what I mean by language and speech will be given later. There is one point I should like to stress here: regardless of how one defines speech, regardless of all the enormous differences in that respect between the various authors who often contend one with another on that issue, every definition refers to signs or symbols comprising human speech.

In speaking, man produces certain phonic *signs* of a particular kind (other authors speak of articulated sound symbols). Communication consists in that the person who produces those phonic signs and the person who hears them understand them in the same way, that is impart to them the same *meanings*. That is precisely the definition of communication advanced by Lund-

27 Cf. G. A. Lundberg, C. C. Schrag & O. N. Larsen, *Sociology*, New York 1954, p. 389.

berg when he says: "Communication can be defined as transmission of meanings through the intermediary of symbols"[28].

Thus we have introduced into the analysis of communication the three fundamental notions which require further investigation: sign (symbol), meaning, speech (language). To understand the sense of communication and to be able to explain sensibly the social conditions of its effectiveness, we must first analyse these three notions and their related problems. Thus the preliminary analysis of the process of communication naturally outlines the programme of further research.

---

[28] Ibid., p. 360.

CHAPTER TWO

THE SIGN: ANALYSIS AND TYPOLOGY

> "We next went to the School of Languages, where three Professors sat in Consultation upon improving that of their own Country.
>
> The first Projects was to shorten Discourse by cutting Polysyllables into one, and leaving out Verbs and Participles; because in Reality all things imaginable are but Nouns.
>
> The other, was a Scheme for entirely abolishing all Words whatsoever: And this was urged as a great Advantage in Point of Health as well as Brevity. For, it is plain, that every Word we speak is in some Degree a Diminution of our Lungs by Corrosion: and consequently contributes to the shorting of our Lives. An Expedient was therefore offered, that since Words are only Names for *Things*, it would be more convenient for all Men to carry about them such Things as were necessary to express the particular Business they are to discourse on.
>
> ... I have often beheld two of those Sages almost sinking under the Weight of their Packs, like Pedlars among us; who when they met in the Streets would lay down their Loads, open their Sacks, and hold Conversation for an Hour together; then put up their Implements, help each other to resume their Burthens, and take their Leave".
>
> (Jonathan Swift: *Gulliver's Travels*)

1. THE COMMUNICATION PROCESS AS THE STARTING POINT IN THE ANALYSIS OF THE SIGN

THE assertion that the social process of communication should be the starting point for an analysis of semantic problems finds telling confirmation in the problems of sign and meaning. If in these problems, which are fundamental for semantics, the social and sociological aspects are neglected, it is easy to end up in a blind alley of verbalism and formalism (history has actual examples of such cases).

In order to be able to answer properly the question as to *how* the process of human communication takes place, in particular, to be able to answer the question, all-important from the social point of view, as to what helps and what hampers effective human communication, we must analyse precisely such categories as "sign" and "meaning", and must fully realize the sense of these terms. But just because both sign and meaning are elements of the communication process, the starting point from which to analyse them must be the whole of the social process of human communication. Any analysis detached from that process would be one-sided, and often entirely warped. Such is the usual fate of the dialectics of the relationship between the part and the whole.

Of course, it is possible to engage in the typology of signs or in philosophical speculation on the essence of meaning — all this in isolation from the social background of the communication process. The extensive history of the problem can readily provide appropriate examples. It is also possible to hold that the social origin of the problem is obvious and has been tacitly assumed, and that such an assumption does not introduce new elements to the analysis of the problem and consequently should not interfere with its course. That, too, can of course be illustrated with historical examples. Yet in both cases we have to do with standpoints which, by separating the analysis of sign and meaning from its natural social background, open the door wide for sterile philosophical speculation.

The problem as to the essence and rôle of the sign, and consequently the problem of the typology of its various forms and varieties, can be seen whole only if and when it is considered as part of the problem as to *how* men communicate with one another.

Let it be clearly understood that we mean here the *human* process of communication. As already mentioned, communication, in various forms, can be observed not only on the human level of development, but also on the animal level. Hence reference is often made — in some specific sense of course — not only to communication among animals, but also to signs and signals in the process of communication among animals. What we are concerned with here are ambiguous concepts which may obscure the issue and bring about numerous misunderstanding.

Obviously, the communication process takes place in the animal world only in so far as the process of *co-operation* is involved, a process of social action *sui generis*. All communication is in its very origin linked inseparably with co-operation (in the broad sense of the word, covering both co-operation proper and struggle). For it is in joint action that we find the need for, and the origin of, communication of the co-operating individuals. This confirms the view of the poet who held that *Im Anfang war die Tat* (*In the beginning was the deed*). It is in practice, i.e., in common action which transforms the world (on the human level we speak of social action), that philosophy (scientific, and not speculative) seeks the solution, at least in the genetic sense, of many problems of consciousness. This holds also for the communication process and the problem of the sign.

Bees in the hive co-operate in finding and collecting honey; similar co-operation can be observed among ants in the anthill, the deer in a herd, etc. In each of these cases what is involved is a specific process of communication between bees, ants, deer, etc. In a sense, a bee which by its "dance" stimulates other bees to a search for honey gives them "signs". All this is very interesting and discloses a variety of problems, not only in the matter of animal psychology, calling for investigation. Nevertheless, it is obvious that when speaking about communication, signs, etc., we have in mind something different when we refer to animals from what we mean when we refer to human beings and human society. For the sake of clarity, and to avoid ambiguity, it is correct to reject obscure analogies and the speculations based on them, and to restrict the sphere of our interest to the specifically human process of communication, of using signs, etc. In referring here to a specifically human process of communication, I pass no judgement whatever on the character of that process in animals; I merely consciously restrict the field of my analysis.

Such a research procedure is not only permissible but even advisable in this case.

Men communicate in various ways, and the origin of the various concrete manifestations of that process are also diverse, especially on the higher levels of the communication process when the motives of communication are not confined to biological matters, requirements of production, etc., but include the need to exchange abstract ideas, to stimulate emotions, etc. Yet men always communicate by means of signs in various forms. Hence the practical and theoretical importance of signs and the need for a definite theory of signs.

Men communicate by means of gestures, phonic language, writing, pictures, signals previously agreed upon, etc. But in all such casses we have to do with signs. Gestures, speech sounds, writing, signals – all these are some form of signs which in turn, arranged in a system, constitute a form of language.

Just because man always communicates with other men by means of signs, all social life is permeated with signs and is impossible without them. Even those famous Balnibarbi scholars of whom Gulliver said that to spare themselves the effort of speaking they carried with them all the objects connected with their conversations, *had* to use signs, however primitive: gestures pointing to objects, imitative gestures, or pictures. No wonder, then, that signs, long since an object of interest in philosophy, have now come to be considered by certain philosophical schools to be the principal subject matter of study. For instance, Susanne Langer, the author of an interesting work *Philosophy in a New Key. A Study in the Symbolism of Reason, Rite and Art*, sees even in the problems of sign and symbol an announcement of a rejuvenation of philosophy which, in her opinion, suffers a crisis caused by the exhaustion of the traditional problems of that discipline. One may view such radical opinions sceptically, yet it is undeniable that the problems of signs do, in various forms, come more and more to the forefront in the investigations undertaken by the various branches of philosophy. And rightly so.

We have so far restricted the sphere of our interest to the specifically human process of communication; now we shall restrict it still more, to the sphere of intellectual communication, thus eliminating those processes which are connected with the transmission from man to man of emotional states by extra-intellectual means. In the communication process thus formulated, certain intellectual, cognitive content is transmitted from man to man by means of such or other signs. When I speak, write, gesticulate, produce signs characterized by a similarity to the objects they denote – or symbolizing certain abstractions or actions – when I give signals established by a convention, etc. – in all these cases the specific sign is for me connected with a definite mental content, and I use it in order to evoke *in someone else* the same content. In other words, we say that in the communication process the sign has *the same meaning* for the persons communicating, and that the communication process consists in the *transmission of meanings* by means of signs.

Two aspects must be distinguished in this connection: communication as *transmission of meanings* and communication as *transmission of convictions*. These two matters are in the literature of the subject not only connected one with the another, but actually confused; a situation which certainly does not simplify the intricate problem of communication. The sense of that distinction will be demonstrated by an example. When someone communicates to me, for example, the thought concerning divine omnipotence, I understand perfectly what he means, but it by no means follows that I agree with him. For it does not suffice to understand the meaning of words or other signs used in a given case in order to share the conviction of the person who pronounces the given words or uses the signs in question. To develop common concordant convictions, people have not only to understand in the same way the thoughts which are expressed, but also to approve the reasoning behind such thoughts. In this book, we shall be concerned only with the process of communication in the sense of transmission of meanings and the rôle of signs in that process[1].

What types of signs appear in the process of human communication, and what is their nature? The reply to that question will involve a specific analysis and typology of signs as an introduction to an analysis of meaning.

As indicated above, the starting point of an analysis of the sign, and consequently of meaning (since sign and meaning are not two independent "entities", but a whole which in the process of cognition is divided into parts or aspects), is the process of communication, i.e., a definite *social activity*. In a Marxist analysis of the issue, it is essential to start from that point, which also constitutes the rational element in certain endeavours to give a behaviourist, pragmatist or operationist analysis (cf. Peirce, G. Mead, or Morris). In approaching the problem thus, we see in the communication process (in particular in the interpretation of that process as an effective transmission of convictions) an attempt to place oneself in the position of the partner in that process. In the literature on the subject, there is a well-chosen comparison with a game of chess: the player must not only envisage his own plan of attack, but also the possible plans of his opponent, i.e., he must estimate his opponent's capacity to apprehend and appraise the various moves. All social dialogue connected with co-operation, and consequently with mutual understanding, consists in such placing of oneself in the position of the partner, and in attempts to envisage his situation. The same applies to a dialogue *sensu stricto*, that is, exchange of thoughts and transmission of meanings *through the intermediary of signs*.

[1] The issue of *effective* communication in the sense of reaching agreement as to opinions, in the sense of conveying convictions, is much broader and includes, as mentioned above, the problem of good understanding as its component part. Those who are interested in the issues of propaganda and in shaping public opinion are above all concerned with that broader sense of communication. This is an extremely important social problem, some aspects of which will be discussed below.

The learned of Balnibarbi used to carry sacks containing a variety of objects in order to spare themselves the necessity for talking. But it was a misconceived idea, not only because it entailed the need to carry great loads. As already indicated, even in such an extreme and absurd case it would not be possible to eliminate the use of signs, such as the gestures of pointing to the objects in question or imitating certain actions. The fundamental misconception, however, consists in something else: those respected scholars could spare their lungs by abstaining from talking, but they could not work the miracle of eliminating thinking in terms of language. That was not possible simply because there is no thinking other than in terms of language, and "true cognition" and "direct cognition" can at the most be a subject of philosophical speculation. I shall not discuss here whether the system of thinking by means, and through the intermediary, of all kinds of signs can be interpreted as a criterion of being man, a criterion distinguishing the human world from the animal world, although everything seems to indicate that such really is one of the possible criteria (inseparable from others, especially the criterion of labour). But it is beyond doubt, and of the greatest importance here, that in the stage of phonic language and the related system of thinking in terms of ideas, every other system of signs, that is every other language *sui generis*, is dependent on phonic language in the sense that it replaces phonic language and in the final stage of communication is *translated* into a phonic language; thus, used to replace a phonic language, it makes a system of signs of other signs (of a phonic language). Failure to acknowledge that fact in the study of the various systems of "languages" is a serious error, pregnant with untoward theoretical consequences: above all, it falsely suggests the equality and autonomy of such "languages". The danger of falling into such an error justifies, among other things, our thesis concerning virtue of approaching the issues of semantics from the point of view of the communication process *as a whole*. It is only on the basis of a social analysis of the problem that the proper hierarchy of the various systems of signs can be recognized, and the inter-relationships between the various "languages" determined.

Such an analysis of signs reveals, first, their variety and, in a sense, the hierarchy of their rôle and importance in the process of human communication; and, secondly, their homogeneity in the sense of sharing a common property, namely that all signs, deliberately produced to serve the needs of the communication process, are *vehicles of meanings*, since all of them are *derivative* with respect to a phonic language as far as their communicative function is concerned.

The rest of this chapter will deal with just that thesis and the related issue of the typology of signs[2].

2. HUSSERL'S TENTATIVE TYPOLOGY OF SIGNS

The vast literature on the subject advancing the various theories of signs (and consequently the various suggestions, often contrasting one with another, as to the typology of signs) implies two conclusions.

First, the very volume and divergency of such suggestions impels rejection of the idea of making a synthesis of them and rather forces an attempt to give a new, independent solution, making use of earlier ideas as specific intellectual stimuli.

Secondly, the analysis of such standpoints shows that the differences between them, including those which pertain to typology, are not only formal or terminological in nature, but

---

[2] When this book had already gone to press I came across the book *Понятие и слово* [Notion and Word] by Л. О. Резников. I regret I have not been in a position to take into consideration here many interesting ideas of that author. I should only like to emphasize that I am in solidarity with many of his opinions and interpretations, especially as far as the analysis of the concept of the sign is concerned.

have underlying philosophical aspects. These issues should be aired so that the problem may be better illuminated and the incorrect opinions on the point refuted.

As already indicated, the starting point of analysis is the process of human communication as a separate entity of a certain social process. In advancing such a theoretical thesis I do not imply that research actually begins from it. No, this is not a thesis adopted *a priori*, but a thesis obtained *as a result* of study and investigations. I have already taken cognizance of this when I referred, among other things, to Marx's proving that the use of such a method is normal in practice.

Thus we start from the process of human communication which, though complicated in its course and functions, is a self-evident fact, a fact that men communicate in action, i.e., in *co-operation* (since all action is social action), by transmitting definite meanings through the intermediary of signs; by so doing, we establish a specific framework and theoretical background for the analysis of signs.

In such a context, the contention that we have to do with a sign only if a given object, property, or material event is included in the communication process, seems simply trivial. We shall see, however, that that statement is not trivial at all, but is of considerable importance for a proper understanding of the nature of signs and their appropriate typology.

We say that the freezing of water is a sign (indication, index) of a fall in temperature, that the halo around the moon is a sign (indication, index) that the weather is going to deteriorate, that – if we pass to another category of examples – black is a sign (symbol) of mourning, that firing a red rocket is an agreed sign (signal) of some action, that a definite sound means this or that since it is a sign (verbal sign) belonging to a given language, etc. But taken "in itself" the freezing of water is a natural process, a natural phenomenon, and no sort of a sign. Likewise a red flare high in the air, black, certain specific vibrations of aerial waves, are "in themselves" material objects, possessing their own properties, constituting actual events, and are not signs. It is only *within the process of human communication* that these natural phenomena, objects, events, etc., become something more, namely those elements of a social process which are called signs.

There is nothing new in this, any more than the requirement is new that an analysis of the elements of the communication process should begin with the social conditioning of that process. Neither is it an exclusive achievement and possession of Marxists, although it is Marxism which potentially creates the most consistent foundation for such analysis. The issue as to how it is that material things and events become signs within the process of human communication, was noticed and perfectly well understood by Peirce, for example. He emphasized forcefully that a thing, a property of a thing, or an event, all function as a sign only if they are interpreted, i.e., if there is someone who in the process of communication acts as an interpreter of the given thing, event, etc., used as a sign. That opinion is now being supported by, for instance, Morris, and forms one of the fundamental ideas of his semiotic, which by the way can be derived from the ideas of Peirce. The same view is held by Susan Stebbing (*A Modern Introduction to Logic*) and others. Thus, the point is not whether the statement is new and who initiated it. The essential point is, in what systems does that statement appear, and what are the consequences drawn from it.

It is to be borne in mind that increased interest in the problems of sign and symbol has opened in contemporary philosophy a new field not only for study and research, but also for philosophical speculation. Suffice it to indicate, by way of example, the basic ideas of Cassirer's theory of symbols to demonstrate that idealistic speculation can use for its purposes all new concepts. Cassirer certainly is a penetrating thinker, and has to his credit considerable achievements in the analysis of, and research on, symbols and symbol systems. Yet his assertions concerning man's allegedly innate faculty of symbolizing, of "creating" reality through symbols, etc., savour of idealistic speculation and cannot be endorsed by anyone who does not accept their idealistic philosophical background.

The first result of a consistent observance of the thesis that a sign is to be analysed in the context of the communication process, that is, that only an object or a phenomenon within that process (i.e., an object or a phenomenon which is interpreted by someone) can be a sign, involves the undermining or even the abolition of the traditional endeavours to classify signs. I invoke here above all the views of Husserl, which have had an enormous influence on the literature concerning signs and meaning.

What is striking is the great ambiguity of the term "sign", both in ordinary language and in scientific attempts to impart precision to terms. Another striking factor is the marked vagueness and even arbitrariness in the terminological distinctions between "sign", "index", "symbol", "signal", etc. No wonder, then, that attempts to explain the function of signs are intimately connected with attempts to establish a typology of sign which would make it possible in turn to establish a hierarchy of signs from the point of view of their extent and content, and thus to bring some order into terminological matters.

What is it that is most striking in the case of such attempted typologies? Probably the division of things and phenomena which function as signs into those which are natural and appear regardless of any purposive human activity and only *ex post* are interpreted by man as signs of something, and into these which are products of man's conscious social activity and have been produced by man *in order* to function as signs. The former are called *natural* signs, the latter, *proper* or artificial signs.

In a sense, we say that the freezing of water is a sign of a fall in temperature, that a halo around the moon is a sign that the weather is going to deteriorate, that wrinkles on a person's face are a sign that he is ageing, etc. In some other sense we say that black crêpe on a flag is a sign of mourning, that the colours of a flag are a sign of nationality, that firing a red rocket is a sign to start the attack, that a monument is a sign of an historic event, that a knot on a handkerchief is a sign to remind one of something, etc. In still another sense, we say that the words we pronounce are phonic signs, that a written sentence is a written sign, that a wink of the eye is a sign of communication between persons, that a definite number of dots and dashes or short and long sounds is a sign belonging to the Morse code, that certain ink marks are mathematical or logical signs, etc. All these are signs in some sense, but they are different signs with different meanings.

When reference is made below to signs *tout court*, that will mean proper signs, i.e., artificial in the sense that they are consciously produced by man for the purpose of communicating with other men. Although the natural signs (indices, symptoms) fall under the general category of "sign", they differ essentially from all other categories of signs, above all in that they are not produced or evoked consciously by man for communication purposes, but exist independently of man as natural processes and are only *ex post* utilized by men as source of information and in such cases function *as if* they were normal signs, i.e., as if they were consciously evoked or produced for the purpose of conveying some information to some person (a similar interpretation of the problem is to be found in Martinak's work – cf. footnote 3). By interpreting "meaning" in the context of interhuman relations in the process of communication (which will be discussed in the next chapter), we may ascribe to the proper signs a meaning in the direct sense of the word, and to the natural signs, a meaning only in some derived sense. This is why — at least for caution's sake, induced by the controversial character of the issue – a clear distinction must be made in analysis between indices (natural signs) and proper (artificial) signs[3].

[3] The terminology adopted in this book and to be used below requires additional explanations.

The division into natural signs and some other signs, which are in some sort of opposition to the former group, has a long standing. There are also

Husserl in his *Logische Untersuchungen* effected an essential division of signs into *Anzeichen* (indices) and *Ausdrücke* (expressions). The former, in his opinion, would have to point to something else and replace or represent that something else, and the latter would express some thought and would be signs *sensu stricto*. If, as the two extremes of the wide gamut of signs, we take, on the one hand, the natural signs (indices) of the type of frozen water or the moon's halo, and on the other the verbal signs, we reach the model of the typology of signs made by Husserl. He

---

various suggestions as to the name of the latter group, and at least some of them require explanations in order to show the motives which have guided me in making my own choice.

The ancients distinguished between the natural sign (*signum naturale*) and the conventional sign (*signum ad placitum*). This preserves a uniform criterion of division, but the division itself does not bear examination, since the latter group would have to include all those signs which are consciously produced by men for communication purposes. Yet not all such signs function on the strength of a convention. This applies above all to the iconic signs, which function on the strength of similarity to the object they stand for (they stand for such objects in the sense that a picture makes us think of the objects which it represents, of the effects usually caused by such an object, of corresponding feelings, etc.). There is a whole scale in that respect: from natural similarity, such as in the case of photographs, to the conventional nature of hieroglyphs or similar written signs (a classical example is offered by the letters of the Hebrew alphabet: their shape is a schematic representation of those objects the names of which are the names of the letters in question: "alef", "beith", etc.). Yet there is no doubt that an iconic sign such as a photograph does not work on the strength of any convention.

Another terminological suggestion, with regard to which an attitude has to be adopted, comes from Martinak (cf. E. Martinak, *Psychologische Untersuchungen zur Bedeutungslehre*, Leipzig 1901). He speaks of real and final signs, explicitly stressing in his terminology that what is characteristic of that group of signs which is in an opposition to the natural signs, namely the fact that men produce such signs in a conscious manner with that end in view which is communication.

The division adopted above in this book in principle follows that of Martinak, yet I consider his terminology not very fortunate, since the prin-

tried to squeeze the full wealth of the phenomena ambiguously referred to as "signs" into that Procrustean bed of extremes.

Two reasons make it advisable to take precisely that typology as an object of analysis: (1) Husserl's system demonstrates, so to speak, in a classical manner, the consequences of disregarding the principle of interpreting socially and historically the problems of sign and meaning; (2) his system has influenced a great many authors. Every work dealing with the problem of signs includes some typology of signs from this or that point of view. Martinak, Bühler, Morris, Carnap, Cassirer, Langer, to quote but a few names, all give their own typologies of signs, but none of them can vie with Husserl's in the matter of influence exerted on others. It might be said that Husserl had his predecessor in Peirce: the latter used a different terminology (index, iconic sign, symbol), but the sense of the division was practically the same[4]; yet Peirce was for many years unknown as an author, and hence his influence could be but small.

Thus the starting point for a critical analysis is the division of signs into indices (*Anzeichen*) and expressions or expressive signs (*Ausdrücke*), with the proviso that according to Husserl

---

ciple of division does not seem to be uniform, in spite of the fact that an appropriate interpretation may easily waive that objection aside (the term "real signs" coincides as to extension with the term "natural signs").

In opposing the proper signs to the natural signs I again start from the communication process. In that process, these are signs which are being consciously produced by men for communication purposes. In my opinion the term "proper signs" is the best term with which to denote them since natural processes function as signs only in a secondary and a derivative sense.

Alternatively with the term "proper signs" I use the term "artificial signs", since I wish to emphasize that in contrast with the natural signs, which are natural processes independent of human activity, the proper signs always are, in one way or another, *products* of human activity, and as such are artificially brought to existence. This I believe to be a very important point, which for a better description of the various categories of signs should also be reflected in terminology.

[4] See above all Ch. S. Peirce, "Logic as Semiotic: The Theory of Signs", in *Philosophical Writings of Peirce*, New York 1955.

only the latter perform the function of expressing thoughts, or, in other words, of *meaning* something. That division undoubtedly takes into account the specific nature of verbal signs, their specific expressive property, which in the literature of the subject is most often called "transparency to meaning". Husserl opposes to the *Ausdrücke* all other signs such as the *Anzeichen*, blurs all the possible difference among the latter (which may be highly significant) and denies to them the function of *expressing* something. Husserl's typology also takes into account – and in that he is certainly right – the specific character of the indices in the sense of natural signs. But at the same time it blurs the difference between the indices so interpreted and the signs of various types, which he lumps together in the same category (I mean here above all such signs as we should call signals, symbols, iconic signs, etc.). Thus, Husserl's *Anzeichen* are not indices (natural signs) in our classification, but all those signs which do not have as attributes the intentional acts (specifically understood by Husserl, and to be discussed in the chapter on meaning), and, consequently, meaning. Thus, Husserl's typology should not be confused with the contention that indices should fall outside the analysis of proper signs, since the extension of his indices (Anzeichen) covers both the indices and all proper signs except the verbal signs. This is the fundamental error of the entire conception, the error resulting from the separation of the analysis of signs from the communication process. Whoever sees that connection, whoever understands that *every* sign is included in the communication process and loses its function as a sign outside the context of that process, that every sign is a thing or an event somehow *interpreted* by someone, must reject as basically erroneous the conception that only *certain* signs are expressive, i.e., express a thought, have a meaning. On the contrary, *all* signs have meanings, express thoughts, and are signs only in so far as they perform those functions. In the communication process, all signs appear in the company of language thinking, or even simply as a specific translation of such (in conformity with an established code). This is so because man is unable to think otherwise than by means of verbal signs in some form, and all other forms of signs are derivative, i.e., they replace verbal signs. The *Anzeichen* theory overlooks that fact, because the signs are detached from the social context of the communication process and treated as something abstract and possessing inherent existence. Thus, Husserl not only separates the *Anzeichen* from the *Ausdrücke*, but even opposes the latter to the former. And yet in fact these two categories are intimately connected one with the other, and not only are they not in opposition, but they appear in combination; I should say that what Husserl called the *Anzeichen* is "infused" with what he called *Ausdrücke*. Consequently, a typology which takes them to be in opposition is based on erroneous initial assumptions.

All the proper signs (and hence a considerable part of Husserl's *Anzeichen*) have meanings. In this sense, they also express something, namely the thought which is contained in the meaning of the given sign. And if the word "to express" is interpreted otherwise, namely associated with information concerning emotional, and not intellectual, experiences, then the indices (natural signs) can also express something in this sense (e.g., tears express sadness, a blush expresses shame or embarrassment, etc.)

The bee communicates somehow with other bees through its "dance"; the stag which by his cry and by the use of his antlers urges the herd to flee, also achieves some sort of communication with the herd. Man sometimes acts similarly in the communication process — for instance when with his hand he stops a pedestrian on the roadway and points to a speeding motorcar. And yet this last is something quite different from the situational communication of animals. That difference exists simply because, behind the ordinary movements and gestures made both by me and by the person with whom I communicate (let us suppose I am abroad in a country the local language of which I do not know), there is a definite content, which we both *translate* for ourselves (often into different languages) – the same gesture of the hand into verbal signs: "Beware, danger!", and we *both* realize that we *understand such* in this way. If, for some reason, such translations into verbal signs differ from one another (e.g., because different gestures of the head are used in Europe and in a large part of Asia to express assent and dissent), then communication simply will not take place. This is self-evident when it comes to signals, symbols, etc.

The same applies to the so-called natural signs, the specific nature of which also makes us set them apart as a separate category. When an avalanche comes down, it is accompanied by the noise of falling stones. But that noise becomes the sign of the fact that an avalanche is coming down, and thereby a signal to run away, only if there are people who properly *interpret* that natural phenomenon. In itself, it is nothing more than a vibration of the air due to natural causes. That vibration becomes a sign (an index) when it is preceived by men and when those men understand of what the noise they hear is a manifestation. This is very important. The simple fact of men's existence does not suffice for a phenomenon to be interpreted and thus to become a sign. Those men must have some knowledge concerning that phenomenon, must understand it in order to be able to interpret it correctly. When a Roman saw a man with a brand on his forehead, he understood perfectly well that he had to do with a slave. We should be rather inclined to interpret the mark on the forehead as a scar left by some accident. If we do not know the meaning of a red spot on the forehead of some Hindu women, we cannot interpret that sign. For a Bushman from Equatorial Africa, who has no appropriate special knowledge, frozen water is merely a hard object with certain definite properties that can be perceived by touch, vision, etc., but not a sign (an index) of the necessary fall of temperature.

Thus, no natural phenomenon is inherently a sign (an index) and consequently does not mean anything "in itself". The situation is different when such a phenomenon occurs within the communication process. But how does it happen that a phenomenon becomes included in that process? By our experience, by our custom. When we become familiar with a given natural phenomenon and its causal or structural regularities, we begin to perceive it as if it were evoked for communication purposes, that is, created as a sign. In such cases it is Nature which is our "partner" in the communication process, Nature "communicates" something to us. That specific anthropologization of natural events blurs the distinction between the index and the artificial sign. A natural phenomenon, without in any degree changing its character, begins to function *for us*, in the context of *our* process of communication (it being assumed that we have come to know the regularities governing the given event), in the capacity of a sign; it begins to express something and is ascribed a meaning. But all this is an adjunct to a natural event, something added to it in the process of communication, and appears only within the framework of that process. From the point of view of natural processes, the function of an index is something secondary and is always related to a definite cognitive process, and further to a definite communication process. In that function an index, like every form of sign, is derivative with respect to communication by words; it is so in the sense that the act of understanding an index is, in the last analysis, always based on thinking in terms and by means of verbal signs.

Thus all signs except the verbal signs shine with reflected light, they somehow replace verbal signs and, when interpreted, are always translated into a language of words (although that translation often takes on an abbreviated form). This is so because we always think by means of a language of words[5].

---

[5] Cushing in his work *Manual Concepts* says that there exist primitive peoples which owing to a greatly developed language of gestures also have a special "manual thinking". That issue, and also the complicated problem of thinking of those deaf-mutes who have not been learned a special language of gestures, is left apart, since it does not invalidate the general thesis about thinking in terms of language of words and about the necessity to translate

This is precisely the point which I have in mind when I say that all signs, as they serve the purpose of human communication, are "imbued" with a language of words, and thereby with the meaning that is specific to that language. Not all signs express thoughts *in the same way*; on the contrary, even these general remarks reveal an essential difference between direct and indirect — substitutive — expression of thoughts, or else a difference between the communicative functioning of the indices on the one hand and of the proper signs on the other. But all the signs are *expressive* in a sense, and must be so if they are to be signs at all.

Thus Husserl's division into *Anzeichen* and *Ausdrücke* is untenable. It fails not only because all signs have in a sense a meaning, as demonstrated above, but also because all signs in a sense *indicate* something. This is admitted by Husserl himself when he says that even the words indicate something, that they are *Anzeichen* of thoughts. It is difficult to agree with that, since it might suggest that thoughts can originate and exist independently of verbal language, and the words are only *ex post* selected as their indices, *Anzeichen*. If our standpoint is that of a specific, organic unity of thinking and language, then we must reject such an idea as speculative, and standing in contradiction to all what psychology and physiology say about thought processes. But in suggesting that conception, Husserl at the same time destroyed the foundations of his own typology. The wrong and inconsistent division (which applies to *both* elements distinguished by it) makes his typology unacceptable in my view.

3. DEFINITION OF THE SIGN

All this (the critical, negative analysis was made with a view to drawing certain positive conclusions) shows clearly that the

---

substitutive signs into that language of words in the normal and the most common form of the communication process.

controversy with Husserl is not at all focused around formal and terminological issues (although these are involved as well). Of paramount interest is: What do we understand by the sign and in what context can its nature be understood and a proper classification be effected of the different variations of the signs?

Every attempt to offer a typology of signs usually begins with a definition of the sign. Otherwise it would be difficult to introduce a hierarchy and a typology of signs. Hence, I too begin with such a definition, but with certain reservations which restrict my plans.

As has been stated above (without any deeper justification, since we still lack elements necessary for that purpose), the sign forms a whole which is analysed into parts and aspects – such as the material and the semantic aspect – by mental abstraction only. It follows from the structure of this book that the problems of meaning must be discussed after the analysis of the typology of signs, since without the analysis it would be impossible to undertake a proper study of such problems. Unfortunately, and this is the usual difficulty with all attempts to offer a systematic exposition of the subject, the lack of an analysis of meaning adds, in turn, something of a difficulty to the analysis of the sign. It is essential, therefore, that I touch upon the definition of the sign only in a most general way, in so far as it is indispensable for further considerations.

Moreover, I shall, in the definition to be proposed, confine myself to proper, i.e., artificial, signs, and that for reasons indicated above, which recommend a separate treatment of the analysis of indices.

In tackling the problem from the point of view of the communication process, that is a process which is *par excellence* social in nature, I always take as my starting point a definite language of which the sign in question is an element, and I try to understand the nature of that element and its functions within the whole. Hence it is beyond doubt that every sign, as an element of some language (words, gestures, code, etc.), must be a signifying sign, that is a sign which, either directly or indirectly, expresses some thought. But there is also this: the explicit functioning of the sign is as *a means* of communication and *for the purpose* of communication. Understanding of that entails far-reaching consequences for the interpretation of the sign and for its definition.

The use of the sign in the communication process (language) leads to at least a double relativization of the sign: it appears in that process not just as an object, a state of things, or an event (which under definite circumstances function as signs), but as a *relation*. By saying that the sign is a relation we abbreviate the following statement: the object, etc., which appears as a sign, is in definite and complicated relations with those persons who use it as a sign; with the reality which it denotes or with which it is connected by the sign-relation in some other way; with other signs with which it makes up a linguistic system and only in the context of which does it become comprehensible, etc. Thus the sign is related to *people who communicate* in a definite, socially conditioned way, and to *the object*. That double relation (and not, as is customary, the referring of the sign to the object alone) leads to a consequence which seems trivial and yet is of great significance for a correct analysis of the sign: the principal function of the sign is to *communicate* something to someone, to *inform* someone about something. That function is undoubtedly common to all categories of signs, and consequently serves as the foundation of the definition of the sign: *Every material object, or the property of such object, or a material event, becomes a sign when in the communication process it serves, within the framework of a language adopted by the persons who communicate, the purpose of conveying certain thoughts concerning reality, that is concerning the external world, or concerning inner experiences (emotional, aesthetic, volitional, etc.) of any of the parties to the communication process.*

Such a definition of the sign is very general and deals with only one (though, in my opinion, the focal) aspect of the problem.

But it undoubtedly grasps that property already mentioned before and common to all the variations of signs – the property of informing about something, of communicating something. Another merit of that definition is the fact that it can serve as the starting point for an effort to classify signs, to suggest a typology of signs.

4. GENERAL FOUNDATIONS OF THE TYPOLOGY OF SIGNS

The task of the typology of signs is to delineate the specific traits of each separate variation of signs against their common background, and to establish connections between them and, possibly, a hierarchy of types of signs.

As mentioned above, the great variety of signs has given rise not only to a rich terminology serving to denote types of signs, but also to a considerable arbitrariness in the use of that terminology. There would be nothing wrong in that if terminological differences were connected solely with different appropriate conventions. In many cases it is in fact so, and then it is essential to understand deeply a convention and its foundations. It has been well known since the time of Plato that there is no natural nexus between the sound of a word and its meaning, and that we are free to change our terminology whenever necessary. But two things to be taken into account in this connection should restrict any too far-reaching arbitrariness in those matters. First, it should be borne in mind that terminological differences may veil the semantic differences revealed – e.g., in different classifications of phenomena – and that goes beyond the limits of conventions. Secondly, there should not, without good and sufficient reasons, be any violation of the actual use of words and the actual meanings of words, since this gives rise to additional complications and adds to confusion, especially in the case of words with a long-established tradition in the ordinary language.

The fact that various authors base themselves on different foundations in classifying signs leads to typologies based on various principles of division. Variety is still greater when it comes to terminology. There would be no point in engaging in a criticism of the various systems; analysis of the problem would thereby become clumsy and obscure, and so it is better to drop all such criticism.

Certainly, some general principles of classification to be found in the literature of the subject may be useful in certain situations. For instance, the division into natural and conventional signs, as referred to above, is of great importance. Morris's division of signs according to their extension (indexical, characterizing and universal) may also turn out to be useful. The same applies to Carnap's distinction between the sign as an act (*sign-event*) and the sign as an inscription (*sign-design*), which goes back to an old conception of Peirce – and also of Wittgenstein – concerning the distinction between the sign as a *token* and the sign as a *type*[6]. But, since it is not possible to agree with Husserl's division into indices and expressions, it is also not possible to agree with Peirce's typology based on the relation the signs and their referents (indices, iconic signs, symbols); with Morris's typology, distinguishing only signals and symbols and deliberately giving those terms meanings different from the current ones; with Bühler's, who ascribes specific meaning to terms and distinguishes signs, indices and symbols; with the typology of S. Langer (natural signs, artificial signs, symbols), or with that of S. Stebbing (expressive signs, suggestive signs, substitutive signs), etc. With reference to all those concepts, the objection may be validly raised that either the principle of division is not uniform, or that the extensions overlap, or that the classification is not exhaustive, or that it is evidently arbitrary, etc. Thus, all such classifications may be used as specific mental stimuli – but I would adopt none of them as my own.

6 When we have written signs, e.g., "cat" and "CAT", each of them is (1) a distinct, individual inscription (*token*), and (2) an individual variation of an inscription of one and the same *type*.

I begin with two distinctions – one of them universally accepted, the other controversial.

First, the signs are divided, as already mentioned, into natural (indices, symptoms) and proper (or artificial).

Second, the proper signs are divided into verbal signs (and written substitutes for such) and all other signs. In a sense (but only in *a* sense), this is an analogy to the distinction Husserl makes with reference to the *Ausdrücke*. The similarity consists in the fact that a clearly distinct character of the verbal signs as opposed to all other signs is recognized; and the difference – in the fact that all the rest is *not* squeezed into the Procrustean bed of the *Anzeichen*. The verbal signs and their specific nature will later be subjected to a more detailed analysis, precisely on account of that specific nature of theirs. For the time being, I only repeat what has already been said: because of the special rôle of the phonic language and of the verbal signs in the process of human thinking and communication, these signs occupy the special, supreme place in the hierarchy of signs.

And now for the classification graph:

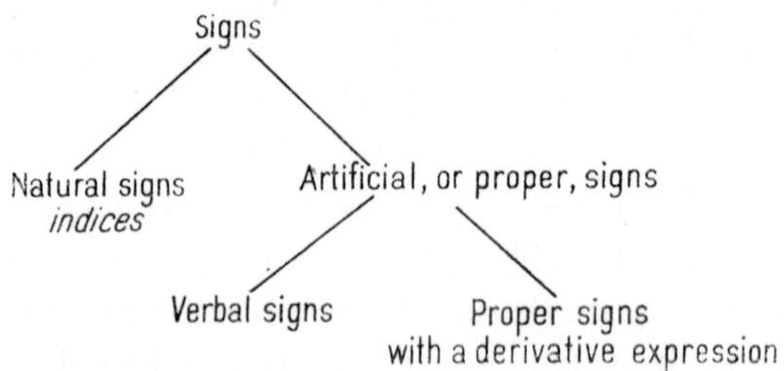

Fig. 1

Thus we have obtained the following result: on the one hand, we have set apart the natural signs (indices) and have opposed them by the artificial, or proper, signs; on the other hand, among the latter we have ascribed a special status to the verbal signs as the basis of the process of human communication and have again opposed them by all other artificial signs. In view of the reservation that an analysis of the verbal signs will be made separately because of the specific nature and importance of the problem, the remaining artificial (proper) signs must be classified and analysed.

It is necessary to realize how far such an analysis is to reach, and what details it is supposed to cover. It is to be borne in mind that, for example, Peirce succeeded in distinguishing over 60 classes of signs. By basing the classifications on different criteria, it is possible to multiply the classes distinguished in one's typology, a process which in some cases may be quite interesting, but in others will boil down to mere scholastic casuistry. In the present instance I am concerned above all with distinguishing large, comprehensive classes of signs and in explaining the sense of the terms relating to them.

It is known that every sign which is not an index (a natural sign), is – in a definite sense of the word – an artificial sign. The majority of such signs are at the same time conventional, in a definite sense of the word also. The signs which are not indices are consciously produced by men for communication purposes. This is achieved either by a natural similarity of certain objects (states of things, etc.) to what they are to signify, or a conventional conferring of definite meanings on objects (states of things, etc.) which lack such a similarity. When we speak of the conventional character of the artificial signs we mean a special, *social* interpretation of conventionality – and such a conventionality appears in the cases of the various categories of such signs, to a certain extent even in those cases where the functioning of something in the capacity of a sign is based on a similarity to the referent, as in the case of maps, hieroglyphs, pictograms, etc., probably with the exception of simple similes of objects, such as photographs. Thus the point is not that such a convention be agreed upon *simply* by the persons communicating *hic et nunc* (although this is possible), or that such an agreement, social and not individual in nature, be concluded at any time in a conscious manner. Artificial signs may be called into existence on the strength of a conscious and deliberate agreement concluded at a specified date (cf. all the codes), but they may equally well owe their origin to the historical practice of the social process of communication (the classical example here being the phonic language). In the latter case, of decisive importance is a definite *action* which in turn arises mainly from the need of many-sided *co-operation*; that action is socially accepted and is being continued naturally, although without any traces of any deliberate convention.

Thus all the proper signs are artificial, and in principle conventional as well. The factor enabling their further division is connected with their function in the human process of communication — the function of direct influence upon human action, in one case, and the function of standing for certain objects, states of things, or events, in the other. By the function of standing for (substituting) something I mean this — that the sign appears instead of some object, state of things, or event, and evokes in the human mind ideas, images and thoughts which are usually evoked by that object, state of things, or event (that substitution also is reflected in human action, although it does not in the least follow that the appearance of the sign should always entail the same results as does the appearance of the object, etc., for which the sign stands).

It might be objected that the proper signs always are signs *for something*, that they are artificial, produced for the purpose of communication, and hence for the purpose of somehow influencing human behaviour. It might also be contended that every sign is a sign *of something*, that it points "beyond itself", and as such performs the function of substitution. All that is true. Nevertheless, there are proper signs the function of which consists in *directly* influencing human behaviour (signals), and proper signs the function of which consists in substitution (substitutive signs) and the influence of which on human behaviour is but *indirect*. In adopting that difference as the criterion of classification, we may further subdivide the proper signs with a derivative expression into signals and substitutive signs, and the latter in turn into substitutive signs *sensu stricto* and symbols.

Here is the graph:

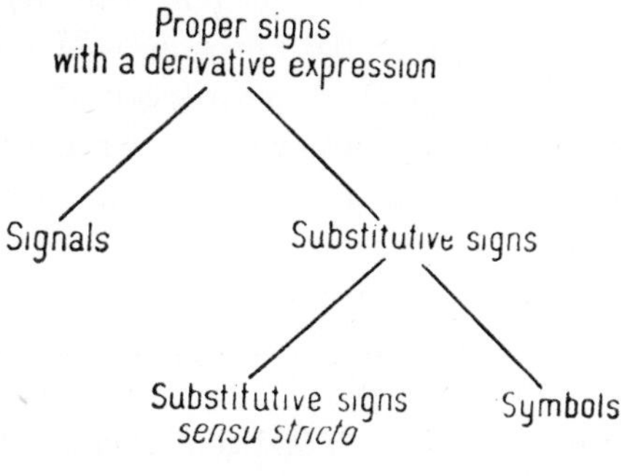

Fig. 2

We now proceed to discuss the various categories appearing in the classification suggested above.

A. *Signals*

In the definition of the signal, the starting point for me is the ordinary sense of the word. Of course, that word is used in the literature of the subject in other, sometimes quite arbitrary meanings also (e.g., for Morris, every sign which is not a symbol is a signal). But I have mentioned, too, that I adopt the directive that the existing meanings of words are not to be violated if not necessary, just because such a violation of linguistic usage would do more harm than good, although the using of words in new meanings, consciously designed in view of some needs, is not only admissible in science, but actually often resorted to.

I am in agreement with the ordinary usage and with the usual meaning of the word "signal" in so far as I understand by it a sign the purpose of which is to evoke, to change, or to make someone desist from, some action.

We usually do not say (although Morris tells us to do so) that the freezing of water is a *signal* of a fall of temperature, or that wrinkles on a person's face are a *signal* of his ageing. On the other hand, it is quite in accord with our language intuition, and in my opinion also with the natural premises of the classification of signs, to say that the firing of a blue rocket was for soldiers a signal for an attack; that the appearance of the green light at a street crossing is a signal for pedestrians to cross the roadway; that the wailing of a siren in wartime is a signal for civilians to seek refuge in shelters against an imminent air raid; that the wailing of a siren of an ambulance car or a fire engine is a signal for all vehicles to leave a free passage; that a bell rung in a school or a whistle blown in a factory is a signal to break or to start work.

What is the point in all such and similar cases? What do they have in common that makes it possible to combine them into a single category, despite all the differences of details?

As already stated, in all such cases we have to do with signs the main objective of which is to evoke, change, or make someone desist from, some action. Thus, these are typical signs *for something*, signs clearly intended to evoke (or to change, or to stop) some definite action as the objective of communication. Thus they are *material phenomena caused especially or utilized in order to* bring about a response, prearranged and agreed upon, whether socially (in a group), or individually, in the form of definite manifestations of human activity.

It is only the element of convention which calls for an explanation of the latter assertion. Signals appear only where an appropriate group of people have concluded an *explicit* agreement by virtue of which a given phenomenon functions for them as a signal.

Thus, if the soldiers in trenches are to understand the appearance of a blue rocket in the sky as a signal for attack, they must be so informed in advance. In such a case, and *only* in such a case, does the firing of the rocket mean for every soldier the order: "Forward! Attack!" In this case the blue rocket, in conformity with an agreed code, *replaces* the appropriate verbal signs. Without precisely *such* an agreement the blue rocket would not be a sign (signal) and would be an ordinary physical phenomenon, lacking the *assigned* property of conveying information. For a third party the blue rocket is not a signal at all (since he does not know the convention agreed upon), and for the soldiers themselves a red rocket would be no signal, because the convention previously agreed upon provided for something different. On the other hand, an accidental firing of a blue rocket by a third party, even one unaware of the consequences of the act, would be understood as a signal, in conformity with the prior agreement.

The same applies to the lights at street crossings, to the movements of the hands of a traffic policeman, to sirens sounded in peacetime and in wartime, etc. In all such cases we have to do with an *explicit agreement* pertaining to the meaning of given physical phenomena which are usually produced by some individuals in order to set up an appropriate activity by others. This is shown by the fact that we *learn* the meaning of the appropriate phenomena (the rules of crossing streets in cities, the meaning of light signals, etc.) and that without learning them we do not understand them.

A further point is that whenever we refer to signals we always mean an object (state of things or event) which is utilized or produced *occasionally*, especially for the purpose of bringing about *the given* action (e.g., the rocket is fired when the attack is to begin; the siren is sounded when the air raid is imminent or is over; the lights at a street crossing are changed when the pedestrians are to be allowed to cross or told to stop; certain verbal signs are uttered or written down, yet they do not appear in their fundamental semantic function but independently of that function play the rôle of a signal, previously agreed upon, to start or abandon some action, etc.); or we mean an object, etc., which exists permanently but *functions occasionally* as a signal, that is when approached and observed by persons who know a given convention (e.g., road signs for vehicles, devices with photocells which at a specified time activate light, sound or other signals to warn of danger, etc.)

Thus the signal can be distinguished from other artificial signs by the following characteristics: (1) *its meaning is always arbitrary, established by virtue of a convention valid within a given group of people*; (2) *its purpose is always to evoke (or change or stop) a certain action*; (3) *its appearance is occasional in connection with the intended action.* The fact that it replaces a certain verbal statement is not to be mentioned as a characteristic, since this holds, as stated above, for all proper signs.

The analysis thus made shows that the signal is a substitute for the corresponding verbal expressions; it replaces them as every code replaces a phonic language. The metaphorical statement that every signal is "imbued" with the phonic language and its meaning, is thus, in the case of signals, explained directly and very simply. The signal has, like every meaningful group of verbal signs, a meaning, although it has such in a different manner, in an indirect and derivative way.

What then is the relation of the "signal" in this sense to the "signal" in e.g. the Pavlovian sense? Let us get it quite clear that we have here to do with two words which have the same shape, but different meanings. In Pavlov's terminology, the "signal" refers to relations concerning physiological stimuli and reactions, by being part of a certain situation, treated as a whole, which brings about definite conditioned responses. Thus in that case the "signal" means the same as a physiological stimulus in a definite sense of the term. No reference is made there to its being "imbued" with meaning and to connections with a phonic language; moreover, the very formulation of the problem eliminates the need to resort to such concepts. I shall not stop for an appraisal of the correctness and virtue of such an approach, but simply confine myself to the statement that in Pavlov's terminology the notion of the "signal" differs completely from that analysed above. For the time being, that statement is sufficient for our purposes.

B. Substitutive signs

The second large class of proper signs comprises substitutive signs. By contrast with signals, they are signs *of something*, signs with the emphasized function of substituting, representing some other objects, states of things or events.

The class of substitutive signs is in turn subdivided into two subclasses according to whether the object a signs stands for is a concrete, material object, or whether the sign, i.e., something material, represents an abstract notion, i.e. something which is connected with the material world, material relationships, material properties, etc., but in itself is not a material object. In the first case we speak of *substitutive signs sensu stricto*, and in the second, of *symbols.*

The problem of substitutive signs *sensu stricto* is comparatively simple. What is involved are material objects which stand for other objects by virtue of similarity or convention. Typical examples of substitutive signs working on the similarity principle (iconic signs) are all kinds of images and similes (drawings, paintings, photographs, sculptures, etc.) and examples of substitutive signs based on convention are all kinds of written signs which stand for speech sounds, their groups, words, sentences, etc. Of course, the division is not a rigid one and there are transition stages between the various types, which I deliberately disregard here in order to avoid complication. The only serious issue here is that of the mechanism of that "substitution" or "representation" of one object by another from the point of view of the mental processes; the problem of meaning is involved, but that will be discussed in the next chapter.

Difficulties arise, on the other hand, when it comes to symbols. This is due mainly to two causes: first, the issue is very controversial and approached from different angles in the very rich literature of the subject; second, the issue at stake here is one of a class (or subclass) of signs which play an exceptionally important rôle in the various fields of social life.

In my system, the symbols are a subclass of substitutive signs and are characterized principally by the following three characteristics: (1) *material objects represent abstract notions*; (2) *the representation is based on a convention which must be known if a given symbol is to be understood*; (3) *conventional representation is based on the representation of an abstract notion by a sign, a representation which outwardly appeals to senses* (and semantically works by exemplification, allegory, metaphor, allusion to mythology, the *pars pro toto* principle, etc).

In such a formulation, which seems highly significant for various reasons, the starting point again is the living intuitive meaning of the term "symbol" which is in agreement with the directive that existing linguistic usage should not be violated unless necessary, and that, so to speak, the semantic *entia* should not be multiplied beyond what is necessary.

For what, in conformity with the ordinary intuitive usage, is it that is called a "symbol"? We are certainly in agreement with such an intuitive usage when we say that the cross is a symbol of Christianity, a crescent – of Islam, and a six-point star – of the Mosaic religion; that the hammer and sickle or a red five-point star is a symbol of Communism, a swastika – of Nazism, and an axe with fasces – of Fascism; that a figure of a woman with a band across her eyes and with a pair of scales and a sword in her hands is a symbol of justice, that the figure of Mars symbolizes war and heroism, that of Eros, love, and a skeleton with a scythe, death; that black symbolizes mourning, purple – dignity, yellow – envy, white – innocence, red – love; that specific colours on a flag symbolize (one's) nation and motherland, etc. In the light of existing linguistic usage, it is doubtful whether, for example, mathematical and logical signs may be considered symbols (although it is often said that they may be). And there is no doubt that the firing of a rocket to start an attack in a battle, a person's photograph, or the fact that water has frozen, etc., cannot be said to be symbols.

Let us analyse those facts and statements from the point of view of the definition of symbol I have suggested.

It is beyond doubt that a symbol is always a substitutive sign, that its function consists precisely in standing for something. It is also beyond doubt that a symbol, like every sign, is something material. Further elements, just those which have to distinguish the symbols from all the other substitutive signs, require certain comments, since they are debatable.

The first issue is as to what is represented by a symbol. I follow in that respect many authors who are justified in protesting against too broad an interpretation of the notion of "symbol", and against a practical identification of the symbol with the sign in general. My assertion is that the characteristic property of the symbol is the representation by a material object (functioning as a sign) of an "ideal object" or, strictly speaking, an abstract notion.

Let us revert to the examples adduced above: this or that religion or faith is an abstract concept; the same holds for the social systems, Communism or Fascism; for such notions as justice, courage, love, envy, innocence, mourning, dignity, nationality, etc. The most profound sense of the symbols — and this is why they are favoured in all mass movements, propaganda literature, etc. — consists precisely in that they *bring abstract concepts nearer to men* by presenting to them abstract ideas in the shape of material objects, that is in a form which is easier to be grasped by the mind and to be preserved in memory. Consequently, as mentioned previously, such material symbols are very convenient for mass movements, since they substitutively convey certain ideas which tend otherwise to be difficult to grasp and to understand; as the material symbol becomes independent of what it represents, as its specific "alienation" develops, a mythologization of such a symbol may also occur. A symbol is not a purely intellectual product, although it is closely connected with a concept. It is equally closely connected with various emotional states and therefore may not only bring abstract concepts closer to men, but also prevent men from coming to know the truth. The multifarious functions of symbols, and in particular their myth-making functions, make them an extremely interesting object of study.

The conventional character of the symbol (in the sense of a social and historical convention) – that is its second specific trait – is linked with the function of representing abstract notions by material objects, which is the proper function of the symbol in the communication process.

To understand *any* symbol, the appropriate convention must be known. Those who do not know the Old and the New Testament, Greek and Roman mythology, who do not know (usually from very childhood) the symbolism of colours as used in Europe, who are not versed in our political life and in the symbolism of the various national emblems and colours – will not understand a single symbol of those exemplified above. By analogy, a European, even an educated European not acquainted with Oriental culture, will fail to understand the symbolism of the Hindu dances, or that connected with Oriental deities, the specific symbolism of colours, smells, etc. This is so because *no* symbol has a natural meaning, on the contrary, *every* symbol has an artificial, conventional sense which must be learned. This is shown by such elementary examples as that in the European cultural circle it is black which is the colour of mourning, whereas in the East it is white; that in our cultural circle it is purple which is the symbolic colour of power and dignity, whereas in China it is yellow; and so on, not to mention the visual symbols of wisdom, courage, virtue, etc., which have nothing in common if compared as between the various cultural circles.

All this explains the third specific trait of the symbol – the sensory (usually iconic) representation of an abstract idea.

The fact that the object represented by a symbol is always an abstract notion was indicated as the first such trait. It has been said that in the case of the symbol we have to do with the substitution of an abstract notion by a material and concrete object, but no explanation has been given as to that material concreteness of the symbol. This is to be dealt with later.

Like every sign, the symbol is a material object or phenomenon. Were it not so, it could not be perceived and could not stand for anything else. But a symbol is, as a rule, not merely a material object, but also a visual image.

The painter, the black and white artist or the sculptor who wants to use his art to present some abstract concept, such as heroism, virtue, love or patriotism, must usually resort to a symbol, in which he has to choose between the alternatives: either his picture will be an allegory conveying the abstract idea in question, or it will be an exemplification conveying what is general through the intermediary of what is particular.

The symbolic representation of abstract ideas frequently resorts to metaphors on which the picture is based (especially in literature). Verbal symbolic images include such formulations as "the bowl of life", "the cup of bitterness", etc.

Mythology is amply drawn on. The serpent of Aesculapius as the symbol of medical art comes from classical mythology, as does Hercules, the symbol of strength, the owl, the symbol of wisdom, etc. And the animal symbols in state emblems (the lion, the eagle, etc.) usually come from ethnic legends.

Representation based on the *pars pro toto* principle also frequently occurs. The cross as a particularly important element in the story of Jesus has thus become the symbol of Christendom.

Of course, it also happens not infrequently that a symbolic image is abstract in character, and in such a case its links with the abstract notion it represents are purely conventional (although sometimes some imaginary explanation through association crops up). This holds for colours (e.g., as symbols of emotions), combinations of colours (e.g., as national symbols in the case of national flags), abstract drawings with mythical or magical interpretations (e.g., the swastika), mathematical and logical signs (the graphic symbols of infinity, negation, etc.)

Gesticulatory, olfactory, etc., symbols are in principle purely conventional. This applies for instance to the symbolism of gestures in Hindu dances, the symbolism of aromas so widespread in the East, etc.

Sound and their combinations, too, can play the rôle of symbolic images by virtue of a convention, most commonly in connection with a certain emotional tone, felt only in a definite cultural circle. For instance, a slow and monotonous ringing of bells with a low tone is perceived by us a symbol of mourning; the same holds, by analogy, for the melody and the rhythm of a certain type of march.

All this is only by way of illustration, and not as any exhaustive enumeration. The gamut of symbols is extremely wide and its possibilities almost unlimited. But in all the cases we have analysed, the factors referred to earlier are involved: the symbol is a material object, state of things, or event; it replaces (represents) an abstract notion, and not any other material object (which is the function of the substitutive sign *sensu stricto*); such a representation is possible only when based on definite conventions (usage, *ad hoc* agreement, etc.)

It is not difficult to notice that such an interpretation of the symbol, organically connected with a definite conception of a typology of signs, and with a criterion of division, adopted for that purpose, is in conformity with ordinary language intuition and is adjusted to the existing sense of expressions. This fact is by no means unimportant or secondary, since the linguistic categories shaped by history offer a certain classification of concepts, based on social appreciation of similarities and differences in content, which means that they pertain to what such categories express as regards relations in the objective world. Names can of course be changed arbitrarily, but if this leads to changes in the classification of phenomena *without adequate semantic reasons*, that is something which science cannot permit. The point is that the terminology adopted should help us to inform others about the real world to which it pertains, and about the relationships in that world, and not hinder us in doing so and consequently in communicating with others. Nothing more forcefully debunks the conventionalist deviation – which in the last score or so years has cast a shadow over correct understanding of the relation between language and reality – than does semantics properly pursued. It is precisely from the position of semantics that one has to oppose the distortions, so frequent in the literature of the subject, in the interpretation of the problem of symbol, the arbitrary classifications of signs, and the resulting arbitrary changes in meanings of the terms used as names for the various categories of signs. It is semantics above all which tells us that terminology is arbitrary in the sense that there is no inherent connection between the phonic sign and the object denoted by it (although there are different opinions on that issue, too), but there is no arbitrariness in establishing a correspondence between the verbal signs and objective reality when it comes to the classification of things and phenomena, when it comes to the cognitive function of language.

As already mentioned, Husserl's typology and Cassirer's theory of symbols, in particular, have spread in the literature of the subject an interpretation of the term "symbol" which stands in contradiction to the existing sense of that word, and thereby to the analysis of that category as performed above. Usually the class of symbols is made to include all the verbal signs, and sometimes (Morris) symbols are identified with signs which are not signals, or the sense of the term is extended so as to cover all signs the meanings of which are not based on a similarity with the object represented (Kotarbińska), or else all the signs which are deliberately used as such are considered to be symbols (Stebbing), etc. These are dangerous practices not only because they obscure, as we shall see later, the highly important specific character of the verbal signs, but above all because they pass over in silence the existence of an important group of substitutive signs with marked common characteristics.

The significance (especially the social significance) of symbols understood in a proper, i.e., restrictive, way is enormous, above all in view of their rôle in shaping public opinion and social myths. That is why we must recognize the achievements of such scholars as Cassirer who succeeded in noticing and spot-lighting the problem, in spite of having mystified it. A proper solution of that problem is still an open issue. Marxism is the trend potentially most suited to undertake that difficult but promising task. So far however the matter remains in the air.

The understanding of the nature and function of symbols depends above all on the criterion adopted for the classification of signs in general. It does not, of course, settle the question, but an error there invalidates a proper analysis of the problem of symbols. It is not possible to understand what a symbol is if Husserl is followed in dividing the signs into *Anzeichen* and *Ausdrücke*, which practice virtually eliminates the possibility of understanding the specific nature of all signs occurring in the process of human communication. The same happens if Kotarbińska is followed in adopting the division (suggested by many authors) into iconic signs and symbols. Such a division is certainly possible, but that dichotomic classification, though formally correct, does not lead to any interesting results and blurs the division in those classes of signs which are observable in practice and highly important from the point of view of the communication process. This is so because the division loses completely the distinction, for example, between the signal, the symbol (in the sense specified above) and the verbal sign. The same objection may be raised with respect to the classifications suggested by Morris, S. Stebbing, S. Langer, and to the resulting meanings of the term "symbol". This criticism once more reminds us how justified is the statement that terminological issues are by no means as arbitrary as might appear at the first glance. It also reminds us the importance of a proper starting point for analysis, and of a proper criterion of the typology of signs.

One more remark to conclude these considerations.

As already indicated, there is no doubt that some other classifications of signs, and the distinction of some other category or categories, may prove advantageous for certain purposes. We have paused here to discuss the principal classification which, in my opinion, is the most important. Within that classification, further divisions may be effected, based on other criteria, and there will be no collision between the two. I should like, however, to devote a few remarks to a group of important signs the analysis of which may involve certain difficulties in the light of the typology adopted in this book. I mean the signs based on physical movements such as gestures, facial expressions, expressive movements of the body, etc. Do not those signs express above all a uniform group, in view of its connection with the human body and consequently with human experiences and psychic states? Is it not a group of signs which is particularly important in view of the fact that it always accompanies the phonic language (gestures and facial expressions), and does it not deserve therefore to be separated as a distinct class or subclass?

First of all it must be said that in the light of the classification we have adopted, based on the functions of signs in the communication process, this is not a uniform group. These bodily signs belong to all the classes we have distinguished: thus, for instance, tears and laughter, being natural phenomena that accompany certain spiritual processes, may be classed as indices; gestures and facial expressions which accompany human speech may also be treated as indices of certain emotional states; a conventional movement of the hand or of some other part of the body may be a signal; a wink may be a substitutive sign *sensu stricto*; an appropriate posture and movement of a part of the body during a dance may be a symbol; and finally certain movements of hands or fingers performed in conformity with a certain code may just be a translation from the phonic language. The apparent uniformity disappears, and the distribution of the signs in question over the categories adopted in our classification presents no difficulty. Thus there is no cause for alarm.

So far we have been discussing the various categories of signs, excluding verbal signs. As previously indicated, our analysis will be concluded by the study of the most important problem in the theory of signs, namely that of verbal signs and their specific nature.

5. THE SPECIFIC NATURE OF VERBAL SIGNS

The significance of the phonic language, and consequently of verbal signs, for the communication process, and thereby for social life, has long been appreciated. And the phonic language and its verbal signs have for long been an object of study and investigation. A deliberate call for such investigation is found in the *Upanishads*, and the study of language is the main subject of Plato's dialogue *Cratilus*. From the times of antiquity to this day, the problem has not ceased to claim human attention. And justly so, for if we realize the social importance of the communication process, in particular its rôle in human co-operation, and its *organic* link with that process, we must focus our attention precisely on the phonic language.

It is possible to engage in the various speculations as to which came first: the phonic language or the language of gestures; it is possible to discuss the rôle and significance of the various categories of signs; it is possible to differ from others on the point as to whether there are various systems of "languages", etc. But it is not reasonably possible to deny that in all the known civilizations the phonic language was and is, not only the principal means of human communication, but also the means without which progress in science, culture and technology would be *impossible*.

All this sounds like a truism and a triviality that might be dispensed with in semantic analysis. But it is only seemingly so, *especially* in semantic analysis. For it follows from that truism, or apparent truism, that the position of the phonic language in social processes is so exceptional that it cannot be explained unless we recognize the specific nature of the phonic language and the verbal signs as compared with all other systems of signs, i.e., with all other "languages". If it is true that all other systems of signs are "imbued" with meaning taken over from the verbal signs, and that they shine with reflected light, then the division into the (phonic) language and "languages", drawing attention to the inequality of these categories, is also justified. And yet the various contemporary semiotics, semiologies, etc. – which after all raise important issues concerning the general theory of signs – blur, if they do not cancel outright, precisely that specific nature of the phonic language and the verbal signs. (This might be explained by the attempt to bring out what is common to *all* signs and thus to formulate a general theory of signs.)

The theoretically erroneous tendency to disregard the specific nature of the verbal signs can also be observed in the terminology that implies a definite classification and characterization of the various classes of signs. True, that terminology is not yet well established, but – especially in the latest literature on the subject – the term "symbol" is most often used to denote the verbal sign. For all the definitional conventions, this fact obscures the difference between the verbal and other signs and simply adds to the confusion. In some cases the term used is just "the sign", which is certainly correct, but by being too general does not help to give precision to the problem (especially if we bear in mind that in these cases the terminology conceals conceptions which certainly do not favour any explanation of the specific nature of the verbal signs).

Let us begin with the statement that although the phonic language consists of signs in the sense defined above, so that a verbal sign (and this *is* a trivial statement) always falls under the general definition of the sign, yet the verbal sign is neither just a sign and nothing more, nor a symbol – in the ordinary sense of the word and in the sense suggested *ad hoc* by the various theories. In the latter case, we have to do not only with an arbitrary change in the terminology adopted, but also (since otherwise the operation would be childishly naive and devoid of any scientific meaning) with a different definition of the symbol, a definition which again obscures the specific nature of the verbal signs.

Thus, the verbal sign complies perfectly well with the general definition of the sign as adopted above, which definition, by recognizing the communication process as the foundation of our analysis, sees in the communicative function of the sign its principal property, and consequently relates the sign both to the object about which it communicates something and to the language in which that something is communicated.

There is no doubt that the phonic language is a definite, *specific* system of signs. But here the issue is opened with the question: a system of what signs?

Can any positive information be found in the literature on the subject? Certainly, yes. Such information concerns above all the way in which a verbal sign means something. Representatives of the most diverse trends seem to reveal fairly common agreement of opinion in that matter; I mean here the issue of "transparency to meaning" of the verbal signs.

If we take authors who independently of one another have written about the specific nature of the verbal signs – Delacroix, Rubinshtein, Urban and Ossowski[7] – we find that each of them uses the expression "transparency to meaning" precisely with reference to the verbal signs, and for each of those authors that property of those signs is associated with their specific nature. In resorting to that metaphor, those authors have in mind that when we perceive verbal signs, then, by contrast with all other proper signs, we do not perceive their material shape as some-

7 H. Delacroix, *Le language et la pensée*, Paris 1924; С. Л. Рубинштейн, *Основы общей психологии* [The Principles of General Psychology], Chap. XI: "Речь" [Speech], Москва 1946; W. M. Urban, *Language and Reality*, London 1951; S. Ossowski, "Analiza pojęcia znaku" [An Analysis of the Concept of Sign], reprinted from *Przegląd Filozoficzny*, 1926, Nos. 1 & 2.

thing autonomous, but just the contrary: that shape is to such an extent confused with meaning that except for the cases of disturbed perception we do not realize the existence of the material aspect for the verbal sign. As to who has the priority right to the formulation "transparency to meaning" – that is not essential; this is an issue that is of interest rather for an historian of the problem. But the fact that the otherwise diverging opinions are in agreement on that point has its implication – at least the implication that we face a conception which has a firm position in the literature on the subject.

When we speak of signs, signals, substitutive signs and symbols, we always speak of material things or events which serve the purpose of human communication, because precisely by virtue of the fact that the communicating parties understand them in one and the same way, each of such signs informs the communicating parties. Each of these signs is in a relation to the object (understood in the broadest sense of the term, so as to cover things, their properties and relations between them, events, psychic processes, etc.) about which it conveys information, and to a definite language within which it functions only as a sign, i.e., means something. But when we speak about the proper signs with the exception of the verbal signs, then it is always a fact that the relation between the material and the semantic aspect of the sign admits of a certain "autonomy" of meaning; this signifies that – except for the iconic signs – meaning is always shaped independently of a *given* sign (in the sense of the material sign-vehicle), as it were outside that sign, and consequently may be combined with another material shape of the sign (e.g., we might change the convention on the road signs without impairing their meaning, that is, what they communicate to us). This is connected with the fact that all those signs function only within a phonic language, and with thinking in terms of ideas, which is specific to that language. This is why we can – and must – have "ready-made" meanings for all the categories of signs which are not verbal signs. This is so because we are simply unable to think otherwise than by means of verbal signs, and all sign-making (except for the use of a phonic language, inculcated in us by our being brought up in society, or, in other words, except for thinking in terms of language signs) is a secondary process, a result of the various conventions (in the broad, historical sense of the term), and as such is always *preceded* by thought, and it is in this sense that it always is "imbued" with thought.

And what about verbal signs, and language as their system? Here the situation is quite different – first of all, because they have nothing "behind them", they are not based on meanings of some other language. This is so because thought and language form a single, indivisible, organic whole. There is no thinking that exists separately and language that exists separately, there is only thinking-and-language. There is no concept that exists separately, and sign that exists separately, there is only concept-and-verbal-sign. Of course, there are people who think that not only can one think without resorting to verbal signs, to language, but that it is just such thinking which is "true". There have been many believers in "true", "direct" cognition, from Plato up to the phenomenologists, intuitionists, adherents of the idea of a mystic union between the cognitive subject and the object of cognition, etc. It is they who sadly repeat after Schiller: "*Spricht* die Seele, spricht die *Seele* nicht mehr". But these are irrationalistic speculations, denied by such disciplines as psychology, the physiology of the brain, etc. From the Marxist position, these opinions were ridiculed – and rightly so – by Stalin, in his *Marxism and the Problems of Linguistics*.

It is just this specific unity of thinking-and-language which gives rise to the "transparency to meaning" of the verbal signs. They *are* meaning, although they are *not only* meaning. A passage from *Die deutsche Ideologie*, quoted previously, refers to consciousness, the real form of which, according to Marx, is speech. Thus the verbal sign is not mere meaning. It is also a sound, the material phenomenon consisting in the vibration of air waves, without which there would be no sign and no communication – if we reject "pure" and "direct" cognition. And this is why the metaphorical formulation "transparency to meaning", although it expresses an idea that is valuable for the understanding of the specific nature of the verbal signs, is insufficient, since it leaves unsolved the real problem of the relationship between the phonic aspect (the sound picture) and the meaning (the conceptual content) of the verbal sign.

It is in this connection that de Saussure has made an interesting comparison between the verbal sign and the sheet of paper one side of which is the sound image and the other, the conceptual content (de Saussure used the terms *signifiant* and *signifié*, being of the opinion that a language sign is a psychic entity composed of a sound image and a concept). He argues further that one side of a sheet of paper cannot be eliminated without destroying the other, and in the same way in a verbal sign the sound cannot be separated from the concept (meaning). This is a metaphor, too, but it somehow sheds light on the problem from a different angle.

To explain the specific nature of the verbal sign, we must engage in greater detail in the analysis of the concept "the verbal sign", since it appears in two different meanings, combined with different theoretical conceptions. In one formulation "the verbal sign" means the sound (in the sense of acoustic vibration or a sound image) with which a definite meaning is somehow connected. In the other, "the verbal sign" is the specific whole consisting of sound-and-meaning, characteristic of really existing entities of the phonic language.

There is no doubt that verbal signs consist not only of meanings but also of the phonic aspect of meanings, that "curse" which in the form of vibrations of the air persecutes the spirit. There is also no doubt – and this is not challenged probably even by the most radical of those who contend that meaning and sound in a verbal sign form an organic unity – that that unity is not absolute, but relative, which means that it can be broken in certain specified cases. This refers not only to such trivial cases as the perception of alien, incomprehensible speech merely as a sequence of sounds. It also covers more complicated and more interesting cases, such as those investigated by Head and others, consisting in aphasia when a person preserves the memory of the phonic form of words but ceases to understand their meanings, or loses the faculty of speech while understanding what is said to him. Both in the case of perception of incomprehensible speech and in the cases of aphasia we have to do with a certain anomaly from the point of view of the process of human communication. That process presupposes the community of speech of the communicating persons as well as a normal state of mind in those persons. And it is here, in view of the *relative* character of the unity of sound and meaning in the verbal sign, that the fundamental problem arises: how is that unity brought about? I have in this connection to anticipate the results of the analysis of meaning and its links with the sign (this is, unfortunately, unavoidable although it breaks the planned exposition of problems), and to engage in the examination of certain issues pertaining to the nature of those links in the case of the verbal signs.

Two competing attitudes are to be found in this connection.

One of them is that of the *associationists* who maintain that sound and meaning exist *independently* of one another and that their combining in the verbal sign is based on the association between a definite sound and a definite ready meaning. Such was the opinion of Delacroix, who held that everything ultimately boils down to an association in human memory between sound and meaning, an association which is arbitrary in nature[8]. The same underlying associationist assumption was also observable in the case of Russell at the time when the periodical *Mind* conducted a discussion on "meaning"[9]. A similar position was occupied by Sapir in his study of language, when in classifying verbal signs as symbols he defined them as sounds *automatically*

---

[8] Delacroix, op. cit., p. 365.

[9] *Mind*, 1920, No. 116, p. 398.

associated with meaning[10]. A variation of the associationist theory assumes the form of the conception of specific association, defended by Martinak who in that respect followed Höfler. That theory consists in asserting that association is indirect, that it takes place through the intermediary of other judgements, and is not a mechanical repetition of the relation, as originally perceived (*judiziöse Association*). Be that as it may, the associationist conception reduces the problem to the mnemonic association of a ready sound with a ready meaning, which consequently must have been somehow ontogenetically shaped outside the language and independently of it. The verbal sign is here treated in the same way as any other sign with relation to which meaning is, as we have seen, "autonomous", i.e., shaped outside and independently of it. This is precisely the Achilles' heel of the whole concept, which not only runs contrary to our sense of the specific nature of the verbal signs and even the simplest analysis of them, but moreover presupposes the object of controversy (it assumes that the verbal signs do not differ from other signs by the nature of their links with meaning). Consequently, the strongest argument against the associationist conception, which at one time was described by K. Bühler as "simply naive" (*geradezu naiv*), lies in the fact that its adherents do not even endeavour to justify their assumptions, even though those assumptions run contrary to our intuition and to the results of analysis of linguistic entities.

The other attitude can be characterized by the interpretation of the relative unity of sound and meaning in the verbal signs as a connection *sui generis*, different from that which is specific to other signs and marked precisely by this — that the meaning of a verbal sign is not "autonomous", that it can neither be shaped nor appear *outside* of that unity which is language-and-thinking, word-and-idea. The only argument, and a very naive one, is that we usually learn foreign languages by looking for appropriate

---

10 E. Sapir, *Language*, New York 1921, p. 10.

sounds to be associated with ready meanings; but that argument can very easily be refuted. It is indeed a fact, but always *on the basis of some known language* by means of which we think and from which we translate into that foreign language. We have learned a foreign language only when we cease to translate, when we start to think in terms of that foreign language, that is, when the links between the sounds of that language with their meanings cease to be for us something "external", based on *ad hoc* associations, and become organic and direct, and the verbal signs become "transparent" to meaning. Thus, there is a difference between the study of a foreign language, and the knowledge of a language already well learned. Our analysis pertains, of course, to the latter case only.

What is meant by the connection between sound and meaning in the verbal sign being *sui generis* — that is another question. One is fully justified in demanding an explanation of these matters. Whoever advances a thesis in science, must prove it. Yet I must make it clear that even if one is unable to give a satisfactory answer to questions pertaing to a theoretical thesis, or even if such an answer is controversial (which is most often the case, especially in the social sciences and the humanities), this fact does not of itself refute the thesis in question. I mention that here, because the thesis concerning a *sui generis* connection between sound and meaning in the verbal sign, although supported by formidable arguments, still lacks a consistent explanation of the nature and mechanism of that connection. The only attempt to offer such an explanation which, in my opinion, deserves attention, namely Pavlov's hypothesis of a second system of signals, will be discussed below.

There is one point more to be mentioned here and now: the arbitrary nature of the connection between sound and meaning. This thesis was submitted by de Saussure[11] who referred to Whitney. It must be emphasized, however, that while de Saussure

[11] F. de Saussure, *Cours de linguistique générale*, Paris 1949, p. 99.

stressed the arbitrary nature of the connection between the *signifiant* and the *signifié* (in which he repeated the old idea, to be found already in Plato's *Cratilus*, that the sounds of words are not connected in any natural way with the objects these words denote), he insisted at the same time that with respect to the given language community the choice of the *signifiant* is not free, but is conditioned socially.

It is obvious that Marxists, in defending the thesis of the organic unity of sound and meaning in the verbal signs, must sharply criticize the conception of the arbitrary connection between sound and meaning (in the sense of its being established by virtue of a convention) which leads to those conventionalist oddities which are to be found in at least part of the neo-positivist literature. It must also be added that that conception had adherents only among formalistically-minded logicians who failed to notice and understand the historical and social character of language and of verbal signs. It has, on the other hand, always been opposed, for fundamental reasons, not only by Marxists, but by linguists as well, regardless of what *trend* they represent. For a linguist such argumentation as that advanced by, for example, S. L. Rubinshtein is quite natural and comprehensible. Rubinshtein criticizes the conception of an arbitrary convention as applied to language signs from the point of view of their genetic, historical analysis, and demonstrates that the verbal sign has its "social" life independent of us, its history independent of our conventions, and is connected with the objective nature of our cognition[12]. A similar argumentation is resorted to by the Soviet linguist Zvegintsev[13]. In particular, he emphasizes that his protest against the conception of the arbitrary nature of the link between sound and meaning is by no means to be interpreted as support by him for the thesis which claims that there is some natural

[12] Рубинштейн, op. cit., pp. 406–407.

[13] В. А. Звегинцев, *Проблема знаковости языка* [The Problem of the Sign-nature of Language], Москва 1956.

connection between the verbal sign and the object it designates. It is very important to bear these two issues in mind.

The view that the link between sound and meaning in the verbal signs is a link *sui generis* is combined with a different conception of such signs: it is not the sound alone which is the sign, with some autonomous "meaning" as its "partner", but the indivisible whole, consisting of sound and meaning, understood as a signifying material object (acoustic vibration). This is the only consistent interpretation of the verbal sign as a *sui generis* link of the unity of sound and meaning, as a *sui generis* sign characterized by "transparency" to meaning. That "transparency" can appear if, and only if, we cease to perceive the material, physical shape of the sign as something independent, with which a no less independent meaning is combined in this or that way. "Transparency" to meaning, so characteristic of verbal signs, appears precisely when we *cease completely* to perceive the material shape of the sign (except for cases of disturbance in the normal process of communication) and are conscious only of its semantic aspect.

Thus, the verbal sign is not any symbol, although the use of that term with reference to verbal signs is now, as referred to above, almost universal in the literature of the subject[14]. The verbal signs should not be confused with that specific and very useful subclass of substitutive signs already analysed, which I have called symbols in conformity with current linguistic intuition, because the verbal sign reveals features of which symbols

---

[14] Let us take note of the characteristic protest by de Saussure who in defending the arbitrary (in a certain specific interpretation of that issue) connection between sound and meaning in verbal signs comes out against calling the latter symbols, because symbols characterize some natural link between the sign and the object. The statement is very controversial, but the intention to introduce terminological distinctions between the various categories of signs is most laudable.

Urban also is against including the verbal signs in a general category of symbols. His argumentation is: if the verbal signs were just symbols, what would be the sense of talking about a symbolic use of language?

in the proper sense of the term are deprived, and is in turn deprived of certain properties that are characteristic of symbols understood in conformity with current usage. And if we impart to the term "symbol" an *ad hoc* meaning, treated in an arbitrary fashion, than we either restrict the class of symbols to verbal signs and, violating the linguistic usage, cease to apply the term "symbols" to those signs which so far have been called so, or we conventionally extend the sense of the term "symbol" so as to cover with it, for example, all non-iconic signs and thus obliterate the specific nature of the verbal signs — which is just what I want to avoid.

The verbal sign is not a signal, nor yet a signal of signals. For all the respect for those suggestions (since thus far they are nothing else but very general hypotheses and suggestions for research) which are contained in the Pavlovian theory of the second system of signals (in which theory the verbal sign is just a signal of signals), it is important not to ignore the contradictions and the dangers of vulgarization that are inherent in that theory. In this field, too, as in any other, worship and fetishization of opinions have detrimental consequences. No one denies that Pavlov was a brilliant scientist. But from that statement it is a far cry to canonizing all his views and hypotheses, and certainly no one is entitled to identify Pavlov's opinions with dialectical materialism (as some authors have done). Anyhow, it is precisely in the name of dialectical materialism that one is bound to protest against the theory of the verbal sign as a signal of signals — at least in that form in which that theory is known at present.

The contradiction consists in that Pavlov, as can be seen from his many statements published in *Pavlovian Wednesdays*, realized perfectly well the specific nature of the verbal sign and phonic language, and yet the traditional formulation of the concept of the second system of signals and of the verbal sign as a signal of signals is a denial of that specific nature of the verbal sign. Hence the danger of a vulgarization of the problem (similar to the vulgarization characteristic of behaviourism).

The primary reservation must be made against the very term "signal". As we remember, a signal in the process of human communication is a conventional sign which replaces a certain *verbal* statement and is comprehensible only as such. Thus, in the process of human communication, the signal is *par excellence* a semantic product, has a meaning and is "imbued" with linguistic meaning, which of course may not be said of the stimuli that produce conditioned reflexes in animals. These phenomena are *qualitatively* different, and therefore the terminology, which after all is to be understood in some metaphorical sense, is not the most fortunate, since it contains the danger of serious misunderstandings. Yet one has to admit that, after all, in every discipline the researcher is free to adopt an arbitrary terminology, on the condition that the sense of the terms involved is sufficiently precise.

But no such argument as that can be used if the term "signal" in a conventional meaning is identically referred both to the animal and the human world. The mechanism of non-conditioned reflexes is the same in man and in the animal. But the mechanism of conditioned reflexes? It is not my business to analyse and criticize physiological theories. But in so far as they encroach on the field of communication processes, I have to adopt some attitude towards them. Now the point is that everything connected with man – and consequently his conditioned reflexes also – is always conditioned *socially*. This general formulation implies that we encounter problems of human communication, and of the rôle of processes that entail consciousness and are inseparably connected with language, without which man cannot think, etc. And the conditioned reflexes that develop in man as a result of certain external influences are not usually formed *outside* the sphere of his consciousness, but within that sphere. This is why we have to do here with a phenomenon that differs *qualitatively* from the reflexes in the animal. Whoever fails to notice that, and seeks to reduce the processes taking place in the human organism to mere physiological stimuli and reactions, as is the case with the behaviourists, simply vulgarizes the problem, since all naturalism in the interpretation of social phenomena is a vulgarization.

Matters become still more complicated when we reach the higher level, namely that of the "signal of signals". The verbal sign would have to be a signal of what signals? Those referred to in the experiments with dogs? If so, then this is a misunderstanding, because except for simple physiological stimuli (e.g., the stimuli produced by food), such "signals" just do not appear in man's social life. Of some other signals? Then which? Undifferentiated terminology prevents us from grasping the differences, and experiments could be informative only if they were treated not from the naturalistic, but from the social point of view, that is not by eliminating those processes which entail consciousness, but by treating such as organic elements of human behaviour, including human reflexes. But experiments of that kind have not been made. The hypothesis of a second system of signals suggests that they should be made, but so far it has not got beyond a suggestion.

Thus, at best we do not know what kind of signals is meant. In a worse situation, we do know, and then we may say that in principle there are no such "signals" in human social processes. What then is that signal of signals? The same signal, only on a higher level, which is a reduction of social processes involving human consciousness to a two-level system of physiological stimuli and reactions? That would be an extreme vulgarization of the problem in the spirit of mechanistic materialism, with which an adherent of dialectical materialism could on no condition agree. For as psychology may not be reduced to physiology, in the same way the issues of epistemology and semantics may not be reduced to pure physiology. And if what is meant is something else, a "signal" in some other meaning, then what is that meaning to be? This we just do not know, and it is better to agree that we have to do with an incomplete hypothesis. But even if we adopt the most favourable interpretation, if we virtually conclude that we do not fully grasp what is being said in that hypothesis, there remains a terminology which is, to say the least, ambiguous and which threatens us with serious misunderstandings and with a possible vulgarization. This is why we have now to conclude that the verbal sign is neither a signal, nor a signal of signals, and that before these matters are clarified experimentally and theoretically, we must rather abandon that terminology.

Thus the verbal sign is not a symbol, not a signal, not any of the other known categories of signs, if their names have a strictly defined meaning at all — it is a sign *sui generis*, a sign that has its own specific nature.

But just because of its specific nature, as a result of which the verbal sign may not be identified with any other sign, it can take over the functions of at least some of those signs. The verbal signs is not a signal, since it has different features and properties from them, but it can function as a signal. The verbal sign in the same sense is not identical with a symbol, but it may assume its rôle. Examples can be multiplied, if a more detailed classification of signs is made. This is one more proof of the special significance and rôle which the verbal sign has in the communication process.

The second characteristic of the verbal sign, which in fact is linked organically with the first (i.e., with the *sui generis* unity of sound and meaning in the verbal sign), is its function and rôle in the process of abstraction.

From the genetic point of view, the verbal sign, like every other sign, is evidently a *product* of the abstraction process. There is nothing strange in this. All cognition and all perception always work on the selection principle. This is connected with the specific requirements of action, which without such selection would not be possible. The same phenomenon is observable in connection with every kind of sign which, in functioning within the framework of human communication, is subject to the general regularities governing all cognition. *Every* sign is a *product* of the abstraction process and at the same time an important *instrument* of that process. There is here, however, a borderline which determines a qualitative differentiation between the verbal signs and all other kinds of sign. The point is that every sign may simplify, formulate something in an abbreviated form, be *pars pro toto*, etc., and may thus be an important instrument of the abstraction process, but in all these cases it always remains connected with *definite* sensory data, with a definite mental image; this refers also to what are known as generic representations. Thinking in terms of ideas requires a different instrument, which is the verbal sign, precisely because of its specific property, "transparency to meaning", which makes it possible to rise to the highest levels of abstraction, inaccessible to other types of sign, and to be separated form concrete sensory data to an extent exceeding the possibilities or other kinds of sign.

As the psychologists tell us, the verbal sign, too, is associated in our mind with representations. But this is a totally different kind of connection with a sensory image what is involved here is either the imaginative associations of objects connected with mental processes and accompanying those processes, or the associations of the images of written signs, words spoken, their sounds, etc. The semantic content of the verbal sign is, however, independent of such associations, which only accompany that content but are not a condition of its existence (and besides they differ as between the individuals who understand a given sign in the same way). Because of the unity of sound and meaning, and because of its "transparency to meaning", the verbal sign has special properties of abstraction. Every word generalizes, wrote Lenin. Similarly Sapir in his *Language* says that cognition becomes communicable only if it is not strictly individual but can be subsumed under some class of things or events, which subsumption is the work of the word. The same is maintained by Susanne Langer and others.

Of course, the rôle of the verbal sign in the abstraction process would require special researches and a comprehensive monograph. In this place I only draw attention to the problem, which is quite sufficient for my purpose.

And finally, the third characteristic of the verbal sign: its special properties from the point of view of a *precise* communication between men. The issue here is so obvious that no lengthy analysis is needed.

One can communicate, and men in fact do communicate, by means of different "languages". Anthropologists testify to the existence of (primitive) tribes that prefer manual "conversation" by means of gestures to verbal conversation. As has already been mentioned, Cushing in this connection speaks of a special style of "manual thinking", different from our thinking in terms of language. All this is neither extraordinary nor impossible. But at the same time one thing is certain: neither the philosophical system of Hegel, nor Einstein's theory of relativity, nor even a grammar of the simplest kind for this or that language could be formulated by means of such a "language". There is a special power, inherent in the phonic language, which makes possible a further development of thinking and its rise to higher and higher levels of abstraction, which makes it possible to discover and formulate increasingly wide and profound regularities in the universe, and thereby enables man to become the master of the world. One may complain about the ambiguity and imprecision of ordinary language, but even such a complaint can only be made by means of that ordinary language and within its framework. This is why the phonic language is not only a particularly convenient and flexible instrument of the communication process, but also an instrument that is exceptionally easy subject to improvement and endowed with almost boundless possibilities of perfecting itself. And this is one of the most important aspects of the specific nature of verbal signs.

*

* *

The analysis undertaken in this chapter was concentrated chiefly on the issues of the definition and the typology of signs. Yet, especially in the part dealing with verbal signs, the problem of meaning could not have been eliminated completely. This is quite natural and normal. An analysis of the sign which would abstract from meaning, and thus from the characteristic function of the sign, would of necessity be incomplete, and hence it may be admitted only when justified by essential reasons. One of such reasons emerges from the plan adopted for my work. It is now necessary to complete that analysis with a discussion of the problems of meaning. To that I shall proceed in the next chapter.

CHAPTER THREE

THE MEANINGS OF "MEANING"

" 'When I use a word', Humpty Dumpty said in a rather scornful tone, 'it means just what I choose it to mean — neither more nor less'. 'The question is', said Alice, 'whether you can make words mean different things', 'The question is', said Humpty Dumpty, 'which is to be master — that's all' ".

(Lewis Carroll: *Through the Looking-Glass*)

"Men content themselves with the same words as other people use, as if the very sound necessarily carried the same meaning".

(John Locke)

I SAY to someone ignorant of French: "Donnez-moi mon chapeau, s'il vous plaît". His only reaction is to reply: "I do not understand you." I repeat the same thing in English: "Give me my hat, please", and the same man smiles and passes me my hat. He understood the meaning of what I had said.

Two persons want to cross the street when the traffic light flashes red. One of the pedestrians stops immediately, while the other, apparently not familiar with traffic regulations, goes on. His companion stops him and explains: "You see that red light? It means that no one may cross the road now; when the green light comes, then you may cross". At the next crossing the learner stops of his own volition when he sees a red light. He now understands the meaning of that sign.

And so it always is when we have to do with signs and with *sign-situations*: such a situation occurs only when the communicating persons understand in the same way the *meaning* of the sign in question.

The problem of meaning emerges in a sign-situation or, to use a different and simpler formulation, in the process of human communication, since that process, if we disregard the issue of telepathy and other forms of alleged "direct" communication, consists in trasmitting thoughts, emotions, etc., by means of signs; it is a process of producing sign-situations. When I speak, write, place road signs or operate beacon lights at street crossings, draw maps or plans, fix "poison" labels on bottles, sew epaulettes on uniforms, hoist signal flags, etc., then in *every* case I am using certain signs for communication purposes (even a mental monologue is, as we know, a dialogue in a masked form), and in each of these cases I produce a sign-situation. Consequently, in each of these cases the problem of meaning emerges.

It has already been said that sign and meaning form a unity which is broken into parts or aspects only by abstraction. There is no sign without meaning (since even an authentic sign which for any reason is not comprehended, e.g., because the language in question is not understood, is nothing more than a material object or event, a blot of ink, sound, etc.); and meanings "by themselves", without a sign-vehicle, exist only in the minds of incurable metaphysicians. Hence, an analysis of the sign, if properly performed, that is an analysis of the sign-situation, an analysis of communication by means of signs, must take into account the sign as a *whole*, as a unity the material sign-vehicle (sound, picture, conventional drawing, etc.) and meaning. In discussing the definition and the typology of signs, we have been taking that unity for granted; although occasionally we have referred to the semantic aspect of the signs, we have been referring to it as to something given and evident. This is not the best method, yet it is unavoidable in all those cases where we have to do with a mutual inter-relationship or with a close connection between the aspects or elements of the phenomenon under investigation. It is high time now to fill that gap, for otherwise both the analysis of the sign and consequently the analysis of the communication process would suffer. The more so since the problem of meaning is extremely important (in view of the importance and frequency of sign-situations in social life, if not for other reasons), and moreover it is neither unambiguous nor universally well understood; on the contrary, it is exceptionally complicated and difficult.

I shall also set now the limits of my interests and indicate those important issues which I intend to analyse, and those which I shall disregard.

C. K. Ogden and I. A. Richards once devoted to the problem of meaning a monograph entitled *The Meaning of Meaning*. It set out to investigate in what senses the term "meaning" is actually used in the literature on the subject (chiefly philosophical). Their Chapter VIII gives samples of the various meanings of "meaning" and shows that the actual usage is marked by a chaos "not dreamed of in our philosophy", although it is precisely philosophers who are principally responsible for the situation existing in that respect. To put an end to that not entirely edifying logomachy, the authors resolved to bring out those senses of the term "meaning" which are in actual use. In Chapter IX, therefore, they demonstrate that there are as many as 16 groups of meanings of that term, some of the groups embracing additional, secondary meanings. In all, they proved the existence of 23 different meanings of "meaning", some of them very remote one from another. The questions arise: Is their list exhaustive? Do not other meanings of that term appear? Is it not possible to conceive of yet other meanings?

These questions are certainly important and interesting from some points of view. We are not, however, interested in a complete list of the possible uses of the term "meaning" in ordinary language and in scientific usage. Moreover, it would hardly be possible to draw up such an absolute list (in view of different uses of the term "meaning" in the various ethnic languages) or in any rigid manner (in view of the incessant developmental processes within languages). We are interested in a certain special group of uses of that term – that group which refers to the interpretation of the "meaning" in relation to the function of the sign in the communication process, the function which makes possible a passage from the sphere of subjective thinking about something to the sphere of inter-subjective transmission of such thoughts so that they are understood by the parties concerned. If we say, most generally and without any claim to precision, that meaning is simply that by which an ordinary material object, a property of such an object, or an event becomes a sign, i.e., that meaning is an element of the sign-situation or of the communication process, then – as we shall see later – we do not eliminate all ambiguity from that term, yet we restrict it considerably. That restriction is important for two reasons: first, it absolves us from laborious semantic analyses exceeding the scope of the issues in which we are interested, and secondly, it enables us to outline more strictly the scope of our positive research.

Thus, we are still concerned with meanings and not with a definite meaning of "meaning". But the essential point is that in seeking a maximum precision of such meanings we should put an end to empty verbalism and empty logomachy, and be able to repeat after Ogden and Richards their motto taken from G. C. Lewis: "A verbal discussion may be significant or devoid of significance, but it is at least well to realize that it is verbal".

The ambiguity of the term "meaning", even in that restricted scope, is explained, first, by the objective many-sidedness of the sign-situation which includes that function of the sign which we call meaning, and secondly, by the diversity of aspects which *we*, as analysts of the sign-situation, extract from that sign-situation by asking various questions, referring to real processes, questions conditioned by the concentration, for practical or theoretical reasons, of our attention on this or that aspect of those processes. This co-operation of objective and subjective factors gives rise to the ambiguity in question.

1. ON THE SIGN-SITUATION

My task, as I understand it, is not only to state that such an ambiguity arises, and to establish those meanings which actually appear when we use the term "meaning" under certain circumstances, but also to adopt an attitude towards the various conceptions connected with those different meanings of the term involved. And that requires something more than the ability to subject a given term to semantic analysis and subtly to bring to light its different senses. One must give a precise formulation to one's own views and take a stand not only in the controversies that divide philosophical schools, but also in the specific issue involved in the process of human communication. That is so because general divisions and general standpoints in philosophical controversies do not automatically produce solutions of special and intricate problems.

The problem of meaning is certainly one of the most important and philosophically most baffling issues of our times. Incessant declarations concerning its importance may already seem boring, but one more repetition is nevertheless worth while, to avoid being suspected of neglecting or underestimating the matter. But then that important issue may be used in different ways – either as a subject matter of scientific analysis (successful and correct or not, but that is a further question), or as a springboard for vertiginous metaphysical speculations. That the second alternative is not merely a theoretical possibility is best proved by Husserl's theory of meaning which, strangely enough, finds adherents even among thinkers who are positivistically-minded. This is why special stress must be laid on the proper starting point of analysis, since that will determine success of failure.

Our starting point has already been defined: it is the real process of human communication, the real sign-situation. But in analysing the problem of meaning one would like, especially in view of the considerable number of attempts and solutions that are clearly metaphysical in character, to add something more to what has been said about that starting point.

First of all, I should like to follow Tadeusz Kotarbiński and to begin by attacking that linguistic hypostasis which is responsible for many a sin of metaphysical distortion of the problem. "There is no such thing as meaning" – in this case that formula directed against hypostases is not just a superficial pedantry (as is proved by Husserl's theory), but a very useful recollection. "Meaning" is a typical term used as abbreviation, which refers not to any entity (whether material or ideal) called meaning, but to men who communicate with one another by using certain objects or events to transmit to one another what they think about the world around them. This is worth remembering – when one plunges into the whirlpool of the problems of meaning – so as to avoid being led astray by the delusive but nevertheless attractive metaphysical thesis that every name has its counterpart in an object, an entity, to which it refers.

One feels an urge here to dot one's *i*'s and cross one's *t*'s as regards the ontological aspect of the issues involved, the more so since the problems of meaning and notion entail some ontological attitude, and a fragmentary treatment of those problems prevents us from discussing all the issues concerned.

First of all, it must be explained that when I say "to exist" or "to be" I understand these words in a materialistic sense. According to that interpretation, all that "exists" or "is" has a material nature and consequently exists irrespective of any cognizing mind, and is an external stimulus of our sensory experiences. Thus there exist things (material objects) which in a broad sense of the word (covering also such things as fields of energy) are manifestations of what is given the abstract name of "matter" (it is in this spirit that the problem is treated by Engels in his *Dialectics of Nature*). This is the *direct* meaning of the word "exists", and this is the proper interpretation of what is known in mathematical logic as the existential quantifier. Thus, the direct meaning of the word "exists" is reduced to two statements: (1) whatever exists has *objective* existence, i.e., independent of any cognizing mind; (2) that existence is existence in the material sense, such as is the attribute of things in the broad understanding of the word. This interpretation of the direct meaning of the word "exists" is characteristic of every form of materialism, and therefore the corresponding theses of pansomatistic reism are unquestionably materialistic.

But things exist not in an isolated form, but in relations which make it possible to speak of a material unity of the world. We also say that there exist connections and relations between things, that there exist traits and properties of things (i.e., that which marks all the elements of a given class or set of things and which in the human mind finds reflection in what are termed abstract notions), that there exist processes or events (certain fragments of the material world, things, somehow change), that there exist attitudes and actions of those fragments of the material world which we call men, etc. In all such cases, when we say "exists" or "is", then the condition of objective existence (in the sense that we have to do not with an arbitrary product of the cognizing mind, but with cognition – in some approximation – of something what occurs independently of the cognizing mind and of all mind in general, although the act of cognition itself has a objective tinge) is satisfied, but in a different manner from the preceding case. Relations, properties, processes, attitudes, etc., are not things (as are men, houses, chairs, stones, etc.), although they always pertain to things, that is, to the material world. Consequently we have to do with some fragment of the material world, but the word "exists" must now be understood in an *indirect* sense (the reists speak in this connection of substitutive abbreviations: instead of saying that things are marked by something, that something happens to things, etc., we say simply that there exist properties, relations, states, etc.). Thus in so far as reism is not identified with nominalism, the reistic standpoint on this issue also coincides with the general materialistic standpoint.

If we say that notions, meanings, etc., exist, then we simply speak of their existence in the indirect sense. To ascribe to them direct existence would be (objective) idealism of the first water, since objective idealism maintains that some ideal entities exist objectively either as the only entities or alongside material entities. Such a philosophical standpoint is, of course, unacceptable to a materialist. Hence the importance of a precise distinction between the various senses of the word "exists", a word the ambiguity of which cannot be eliminated in ordinary (natural) language; hence also the importance of the struggle with hypostases, especially in the case of discussions so subtle and slippery as are those pertaining to meaning, notion, etc.

It is also worth while now to be precise about the matter of the philosophical aspects of the communication process (see pp. 125–127 above). In particular, I refer here to the reply to the question, "What does it mean that different men experience the same states of mind?" We have agreed that one of the conditions of the development of "the same states of mind" is the reflection of one and the same object by minds that possess the same structure. What is and what can be that "object", reflected by the mind and giving rise to "the same experiences"? We absolutely reject the existence of certain ideal objects – a conception dear to the hearts of such thinkers as Bolzano, Frege, Brentano, Husserl and others. From the materialistic point of view, only one solution is possible: the object which in the relation of cognition is the common counterpart of various subjects is the material world, which manifests itself concretely in the form of things (in the broad sense of the word). All connections, relations, properties, attitudes, actions, etc., are objects of cognition not in the sense of some independent material or ideal objects, but as *objectively* occurring relations, properties, attitudes, etc., of some fragments of the material world – *things*. Thus, they are an objective object of cognition only in so far as they are attributes of those fragments of the material world which always are objects in the essential and direct sense of the word (this is an analogous issue to "existence" – in the direct and the indirect sense of the word – as discussed above).

Having made this brief explanation of my understanding of the words "object" and "exists", I revert to the main course of my analysis. Two problems must be formulated precisely — what is a sign-situation where that which we call meaning appears; and what do we mean by meaning?

Many references have already been made to the communication process as the foundation of an analysis of sign and meaning. Consequently, we have referred to the sign-situation, because whenever we have to do with communication, we likewise have to do with a sign-situation: for we communicate only and exclusively by means of signs. That thesis is correct enough, yet it conveys but little. To add something on the subject we have to analyse the sign-situation. For that purpose I should like to present three conceptions — of Ogden and Richards, of Johnson, and of Gardiner. The choice is not accidental in so far as all these conceptions resort to schemes similar and yet different and somehow complementary, and as such form steps leading to what in my opinion is a correct interpretation of the problem.

Ogden and Richards are authors of a now classical book on the theory of meaning[1] and undoubtedly have in that respect considerable achievements to their credit. This fact explains why their diagram of the sign-situation is considered almost classical, in spite of the fact that the idea it expresses had been formulated earlier (cf. Russell). Since I am not interested in chronological priority, but in a typical standpoint on the issue we are analysing, the work of Ogden and Richards can well be taken as the representative of that standpoint.

Ogden and Richards stand for a causal theory of meaning, since they claim that between the various elements of the relation of meaning there is a causal nexus. We are, however, interested not in that aspect of the problem, but above all in the formulation of the sign-situation (and, consequently, meaning) as a definite *relation*.

Ogden and Richards distinguish the following three elements of the sign-situation: the symbol (which in their terminol-

[1] C. K. Ogden & I. A. Richards, *The Meaning of Meaning*, London 1953.

ogy is the same as the sign), the object (referent), and the intervening thought (reference). The somewhat artificial terminology (referent, reference) is explained by their unwillingness to use existing terms, such as "object", in view of their being burdened with a definite semantic tradition.

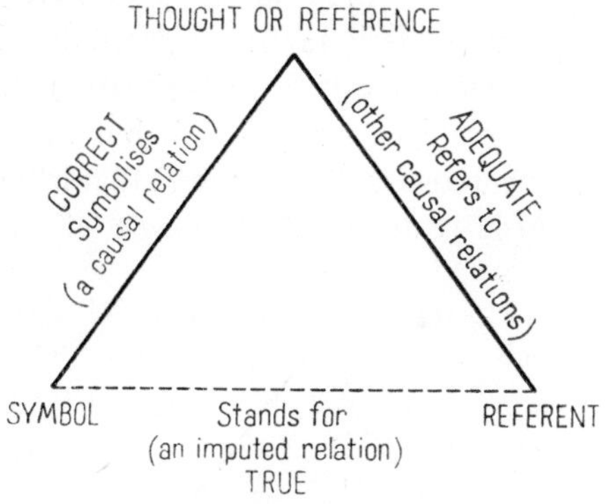

Fig. 3

The situation is clear. The authors refer to communication and to the sign-situation, the latter being in their opinion reducible to the three elements shown in the diagram: the *symbol* symbolizes something and evokes an appropriate *thought* which refers to the *referent* (object). The relation between the symbol and the referent is an indirect one; a direct relation (along the base of the triangle) occurs only in those exceptional cases when we have to do with a similarity between the symbol and the referent (i.e., in our terminology, when we have to do with an iconic sign). It is worth while drawing attention to the vigour with which the authors reject the suggestion that the sign-situation is characterized only by a relation between the symbol and the thought. Such a standpoint (they quote Baldwin's *Thoughts and Things* as an example) they treat as solipsist, and they stress the necessity of "explicitly recognizing the world beyond us"[2]

[2] Ibid., p. 20.

in our analysis of the sign-situation. Yet they remain silent when it comes to *men* who communicate with one another.

These appear in Johnson's diagram. Johnson's book[3] is not a work of any signal significance, but is a rather typically American work concerning the social sciences. I have chosen it as an illustration because its author adopts the scheme of Ogden and Richards but interprets it in an entirely different way. Here, too, there are three elements of the sign-situation (Johnson refers explicitly to the communication process), but they are different and their arrangement also is different, and that in a characteristic manner. Here, then, is Johnson's "triangle of reference":

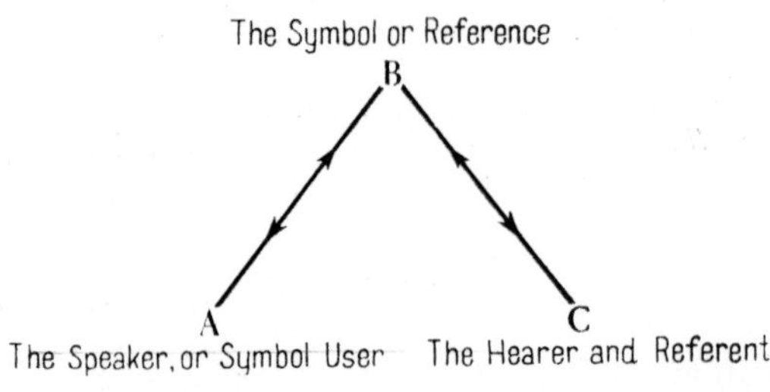

Fig. 4

Not only the scheme but the terminology (reference, referent) are clearly borrowed from Ogden and Richards. Johnson gives the terms an entirely new sense ("reference" is used not as "thought" but as "frame of reference", and "referent" not as "object" but as "the person who is spoken to"), yet this only results in confusion. One may legitimately object to such terminology as "the symbol or reference" and "the hearer and referent", but my point concerns something else: in the fundamental change of the entire sign-situation, in which the relation "symbol-referent" through thought is replaced by the relation "speaker-hearer", then that relation is that of men who com-

[3] E. S. Johnson, *Theory and Practice of the Social Studies*, New York 1956.

municate one with another through the intermediary of the sign. The author somehow links the symbol with thought (although it is not clear in what that link is to consist), and passes over in silence the referent, i.e., the object which is spoken about.

Gardiner's work[4] offers a still different picture. Gardiner represents a consistently realistic and consistently social theory of communication (and, consequently, of the sign-situation), and so avoids a fetishization of the sign-relation and the meaning-relation.

Gardiner is an eminent linguist. Here are two of his characteristic statements which, although chosen especially for my purpose, are by no means exceptional in his work:

"As a first approximation, let us define speech as the use, between man and man, of articulate sound-signs for the communication of their wishes and their views about things. Note that I do not deny the thought-element in speech, but the emphasis of my definition does not lie on that element. The points which I wish to stress are, firstly, the co-operative character of speech, and, secondly, the fact that it is always concerned with things, that is to say with the realities both of the external world and of man's inner experience"[5].

"Thus the speaker, the listener, and the things spoken about are three essential factors of normal speech. To these must be added the actual words themselves"[6].

Gardiner did not draw any diagrams of the sign-situation, but one can easily reconstruct such a diagram on the strength of his statements. But then one will have to resort to some geometrical figure other than a triangle, because, according to Gardiner, the description of the sign-situation requires at least four elements. First of all, there are the two men who communicate one with another, then there is the object concerning which they communicate, and finally the sign, linked with the

[4] A. Gardiner, *The Theory of Speech and Language*, Oxford 1951.

[5] Ibid., p. 18.

[6] Ibid., p. 28.

thought, by means of which communication takes place. If the sign and the thought are treated separately, the number of the elements in question rises to five. The geometrical shape is irrelevant here (it might a trapezoid, or two triangles with a common base, etc.). The important point is that he grasped the essential elements and relations occurring in the sign-situation. It is for that reason that I consider Gardiner's standpoint to be a correct one.

First of all (and this is, as we shall later see, extremely important for the analysis of meaning), an end is put here to a specific fetishization of the sign and of the sign-situation, so common in the literature of the subject. In other words: the suggestion is rejected that the sign-situation means a relation between signs or a relation between the sign and the object, between the sign and thought on the one hand and the object on the other, etc. (such a suggestion comes from lexical and logical operations and from partial analyses of "what the word 'x' means", "what 'the red flag' means", etc., that is, from all those analyses which suggest that signs have some sort of independent existence). The fact that the sign-situation develops as *a relation between the men who communicate with one another* and "produce" signs for that purpose, is well understood and explicitly indicated. In discussing the struggle against the fetishization of the sign, I have borrowed something from Marx who in *Capital* coined the term "fetishism of commodities" in connection with a problem which very much resembles ours. We are seeking the sense of "meaning", and Marx wanted to explain the sense of "value". In the course of his analysis, he realized that people who investigated the exchange of commodities on the market succumbed to the notion that commodities exchanged themselves so to speak by themselves, so that the relations of economic value were relations between commodities. To Marx goes the credit of proving that in fact they are relations between producers of commodities, that is men, so that they are *social* relations, social labour is "embodied" in commodities, and becomes the foundation and measure of exchange relations and of what we call value. The discovery of the "fetishism of commodities" was indeed a revolution in the interpretation of economic relations. An analogous phenomenon is now observed in the case of meaning and the sign-situation: here, too, a specific "sign fetishism" prevails and to a considerable extent hampers the understanding and solution of the problem. Considerable scientific credit must be ascribed to those who abolish or at least oppose that fetishism by drawing attention to the apparently trivial fact that the sign-situation is a relation between men who "produce" signs (or use them). This credit holds good even if it is not possible to agree with other assertions of theirs. I mention this because *on that point* Gardiner was neither the first nor the only one to advance such an opinion. Leaving the Marxist conception apart for the time being, it must be stated that the understanding of that point, essential for the theory of communication, is to be found in principle in all the pragmatists and behaviourists, and also in adherents of other trends who have been influenced by pragmatism (for instance Morris, who is connected with neo-positivism, and Urban, who is connected with Cassirer; both are Americans and both have been influenced by pragmatism). The exceptional position and rôle of Gardiner consists in his having succeeded in combining his struggle against "sign fetishism" with a consistently realist (one should rather say: materialistic) interpretation of the relation between the sign and the objective reality.

Gardiner, of course, is concerned with language and speech, and consequently he speaks of verbal signs. But this fact does not limit the significance and the general validity of what he says. Linguists, he maintains, have never forgotten the rôle of words (verbal signs) in the communication process. On the contrary, the importance attached to the rôle of those signs veiled all their other elements, that is the men who communicate with one another, and the objects to which the communication process pertains and without which the signs would lose all sense. This is why Gardiner wrote:

"... The statement that speech serves to express thought simply ignores the fact that I can speak about this pen with which I am writing, about my house, my books, my family, and, in short, about everything else in the world. *If linguistic theory is ever to make wide appeal, it must clearly be placed upon a more realistic basis than at present.* The rudest villager knows that he can talk about all the various things which he can see or touch. Why, then, should that truth be hidden from the theorist of language?"[7].

It is not difficult to observe that in the course of the analysis presented here and especially as a result of a proper selection of texts, we have obtained a positive answer to the question as to what is to be meant by the "sign-situation". The criticism of "sign fetishism" inherent in the scheme suggested by Ogden and Richards was contained *implicitly* both in the text of Johnson and in that of Gardiner. The criticism of idealism in the interpretation of the sign-situation is contained *explicitly* in the words of Gardiner who at the same time notes the rôle of the thought element in the communication process, although in the case of the word he combines sign and thought into an indivisible whole. All in all, in declaring oneself to be in solidarity with Gardiner, one may say that *the sign-situation occurs when at least two men communicate one with another by means of signs in order to transmit one to another their thoughts, expressions of feelings, will, etc., connected with some object (universe of discourse) to which their communication pertains.* In other words, whenever the sign and the sign-situation occur, the sign must refer to some object (directly or indirectly), and there must be at least two partners in the process of communication by means of that sign: he who uses the sign in order to convey his thoughts, and he who perceives and interprets it (and consequently, understands it). Thus, the sign-situation turns out to be something extremely common, as common as is the process of communicating by

---

[7] Ibid., p. 22 (italics – A. S.)

means of signs, the only process of human communication, that is, which we know in practice.

The problem of meaning, too, is rooted in the sign-situation, since meaning is, as we have seen, inseparably connected with the sign. A sign without meaning is an inherently contradictory notion, for only what we call meaning turns material objects and events into signs; meaning without a sign is a product of idealistic speculation in the same way as is motion without matter that moves.

Thus we are in possession of a start-line for our attack on the problem of meaning, for the assessment of other people's standpoints, and for the formulation of a view of our own. Let us begin with a list of the *possible* interpretations of meaning, so drawn as to include both the opinions which are in fact represented, and also such important combinations as can be obtained by manipulating the elements of the sign-situation:

(1) meaning is the object, of which the sign is the name;

(2) meaning is a property of objects;

(3) meaning is an ideal object, or an inherent property of thought;

(4) meaning is a relation:

  (a) between signs,
  (b) between the sign and the object;
  (c) between the sign and the thought about the object in question,
  (d) between the sign and human action,
  (e) between the men who communicate with one another by means of signs.

Of course, like all classification, this one commits the sin of schematism, but it enables us to take into account and put in order the most important opinions held in that matter, and at the same time, through the exposition and criticism of other people's views, it leads systematically to the presentation of our own standpoint.

2. MEANING AS A REAL OR IDEAL OBJECT

Nothing is simpler than to take such elements of the sign-situation as the object to which communication pertains, or the thought about that object – which is inseparably connected with the sign that stands for it – to divorce them from that sign-situation and thereby to impart to them some absolute character. The more so since the concentration of our attention and interest on such elements is not always due to an erroneous theoretical standpoint, but is often dictated by practical needs. Consequently, although the identification of meaning with the object denoted is from the theoretical point of view simply in contradiction with its identification with the thought about that object, the two solutions are of the same type and may as such be treated, in a sense, jointly.

A. "Meaning" as the object denoted

The differentation between "meaning" and "denotation", which played such an important rôle in Frege's analysis[8], was forgotten, and then again brought to light by Russell[9]. Thus, the issue is linked with the names of these two logicians and philosophers (from the formal point of view, the issue was also raised by Husserl in *Logische Untersuchungen*, Vol. II, Pt. 1, p. 47, but that differentiation acquires, in the light of his theory of intentional acts, a special character and would require separate analysis).

Frege postulates two expressions: "the morning star" and "the evening star", and raises the problem of their meanings. His conclusion is that in a sense the meanings of these expres-

[8] G. Frege, "Vom Sinn und Bedeutung", in *Zeitschrift für Philosophische Kritik*, 1892; there is an English-language version in *Translations from the Philosophical Writings of Gottlob Frege*, Oxford 1952.

[9] B. Russell, "On Denoting", *Mind*, 1905; quoted after B. Russell, *Logic and Knowledge. Essays 1901–1950*, London 1956.

sions are identical, but in another sense they are different. When we ask "What is meant by 'the morning star'?", "What is meant by 'the evening star'?", and bearing in mind *the object* which these expressions (of which they are names) denote, then the meanings of the two expressions are identical, for the object which they denote is one and the same. But when we consider *the content* of these expressions, the way in which they denote their designata, then their meanings appear different. This can be demonstrated by the fact that people may reach a linguistic agreement concerning these expressions and formulate their definitions without realizing that they refer to one and the same object. There is nothing strange in that, since we have to do with different questions and consequently with different meanings of "meaning". Frege reserved distinct terms for each: "Bedeutung" for the former (translated as "denotation" by Russell and as "reference" by Black), and "Sinn" for the latter (translated as "meaning" by Russell and as "sense" by Black). In the former case, when we ask "What does ... mean?", we ask in the sense of "What is ...?", and we are concerned with an object, the designatum of the name. In the latter case, we ask about the content of the name. Therefore Frege is correct in stating:

"A proper name (word, sign, sign combination, expression) *expresses* its sense, *stands for* or *designates* its reference. By means of a sign we express its sense and designate its reference"[10].

I do not raise here the issue of denotating sentences, which is the main subject matter of the analysis carried out by Frege and above all by Russell (it is the foundation of Russell's theory of descriptions). We are here interested principally in the distinction between meaning and denotation. That distinction is equivalent to the statement that in a certain sense "meaning" is identical with the object of which the given expression is the name (I understand here the term "expression" in a broad sense, covering both verbal signs and the combinations of such).

---

[10] Frege, op. cit., p. 61.

This is an indubitable fact which leads to the following conclusion: in view of the clear difference existing between these meanings, and in view of the specific character of the question "What does ... mean?" one should, in order to avoid misunderstandings, use different terms. This was done by Frege. Kotarbiński[11] followed the same course. Consequently, we note this specific meaning of "meaning" in the case of names, but must insist that we have here to do with a special case (that of names) and that such ambiguity can to a large extent be eliminated by a consistent use of distinct terms, "meaning" and "denotation".

Frege's idea goes back to the tradition of the denotation and the connotation of ideas as formulated in the conception of J. S. Mill, although the two ideas are not identical. But then the adherents of the opinion listed in the classification above under (2) go back directly to Mill's conception. They understand "meaning" as an inherent property of the object to which the sign refers. The "object" is understood here in a specific way, as an ideal object, a notion. In that case, the sum of the properties that constitute the essence of the notion understood as an objective entity, i.e., its connotation, is equivalent to meaning. Thus meaning is inherent in the object, and it might equally be said that meaning *is* the object, since it is equivalent to its essence. Of course, I take no responsibility either for these "objects" or for "essences". I have merely related a certain point of view in order to realize those meanings of "meaning" which may be encountered in practice. The other extreme, within the type of the solutions of the problem of meaning which we are now discussing, is represented by Husserl's theory.

B. The conception of intentional meanings

In our classification, Husserl's theory is listed under (3), which groups theories interpreting meaning as an ideal object, or as an inherent property of thought. Should we take Husserl's

[11] T. Kotarbiński, *Elementy* ... [Elements ...], Lwów 1929.

statements at face value, we would not have to include his theory in this class, since Husserl vigorously disclaims such a conception. I must therefore justify my classification, but of that — anon. I must now begin with another explanation — as to why I devote to Husserl's conception so much attention, out of all proportion if compared with my treatment of other theories.

For this there are two reasons: the influence of Husserl's theory upon contemporary philosophy in general, and its influence upon Polish philosophy in particular. The latter point seems to me decisive. The fact that such positivistically-minded thinkers as Ajdukiewicz[12] and Czeżowski[13] have been influenced precisely by Husserl's theory of meaning is, to say the least, striking, and is in my opinion a serious philosophical misunderstanding. Regardless of all our likes or dislikes concerning the positivist trends, it must be conceded that they are beyond all doubt in direct contrast with the initial assumptions of Husserl's phenomenology. Husserl's philosophy is undoubtedly a product of a brilliant mind, but at the same time it proves that an alliance between precision of formulations and an idealism that borders on mysticism is not impossible, and that no undue importance should be attached to the postulate of formal correctness and precision of analysis. I am not one of those adherents of the Lwów-Warsaw school who are so "radical" in their opinions that, following the neo-positivists in that respect, they are ready to consider as nonsense any exposition which does not comply with their criteria of what is scientific. Therefore I do not say that "I do not understand" Husserl. I do understand the sense of the words in his books, although I often find that difficult. But I do not understand how people who advocated the principles of a rigorously scientific character in philosophical theses can fall in with the mysticism of Husserl's concep-

---

12 K. Ajdukiewicz, *O znaczeniu wyrażeń* [On the Meaning of Expressions], Lwów 1931.

13 T. Czeżowski, *Logika* [Logic], Warszawa 1949.

tions of intentional act, etc. Is that just a misunderstanding? Or is it an "indulgent" interpretation of what Husserl says, an interpretation disregarding context? This, however, is not the most important point. What is important is the fact that Polish philosophy, the traditions of which are so alien to phenomenology, did prove susceptible to Husserl's ideas. This fact indicates that the problem should be given more attention than would seem necessary at first glance.

It is a truism to say that in order to understand any idea belonging to a philosophical system one has to interpret that idea *in the context* of that system. This remark is addressed to the adherents of the intentional conception of meaning. The interpretation of Husserl's theory of meaning and of intentional act does involve his entire system including his *epoché*, *eidos*, *Wesenschau*, the theory of universals, the phenomenological method, etc. Otherwise it would not be possible to understand what an "object" means in his system, what is an intentional act that contains as object, etc. Unfortunately, there is not a word about that in the works of Polish adherents of the intentional conception. On the contrary, when reading those works it would be easy to be misled into believing that Husserl's theory represents a variation of the psychological theory, which is concerned with the dispositions of men using a certain language. How sharply Husserl would protest against such a flagrant misunderstanding of his basic ideas! It is not my intention to expound here the extremely complicated theses of Husserl's philosophical system and all the resulting implications for the problem of meaning (and it must be borne in mind that *all* his more important theses have such implications). I should only like to present (in the form of quotations, as far as possible) at least those of his theses without which — in my opinion — it is not possible to understand the conception of intentional act and, consequently, Husserl's theory of meaning.

I shall begin by stating the well-known fact that Husserl is an idealist who, in continuing Platonic traditions, not only recognizes the existence of ideal entities, but also considers meaning to be such an entity.

Let us be fair: Husserls does not admit he is a Platonist, and even disclaims that *expressis verbis*:

"Die Bedeutungen bilden, so können wir auch sagen, eine Klasse von *Begriffen* im Sinne von '*allgemeinen Gegenständen*'. Sie sind darum nicht Gegenstände, die, wenn nicht irgendwo in der 'Welt', so in einem τόπος οὐράνιος oder im göttlichen Geiste existieren; denn solche metaphysische Hypostasierung wäre absurd"[14].

Yet the old Marxian principle that men, like social classes, should be judged not by what they think of themselves, but by what they actually do, makes us sceptical. And our scepticism grows as we read on:

"... Wer sich daran gewöhnt hat, unter Sein nur 'reales' Sein, unter Gegenständen reale Gegenstände zu verstehen, dem wird die Rede von allgemeinen Gegenständen und ihrem Sein als grundverkehrt erscheinen: dagegen wird hier keinen Anstoss finden, wer diese Reden zunächst einfach als Anzeigen für die Geltung gewisser Urteile nimmt, nämlich solcher, in denen über Zahlen, Sätze, geometrische Gebilde u. dgl. geurteilt wird, und sich nun fragt, ob nicht hier wie sonst als Korrelat der Urteilsgeltung dem, worüber da geurteilt wird, evidenterweise der Titel 'wahrhaft seiender Gegenstand' zugesprochen werden müsse. In der Tat: logisch betrachtet, sind die sieben regelmässigen Körper sieben Gegenstände, ebenso wie die sieben Weisen; der Satz vom Kräfteparallelogram *ein* Gegestand so gut wie die Stadt Paris"[15].

Has not Husserl made a mistake, then, in assessing his own opinions and their genealogy? But that is a secondary issue. What is important is that Husserl represents the standpoint of objective idealism as concerning ideal entities, and meanings in particular. And that fact is beyond dispute:

---

[14] E. Husserl, *Logische Untersuchungen*, Vol. 2, Pt. 1, Halle 1913, p. 101.

[15] Ibid.

"Natürlich ist es nicht unsere Absicht, das *Sein* des *Idealen* auf eine Stufe zu stellen mit dem *Gedachtsein des Fiktiven* oder *Widersinnigen* ... *Die idealen Gegenstände* ... existieren wahrhaft. Es hat evidenterweise nicht bloss einen guten Sinn, von solchen Gegenständen (z. B. von *der* Zahl 2, von *der* Qualität Röte, vom *dem* Satz des Widerspruches u. dgl.) zu sprechen und sie als mit Prädikaten behaftet vorzustellen, sondern wir erfassen auch *einsichtig* gewisse kategorische Wahrheiten, die auf solche ideale Gegenstände bezüglich sind. Gelten diese Wahrheiten, so muss all das sein, was ihre Geltung objektiv voraussetzt ... Gilt uns alles, was ist, mit Recht als seiend und als so seiend vermöge der Evidenz, mit der wir es im Denken als seiend erfassen, dann kann keine Rede davon sein, dass wir die Eigenberechtigung des idealen Seins verwerfen dürfen. In der Tat kann keine Interpretationskunst der Welt die idealen Gegenstände aus unserem Sprechen und Denken eliminieren"[16].

This needs no comment. And if there is any difference between his standpoint and Platonism, then it is such as the difference between a green devil and a yellow one. Anyhow, his views on ideal entities in general are closely connected with his view of meaning as an ideal entity, since for Husserl meaning is an objective ideal entity. Whoever fails to see and understand that, blocks his road to understanding the theory of intentional acts and the intentional conception of meaning.

"Wir haben bisher vorzugsweise von Bedeutungen gesprochen, die, wie der normalerweise relative Sinn des Wortes Bedeutung es schon besagt, Bedeutungen von Ausdrücken sind. An sich besteht aber kein notwendiger Zusammenhang zwischen den idealen Einheiten, die faktisch als Bedeutungen fungieren, und den Zeichen, an welche sie gebunden sind, d. h. mittels welcher sie sich im menschlichen Seelenleben realisieren. Wir können also auch nicht behaupten, dass alle idealen Einheiten dieser Art ausdrückliche Bedeutungen sind. Jeder Fall einer

---

[16] Ibid., pp. 124–126.

neuen Begriffsbildung belehrt uns, wie sich eine Bedeutung realisiert, die vorher noch nie realisiert war. Wie die Zahlen – in dem von der Arithmetik vorausgesetzten idealen Sinne – nicht mit dem Akte des Zählens entstehen und vergehen, und wie daher die unendliche Zahlenreihe einen objektiv festen, von einer idealen Gesetzlichkeit scharf umgrenzten Inbegriff von generellen Gegenständen darstellt, den niemand vermehren und vermindern kann; so verhält es sich auch mit den idealen, reinlogischen Einheiten, den Begriffen, Sätzen, Wahrheiten, kurz den logischen Bedeutungen. Sie bilden einen ideal geschlossenen Inbegriff von generellen Gegenständen, denen das Gedacht- und Ausgedrücktwerden zufällig ist. Es gibt also unzählige Bedeutungen, die im gewöhnlichen relativen Sinne des Wortes bloss mögliche Bedeutungen sind, während sie niemals zum Ausdruck kommen und vermögen der Schranken menschlicher Erkenntniskräfte niemals zum Ausdruck kommen können"[17].

This, again, calls for no comment. Husserl's standpoint on the issue of meaning is presented plainly and clearly. Contrary to the principle adopted in the present work, I confine myself almost exclusively to quotations. This is deliberate: not only does a quotation present its author's opinion in the most authoritative way, but also we have to do here with opinions which look somewhat strange to a modern author, so that he might easily be suspected of having distorted them or presented them inexactly.

Husserl's opinions as quoted above are nothing extraordinary in the context of his system: this is proved by his interpretation of sentences belonging to so-called pure logic. When speaking of the vacillation of meaning of words, Husserl makes a distinction as between individual psychic processes in which meaning is vacillating and changeable, and meanings as ideal entities which are unchanging. Thus meaning always is one and the same, but its expressions can be various and changeable. Now there is a

[17] Ibid., pp. 104–105.

direct passage from unchanging meaning of so-called pure logic and its tasks.

"In der Tat hat es die reine Logik, wo immer sie von Begriffen, Urteilen, Schlüssen handelt, ausschliesslich mit diesen *idealen* Einheiten, die wir hier *Bedeutungen* nennen, zu tun..."[18].

This is quite comprehensible when it is realized that for Husserl, who in that matter is faithful to Bolzano's tradition, meaning as an ideal entity is identical with a proposition (as opposed to "sentence" and "judgement"). For him, there is a difference between acts of judgement, experienced actually and changeable; and ideal content or proposition as the unchanging partner of different statements. This distinction between the two kinds of judgements is analogous to Peirce's distinction between *token* (experience of a *given* sign-situation) and *type* (a certain type of experience of sign-situations). The difference between Husserl and Peirce is that the former ascribes to propositions the status of ideal entities which are absolutely identical with meanings and are the domain of "pure" logic.

"Die Idealität des Verhältnisses zwischen Ausdruck und Bedeutung zeigt sich in Beziehung auf beide Glieder sofort daran, dass wir, nach der Bedeutung irgendeines Ausdrucks (z. B. *quadratischer Rest*) fragend, unter Ausdruck selbstverständlich nicht dieses *hic et nunc* geäusserte Lautgebilde meinen, den flüchtigen und identisch nimmer wiederkehrenden Schall. Wir meinen den Ausdruck *in specie*. Der Ausdruck *quadratischer Rest* ist identisch derselbe, wer immer ihn äussern mag. Und wieder dasselbe gilt für die Rede von der *Bedeutung*, die also selbstverständlich nicht das bedeutungsverleihende Erlebnis meint"[19].

The matter is quite clear, and the mechanism of building a system based on objective idealism can be seen in detail. Husserl's starting point for constructing meaning as an ideal entity is the fact that when we have to do with any statement, e.g.,

---

[18] Ibid., pp. 91–92.

[19] Ibid., pp. 42–43.

"the square is a quadrangle having equal sides and equal angles", we are concerned with a certain thought which repeats itself whenever that statement is actually reproduced, provided that its sense is understood, but regardless of the individual differences between the psychological acts which accompany the various occurrences of that statement. For Husserl, this is sufficient proof that meaning must exist as an ideal entity, regardless of the concrete experiences of judgements having that meaning.

"Mein Urteilsakt ist ein flüchtiges Erlebnis, entstehend und vergehend. Nicht ist aber das, was die Aussage aussagt, dieser Inhalt, *dass die drei Höhen eines Dreieckes sich in einem Punkt schneiden*, ein Entstehendes und Vergehendes. So oft ich, oder wer auch immer, diese selbe Aussage gleichsinnig äussert, so oft wird von neuem geurteilt. Die Urteilsakte sind von Fall zu Fall verschieden. Aber, *was* sie urteilen, *was* die Aussage besagt, das ist überall dasselbe. Es ist ein im strengen Wortverstande Identisches, es ist die eine und selbe geometrische Wahrheit. So verhält es sich bei allen Aussagen, mag auch, *was* sie sagen, falsch oder gar absurd sein ... Als Identisches der Intention erkennen wir sie auch jeweils in evidenten Akten der Reflexion; wir legen sie nicht willkürlich den Aussagen ein, sondern finden sie darin"[20].

That conception of meaning as an objective entity amounts to objective idealism. As we shall see later on, in Husserl's case it is intimately connected with subjective idealism. But let us not be misled by that apparent opposition. The ideal objects and absolute ideas in systems of objective idealism, absolute idealism, etc., are nothing but individual consciousness, artificially shifted into the supra-individual sphere and thus transformed into something absolute. In this interpretation, objective idealism is but a transformation of subjective idealism. In Husserl's case, the mechanism of that transformation (as demonstrated above)

---

20 Ibid., p. 44.

is obvious. The individual acts of understanding certain expressions are taken as the starting point: what is common to these individual experiences (after the rejection of their variable elements connected with the individualities of the persons concerned with the situation of a given experience, etc.) is extrapolated, and in this way is *constructed* what is said to be a proposition or meaning in the ideal sense of the word. That it *is* a construction and *what* construction it is, can be shown (contrary to Husserl's assertions that what is involved here is an act of direct *Wesenschau* supported by the testimony of self-evidence) by what Husserl says himself, as here quoted extensively. Hence Husserl's theory can be headlined – "Meaning as an ideal object or as an inherent property of thought", since meaning interpreted as an ideal entity is but an absolutized and inherent property of thought connected with certain experiences in understanding expressions. This is confirmed by the intimate links between that conception and the theory of intentional acts.

Now that we know, probably clearly enough, how Husserl understands meaning as an ideal entity, let us pass to intentional acts and to the intentional conception of meaning, which has found reflection in Polish philosophical literature.

Whoever would understand the conception of intentional acts, as conceived by Husserl, and apply it to the problem of meaning, must bear in mind not only meanings as *ideal objects*, but also the entire theory concerning the *essence* of things and the *direct seeing* of things. True, the conception of *epoché*, *eidos*, and *eidetic seeing*, fundamental to the phenomenological method, developed in the period that followed *Logische Untersuchungen*, wherein the theory of meaning and the theory of intentional acts were formulated; yet that work already includes ideas that came to be the foundations of those theories. This refers above all to the idea of a direct seeing of meaning as an ideal entity, and the realization of the consequences resulting therefrom for the intentional theory of meaning.

"Was 'Bedeutung' ist, das kann uns so unmittelbar gegeben sein, wie uns gegeben ist, was Farbe und Ton ist. Es lässt sich nicht weiter definieren, es ist ein deskriptives Letztes"[21].

We have to do not only with a direct perception of meaning, but also with a criterion which makes it possible to single out the same meaning in all individual statements, namely the criterion of self-evidence. That criterion, together with the theory of intentional acts and of intentional objects, was taken over by Husserl from his master, Franz Brentano.

"... Es handelt sich dabei auch nicht um eine blosse Hypothese, die sich erst durch ihre Erklärungsergiebigkeit rechtfertigen soll; sondern wir nehmen es als eine unmittelbar fassliche Wahrheit in Anspruch und folgen hierin der letzten Autorität in allen Erkenntnisfragen, der Evidenz"[22].

Only when we have understood that meaning, in Husserl's view, is an ideal entity, "a unity in plurality", a unity of species, only when we have understood that meaning is accessible to us in direct perception (*Schau*), can we understand the intentional conception of meaning.

Let us begin by recalling the elementary facts concerning the theory of intentional act. As already indicated, that theory was taken over by Husserl from Franz Brentano who was in turn a transmitter of scholastic tradition, where, in the last analysis, the conception of intentional acts is rooted. But, without reaching so far back, one has, in order to understand Husserl, to become acquainted not only with Brentano's *Psychology*, to which Husserl refers *expressis verbis*, but also with Brentano's correspondence with Marty, Krause, and others, on the subject of intentional objects[23].

Even a nodding acquaintance with the theory of intentional acts shows that it would be an unfortunate error to identify the intentional act, as understood by Husserl (and consequently

[21] Ibid., p. 183.

[22] Ibid., p. 100.

[23] Cf. the posthumous collection *Wahrheit und Evidenz*, Leipzig 1930.

his intentional conception of meaning), with the thesis that when we express certain words we have certain definite dispositions to understand that state in such and such a way. The theory of intentional acts embraces a thesis about such or other psychic dispositions concerning the meaning of expressions, but at the same time it includes a lot of other theses, such as a soberly thinking man must consider to be at least strange, theses which are taken over as part and parcel of the theory of intentional acts.

According to Brentano (Husserl adopts his theses), the differences between the various types of experience consist in "the manner of reference of consciousness to a certain content" or, in the mediaeval scholastic terminology, in their *intention*. Husserl says:

"... In der Wahrnehmung wird etwas wahrgenommen, in der Bildvorstellung etwas bildlich vorgestellt, in der Aussage etwas ausgesagt, in der Liebe etwas geliebt, in Hasse etwas gehasst, im Begehren etwas begehrt usw. ... Nur eins halten wir als für uns wichtig im Auge: dass es wesentliche spezifische Verschiedenheiten der intentionalen Beziehung, oder kurzweg der Intention (die den deskriptiven Gattungscharakter des 'Aktes' ausmacht) gibt. Die Weise, in der eine 'blosse Vorstellung' eines Sachverhalts diesen ihren 'Gegenstand' meint, ist eine andere, als die Weise des Urteils, das den Sachverhalt für wahr oder falsch hält"[24].

Thus, every experience in which there is a reference — a relation of consciousness — to a certain content or, in other words, to an intentional object, is an intentional act. As we shall see, the content of consciousness and the intentional object are one and the same. The difference in intention depends on the difference in that content or intentional object. But let us not suppose that we have here to do with a real relation between consciousness and object, or that the intentional act and the intentional object are two things really appearing in consciousness[25].

[24] Husserl, op. cit., pp. 366–367.

[25] Ibid., p. 371.

There is only an intentional experience, the characteristic trait of which consists just in the given intention.

"... Je nach ihrer spezifischen Besonderung macht sie das diesen Gegenstand Vorstellen oder das ihn Beurteilen usw. voll und allein aus. Ist dieses Erlebnis präsent, so ist *eo ipso* – das liegt, betone ich, an seinem eigenen *Wesen* – die intentionale 'Beziehung auf einen Gegenstand' vollzogen, *eo ipso* ist ein Gegenstand 'intentional gegenwärtig'; denn das eine und andere besagt genau dasselbe. Und natürlich kann solch ein Erlebnis im Bewusstsein vorhanden sein mit dieser seiner Intention, ohne dass der Gegenstand überhaupt existiert und vielleicht gar existieren kann; der Gegenstand ist gemeint, d. h. das ihn Meinen ist Erlebnis; aber er ist dann bloss vermeint und in Wahrheit nichts"[26].

Husserl explains his idea by way of the example of how we imagine Jove. Jove is an intentional object of what I imagine, but in analysing my experience I find that object neither *in mente* nor *extra mentem*. It is simply nowhere, and yet the imagined picture of Jove is a true experience. But the most interesting is Husserl's assertion that nothing changes when the object of intension does exist.

"Existiert andererseits der intendierte Gegenstand, so braucht in phänomenologischer Hinsicht nichts geändert zu sein. Für das Bewusstsein ist das Gegebene ein wesentlich Gleiches, ob der vorgestellte Gegenstand existiert, oder ob er fingiert und vielleicht gar widersinnig ist. *Jupiter* stelle ich nicht anders vor als *Bismarck*, den *Babylonischen Turm* nicht anders als den *Kölner Dom*, ein *regelmässiges Tausendeck* nicht anders als einen *regelmässigen Tausendflächner*"[27].

A strange theory, that: it refers to a reference of consciousness to content, and to an object of the intentional act, only to state in the end that not only *is* there *no* object, but that there *cannot*

---

[26] Ibid., pp. 372–373.
[27] Ibid., p. 373.

be one at all, since *ex definitione* there is only and exclusively an act of consciousness as an intentional act. Elsewhere in his work[28], Husserl explains that content expressed in the objective sense is identical with meaning and object. All this is considerably clarified by the later development of his theory. In the light of the phenomenological *epoché* those judgements which do not pertain to pure consciousness and thereby to *eidos*, to the essence of things, are subject to suspension. *Eidetic reduction* suspends the judgements concerning the individual existence of the object, and *transcendental reduction* goes still further by suspending all that is not a correlate of pure consciousness. In this way, as J. M. Bocheński correctly remarks, there is left of the object only what is given to the subject[29]. The real world is totally referred to pure consciousness, and deprived of its independent and absolute character; it thus becomes only an "intentional object", a content of consciousness.

This is subjective idealism of the first water, and seems to be at variance with the objective idealism of Husserl's theory of ideal entities, including meanings. That duality is revealed both in the development of Husserl's own theory, and in the development of the phenomenological school. Finally, we must concern ourselves with one point more: does Husserl somehow bridge the gap between the objective idealism of his conception of meaning as an ideal entity and the subjective idealism of his conception of intentional acts? Does he formulate any uniform theory of meaning?

Yes, and no. Yes — in the sense that he clearly combines the two conceptions into a whole in a manner which I shall demonstrate below. No — in the sense that the inner split into objective and subjective idealism remains, and both conceptions are connected by a bridge that is very narrow and unsteady (from the point of view of the uniformity of the theory).

---

28 Ibid., p. 52.

29 J. M. Bocheński, *Contemporary European Philosophy*, Berkeley and Los Angeles 1956, pp. 137–140.

Husserl thus bridges the gap:

"... Die mannigfaltigen Einzelheiten zur ideal-einen Bedeutung sind natürlich die entsprechenden Aktmomente des Bedeutens, die *Bedeutungsintentionen.* Die Bedeutung verhält sich also zu den jeweiligen Akten des Bedeutens ... wie etwa die Röte *in specie* zu den hier liegenden Papierstreifen, die alle diese selbe Röte 'haben' "[30].

And elsewhere:

"... *Denselben* Wunsch hegen mehrere Personen, wenn ihre wünschende Intention dieselbe ist. Bei dem einen mag der Wunsch voll ausdrücklich sein, bei dem andern nicht, bei dem einen mit Beziehung auf den fundierenden Vorstellungsgehalt anschaulich klar, bei dem andern mehr oder minder unanschaulich usw. In jedem Falle liegt die Identität des 'Wesentlichen' offenbar in den beiden oben unterschiedenen Momenten, in derselben Aktqualität und in derselben Materie. Dasselbe nehmen wir also auch für die ausdrücklichen und speziell die *bedeutungsverleihenden* Akte in Anspruch, und zwar so, dass, wie wir es oben vorweg ausgesprochen haben, ihr *Bedeutungsmässiges*, d.h. das in ihnen, was das reelle phänomenologische Korrelat der idealen Bedeutung bildet, mit ihrem intentionalen Wesen zusammenfällt"[31].

Thus the situation is clear. According to Husserl, the individual intentional acts are, as it were, specifications of ideal meaning; their intentional objects coincide with the phenomenological (i.e., appearing in consciousness) correlate of ideal meaning. Meaning is thus an ideal entity manifesting itself in intentional acts owing to a direct, eidetic, "seeing" (*Schau*) of the essence of things. Is that "bridge" satisfactory? Let the adherents bother about that, since for opponents such *Schönheitsfehler* is a trifle as compared with the basic thesis of the theory.

We have presented Husserl's theory of meaning. I hold Husserl to have been a brilliant philosopher, marked by extra-

---

30 Husserl, op. cit., p. 100.

31 Ibid, pp. 420–421.

ordinary precision of thought. This is precisely why he has become one of the greatest intellectual trouble-makers of our times. It is only Bergson who can vie with him in that respect. What does that trouble-making consist of? In propagating metaphysical, anti-scientific opinions. In Husserl's case, that occurred, so to speak, in the full glory of precision, which inevitably made a great impression on readers.

My attitude – that of a philosopher who adopts the standpoint of dialectical materialism – to Husserl's philosophy of meaning, is self-evident and unequivocal. In my opinion the ideal entities, eidetic seeing, eidetic reduction, transcendental reduction, intentional acts, etc., are products of anti-scientific views, belated aftermath of the various systems of idealistic philosophy. Why? First of all, because Husserl's ideas are in clear opposition to the requirements of the scientific method in thinking, which is hostile to all kinds of intuitions and demands, among other things, inter-subjective communicability of the facts under investigation and the possibility of verification of the results of research. As I have said, I do not maintain that all that is an unsense, mere rubbish clad in a grammatical garb. Nor do I say that "I do not understand" what has been said. My "liberalism", as compared with the attitude of the positivists, is due to the fact that I am more sceptical about the possibility of solving philosophical controversies. In his concluding lecture on logical atomism (a series delivered in 1918), Bertrand Russell reflected on the relation between philosophy and science. One perhaps cannot agree with everything Russell says, his assessment of the rôle of philosophy is certainly too pessimistic, but nevertheless his opinion is an interesting one and contains a lot of truth.

"... I believe the only difference between science and philosophy is that science is what you more or less know and philosophy is what you do not know. Philosophy is that part of science which at present people choose to have an opinion about, but which they have no knowledge about. Therefore every advance in knowledge robs philosophy of some problems which formerly it had ... And of course the moment they become soluble, they become to a large class of philosophical minds uninteresting, because to many of the people who like philosophy, the charm of it consists in the speculative freedom, in the fact that you can play with hypotheses. You can think out this or that which *may* be true, which is a very valuable exercise until you discover what *is* true; but when you discover what is true the whole fruitful play of fancy in that region is curtailed, and you will abandon that region and pass on"[32].

The fact that philosophical controversies continue for millennia and that the basic standpoints in those controversies have survived millennia, the fact that to this day there are discussions like those which Schiller so well described in his *Xenien*:

> "Einer, das hőret man wohl, spricht *nach* dem andern.
> Doch keiner
> *Mit* dem andern; wer nennt zwei Monologe Gespräch?"

— all this seems to confirm the truth of at least some of Russell's statements, seasoned as they are with bitter irony. What then if I reject Husserl's theory as a product of imagination, if Husserl and his followers reply with equal *aplomb* that it is precisely their standpoint which is scientific and that I am in the wrong? What if I demand a scientific proof of the existence of ideal entities, if my opponents adduce evidence as a proof which in their eyes is a most scientific one? I can multiply arguments demonstrating that the standpoint of my opponents is anti-scientific; I also can, if I feel forced to it, describe their opinions from the sociological point of view and ascribe to them a definite function in the class struggle. I personally think that all that is justified and methodologically correct. But it has one fundamental

[32] B. Russell, "The Philosophy of Logical Atomism", in *The Monist*, 1918, quoted after B. Russell, *Logic and Knowledge*, p. 281.

defect: it does not suffice to *convince the opponent* if he sticks to his original assumptions. And this makes all the difference between philosophy on the one hand and such sciences as mathematics, chemistry or any other experimental discipline on the other. In the exact sciences, calculus or experiment usually settles the question. In philosophy it is not so; this is testified by the history of philosophy and the present situation in philosophy. I do not want to engage in a discussion as to *why* it is so, nor do I believe that this fact ultimately discredits philosophy. But at least one has to acknowledge that state of things in detail and draw appropriate conclusions. Neither my Marxist companions nor the numerous positivist-minded Polish philosophers wanted to draw such conclusions. And the basic conclusion is: the adherent of a philosophy with which one does not agree may neither be ignored nor accused of preaching nonsense.

What then is a philosopher to do in such a situation? First of all, he should take cognizance of the fact that opposing views do exist. This leads to further consequences. Since the views with which I do not agree are alien to me and even, according to my conviction, detrimental to the progress of human knowledge, I must, as a philosopher, oppose and fight them. But since I operate in a field in which victory may be won *only* by convincing my opponent by appropriate argumentation, I must familiarize myself with his opinions in order to be able to combat them properly. All this makes my victory only *possible*, but in no way certain. But in order not to be at a loss on that slippery ground of philosophical problems, where one moves in a different way from where one is on the firm ground of the exact science, one thing is necessary: one must realize not only that there are different *ways* of solving philosophical problems, but also that these are *different* ways. And if one sees and understands those differences one must clearly realize *which way* and *to where* one is going. From the point of view of a maximalist, this is certainly not much, but in fact the requirement is no small one.

3. MEANING AS A RELATION (1)

Among the theories which interpret meaning as a relation, those two which were listed last, merit special attention. Consequently, these two will now be examined in detail, whereas the rest will be accorded only cursory treatment.

When we ask "What does the word ... mean?" we are often concerned with a translation of that word into a language we know. This is especially so when we ask about the meaning of words in a language we do not know or about a word we do not know in a language which in principle is known to us. If, when learning French, I ask "What does 'la chaise' mean?", I obviously want to know the translation of 'la chaise' into English. Consequently – I rest perfectly satisfied with the reply that "'la chaise' means in English 'the chair'" and I am satisfied that I have come thereby to know the meaning of that word. It is also similar when I ask in English about the meaning of a term I do not know, for example, a technical term. I have said "similar", because the mechanism of explanation in this case is different. What is involved here is not just a replacement of a word in one language by its equivalent in another language, but a definition of a term. For instance, I ask "What is a 'differential gear' " and I obtain such an answer as "A differential gear is ...", for I actually wanted an explanation as to what a differential gear is.

In these cases meaning is as much as a relation between signs, a relation between the definiendum and the definiens, such that the definiens may be either a verbal sign in a language that is known to us or a definition of a word given in that language. Meaning of this type is called lexical meaning. This is one the most commonly used meanings of "meaning", very important in practice.

When it comes to "meaning" understood as a relation between the sign and the object or the sign and the thought about an object (according to others: the idea of an object), that is that particular meaning of "meaning" which prevails in semantics as pursued by logicians, then a critical discussion on a broader theoretical basis is required. We shall revert to that issue when analysing the last point of our list, in connection with the theory of meaning based on Marxist principles. For it is only in such a context that we shall be able to assess properly the merits and demerits of the conceptions enumerated here.

The other extreme, opposite to a psychological or mentalistic conception of meaning, is tenanted by the biological conception, or all those variations which connect the meaning of a sign with such reactions of the human body as manifest themselves in action. In the light of that conception, meaning implies the relation between the sign and the biological reaction of the human organism to that sign or — in a social interpretation — the relation between the sign and human action in a broad sense of the term. If we approach the biological conception from that angle, there are revealed the links which connect the Pavlovian theory not only with pragmatism, operationism, and Morris's semiotic, but also with certain neo-positivist ideas.

The anti-mentalistic character of that conception of meaning is most clearly marked in the case of Pavlov's reflex theory. First of all, that theory eliminates the category of meaning and interprets the sign-situation, and consequently the communication process, in terms of stimuli and reactions. The specific nature of human communication, i.e., communication by means of a phonic language, is reduced to a *more complicated* system of stimuli and reactions to them; this is achieved by the introduction of an additional, higher level of stimuli as signals. It would be superfluous to expound here the elements of the theory of conditioned reflexes; I shall abstain also from repeating my reservations concerning the term "signal" in general, and the term "signal of signals" in particular. It will suffice to state that in the light of Pavlov's physiological theory, the category of meaning (in the sense adopted above) disappears, and the relation which in the mentalistic interpretation bears the traditional name of "meaning" is tantamount to the relation between the sign ("signal" in Pavlov's terminology) and the reflex associated with that sign. In other words, it is claimed that what is traditionally called "meaning" is in fact a reflex of human organism to the sign (signal).

In his theory, Pavlov was not concerned with the philosophical aspect of the problem of meaning, and confined himself to the study of certain specific physiological reactions of human organism. Nevertheles, his theory has important, though indirect, philosophical implications. These implications appear directly in those *philosophical* trends which solve the problem of meaning after the fashion of the biological conception.

First of all, I mean here pragmatism. Not pragmatism as interpreted by James, but the authentic pragmatism which originates with Peirce and then follows various channels and combines under the common name tendencies which often differ very much one from another, from radical subjectivism to opinions which in certain points come close to materialism. It is precisely with pragmatism that is connected the tendency towards a behaviouristic interpretation of meaning.

When I refer to solutions after the fashion of the biological conception, I have no sort of idea of taking over some elements of that conception, but refer to a similarity of solutions, to their congeniality. This applies of course to Peirce who expounded his ideas long before Pavlov.

In his article "How to Make our Ideas Clear" (1878), Peirce formulated the basic concepts of his pragmatism; they included the thesis that meaning is nothing but the practical consequence of thought as manifested in action. He says:

"... The whole function of thought is to produce habits of action ... To develop its (i.e., thinking's – A. S.) meaning, we have, therefore, simply to determine what habits it produces, for what a thing means is simply what habits it involves"[33].

[33] Ch. S. Peirce, "How to Make Our Ideas Clear", in *Values in a Universe of Change* (*Selected Writings of Charles S. Peirce*), Stanford University Press 1958, p. 123.

And then he concludes:

"It appears, then, that the rule for attaining the third grade of clarity of apprehension is as follows: consider what effects, which might conceivably have practical bearings, we conceive the object of our conception to have. Then, our conception of these effects is the whole of our conception of the object"[34].

That idea Peirce next developed in the articles published in 1905 in *The Monist*[35], in order, above all, to protect pragmatism against being vulgarized by the epigoni. The idea itself is very simple: meaning amounts to effects manifested in action, definite habits of action. Effects of what? Habits connected with what? Peirce explains in the paragraph on thinking. But he understood perfectly well the function of the sign in the communication of thoughts and the connection between meaning and sign. Thus, we find here the idea which Pavlov developed later on, although the starting point of interests was quite different in each case. That idea came to rest later at the root of the various interpretations within pragmatism itself, and at the same time exerted influence on other philosophical trends.

Within pragmatism, the two extreme tendencies concerning that issue were represented by F. C. S. Schiller on the one hand, and by George H. Mead on the other.

In 1920, *Mind* published materials from a symposium on meaning. The principal participants in the discussion were Schiller, Russell and Joachim. Schiller, starting from a pragmatist position, ascribed a purely subjectivist and voluntaristic character to the theory that meaning amounts to effects manifested in human action.

"What if meaning be neither an inherent property of objects nor a static 'relation' between objects at all, not even between the object and a subject, but essentially an *activity* or *attitude* taken up towards objects by a subject and energetically projected

---

[34] Ibid., p. 124.

[35] They are the articles "What Pragmatism Is?" and "Issues of Pragmatism".

into them like an α particle, until they, too, grow active and begin to radiate with 'meaning'? Here, if anywhere, would seem to lie the clue to the mystery of 'meaning' "[36].

Schiller then immediately ranges himself on the side of a voluntaristic interpretation of meaning, and states that "meaning is essentially personal", so that meaning is relative with respect to the whole personality of the subject[37].

Another interpretation of the problem, one in conformity with the basic assumptions of Peirce, is given by George H. Mead[38]. That author reveals, however, effects of the direct influence on him of the Pavlovian theory, although he speaks not of reflexes of human organism, but of responses. At the same time, Mead interprets the problem of meaning from the social point of view, in the context of the communication process. A few of his statements, those which are representative of his ideas, are quoted below by way of example.

"Meaning arises and lies within the field of the relation between the future of a given human organism and the subsequent behavior of this organism as indicated to another human organism by gesture"[39].

"Meaning is thus not to be conceived, fundamentally, as a state of consciousness, or as a set of organized relations existing or subsisting mentally outside the field of experience into which they enter; on the contrary, it should be conceived subjectively, as having existence entirely within this field itself. The response of one organism to the gesture of another in any given social act is the meaning of that gesture"[40].

"... Meaning involves a reference of the gesture of one organism to the resultant of the social act it indicates or initiates, as adjustively responded to in this reference by another organism;

---

[36] *Mind*, October 1920, No. 116, p. 389.

[37] Ibid., pp. 390, 391.

[38] G. H. Mead, *Mind, Self and Society*, Chicago 1955.

[39] Ibid., pp. 75–76.

[40] Ibid., p. 78.

and the adjustive response of the other organism is the meaning of the gesture"[41].

The contentions of that trend in pragmatism which sees meaning as being effects manifested in human action, as being the results of communicating thoughts by means of signs, are in harmony with the tendencies which in the 1920's and '30's appeared in Russell's logical atomism, in logical empiricism (neo-positivism), in operationism and in semiotic. All these trends are interconnected, influence one another, and follow similar courses in their approaches to meaning. This refers above all to certain general conclusions from the practical experience of experimenters (chiefly in the case of operationism) and representatives of the natural and the exact sciences (neo-positivism) who combatted, at least subjectively, the metaphysics of traditional philosophy. Another point is, whether or how far they succeeded in that combat, and how far they themselves laid foundations for a new metaphysics. Yet, despite all criticism aimed at the philosophy connected with positivism, it must be said that its endeavours to find a practical interpretation of meaning indicated an important problem.

Operationism is undoubtedly the most interesting in that respect. Its founder, Bridgman, behaves as a physicist who tries to explain, for the purpose of the discipline he represents, certain general theoretical categories, in doing which he takes into account above all the great revolution effected in a number of concepts by Einstein's theory of relativity. I cannot say whether there were any connections and exchange of ideas between Bridgman and the Vienna Circle; anyhow, the problems of meaning and of meaningful statements, which played such an important rôle in the evolution of neo-positivism, stands out in full relief precisely in the case of Bridgman's views. Two theses are involved here. First, that meaning is equal to the sum of the operations corresponding to a given term; or, in other words, that the

[41] Ibid., p. 81.

meaning of a term is to be sought in what one does, and not in what one says. Second, that a question has a meaning (in the sense that it is sensible, and not purely verbal) when one can point to the operations resulting in answer to that question. These two theses are in close harmony with the standpoint of Peirce, on the one hand, and with that of the neo-positivists, to be discused below, on the other.

Bridgman writes:

"We evidently know what we mean by length if we can tell what the length of any and every object is, and for the physicist nothing more is required. To find the length of an object, we have to perform certain physical operations. The concept of length is therefore fixed when the operations by which length is measured are fixed: that is, the concept of length involves as much as and nothing more than the set of operations by which length is determined. In general, we mean by any concept nothing more than a set of operations; *the concept is synonymous* with *the corresponding set of operations.* If the concept is physical, as of length, the operations are actual physical operations, namely, those by which length is measured; or if the concept is mental, as of mathematical continuity, the operations are mental operations, namely those by which we determine whether a given aggregate of magnitudes is continuous"[42].

And further on he thus formulates his ideas:

"For of course the true meaning of a term is to be found by observing what a man does with it, not by what he says about it"[43].

That concept of meaning is connected with the concept of meaningfulness of statements, which has played such an important rôle in the neo-positivist campaign against metaphysics.

"If a specific question has meaning, it must be possible to find operations by which an answer may be given to it ... I believe

[42] P. W. Bridgman, *The Logic of Modern Physics*, New York 1927, p. 5.

[43] Ibid., p. 7.

that many of the questions asked about social and philosophical subjects will be found to be meaningless when examined from the point of view of operations"[44].

The question of meaningful and meaningless statements brings us to a certain point which will enable us to understand better the appropriate conceptions of the neo-positivists, namely the ambiguity of the expression: "That statement has meaning". In one case, reference is made to meaning in the traditional sense of the term, which implies that a given statement conveys some content to the listener or reader. Such statements are contrasted with *nonsense*, that is such sequences of words as in view of their disagreement with the grammatical rules of the language involved (e.g., "Horse by though seven still") or in view of the incomprehensibility of certain words (e.g., "Woggled diggles are miggling") convey no content. In the second case, the point in question is the meaningfulness of such statements as can be decided upon in practice, as contrasted with *unsense*, i.e., such statements as have the grammatical form of sentences and are comprehensible, but cannot be decided upon in practice and consequently must be recognized as purely verbal. Thus, unsense has a verbal meaning (that is, some sense) and is not a nonsense, but being an undecidable and unverifiable statement is devoid of practical importance and cannot be considered a scientific statement. That distinction between sense and unsense was enlisted by the neo-positivists in their campaign against metaphysics.

The basic ideas on meaning of the pragmatists and the operationists are found in neo-positivism to be one of the elements in that oft-changing trend, non-uniform in its conceptions.

Historically, neo-positivism (logical empiricism) was shaped under the overwhelming influence of Russell's logical atomism, chiefly though the intermediary of Wittgenstein. Consequently, it is desirable to begin a presentation of the neo-positivist views

---

[44] Ibid., pp. 28-30. An interesting exposition of that standpoint is to be found in *Operational Philosophy* by Anatol Rapoport, New York 1953.

with Russell's and Wittgenstein's opinions on meaning. This is neither easy nor simple, since their opinions are complicated, by no means uniform, and often (cf. Wittgenstein) marked by even radical evolutions.

Russell has two interpretations of meaning as a relation. At least one of them is evidently influenced by pragmatism and behaviourism, namely that which maintains that the meaning of signs is to be sought by observing how they are being used. In his article "On Propositions: What They Are and How They Mean"[45] (1919), which later became the foundation of the 1920 symposium, Russell makes explicit reference to behaviourism[46], and adopts the standpoint of that theory concerning the so-called demonstrative use of language, consisting in pointing out the properties of actually existing virromment. To understand expressions of a language means here: a) to use them in appropriate conditions, and b) to act in a definite way on hearing them. Between the sign and its meaning there is a causal relation in the sense that the signs are evoked by appropriate events, and also in the sense that they in turn evoke other events, namely human action.

Russell concludes quite in the behaviourist spirit (as noted by F. C. S. Schiller, who opposed his conception of meaning-images):

"It is not necessary to 'understanding' of a word that a person should 'know what it means', in the sense of being able to say 'this word means so-and-so'. A word has a meaning, more or less vague; but the meaning is only to be discovered by observing its use; the use comes first, and the meaning is distilled out of it. The relation of a word to its meaning is, in fact, of the nature of a causal law, and there is no more reason why a person using a word correctly should be conscious of its meaning than there is for a planet which is moving correctly to be conscious of Kepler's law."

---

[45] In B. Russell, *Logic and Knowledge*, pp. 285–320.
[46] Ibid., p. 291.

"He [a man] 'understands' a word, because he does the right thing. Such 'understanding' may be regarded as belonging to the nerves and brain, being habits which they have acquired while the language was being learnt. Thus understanding in this sense may be reduced to a mere physiological causal law"[47].

But in his theory of meaning Russell did not maintain a consistently behaviourist position. In thinking, verbal signs are used for "narrative" purposes, and their function consists in describing images retained by memory or produced by imagination (we would say rather: reproduced and produced ideas).

"These two ways of using words may be spoken of together as the use of words in 'thinking'. This way of using words, since it depends upon images, cannot be fully dealt with on behaviourist lines. And this is really the most essential function of words: that primarily through their connection with images they bring us in touch with what is remote in time or space. When they operate without the medium of images this seems to be a telescoped process. *Thus the problem of the meaning of words is reduced to the problem of the meaning of images*"[48].

Thus, in Russell's case, the behaviourist interpretation of meaning is accompanied by a second one, whereby the meaning of signs is reduced to images or reproduced and produced ideas. While in the light of the first conception meaning belongs to the field of physiological reactions of human organism, in the light of the second it belongs to the sphere of psychological experience. Yet in both cases the sign is linked with meaning by the bonds of a causal relation.

The whole conception, in no way uniform, is however dominated by the pragmatist ideas of linking meaning with action and of seeking meaning in action. Replying to F. C. S. Schiller's objections at the 1920 symposium, Russell wrote:

"Meaning, in my view, is a characteristic of 'signs', and 'signs' are sensible (or imaginal) phenomena which cause actions

47 Ibid., pp. 300–301.

48 Ibid., pp. 302–303 (italics – A. S.).

appropriate, not to themselves, but to something else with which they are associated. The possibility of action with reference to what is not sensibly present is one of those things that might be held to characterize mind"[49].

This point is still clearer in the case of Ludwig Wittgenstein, a disciple of Russell's, who acted as intermediary between the latter and continental philosophers; the clarity is the greater if we take into account the evolution of his views from *Tractatus Logico-Philosophicus* to *Philosophical Investigations* (that book, published posthumously, presents Wittgenstein's views as shaped over a period of some dozens of years).

In this *Tractatus*, he still represents the conception of meaning-images, although even there different tunes can be heard. He says for instance:

"3. 262 What does not get expressed in the sign is shown by its application. What the signs conceal, their application declares"[50].

In *Philosophical Investigations*, the identification of meaning with the application of the sign is already effected consistently. Wittgenstein even comes to the conclusion that in the words, apart from the way in which they are *used*, there is nothing else that might be called meaning[51]. His standpoint can be reduced to the following:

"43 For a *large* class of cases — though not for all — in which we employ the word 'meaning' it can be defined thus: the meaning of a word is its use in the language"[52].

Wittgenstein does not repeat the ideas of the pragmatists and the behaviourists in spite of the fact that his reasoning is on the same plane as theirs. Meaning is the relation between sign and action, but an action of a particular kind, namely that which consists in using the sign in speech.

---

[49] *Mind*, October 1920, No. 116, p. 402.

[50] L. Wittgenstein, *Tractatus Logico-Philosophicus*, London 1933.

[51] L. Wittgenstein, *Philosophical Investigations*, Oxford 1953, p. 3.

[52] Ibid., p. 20.

Now the neo-positivist conception of meaning becomes fully comprehensible against the background of all these views. It is for us a matter of secondary importance whether we have to do with congeniality or merely with an ordinary reception of views of other trends and other thinkers. We only wish to high-light a certain standpoint, and to show its variations in order to extract what is typical in them for a conception of the meaning of "meaning".

Among the former members of the Vienna Circle that problem was analysed by, in particular, Moritz Schlick and Rudolf Carnap.

Schlick raised the problem of meaning in his *Allgemeine Erkenntnislehre*, and later reverted to it in the various articles and papers published in the collection *Gesammelte Aufsätze*. I refer in particular to his article "Meaning and Verification"[53].

Schlick's starting point, later adopted by the Vienna Circle as a whole, was that the meaning of a sign is the same as the method of its verification. Hence a transition to the concept of unsense – that is, statements which have the grammatical form of a sentence but are devoid of sense since they are unverifiable. Schlick combined that typically operationist conception with the view of Wittgenstein (to whom he referred *expressis verbis*) that the meanings of expressions are manifested in the way in which they are used in speech. That combination of the two conceptions appears most clearly in the article "Meaning and Verification", mentioned above.

"Thus, whenever we ask concerning a sentence, 'What does it mean?', what we expect is instruction as to the circumstances in which that sentence is to be used ... Stating the meaning of a sentence amounts to stating the rules according to which the sentence is to be used, and this is the same as stating the way in which it can be verified (or falsified). *The meaning of a proposition is the method of its verification*"[54].

---

[53] First published in *Philosophical Review*, Vol. 44, 1936.

[54] In M. Schlick, *Gesammelte Aufsätze*, 1926–1936, Vienna 1938, p. 340.

The situation is somewhat different in the case of Carnap. He, too, had undergone a considerable evolution from the period of logical syntax, when he asserted that a logic of meaning is superfluous, to the period of semantics (*Introduction to Semantics*) in which he explicitly renounced that assertion. In the course of that evolution the concept of "meaning" appeared in his works: originally he interpreted meaning exclusively as the designatum of the name (cf. his introductory article to *The International Encyclopedia of Unified Science*, entitled "Logical Foundations of the Unity of Science"). Yet throughout that period Carnap was interested in something else, namely in the *meaningfulness* of sentences, understood as their capacity for verification in some form. This is a fascinating problem in the evolution of neo-positivism, most clearly marked in the evolution of Carnap's views. The requirement of a full verifiability of sentences was connected with the standpoint on meaning of Wittgenstein[55] and Schlick. The requirement of falsification appeared under the influence of Popper. Later on, Carnap adopted a more moderate position (*Testability and Meaning*) in that he required only a gradual confirmation, and not a full verification or falsification. But, as indicated with reference to Bridgman's views, these are only related matter, and not fully coincident.

Finally, a brief mention of the concept of meaning as represented by Morris's semiotic.

So far, I have more than once indicated a similarity between such and such views on the one hand and pragmatism and behaviourism on the other; here we have to do with an obvious connection with such views, since semiotic was born in the union of neo-positivism with pragmatism. This is why those tendencies which we have previously called the biological conception, emerge in semiotic with particular clarity. Meaning is interpreted in terms of physiological reactions of human organism, and the term itself is most willingly avoided.

[55] L. Wittgenstein, *Tractatus* ..., 4.003.

In referring to Morris's views, it is necessary to make a clear distinction between the opinions contained in his *Foundations of the Theory of Signs*[56] and those formulated later on in his book *Signs, Language and Behaviour*. In my opinion, his earlier and more modest work is much better than his system as developed in that book. In *Foundations*, Morris sets forth a reasonable conception of meaning. Stressing the ambiguity of that term, he firmly opposes all Platonizing interpretations. In conformity with his conception, meaning is a term that belongs to the social process of semiosis ("sign-situation" in other terminology). That term becomes comprehensible only in the context of such process and the terms related to the latter concept.

"Nothing is intrinsically a sign or a sign vehicle, but becomes such only is so far as it permits something to take account of something through its mediation. Meanings are not to be located as existences at any place in the process of semiosis but are to be characterized in terms of this process as a whole. 'Meaning' is a semiotical term and a term in the thing-language; to say that there are meanings in nature is not to affirm that there is a class of entities on a par with trees, rocks, organisms, and colours, but that such objects and properties function within processes of semiosis"[57].

The aspect is quite different when it comes to Morris's fundamental work on signs – marked by vast claims and insignificant results. I fully agree with the criticism of its ideas as made by Max Black[58] and J. Kotarbińska[59].

Morris wanted to handle the problem of the sign from the behaviourist point of view, and therefore postulated a complete renunciation of the category of "meaning".

[56] In *International Encyclopedia of Unified Science*, Vol. 1, No. 2, University of Chicago Press, 1938.

[57] Ibid., p. 45.

[58] M. Black, "The Semiotic of Charles Morris", in M. Black, *Language and Philosophy*, New York 1949.

[59] J. Kotarbińska, "Pojęcie znaku" [The Concept of Sign], in *Studia Logica*, 1957, Vol. 6, pp. 57–133.

"The term 'meaning' is not here included among the basic terms of semiotic. This term, useful enough at the level of every-day analysis, does not have the precision necessary for scientific analysis. Accounts of meaning usually throw a handful of putty at the target of sign phenomena, while a technical semiotic must provide us with words which are sharpened arrows. 'Meaning' signifies any and all phases of sign-processes (the status of being a sign, the interpretant, the fact of denoting, the significatum), and frequently suggests mental and valuational processes as well; hence it is desirable for semiotic to dispense with the term and to introduce special terms for the various factors which meaning fails to discriminate"[60].

The declaration is reasonable. But the execution? One has to agree with Black that nothing remains of that strident announcement except the declaration itself. Morris replaces the term "meaning" by the term "significatum" (in doing which he avails himself of the fact that in English there are two synonymous words, "to mean" and "to signify") as being the equivalent of the conditions under which a sign denotes something[61], and then distinguishes between the individual variations of that "significatum" according to the dispositions of the human organism to react in definite ways to preparatory stimuli.

*

* *

It is time to sum up what been said so far and to draw more general conclusions.

To avoid misunderstandings, I must emphasize once more that my sole object has been to show a certain *type* of solution of the problem of meaning. Consequently, I do not claim that the views described here belong to one and the same philosophical trend; on the contrary, there are sometimes considerable differences between them. Nor do I claim that the theory of meaning

60 Ch. Morris, *Signs, Language and Behavior*, New York 1946, p. 19.
61 Ibid., p. 18.

is characteristic of such trends; on the contrary, it is sometimes in opposition to other theories within the same system (as in the case of neo-positivism). I only maintain that there is a certain type of solution of the problem of meaning which is common to various philosophical schools and trends.

That solution was born of opposition to metaphysical concepts of the Husserlian type, where meaning is transformed into a sort of ideal entity, or against mentalistic or psychologistic concepts, which locate meaning in man's spiritual life and resort exclusively to psychological categories. Such views are opposed by the concept of meaning as a specific relation between the sign and certain reflexes of organism, or a conscious reaction in the form of a definite action evoked by the given sign. Thus, in the light of that conception, "meaning" means the equivalent of a relation between the sign and the reaction it evokes, or, more briefly but with less precision, of the action evoked by the sign. Psychological categories are here replaced by categories of objective behaviour, the action of human organism, and in this way we acquire objective data which enable us to define meanings and differentiate between them, data which can be observed intersubjectively.

How is that conception to be evaluated?

It has two unquestionable virtues. First, the opposition to Platonizing metaphysics and idealistic mentalism gives rise to a tendency to interpret meaning as a relation *sui generis*. Second, the same source gives rise to a tendency to interpret meaning in terms of objective reactions of organism or conscious action.

Yet it also has obvious shortcomings. First of all, these theories which take as their foundation the relation between sign and action, tend, at least to some extent, to fetishize the sign, as indicated above. In other words, they fail to notice that meaning is above all a social relation between men who act and who communicate with one another. Next, while developing out of an opposition to a one-sided interpretation of meaning, they fall into the other extreme: they simplify the problem in the behaviourist spirit. There is no doubt (as has been pointed out by, among others, Russell) that the behaviourist approach fails completely when it is required to explain communication on abstract subjects, such as the understanding and interpretation of a philosophical treatise, a lyrical poem, etc.

Of course, one might draw attention to a number of other shortcomings, inconsistencies or simple mistakes in the conceptions discussed above. But it seems that the best way of criticizing erroneous views is to formulate a more satisfactory positive conception. That I shall now attempt.

4. MEANING AS A RELATION (2)

One of the ways of interpreting "meaning" is to conceive of meaning as of a specific relation between the persons who communicate with one another. It is within this conception that I intend to expound the Marxist standpoint on the issue under discussion.

My declaration requires certain explanation in order to avoid misunderstandings: I have to explain what is meant here by "to expound the Marxist standpoint."

It might mean, first, that the author is going to present the opinions of the Marxist classics on the given subject, drawing on the appropriate writings. This is not the point in this case since no theory of meaning is to be found in the works of the Marxist classics. They simply did not tackle the subject, except to the extent of chance remarks on language and meaning.

Alternatively it might mean that the author wants to subject the problem concerned to an analysis from the Marxist point of view, making use of the Marxist method. This is in fact my intention and this is how my declaration is to be understood. But from this definite deductions can be made. The study of a problem from a certain methodological standpoint does not imply a monopoly of correct solutions. Not only because a researcher may commit an error and be mistaken in his analysis, but also because different people, in using the same method and starting from the same theoretical assumptions, may in concrete matters reach different, and even in some respects contradictory, conclusions. The results of research and the conclusions drawn from research are determined not only by the methodological and theoretical assumptions made, but also by knowledge concerning the problem involved, general knowledge which forms the background of the problem under investigation, individual talent for research, creative inventiveness, etc. Be that as it may, from the fact that two persons adopt similar basic assumptions, that they speak *in the same manner*, it does not follow that they must always say the *same thing*, that is, come to identical research results. This refers in particular to such difficult, intricate and extremely controversial issues as is the problem of meaning. Consequently, by declaring that I want to expound the Marxist point of view on that issue I wish to say only this — that I start from Marxist assumptions. I do not in any wise claim that what I shall say will be "authentic" Marxism and that every Marxist at variance with me on that subject should be anathematized. I find it the more necessary to stress that point because the literature of the subject based on Marxist principles (primarily theoretical linguistic studies, since Marxist philosophical studies on language, and in particular on meaning and the theory of signs, are very scanty) does not include a single item which I would fully endorse and on the other hand includes items from which I should like vigorously to dissociate myself. Hence, I have to admit that the problem is controversial and to present my own view as one of the possible solutions.

A. Meaning as a relation between men who communicate with one another

I have often repeated the thesis that all effective analysis of the signs and meaning should start from an analysis of the social process of communication or, in other words of sign-situation. Consequently, I shall begin from that point.

The problem of meaning appears wherever we have to do with signs in the process of human communication. In this sense, meaning is a definite relation between men who communicate with one another. It is that meaning of "meaning" with which we are concerned now; other meanings of that term are outside the scope of our interest.

What is meant when we say that meaning is a definite social relation? This means more or less: someone wants to incite someone else to action, to inform him about his thoughts, feelings, etc., and with that end in view resorts to a sign — a gesture, a word, an image, etc. If the intended effect has been achieved, i.e., if the appropriate thoughts have in fact been conveyed to the other party (as can be inferred from the reply or other behaviour of that other party), then we say that the meaning of the sign has been understood by the hearer. What we call meaning appears where a complicated social process takes place, a process which we have referred to above in analysing the concept of sign-situation. The following elements are indispensable for the occurrence of that process: (1) two persons (classes of persons) who communicate with one another, that is, who think; (2) that something to which the sign refers; (3) the sign by means of which thoughts are conveyed. But material objects or events become signs only when they enter into definite intricate relations with men who use them as signs; with reality to which they are somehow referred (as names, pictures, etc.); with the system of signs, i.e., language, within which they function. It is only in such a context that an object or event becomes a sign or, in other words, has a meaning. Thus, if we do not believe in the mysticism of inherent meanings, meanings as ideal entities, in which their material vehicles participate, then we have to admit that for all the ambiguity of the term "meaning" (even in the narrower sense of the word, with which we are concerned here), it is always a certain system of *social relations* which is involved. Similarly, human cognition is a social relation, since it is relation between the cognizing subject (but shaped by life in society) and the object of cognition; what we call "reflection" (in the theory of cognition), etc. The question practically consists in a better appreciation of *what* relation it is which is called meaning, or what *system of relations*.

There are specific relations between all the elements of the sign-situation: between the men who communicate one with another; between men and reality; between men and signs; between signs and reality; between signs and other signs in a certain system of signs. These are relations of various types, situated, as it were, on various planes, above all on the psychological plane and on the plane of human attitudes and actions. But it is always *human communication* which is decisive in such relations. It is always in that context that the sign-situation, the sign and meaning are comprehensible. The separation of a fragment of such relations (the relation between the sign and its designatum; the relation between signs; the relation between the producer of signs and the signs, etc.) may be necessary for research purposes and is of course permissible; but it is not permissible to treat such a fragment as an independent whole, since this involves, as we have seen above, the danger of various "fetishisms".

Thus, meaning is, first, a relation or a system of relations between men on the psychological plane. We may also refer to a psychological aspect of meaning, namely the relation between men who act and feel, and who communicate with one another, that is comprehendingly convey to one another their thoughts which refer to some reality in the broadest sense of the term. A closer explanation of the sense of that relation, and an analysis of its elements, would require volumes. For virtually each of these elements could be the subject matter of a separate monograph: beginning with the issue of a social individual, i.e., a human individual shaped in society, whose every step, both as regards action and thought, is at once individual and social; through the problem of reality as the subject of cognition and communication through the issue of the sign as the intermediary in that process; to the problem of the interpretation of the process of comprehending and communication in individual and social psychology. It can be seen that we touch here upon extremely complicated problems which moreover are inseparably interconnected. Thus we must of necessity use concepts which are not explained to the very end, and must move with apparent ease on very slippery ground.

With this reservation in mind, we may say that, on the psychological plane, by meaning we understand that which enables the sign to perform the function of an intermediary in the process of human communication, that is, in the process of conveying thoughts from one person to another. That "something" is an intricate system of interhuman relations whereby a material object becomes a sign. An explicit reservation must further be made here to the effect that we neither refer to the origin of that relation, nor explain how it happens that material objects and events can perform, under definite conditions, such complicated cognitive and communicative functions; we merely state certain facts.

A quite different view point is made possible by the analysis of human actions and behaviour. Here, too, we are concerned with definite relations between men, *the same* as those referred to above, but seen in the aspect of objective human behaviour in practical, mental, etc., action.

In other words, it might be said that meaning belongs both to the sphere of human action and to the sphere of human thought. For in fact these two spheres are inseparably connected one with another. If we notice these two aspects of the meaning relation, we are protected against mentalism, which is nothing more nor less than ascribing absolute importance to one aspect of the sign-situation. In an objective interpretation, mentalism leads to the conception of meanings as ideal entities; in a subjective interpretation, it leads to psychologism, which believes meaning to be a subjective property of autonomous mental processes.

To treat meaning as definite interhuman relations (which, in my opinion, is extremely important for a correct analysis of the complicated issue) in no way protects us against the ambiguity of the term. For, starting from that theoretical assumption, one may by "meaning" understand either the whole of the relations which make up the sign-situation (the process of semiosis), or a fragment of those relations (the relation between the sign on the one hand and the object or the thought about the object on the other), or the designatum or the denotatum of the sign (i.e., an object of communication regardless of whether it actually exists or not, or such an object existing in reality), or the relation between the sign and the system of signs (language) or between the sign and the signs or another language, etc. In the literature of the subject all these meanings of "meaning" appear in more or less pure form. In our analysis, too, we might draw attention to an ambiguous—in this sense of the word—use of the term "meaning". There is nothing detrimental in it, the more so since we are here concerned not with a pedantic distinction between the various shades of the meaning of "meaning", but rather with a theoretical view of the foundation on which all these meanings rest. Now, to explain that aspect of the problem requires the adoption of some definite standpoint on the issue of the origin of meaning, that is, the origin of that specific property which transforms material objects and events into signs, turning these objects and events into extremely important intermediaries in the communication of men *among themselves* and – if it may be so expressed – *with themselves* (since a mental monologue is but a form of a dialogue).

B. The origin of meaning

The problem of the origin of meaning, of the factors contributing to that origin, is important not only for the explanation of the thesis that meaning is a definite social relation; it is equally important for a proper interpretation and solution of the very difficult issue of the relation between meaning and notion.

This reveals the third plane on which the problem of meaning is to be examined, namely the logical plane. In this connection I must emphasize that both the above approach to the problem and my further explanations of the origin of meaning deviate considerably from customs prevailing among logicians. Objections which might possibly be raised on that score would not be justified, since a one-sided formal logical analysis of such problems as that of meaning is certainly detrimental to the issue at stake. This is testified by such authorities fully recognized in logic circles as Russell and Wittgenstein.

In his well-known work published in 1919, "On Propositions: What They Are and How They Mean," Russell thus assessed the contribution of logicians to the analysis of meaning:

"Logicians, so far as I know, have done very little towards explaining the nature of the relation called 'meaning', nor are they to blame in this, since the problem is essentially one for psychology"[62].

Many years later, when his life was already drawing to a close, Wittgenstein wrote:

"23 It is interesting to compare the multiplicity of the tools in language and of the ways they are used, the multiplicity of kinds of word and sentence, with what logicians have said about the structure of language. (including the author of the *Tractatus Logico-Philosophicus*)"[63].

What these two statements have in common is the understanding of the fact that the approach to the problems of language, meaning, etc., exclusively from the point of view of formal logic, impoverishes the entire issue. Anyhow it must be said that a protest against psychologism may not lead to separating the issues of men's psychic life from psychology. Far less may it lead to a separation of issues of social life from that life and its manifestations in human action.

---

[62] In B. Russell, *Logic and Knowledge*, p. 290.

[63] L. Wittgenstein, *Philosophical Investigations*, p. 12.

In asking about the origin of meaning, we ask about the origin of those interhuman relations which appear in the communication process, we ask how it happens that material objects and events perform the function of vehicles of human thoughts, emotions, etc. This is *par excellence* a psychological and epistemological question; it is in principle outside the sphere of interest of the logicians who either abstract from the problem of meaning or take it as given. But how can one develop the theory of the sign without first answering the question, what are sign and meaning? And in turn, how can one answer that question without first investigating *the origin* of sign and meaning, that is without tackling problems belonging to epistemology, psychology and sociology? Of course, not every discipline concerned with signs and meanings must handle these problems in all their aspects, but no discipline, including formal logic, may aspire to a full comprehension of such problems if it passes over in silence the fundamental questions.

In reply to the question posed above (what are sign and meaning?) it must be made clear that the origin of meaning is connected with the social practical activity of men, as shaped in history, activity an inseparable part of which is the process of thinking.

Let us recall here that — in conformity with what has been said in the preceding chapter concerning the relation of the verbal sign to other types of signs — when I refer simply to meaning I have in mind the meaning of the phonic language and of the verbal signs, whereas the meanings of other signs are treated as derivative with respect to signs of the phonic language, as specific translations of the latter. In view of the inseparable, organic links between language and thinking, the question as to the origin of meaning is intimately connected with the question as to the origin of human thought processes. But then that question lets in all the issues of epistemology and the related aspects of social life. Here again I must regret that I shall not be able to raise all the issues involved by the problem we are interested in, but shall have to confine myself to the principal ones.

When men communicate one with another by means of signs, the sign-situation consists in the fact that the cognitive content which is, so to speak, the private property of a thinking individual, becomes socially communicable by means of signs. This is so because the signs in question are similarly understood on a social level. The mechanism of that "being similarly understood" consists in that the sign (above all the verbal sign) is connected (the nature of that connection will be discussed below) on a social level with similar thought processes and with similar reactions in the form of action (these are the psychological and the behavioural aspects of meaning). Thus, we may equally well ask about the origin of meaning and about the origin of a similar understanding (interpretation) of the sign. These are in fact two approaches to the same problem.

Meaning and similar understanding, and consequently similar thought processes (but not only such – the same applies to similar reaction in behaviour), are interconnected. I shall ignore the nature of that connection and shall concentrate on the actual similarity of thought processes. By what is it evoked, and by what is it conditioned? Certainly by a considerable number of factors, including the relation: the cognizing subject – the object – the sign, which comes to the forefront. It is an intricate relation since it is in fact a complex of relations taking place between its various elements: the subject – the object, the sign – the object, the subject – the sign.

The meaning of the sign cannot be separated from cognitive thought, which is a subjective reflection of objective reality (the term "reflection" is used here in its specific philosophical sense, not here discussed). In a sense, meaning and the reflection of the object in thought can be said to coincide.

Does all this agree with the thesis that meaning is a relation? Certainly. It has already been stated that reflection in the sense of a (cognitive) act is a specific relation also.

Thus, meaning is moulded in the process of reflection of the objective reality in the human mind. But here again we are not concerned with any simple, one-directional relation, for meaning is in a sense a product of the cognitive process of reflection in the human mind of the object to which the sign refers. But at the same time it is an element, and even an instrument, of that process, since without the sign there is not only no communication, but no process of thinking and cognition in general (in particular, because without the sign, and especially the verbal sign, it is impossible to attain to that level of generalization and abstraction which is necessary for thinking in terms of ideas).

Thus at the root of the origin of meaning there is the same process of a generalizing reflection of reality[64], as in the case of thinking in terms of ideas. As in the case of the cognitive process, the process of reflection, the practical experience of human social history rests at the root of the origin of meaning.

Man acquires knowledge of reality by influencing and transforming it. This thesis, which is the principal assumption of Marxist epistemology, may appear trivial. But let us bear in mind that if we accept it, then that implies the recognition of at least two such philosophical "trifles" as the existence of material reality and the reflection of that reality in human consciousness. These are theses which are infrequently to be met with in contemporary philosophy. From the point of view of Marxist philosophy, it is an uncontestable fact that practical experience is at the root of the process of human cognition, in the sense of its origin, its goal, and the criterion of its truth alike. Consequently, that philosophy acquires a new viewpoint on the origin of the meaning of signs (verbal signs above all) and discovers a new aspect of such origin,

---

64 When we have to do with a name of an empty class, that is a name that has a designatum, but no real denotatum, e.g., when reference is made to such imaginary objects as fauns, devils, centaurs, etc., or to abstract properties, such as heroism, here too there is a reflection of reality, although in an indirect way. Ideas of imaginary objects consist of fragments of reality, and abstract properties are reflections of properties, relations, attitudes, behaviour, etc., that are common to elements of a set of objects, i.e., individual material objects (see pp. 219–220).

Intricate social conditions in the form of cognitive and semantic processes are based on human social practice and, conditioned by that practice in a multiple manner, develop on its basis.

When practice intervenes in semantic relations, it is accompanied by the historical element as one of the important factors of the origin of those relations. We are here concerned with a problem which is perfectly well known to linguists and anthropologists who study linguistic meaning. If meaning is genetically conditioned by social practice, then historical changes in that practice must have repercussions in the field of semantic relations which it conditions. This is confirmed by linguistic semasiological studies which often base on this fact their hypotheses concerning the evolution of linguistic meanings (this is especially true of the sociologically-minded trends, such as Meillet's school). This is also a natural explanation of the thesis concerning the national specific features of languages, which refers above all to their semantic aspect in the broad, linguistic sense of the term.

Only such a genetic approach to the problem of meaning, which enables us to interpret it as specific interhuman relations giving rise to the reflection of the objective reality in human minds, conditioned by practical human activity, makes it possible to solve the question of the arbitrary nature of the sign and of conventionalism in linguistic matters. The question is interesting not only from the linguistic but also from the philosophical point of view. (The latter issue, which has wrought so much havoc in philosophy – this refers above all to neo-positivism broadly understood – proves most tellingly that the genetic aspect may not be disregarded in problems of meaning).

Attention was directed in the previous chapter to the problem of the arbitrary nature of the sign. De Saussure's thesis that there is no natural link between the linguistic sign (including its semantic aspect) and the reality to which that sign refers, is, as we know, in conformity with the philosophical standpoint known since the times of Plato. That standpoint was supported *expressis verbis* by Marx when he wrote in *Capital* in connection with the analysis of value: "The name of a thing is something distinct from the qualities of that thing"[65]. But that concept has nothing in common with the view that language is a game with rules fixed by convention, and consequently something that may be changed in an arbitrary fashion (reference is here made to natural languages). This is understood by linguists as well as by sociologists and psychologists who are interested in the study of language problems. I shall refer here to the opinion of the Soviet psychologist whose judgement in these matters I hold in very high esteem, namely S. L. Rubinshtein: "... The sign is fixed arbitrarily, the word has its own history, owing to which it lives its own life, independently of us"[66]. De Saussure, as a linguist who was interested in the study of actual social conditions, also made an explicit reservation against interpreting his opinions in the spirit of conventionalism. Such an interpretation had its say only as regard philosophy.

C. *Meaning and notion*

In order to understand well what we mean when we speak about meaning, it is necessary to analyse the relation between the verbal sign and notion, and that for two reasons. First, it will help us to understand better the meaning of "meaning". Second, it will enable us to uncover certain deeply rooted idealistic views on the relation between meaning and notion, views which, as we shall see, can be encountered even in Marxist circles.

Theoretically, there are two possible solutions to that problem: either the meaning of a word and a notion are two *different* phenomena between which such or other relations may exist, or we have to do with the same phenomenon examined from dif-

---

[65] K. Marx, *Capital*, Vol. I, Foreign Languages Publishing House, Moscow 1954, p. 100.

[66] С. Л. Рубинштейн, *Основы общей психологии* [Principles of General Psychology], Москва 1946, p. 405.

ferent aspects and connected with the cognitive process as a whole. The first opinion prevails in the literature of the subject, including Marxist works. In my opinion it is essentially erroneous and based on a mystification. Consequently, I defend the second opinion and propose to devote this section to its defence.

Usually, the problem is formulated thus: meaning is a linguistic category, whereas notion belongs to the sphere of mental processes, and as such to the field of interest of logic, psychology and epistemology. Now, I claim that such a division of the field to which the categories of meaning and notion belong is erroneous, and that both meaning and notion belong — at least in some respect — to the field of thought (mental) processes properly understood, which by no means excludes specific linguistic interest in the problem of meaning.

It is also possible to find such formulations as: "the word expresses notion", "the word realizes notion", "notion rests at the root of meaning", "notion and meaning are interconnected, but they do not coincide", etc. Now, I assert that such a distinction between meaning and notion, and even opposition of meaning to notion, is pure speculation completely lacking any confirmation in the sciences which investigate the corresponding mental and linguistic processes, and is a tribute paid to the myths of Platonism and nominalism. That tribute is often paid even by those philosophers who themselves issue a call to fight against idealistic mythologization of the problem.

Are the opinions mentioned above to be encountered in fact? Indeed, they are. There is nothing particularly interesting or strange in the fact that, for instance, the intuitionists sharply oppose the word and its meaning to "true" cognition. Likewise, there is no reason to be surprised that Husserl separates notion from meaning, and even opposes one to the other. Nor do we find anything unexpected in, for example, Schlick's neonominalism. Let them so think; such are their views, and the conception of the relation between meaning and notion is no deviation from others of their conceptions.

The situation is different when it comes to the Marxists. If the objections raised above also pertain to some of them, then this is an interesting fact and, to say the least, strange. It is worth explaining how people who declare themselves to be adherents of dialectical materialism come objectively to expound idealistic views in this or that version. And I claim that it *is* so, and consider the present controversy to be a "family quarrel". Documentation to that controversy can be found e.g., in Zvegintsev's *Semasiologia*[67] and in articles by Kovtun and S. A. Fessalonitsky[68], who relate the various opinions held by Soviet authors on the issue. I wish to emphasize that (except for a few somewhat secondary points) I fully agree — both as regards his criticism and the formulation of his own views — with the opinion of P. S. Popov, expounded lucidly in his article "Znacheniye slova i poniatiye"[69].

Let us begin with the question as to whether in fact, when we speak of meaning and notion, we speak of *different* phenomena and categories, phenomena and categories belonging to *different* spheres of human activity? Such an idea is suggested by the majority of the authors mentioned in this connection. Let us take Zvegintsev as an example:

"In all those cases when the sign of equality is placed between notion as a logical category and meaning, words are deprived of all those specific characteristics which transform them into elements of language ...

"As has been pointed out already, the forms of the mutual relations between the two phenomena, closely inter-connected — notion and word — should be understood as the relation

---

67 See e.g. pp. 110–112, 138 et passim.

68 Л. С. Ковтун, „О значении слова" [On Meanings of Words] in *Вопросы языкознания* 1955, № 5; С. А. Фессалоницкий, "Обзор литературы по вопросам связи языка и мышления" [A Review of the Literature Concerning the Connections Between Language and Thinking], in *Вопросы языкознания*, 1953, № 3).

69 *Вопросы языкознания*, 1956, № 6.

of mutual influence, and not as one functioning instead of, or in place of, the other. It is precisely in the mutual influence of word and notion that the formation and development of both notion and the meaning of the word takes place, but each of these phenomena is subordinated to its own regularities, follows its own path, so that they cannot be examined as equivalent phenomena"[70].

I pronounce or hear pronounced the word "horse" and at the same time I experience a thought connected with that fact. They say that when I experience that act of thought I understand the *meaning* of the word "horse", but that there also appears in it the *notion* "horse". As the above quotation from Zvegintsev's work shows, there are authors (probably the majority) who assert in addition that in such cases we have to do with phenomena which, although somehow interconnected, are *different* one from another.

While still for the time being leaving undecided the issue of the identity of the meaning of the word and notion, we may state that in both interpretations we have to do with intricate relationships occurring in the cognitive process and in the communication process. But these relationships are always connected with human psychic life, they are cognitive relations. Any attempt to overstep the framework of such relations leads — as was the case of Husserl — directly to the metaphysics of Platonic ideal entities. Consequently, whoever chooses to avoid Platonism must ask himself: what is the difference between notion and meaning if in both cases we have to do with the relation of reflection by the mind of the objective reality by means of signs? Before we pass to conclusions, let us hear those who defend the thesis that notion and meaning are different categories.

There are two principal variations of their argumentation. Starting from apparently opposing positions they are in fact based on a common foundation.

---

[70] В. А. Звегинцев, *Семасиология* [Semasiology], p. 142.

Such authors as Zvegintsev in his *Semasiologia* quoted above, or Gorsky in his articles published in *Voprosy filosofii*[71], assert that the difference consists in the fact that a *scientific notion* is richer than the ordinary (universally accepted) meaning (of words) since it contains all the essential traits of its designata, including the regularities which govern such designata. They do not deny that ordinary meanings of words coincide with ordinary (every-day) notions, but the existence of *scientific* notions eliminates, in their eyes, the possibility of treating notions and meanings as equivalent categories. The adherents of similar opinion occasionally add that words live long and their meanings (they claim) do not change, whereas notions are changeable and grow richer as science and the world scientific knowledge develop. A criticism of such opinions can be found in Kovtun's article quoted above; I fully agree with his fundamental arguments.

Thus the argumentation of those who would separate notions from meanings is based principally on the claim that in each of these phenomena we have to do with some other cognitive content. In conformity with the reasoning adduced above, that content would be broader in the case of notions. Let this be illustrated by a quotation from *Semasiologia*:

"If we identify notion as a logical category with the meaning of a word, this means that we assume that in the meaning of a word is reflected the entirety of general and essential traits of a definite class of object, with due consideration of the intricate connections of, and relations between, these traits, as established by science at a given level of its development. If this

[71] Д. П. Горский, "К вопросу об образовании и развитии понятий". [Concerning the Formation and Development of Concepts], in *Вопросы философии*, 1952, № 4, and "О роли языка в познании" [On the Rôle of Language in the Process of Cognition], ibid., 1953, № 2. It must be added that Gorsky has changed his opinion and now defends the view, which in my eyes is a correct one, that the meaning of a word coincides with the content of the concept; see his "Роль языка в познании" [The Rôle of Language in the Process of Cognition], in the collection *Мышление и язык* [Thinking and Language], Москва 1957, pp. 82, 85.

is to a certain extent justified with respect to scientific terms, which by means of words appearing here in the capacity of mathematical or chemical formulae fix the results of scientific generalizations, it certainly cannot be applied to words of ordinary language. But scientific terms have a limited range of use and often never leave a very narrow circle of specialists. It is therefore quite clear that the mutual interaction between notion and the meaning of a word should not be investigated by reference to the example of terms"[72].

It is obvious that there is an essential difference between an every-day, colloquial meaning, or a manner of understanding of the word "horse", and a scientific definition of the corresponding notion. Anyone can easily check that for himself by referring in ordinary language dictionaries and in scientific encyclopaedias the same item — "horse". But what are the consequences? Probably only this — that we are referring to wrong places and make unjustified comparisons. Scientific notions should be compared with *scientific terms* and their meanings, and words used in ordinary language and their meanings, with their corresponding ordinary notions. We shall not here go into details concerning the definition of notion, but it is self-evident that since we reject the existence of notions as certain ideal entities, then we must seek them in the field of reflection by human mind of the objective reality; but we have to bear in mind that it is a specific reflection, inseparably connected with the verbal sign (anyhow for Marxists, and also for the overwhelming majority of linguists, notions without words are merely products of imagination). There are different acts of reflection, and there are also different notions. These differences are conditioned not only by our knowledge of the world — which determines our way of seeing it and reflecting it in our minds — but also by the social context of that reflection. Even a most eminent veterinary surgeon, when he describes a military parade involving horses,

[72] В. А. Звегинцев, *Семасиология* [Semasiology], p. 143.

does not, at that moment, have in mind a *scientific* notion of the horse and does not develop in his mind all the essential characteristics of that animal, as he undoubtedly does when lecturing on the horse, its diseases, its anatomy, etc. Thus, there are ordinary notions (in the sense of being very common) and scientific notions. There are also ordinary meanings of words and meanings of scientific terms. It is obvious and easily comprehensible that scientific notions differ by the breadth, depth and precision with which they reflect reality from those contents which appear in ordinary meanings of words. But in no case is it possible to find essential differences between a scientific notion and the meaning of a scientific term.

The second type of argumentation in favour of the difference between notion and meaning starts, as indicated above, from an opposite position: its adherents claim that the meaning of a word is broader than notion since it includes emotional, aesthetic, etc., elements which have no part in notion[73]. Here, too, scientific notion, a product of scientific abstraction, is compared with ordinary meaning of a word or even with an entirety of psychic processes taking place in a person's mind in connection with a given statement, with the entire emotional, aesthetic, etc., context of such processes. Those who defend such a view behave like people of whom Marx once said that having formed an abstract notion of a fruit in general, a notion which disregards the concrete shapes of an apple, a pear, etc., would like to touch that fruit-in-general, taste it, etc. A scientific notion is in fact in a sense semantically broader, and in a sense semantically narrower than an ordinary meaning of a word. But — let us repeat once more — the issue evaporates if we compare ho-

---

[73] That opinion is defended e.g. by В. М. Богуславский in his work "Слово и понятие" [Word and Concept] in the collection *Мышление и язык* [Thinking and Language], pp. 245 ff. It is worth while mentioning that Boguslavsky also accepts the view that a concept is extensionally broader than the meaning of a word, and uses these arguments to show that a concept and the meaning of a word are two different categories, belonging to various fields.

mogeneous categories: a scientific notion with a scientific term and on ordinary meaning of a word with an ordinary notion.

The argument that words have a long life and have unchanging meanings, whereas notions are changeable and continue to develop, is equally groundless, for it assumes what has still to be proved – a difference between notion and the meaning of a word. Moreover, such an assumption is notoriously wrong and unacceptable for, e.g., a linguist, who knows very well that meanings of words change as much as notions. The study of such changes and the law which governs them is daily bread to him.

Thus the argumentation which I have found in the literature of the subject in favour of the thesis concerning the difference between notions and meanings of words turns out to be completely futile. It would be difficult to accept conviction that notions and meanings of words belong to different fields and form different categories. Let us now see what are the philosophical consequences of the thesis which I am criticizing.

It has been said before that view that notion and the meaning of a word are different categories in usually accompanied by statements like "The word realizes the notion", "The word expresses the notion", "Notion lies at the root of meaning", etc. Dozens of examples might be adduced to support that point (the criticism contained in the work by P. S. Popov, quoted above, is extremely instructive in that respect). Now, it is hard to resist the impression that the authors of such and similar formulations pay, whether they want to or not, a double ransom: on the one hand to linguistic hypostases and related objective idealism, and on the other (indirectly), to nominalism. I shall now endeavour to substantiate my opinion.

As stated above, the meaning of a word is tantamount to definite interhuman cognitive relations, inseparably connected with the act of cognition, and therefore with a psychic act. I say "There are horses over there" and I understand that sentence in the same way as does the person I address; in other words, I experience the understanding of the meanings of those words.

What is implied, then, if e.g., the word "horses" realizes or expresses the notion "horses", that that notion rests at the root of the meaning of that word, etc.? The sense of such a statement is univocal: apart from meaning as a cognitive relation, which always appears in some and someone's psychic acts, there is also such an entity, namely notion, which exists *before* meaning and *independently of* meaning, since otherwise it could not "rest at the root, "be realized," "be expressed," etc. This is objective idealism of the first water, and beyond help.

The opinion that meaning is a subjective, and that notion is an objective category, is very popular, and due above all to logicians.

Russell had enough courage to admit to Platonizing in his mathematical and logical conceptions based on such "entities" as numbers, classes, relations, etc. Not all logicians share his courage, but the influence of Platonism is widespread in contemporary logic and the study of the foundations of mathematics. This is due to two causes. One of those causes is the succumbing (regardless of all declarations and warnings) to linguistic hypostases, that is the common suggestion that where there is a name (e.g., "class", "notion", etc.) there must be a real entity designated by that name. The other is suggestion due to one's own mental constructions, a state of being entangled in the meshes of one's own abstraction process.

I shall begin not with notion, but with the still more glaring issue (perhaps because it is less popularized) of the two forms of judgement: as acts of judgement, and as propositions (judgements in the logical sense).

Like the process of thinking, the communication process takes place not through detached, isolated words, but through sentences. Certainly, in every-day speech we do occasionally resort to single words, e.g., "Attention!", "Avalanche!", "Lord!", etc., but these are obviously undeveloped, abbreviated forms of sentences (in other words, sentence equivalents). The sentence, too, serves the purpose of expressing thoughts, and it is only in the context ofa sentence that words acquire meaning by establishing, in the given case, one of the many meanings connected with a given sound. There is of course the traditional grammatical formulation tha. the sentence consists of words and the assertion of many logicians that the sentence is a relation between notions, but psychologists (e.g. Wundt) and philosophers of language (e.g. Marty, Meinong) have long since come to consider sentences and propositions as the two fundamental units of language and thought, and consequently they explain words and notions by placing them in the contexts of sentences. We utter a sentence — for instance "There are horses over there" — and at the same time we think that there are horses over there; we thus experience an appropriate act of judgement. Some authors assert that there is also a proposition (in the logical sense — a judgement *an sich*) the expression of which is the sentence.

What is the origin of that judgement in the logical sense (i.e., proposition)? The need to interpret what Peirce called "token" and "type" in inscriptions. Now here is the sentence written: "There are horses over there". I read that inscription, experience an appropriate judgement and thereby "consume" that inscription as a "token" (in Carnap's terminology, "sign-event"). But the inscription remains, and with it remains the possibility of its being "consumed" many times. It then appears as a "type" (Carnap: "sign-design"), which is characterized by the fact that whenever someone pronounces it comprehendingly, he thereby experiences a definite judgement, namely, that there are horses over there. Each individual case of "consumption" of that inscription is combined with the individual specific experience of a given judgement; the experience of a veterinary surgeon will differ from that of a municipal tax-collector, and the experience of a cowboy will differ from that of a horse-racing fan, etc. All this depends on the type and scope of knowledge about horses, individual past experience, emotional associations, and the like. Yet in all such cases there is some content that is common to all those different individual judgements, something which accounts for the fact that every person who knows English understands the meaning of the sentence in question. Why is that so? There are two explanations possible. One of them simply refers to a similar form of experiencing the meaning of the words spoken out in a given sentence context, characteristic of all those persons who know the language involved. That phenomenon is explained from its various aspects by grammar, the physiology of the brain, etc. But there is also the other explanation: apart from the changing individual judgements, there is some judgement immutable in itself, which is some entity and is, as it were, the standard of all utterances and experiences of that judgement. This is metaphysics of the Platonic type, as endorsed by many. There are mathematicians who claim that it is not possible to build the set theory without admitting that classes exist as real ideal entities, and there are logicians who maintain that propositions as real ideal entities are indispensable. It would be possible to prove (in my opinion, quite irrefutably) that we have here to do with a mystification, that one's own logical construction, obtained by abstraction of those elements that are common to many acts of judgement, is transformed into an independent entity which moreover appears as the standard of those actual acts of judgement. But all this does not seem adequately convincing, so that the unconvinced include even adherents of materialism.

Now the situation is analogous in the case of word and notion, the only difference being that notion stealthily performs both rôles, which in the case of the pair: proposition – judgement are distinguished terminologically. Yet in the case of notion, too, it is possible to distinguish terminologically the act of experiencing notion, and notion in the logical sense. The latter is a product of abstraction, a specific cognitive and logical construction reflecting something which objectively appears, in reality: common properties or traits, common regularities, etc., characteristic of a given class of objects. But no material entity can be a notion. Only an idealist of a peculiar kind, one who hypostatizes a product of his own mind and transforms it into an independent entity, can accept such an entity.

What then is the origin of such views when held by materialists, and by Marxists in particular? They arise from the fear of a nominalist distortion of the problem. This will now be explained in more detail.

As opposed to conceptual realism, the nominalistic doctrine stated traditionally that general concepts are *flatus vocis*, arbitrary verbal constructions. Both materialistic tendencies (negation of ideal entities) and subjective-idealistic tendencies (negation of an objective correlate of notions, e. g., in the case of Berkeley) used to refer to nominalism. In the contemporary philosophical context, neonominalism opened the door wide for the subjective-idealist tendency. Hence, Marxist philosophers see in a nominalistic interpretation of notions (e.g., in the interpretation of Schlick, who simply negates them) a danger of subjective idealism. And rightly so. For in that interpretation the cognitive relation of *reflection* of the object by the subject disappears, as also does the objective correlate of notion as a generalizing reflection of reality; what remains is the *flatus vocis* and a subjective interpretation of mental processes and their products.

In his endeavour to escape that danger, the materialistically-minded philosopher occasionally falls into the wide-spread arms of conceptual realism.

Consequently, the conclusions of these considerations concerning what is said to be a difference between meaning and notion are as follows: not only are there no positive arguments in favour of the conception that meaning and notion belong to different fields, but even a negative argument discloses clearly the idealistic consequences of such a conception.

Yet its defenders have in mind certain real theoretical problems which we do not eliminate by proving the incorrectness of such or other solutions. Is it not possible, then, to suggest a rational solution of that problem, a solution free from the dangers of idealism? In my opinion, this *is* possible.

The controversy between anti-psychologism and psychologism in modern philosophy is focused around the interpretation of psychic processes and the products of such. It is a fact that spiritual processes (we are here interested mainly in *mental* processes) are always *eigenpsychisch* that is, are always "private", are always *hic-et-nunc* processes and processes of *a given* individual. Thus they belong to the sphere of psychic existence and are subject to psychological analysis without which they cannot be understood. But at the same time, it is a fact that there is something in those processes which goes beyond the strictly "private" sphere, that men experience certain thoughts in a similar manner, that "private" psychic processes include elements which are somehow to be found in all men who know the given language and have a certain knowledge concerning the world; these elements are classified in the categories of "notion", "meaning", etc. Now these elements, too, are somehow connected with psychic life and psychic experiences, but cannot be explained *exclusively* in terms of subjective experience. If psychologism represents the tendency to treat the products of human thought *only* as *eigenpsychisch* (and from the historical point of view it did represent that tendency), then it is a conception inadequate theoretically, and is not without reason exposed to the attacks of anti-psychologism (by which I do not at all want to imply that the latter standpoint is automatically correct and flawless).

Both psychologism and anti-psychologism thus find a real basis in the analysis of human spiritual processes and such of their products as notions, meanings, etc. At the same time, these two trends can successfully expose one another, each pointing out the one-sidedness and limitations of the other; consequently, both are unacceptable to a sober researcher. Psychologism usually adopted the standpoint of subjective idealism and was then helpless in face of the problem of regularity and communicability of psychic acts. On the other hand, traditional anti-psychologism is criticized by those who, in the name of scientific sobriety, come out against the fideistic conceptions of the ghosts of "notions in themselves" or meanings as "ideal entities".

The analysis of the thought process reveals the apparent character of the conflict. The thought process is a cognitive process, that is, it is always someone's thought about something, it always transforms the sense data and is objective in the sense that it provides information about reality which exists objectively and independently of human mind. Of course, an epistemological discussion only begins here – a discussion which draws a clear line of division between the adherent of such or other theory of reflection and the opponents of that theory (whose opinions too are very much differentiated). But one fact remains beyond dispute (unless we insist on some metaphysical conception and deliberately reject the testimonies of science, above all psychology and physiology); that fact is that the thought process as a cognitive process takes place not only *with the help* of linguistic means (verbal signs), but also *in an organic unity* with linguistic processes. One might quite well use interchangeably the expressions "to think" and "to experience linguistic processes", since in both cases we refer to the same process of thinking, the only difference being that of a stress on one of its aspects. For there is no separate thought process and separate process of linguistic experience, but there is always the homogenous process of thinking *and* linguistic experience.

From our point of view, this is the focal issue here. The process of thinking *and* linguistic experience will be neither analysed nor explained as yet; we shall revert later on to that problem which is of immense importance not only to epistemology, but also to linguistic and to semantics in its broader theoretical aspect. But certain conclusions must be drawn here and now.

We always think in terms of integrated thoughts which take on the form of this or that proposition – consequently, of a sentence. That sentence does not express the proposition – as it is usually formulated – but is inseparable from it: a proposition without its given verbal form cannot be expressed, and cannot even be formulated in one's mind. Thus, proposition and sentence are not different categories, or even distinct and separate wholes, in spite of the fact that propositions (and judgements) are studied by logic and psychology, and sentences, by linguistics and logic. The thought process always appears in a verbal form – more strictly, it is always linguistic. It is not true that we experience independently a proposition as our thought about something, and some language processes in the sense of understanding the appropriate words and their combinations. Neither it is true that the thought is *later on* joined by its linguistic expression (sentences with appropriate meaning). A sentence is not any expression of any thought or proposition because no such situation is possible in which a thought, or a proposition, without words (even in one's mind) develops *first* and is *later* joined by the words which express it.

Now, what has been said about the integral thought processes, and about such indivisible units of those processes as proposition-sentences, refers *in toto* to such elements as notion-verbal expression (that is, a verbal sign or a combination of such signs). I disregard here the intricate problem of the relations between proposition and notion and between sentence and word, since that transcends the limits of our present analysis. I shall only focus attention on that aspect of the problem which was the starting point of this discussion, namely the relation between notion and verbal expression (a verbal sign or a combination of such signs), the relation between the content of a notion and the meaning of a word (which by way of abbreviation is called the issue of the relation between notion and meaning).

It is necessary to begin with the statement that there are no separate acts of experiencing a notion on the one hand and experiencing a corresponding meaning on the other. When we pronounce with comprehension the word "horse", this is accompanied by a thought process which is the process of understanding that word, or the processes of experiencing its meaning. Nothing else which would be a separate experience of the notion "horse" appears in real cognitive processes. Is then notion a fiction, as was claimed by, for instance, Schlick? By no means! I mean by notion that same product of a generalized reflection of reality which, when examined from the point of view of human communication, is called "meaning".

This statement implies a number of significant consequences, first of all for the interpretation of the interrelations between notion and meaning (the former being understood here not as an act of experiencing a notion, but as the content of a notion). This reveals their *identity*, which is usually veiled by different terminology and obscured by the fact that the analysis of the same cognitive process is approached from various aspects.

And what are the difficulties which may arise from the fact that a certain mental process is analysed as to its various aspects?

The issue of differences in content between notion and meaning is rather simple. As has been pointed out above, these differences appear only when different cognitive processes come in question (for instance, a scientific notion differs from the ordinary meaning of a word, but does not differ from the meaning of that word when used as a scientific term). This point may now be considered elucidated.

There is, however, a serious problem still requiring explanation – how is it possible to pass from an individual act of experiencing a notion or a meaning to the intersubjective communicability of that act and to its repetition within a language community? That problem rests at the root of the speculations on propositions, notions, and meanings, as ideal or intentional entities, etc.

Let us again begin with the statement that every spiritual process, and consequently every thought process, is individual, *eigenpsychisch*. In that sense it is subjective. But at the same time it is an objective process in the sense that it always involves the relation "the subject – the material object". That contention, which is a very essential point in the Marxist theory of reflection, will help us solve the problems which interest us.

First of all, the problem of the repetition of psychic processes connected with definite linguistic expressions (the mechanism of that relation is disregarded here). If we emphasize only the subjective aspect of the cognitive process, namely the fact that it is *eigenpsychisch* (and this is usually done by psychologistic trends), the problem becomes in fact insoluble without the interference of some ideal entities which are the ideal pattern of all acts of judgement, the intentional object, etc. But it suffices to take into account the fact that cognitive acts of subjects which have the same perceptive apparatus, acts relating to one and the same object, are the same (or analogous) for most natural reasons. One has here to agree fully with the argumentation of the naturalists that to understand that repetition of psychic acts no "transcendental 'I'" is necessary; we may add that no ideal entities construed by conceptual realism, no propositions as real ideal objects, etc., are necessary either.

When I say "There are horses over there", and those words are heard by someone who understands English, then both of us understand those words as the information that there are horses in the place which I indicate. Both of us understand these words in the same way, since we know the verbal signs concerned, and these signs are connected in our minds with corresponding perceptive or reproductive representations developed in the process of a cognitive reflection on reality by our minds. In each individual case, these cognitive acts include lots of other experiences connected with our knowledge of the object involved, and with personal emotions which develop as a reaction to the given object (reminiscences, artistic tastes, different systems of values, etc.). But in each of these acts there is always, apart from the elements which account for the differences between them in view of their specifically individual nature, an element which makes them similar owing to which the understanding of the given words is similar, though not identical.

This applies not only to a "common" understanding by listeners of a statement made *hic et nunc*, but also to those cases in which the statement is treated as a "sign-design" and not as a "sign-event". Let us suppose that we still have to do with the inscription "There are horses over there". Whoever reads that inscription in the future comprehendingly (knowledge of English is assumed) or whoever in the future pronounces them comprehendingly, that person will experience – as has been stated above – a psychic act similar to ours. He will understand the sense of the sentence and meanings of the individual words, and will experience psychically the appropriate proposition and notions. Why? Not because there is any proposition as an ideal entity which is actualized in individual experiences, but because in men who understand a given language, similar cognitive experiences are connected with a given statement (the normal state of minds being assumed), which is in turn due to the reflection of the same reality by perception apparatuses which are built and function in the same way. The thing as such is quite simple, although the mechanism of the process is extremely intricate. It does not suffice to refer to language rules the observance of which conditions a similar understanding of statements. That the observance of language does that, is true; but only partially true, since a further explanation is required. What is the origin of those language rules? If we rest satisfied with that partial explanation then we again mystify the problem, this time from the position of nominalism, and open the door wide for conventionalism. Such was the case of the numerous positivist interpretations of the issue with which we are concerned.

Those who are in favour of transforming products of psychic life into ideal entities, refer in their arguments to the differences between, on the one hand, a psychic act treated as a whole and connected with experiencing a certain statement (or with the perception of definite objects, also connected with definite language-and-thought processes), and on the other, the understanding of certain meanings or notions connected with that statement when we ask ourselves or other people such a question as "What does the word ... mean?" or "What is ...?"

It must be clearly realized that the defenders of the alleged difference between meaning and notion, who treat either the former or the latter as *eigenpsychisch* and correspondingly transform the second element of the pair "notion – meaning" into something which is given intersubjectively (as a logical or other entity), have in fact another relation in mind: namely that between, on the one hand, a concrete psychic act (in the sense of a full experience) and, on the other, such products of conscious cognitive reflection, which abstract from many factors, as notion or meaning.

When I utter the sentence "Pigs are mammals" and that statement is heard by people who understand the language I use but differ as to their origin, religion, education, etc., then while they understand that statement in the same way they may differ considerably in the ways they experience it. For the psychic act of understanding that statement will include not only their knowledge of pigs and mammals (differing widely e.g., in the case of a village veterinary surgeon and a London sales girl), but also their emotional reactions connected e.g., with religious prejudicies (a Christian vs. a Muslim), aesthetic evaluations and/or associations (one person may think about a dirty hog wallowing in mud, and another about an amusing, pink, rollicking piglet), certain personal reminiscences, etc. There is no doubt that every psychic act, including those which are *par excellence* cognitive acts, has not only a cognitive content (intellectual description), but also a content consisting of personal emotions (moral valuation, aesthetic assessment, etc.). If that integral psychic act connected with a given statement is called meaning or notion (both cases can be found in the literature of the subject), then of course meaning or notion so understood is transformed into something "private" not only in the sense of the subjective nature of the experience involved, but also in the sense of incommunicability. It is not to be wondered at, then, that in such a case to a "private" meaning or notion one may oppose its "public" partner in the form of the other element of the pair "meaning–notion". But this is only a terminological arbitrariness which merely complicates the issue, for in the proper and original sense of these words neither "notion" nor "meaning" are names of the relation with which the complete psychic act is connected. "Notion" and "meaning" are names of the relation with which are connected *certain particular acts*, based on the specific process of abstraction which is indispensable if one is to answer the question "What does the word ... mean?" or "What is ...?"

All this should not be understood to imply that a conscious process of abstraction takes place every time, and that only then we have to do with meaning or notion. Such conscious processes are very rare, and in principle are elements of research work. Usually, all this takes place through spontaneous learning of a given language, in which process the social experience of a given society is transmitted through language to a member of that society. Hence we usually do not notice that process and remain unconscious of it. On the other hand, scientific (psychological, philosophical, linguistic, etc.) research reveals the selective and abstract character of such categories of the cognitive process as notion and meaning. Of course, the case of scientific notions and meanings of scientific terms seems different from that of ordinary notions and meanings in ordinary language. Although that difference may be of great cognitive significance (especially when it comes to understanding the regularities governing a given phenomenon), nevertheless we have to do only with *a difference in the degree of abstraction.* Notion and meaning are always a result of the work of the mind on some sense data, they are always products of abstraction and selection, and hence they always differ from the cognitive process taken as a whole, with its emotional elements, etc.

Thus notion and meaning are products of abstraction performed on the cognitive process by means of verbal signs. The character of notions and meanings – ordinary in one case, and scientific in the other – depends on the character of that abstraction. The said abstraction, and consequently all notions and meanings, always originates in the intricate system of social relations, as perceived by human consciousness. According to whether a given thought-and-language product is interpreted from the point of view of the thought process or the language process (that is, according to whether we emphasize the one aspect or the other), it appears either as a notion (the content of a notion) or as a meaning of the word. There is no other difference between notion and meaning (of the same type).

Such an interpretation does not lose anything dear to the heart of the gnoseologist, the linguist or the logician. The gnoseologist finds here reference of the cognitive process (in the form of notion or meaning) to objective reality; the linguist, the full and living content of the cognitive process which is manifested in the meaning of words; the logician, the exact and precise content of a scientific notion or a scientific term, which he develops in the form of an adequate verbal or real definition. And all this does without ideal entities and the nominalist interpretation of words and notions as the *flatus vocis*.

So to the conclusions:

(1) The thesis that notion and meaning are different categories with different contents is not acceptable, because the arguments which are supposed to support that thesis prove to be in error, and the adoption of that thesis would imply adoption of objective idealism.

(2) On the contrary, it is to be concluded that notion and meaning are identical as to content, and the difference between them consists only in the fact that the same cognitive process is interpreted from two points of view, different but inseparably linked with one another – that of the thought process in one case, and that of the language process in the other.

(3) Differences as to content, said to appear as between meaning and notion, are in fact differences between a scientific and an ordinary notion, between the meaning of a scientific term and the meaning of words as used in ordinary language.

(4) In order to avoid misunderstandings and logical slips, it is necessary to distinguish as to content between: integral psychic acts which along with cognitive elements include emotional and other elements; ordinary notions and meanings of words; scientific notions and meanings of scientific terms, which like the ordinary ones, are results of a specific abstraction process applied to an integral psychic process and are therefore communicable.

D. The mechanism of the links between sign and meaning

The theories of the sign and meaning can be classified by taking as the criterion of division the views on the character of the links between sign and meaning (this is, e.g., the procedure used by J. Kotarbińska in her paper on the theory of the sign). If we do so, we obtain two large groups of such theories: those which see the links between sign and meaning in association, and those which see it in some specific intentional act. This obviously refers to the psychic aspect of the problem, the psychological mechanism of the links between sign and meaning. I personally do not think that this is the main or decisive issue in the theory of the sign, but it is certainly one of those issues which help us to gain a better insight into the problems of sign and meaning. That is why it is worthy of analysis.

A reference to the links between sign and meaning should not restrict the problem to the meanings of verbal signs. As we already know, verbal signs are of a special nature and hence in their case the links between sign and meaning are specific and different from the case of the remaining categories of signs. This is so because, not to look for other reasons, all other signs are in a sense derivative with respect to verbal signs, and are, in the last analysis, translated into verbal signs. All proper signs except the verbal signs resort to an actual, ready meaning which is, so to speak, "behind them" and is connected with a sign understood autonomously, that is with a definite material object or material event. The situation is quite different with the verbal signs which have no meanings "behind them", are organically linked with their respective meanings and in this sense are, as it is often expressed, "transparent to meaning".

All the proper signs (again except for the verbal signs–analysis of that point will be made later) are linked with their respective meanings by associative links.

This is explained quite simply. As we know, proper signs are artificial signs and are in a way conventional. Definite meanings (or notions, if you prefer it that way) are combined in a purposive and deliberate manner with material sign-vehicles, that is signs in the narrower sense of the term. The sign (in that narrower sense) and meaning are here autonomous, as has been rightly pointed out by Zvegintsev in his cited work on the sign-nature of language[74]; moreover, they are not bound by the rules of the system concerned (e.g., syntax, etc.). That is why the form of the sign-vehicle (i.e., sign in the narrower sense) may be changed in those cases without involving a change in meaning.

For instance, there is a road sign in the form of a triangular board, yellow with red edges, with a black curve in the middle. Whoever knows the road signs also knows that this means: "Beware! Sharp bend in the road!" There is nothing to prevent us from changing the shape and the colour of the board and the shape and the colour of the central drawing; the meaning of the road sign "Beware! Sharp bend in the road!" will not be changed, provided that the convention remains unchanged. The meaning of the expression "Beware! Sharp bend in the road!" is conveyed to us by the sign adopted by a convention. But that meaning exists regardless of the given form of the sign, as the meaning of a definite verbal expression which we combine with this or that material sign-vehicle that exists independently, autonomously and has, besides its meaning, other values as well (e.g., aesthetic

[74] В. А. Звегинцев, *Проблема знаковости языка* [The Problem of the Sign-nature of Language], Москва 1956.

values such as shape, colour, etc.). On what basis, then, do we combine the image of the sign with the thought "Beware! Sharp bend of the road!" On the basis of association which we have developed in the practice of using the given language, in a close connection with the knowledge of convention (from which it does not follow that everything what we associate with a given sign belongs to its meaning).

A similar analysis can be performed in every case of a signal, a symbol, or a substitutive sign *sensu stricto* – that is, in every case when the material form of the sign is joined to a ready meaning of an expression, in other words, when the meaning of a sign is given not directly but through the intermediary of a verbal sign.

The situation changes when we proceed to analyse the verbal signs. Then the associationist conception can hold its ground in special cases only.

First of all, in learning a language.

The child learns a language by association. Let me refer, a trifle spitefully, perhaps, to the testimony of a saint. This is what St. Augustine says in his *Confessions*:

"So I began to reflect. [I observed that] my elders would make some particular sound, and as they made it, would point at or move towards some particular thing: and from this I came to realize that the thing was called by the sound they made when they wished to draw my attention to it. That they intended this was clear from the motions of their body, by a kind of natural language common to all races which consists in facial expressions, glances of the eye, gestures, and the tones by which the voice expresses the mind's state – for example whether things are to be sought, kept, thrown away, or avoided. So, as I heard the same words again and again properly used in different phrases, I came gradually to grasp what things they signified; and forcing my mouth to the same sounds, I began to use them to express my own wishes"[75].

[75] St. Augustin, *Confessions*, trans. by F. J. Sheed, London 1943, p. 11.

Psychologically, there is no other way for an infant to learn a language than by way of associations. The meanings of words, especially when it comes to abstract terms, are learned by the child in action combined with speaking, by numerous repetitions of specific definitions in use.

When an adult who already knows some language is learning a foreign language he also has to do with associations, but of a quite different type. In his case, there is an association of sounds of foreign language words with the words of his mother tongue. That is why in the initial stage of learning the foreign language he thinks in his native language and translates into the foreign language he is learning. He will, of course, really know that (foreign) language only when he ceases to translate and begins to think in that newly-learned language.

But here ends the application of the associationist theory to the verbal signs. All attempts to interpret the meanings of words in terms of that theory are complete failures. Meaning is then treated as the images, representations, thoughts associated with the sounds of words. Such was the standpoint of Russell at the time of the well-known discussion in *Mind* (he then compared language processes to the dancing of the bears provoked by the tune which formerly used to be played when the bears were placed on a hot floor); a similar position was at one time held by Wittgenstein, and among Polish linguists too, e.g. Szober. In the criticism of that opinion, I agree with the arguments set forth by Ajdukiewicz. The interpretation of the verbal signs as sounds with which certain independently existing thoughts are associated is due to a complete disregard of the nature of language processes and thought processes. Not only are there no thoughts existing independently of speech sounds (which is closely connected with the rôle of verbal signs in the abstraction process on the level of thinking in terms of notions), but also there is no thought independent of a system of such signs, that is the syntax of the language concerned, etc. All attempts to reduce meanings of words to associations with images of objects or with representations, extremely primitive even with respect to names, become absolutely unacceptable when it comes to words that are not names and to more complicated combinations of signs in sentences.

Solidarity with the criticism of associationism by no means amounts to solidarity with the alternative proposal advanced by the majority of the critics in the form of the intentional conception of meaning. As I have said, in the case of such philosophers as Ajdukiewicz I consider his acceptance of intentionalism to be a misunderstanding due to a wrong interpretation of Husserl's standpoint. I have previously striven to present that standpoint in the most faithful and unbiased manner, namely by quoting Husserl himself. Let us now see what Ajdukiewicz said on that subject in his paper "On the Meaning of Expressions":

"According to Husserl, that 'act of meaning', or the use of a given phrase as an expression of a certain language, consists in the fact that a sensory content appears in consciousness, by means of which one might think visually about that phrase, should that content be joined by an appropriate intention directed to that phrase. But when a given phrase is used as an expression belonging to a certain language, then that sensory content is joined by another intention, not necessarily a representative one, which is however in principle directed to something other than that phrase itself. Together with the sensory content in question, that intention makes up a uniform experience, but neither the experiencing of that sensory content, nor that intention is a complete, independent experience. Both the one and the other are non-independent parts of the experience as a whole. The meaning of a given expression (as a type) would be, according to Husserl, the type under which that intention joined to the sensory content must fall if the given phrase is to be used as an expression belonging precisely to that language"[76].

The misunderstanding clears. To put it as mildly as possible, that whole passage has — except for the word "intention" —

[76] Ajdukiewicz, op. cit., pp. 19–20.

little in common with Husserl's intentionalist conception. It is not permissible to lose on the way all the luggage of Husserl's metaphysics, without which the interpretation of that author's opinions becomes quite arbitrary and alien to phenomenology. That is why the word "intention" has with Ajdukiewicz a different meaning from that it has with Husserl. It seems that such Polish authors as Ajdukiewicz and those who follow him (Czeżowski, Kotarbińska, and others) are in error in admitting that their views are related to Husserl's. When we analyse what Ajdukiewicz really means by "intention" we find rather certain connections with behaviourist semiotic. Ajdukiewicz has in mind rather a certain readiness to use language in such and such way and not otherwise, and consequently he means certain psychic dispositions. This is not a phenomenological conception; the idea has nothing in common with phenomenology, but plays an important rôle with Morris and others. But that is a secondary point: my intention is not to discuss that issue or to criticize the relative views of Ajdukiewicz, since the problem under discussion is *par excellence* a psychological one, even in the physiological aspect of that term – and such issues are not decided by philosophizing. There also comes a moment in which the method of imparting precision to ideas or notions encounters its natural limit. Such is, at the moment when we have already performed all the preliminary operations, that is when we have rejected all the wrong theories, given precision to the sense of words, etc., precisely the case of the issue of the nature of the links between speech sounds and their meanings. No deduction can provide an answer to the question – in what does the link between sounds and meanings, now under investigation, actually consist? It is a matter which requires experimental studies, and as such belongs above all to experimental psychology and the physiology of the brain. A philosopher can at the best adopt a certain attitude towards such or other proposals as to how to solve the problem, proposals submitted by such experimental disciplines, and that is all. I think it reasonable to confine myself to the statement that the link between sound and meaning in the verbal signs is a connection *sui generis* and does not consist in association. For the rest, as has been said – it belongs to psychology and physiology. Certainly, the results of research in those disciplines are not entirely satisfactory so far; in particular, it does not seems possible to accept the Pavlovian hypothesis concerning the second system of signals as definitively formulated and proved, and consequently as one which fully explains the nature of the verbal signs and the mechanism of the functioning of thought-language. All this is true. But philosophers can only wait for further progress to be made by experimental sciences in the field they are interested in.

5. THE LINGUISTIC APPROACH TO THE ISSUE OF MEANING

References to linguistic meaning are frequently found in the literature of the subject. That might suggest that linguistics has its own, distinct, theory of meaning. This is an obvious misunderstanding, to be refuted at the outset. A theory of meaning – which above all answers such questions as: What is meaning? How is it connected with sign?, etc. – does not and cannot vary according to the discipline concerned. On the contrary, every author, regardless of his speciality and consequent approach to the problem, if he formulates a theory of meaning, always formulates it as a general theory with universal validity.

What, then, lies behind the term "linguistic meaning"? Simply what is indicated in the title of this section, namely an approach to the issue of meaning from the point of view of linguistic interest, that is of those questions which are theoretically significant in specifically linguistic research. This is as natural and comprehensible as the fact that the logician, the sociologist, etc., investigates linguistic problems from the point of view of his specific interest.

What, then, are the theoretical aspects of linguistic interest in the issue of meaning? They have been outlined in a most general manner in the first part of this book, when the nature and scope of semantic interests of linguistics was tentatively explained. But there, the issue of meaning was one of the many issues involved; at present it comes back as *the* issue, which may shed additional light on the questions we are discussing.

As opposoed to the philosopher and the logician, the linguist is in principle not interested in what meaning *is*, but he wants to know what *happens* to meaning, that is, of what (of what language units) it is an attribute, in what way verbal signs mean something, how meaning changes, etc. I agree with Quine[77] that it is possible to study the regularities of something even without knowing what that something is (e.g., ancient astronomers knew very well the movements of planets without knowing what planets are).

According to Quine, there are three principal spheres of the linguistic interest in the issue of meaning:

(1) grammar – the study of those forms which have meaning;

(2) lexicography – the study of synonyms, i.e., expressions which have similar meanings; thus the subject matter of lexicography is to identify meanings, that is to list pairs of synonymous expressions in a language or in a pair of languages;

(3) semantic changes (called by de Saussure diachronic analysis) – the study of changes in meanings and of regularities in such changes.

This classification seems to be particularly lucid and convenient for the presentation of certain general theoretical issues connected with meaning. It is obvious that the linguistic aspect of the issue of meaning is a specialized matter which can be analysed and solved only by linguistic means, applied to concrete comparative material taken from the field of language phenomena. Thus it is not a specific domain of philosophizing, for no general philosophical or logical considerations can replace

---

[77] W. v. O. Quine, "The Problem of Meaning in Linguistics", in W. v. O. Quine, *From the Logical Point of View*, Cambridge (Mass.) 1953.

a concrete linguistic analysis, or refute the results of such. Yet linguistic analysis has broader theoretical implications which are interesting also for a philosopher, and consequently are worth drawing attention to here.

First of all, it is desirable to interest ourselves in the linguistic search for the least meaningful element in language. This is an important problem – not only a linguistic one – involving the general theory of the sign: when have we to do with a verbal sign and what linguistic element is the phonetic vehicle of meaning? We have previously followed Kotarbińska in adopting a division into language signs and verbal signs at the root of which lay precisely the distinction between signs proper (in the sense of elements endowed with meaning) and such phonic elements as give meaningful entities only in definite combinations. In making such a division of the signs belonging to the phonic language, we assume that we know what verbal signs are. But in fact, we simply take over the results of linguistic research and leave detailed analysis to the linguist. This is natural, since the issue can and should be solved above all by the linguist. But let us take at least a look at the problems which he has to face, since in certain circumstances the knowledge of those problems and the solutions of them can also prove significant for specifically philosophical investigations into linguistic questions.

When we speak of verbal signs we assume, as is indicated by the terminology we use, that the word is the least phonic-and-semantic unit (element) of language. But what does that mean? What is a word? Having asked that question we encounter difficulties of two kinds. The first is that there are expressions which formally consist of several independent words and which as an "equivalent" of a single notion (let us bear in mind that we have rejected the conception that independent notions and meanings enter into relations with one another) have the semantic function of a single word (e.g., "the author of *Romeo and Juliet*"). The second difficulty is that the language element which the grammarians call "the word" is often a compound whole the parts of which (e.g., the stem of the word, prefixes, suffixes) have specified meanings. This point requires a more detailed analysis. The issue is further complicated by the fact that among linguists themselves there is no universal agreement on the most fundamental appropriate problems; moreover, the terminology is not well established, and occasionally shows striking differences when the works of different authors are compared. Structuralism, phonology, the behaviourist trend, and psycholinguistics represent in many respects different standpoints.

The point is that when we listen comprehendingly to someone's speech and perceive such phonic units as the syllable, the word and the sentence, then from the theoretical point of view the principal difficulty consists in drawing a strict line of demarcation between the word and the other linguistic units. In analysing the verbal signs, we notice a number of their component elements, above all — according to some authors — the phonemes, the morphemes and the semantemes. Whereas the phoneme is the least phonic unit in the system of a given language (and as such is not merely identical with a sound), and the problem of its "meaning" is confined to definite functions within that system, owing to which it serves to form and to distinguish words, the morphemes and the semantemes clearly perform semantic functions. By the semantemes I mean here (following the definition given by Vendryes) those language elements the meaning of which coincides with the content of the given notion (e.g., horse), and by the morphemes, those elements which are non-independent parts of words and express relations (e.g., horse-*s*). That terminology more or less coincides with the differentiation into stems on the one hand and affixes and flexional elements on the other. It is not my intention to enter here into the details of linguistic controversies (whether factual or terminological) around such matters. What is important for us is the distinction made by the grammarians between the special categories of meanings: *lexical* and *grammatical* (which is a result of the distinction of semantemes and morphemes in words).

This touches upon the question raised at the beginning, and very important for understanding of the whole problem – namely the question of differences in the approach to meaning between philosophy and linguistics. The linguist is not interested in the "essence" of meaning, he does not ask, *what meaning is*, but asks, *how* linguistic entities *mean something*. This is the origin of the differentiation between lexical and grammatical meaning, and also the distinction between other categories of meaning, such as principal and marginal meaning, autonomous and synsemantic meaning, etc. This must be realized clearly if a serious confusion of ideas is to be avoided.

Lexical meaning involves no particular difficulties. It is merely meaning in the sense of the appropriate notion experienced in connection with the use of the word in question. And the linguist does not ask, what meaning is, but what it implies in the given case, that is, he asks about a synonym in the same or some other language. The lexical description of the word "horse" coincides with the content of the notion "horse".

On the other hand, grammatical meaning is connected with the morphemes concerned. It is always connected with lexical meaning; it refers to the properties and relations of the given verbal signs, and through their intermediary to the properties and relations of the real objects which are reflected in thought-language (e.g., gender, number, tense, various relations, etc.).

Syntactic meaning is, so to speak, an extension of grammatical meaning; it is sometimes interpreted so broadly that the meaning of morphemes (grammatical meaning) becomes one of its elements. In the case of syntactic meaning, we always have to do with some meaning added to the lexical meaning, and referring to certain relations, properties, and so on, of objects, actions, etc. This, in turn, is connected not only with morphemes, but also with the order of words fixed by the syntactic rules and with what are known as auxiliary words. Syntactic rules are particularly important in those languages where poorly developed morphology forces the hearer or reader to establish, on the strength of the order of words only, relations between the words in a sentence[78].

A rôle similar to that of the morphemes is played by such words as "and", "or", etc., called sentential conjunctions (identical with sentence-forming functors or operators), definite and indefinite articles to be found in certain languages (e.g., "the" and "a" in English) and other auxiliary words (e.g., the auxiliary verbs in such forms as "I *have* come"). They differ from the morphemes in that formally they are separate words, whereas the morphemes are always syllables or strings of syllables organically connected with a word. This difference, however, is purely formal, since auxiliary words can appear only in the company of other words and add to the meaning of such. The separation of them is a secondary issue, which is being solved in various manners in the various ethnic (natural) languages, and can be explained on historical grounds.

The question raised above leads to the division of language signs into autosemantic and synsemantic. That division, which harks back to Aristotle's division of language signs into categorematic (those which can play the rôle of subject or predicate in a sentence) and syncategorematic (those which cannot independently perform such functions), has been introduced by Anton Marty[79]. The division into autosemantic and synsemantic signs does not coincide with the Aristotelian classification, or with the division into words and such word parts as morphemes. Nevertheless, it is the same idea of distinguishing between those signs which in a given language and sign system have independent meanings, and those which can perform their semantic

---

[78] Let us take an example drawn from *Logic and Language* by B. F. Huppe & J. Kaminsky, New York 1956, p. 77: "Keep the home fires burning — Fires keep the home burning — Keep fires burning the home — Keep home the burning fires".

[79] See above all his *Untersuchungen zur Grundlegung der allgemeinen Grammatik und Sprachphilosophie*, Vol. 1, Halle a. S. 1908.

functions only in the company of certain other signs, as the parts or adjuncts of such other signs.

Other issues that are interesting from the general theoretical point of view are the distinction between *principal* and *marginal* meaning, and between *universal* (usual) and *occasional* meaning. This is important not only in lexicography but also in the semantic analysis of statements in ordinary and scientific language; it involves the study of polysemy and homonymy of words — that is, those cases in which the same phonic form of the sign covers different, although related, meanings (polysemy), or totally different meanings (homonymy), or even contradictory meanings (antonymy such as, e.g., in the case of the German word "aufheben" which according to circumstances may mean both "to abolish" and "to preserve"). Now, especially in the cases of polysemy it is essential to extract the principal meaning of the word concerned, around which marginal meanings are grouped historically, in conformity with certain regularities studied by linguistics. The distinction between usual (universally adopted) and occasional meaning is simply a special case of the differentiation indicated above. Occasional meaning is shaped in a new context in which a given word appears, which is made use of by literature — in the form of metaphors (literal and metaphorical meaning).

Now that distinction between, on the one hand, principal and usual meaning and, on the other, marginal and occasional meaning, indicates the extremely important issue of the rôle of context in the meaning of verbal signs. Marginal and occasional meanings result, as already indicated, from new, specific contexts of the verbal signs concerned. But the question has broader aspects in view of the notorious ambiguity (in the sense of polysemy and homonymy) of every verbal sign. The standpoint adopted by Kurylovich is worth quoting here; in his article in Russian "Zametki o znachenii slova" ("Notes of Meanings of Words") he expresses his scepticism concerning the category of universal (common) meaning and lays particular stress on the grasping of principal meaning. He says:

"Universal meaning is an abstraction; the future will show whether and how far it is useful and applicable to concrete linguistic problems. My personal protest against the introduction of that notion is based on the impossibility of integrating elements that are different *qualitatively*, namely communicative content and emotional (stylistic) shades. In my opinion, the most important is *principal* meaning, that which is not defined by a context, whereas the remaining (partial) meanings add elements of the context to the semantic elements of principal meaning"[80].

I agree with those who – contrary to the universal complaints (especially among the logicians) concerning the imperfection of language due to the ambiguity of its expressions – assert that not only the ambiguity but also the vagueness of verbal signs is a necessary phenomenon, even advantageous from the point of view of the communicative effectiveness of language[81]. This is not tantamount to an approval of obscurity, since vagueness and obscurity are two different notions. Whereas the vagueness of an expression is due (I repeat here the idea of M. Black from his essay on "Vagueness") to the reference of the sign to many objects in the field of reference, obscurity arises from the association of a limited number of alternative meanings with the same phonetic form. Thus the point is to enable the hearer (the interpreter of the sign) to make a selection among those alternative meanings, a selection achieved through the context in which the sign stands. Obscurity is related to the context, as Black says in his *Critical Thinking*[82]. This is a correct concept, bringing out the broader, theoretical sense of the issue of context.

---

[80] *Вопросы языкознания*, 1955, № 3.

[81] See above all Max Black, *Language and Philosophy* (the essay on "Vagueness"), and *Critical Thinking* by the same author (New York 1952, the chapter on "Ambiguity"). The same issue is discussed by Bertrand Russell in *The Analysis of Mind* and in an essay also entitled "Vagueness".

[82] Cf. e.g., p. 198.

Linguistic studies on meanings of words have not only shown that words take of definite meanings (that is, the choice of one of the many possible meanings is made) only in a context which establishes a definite universe of discourse, but have led also to the extremely interesting theory of semantic field and to experimental methods of the measurement of meanings.

The theory of semantic field can be traced back to, above all, German tradition (Herder, Humboldt) and in contemporary linguistics is associated with the names of L. Weisgerber, Jost Trier, Porzig, Ipsen and others. From the philosophical point of view it has been developed by Karl Bühler (*Sprachtheorie*, Jena 1934). Its ideas are aimed chiefly against an isolated study of language elements and emphasize the integral nature of language systems and the influence of context on the meanings of expressions. That rational idea is, however, overlaid by thick strata of idealism, especially in the German tradition (Weisgerber, Trier). According to Trier, language "creates" reality. "Semantic field" is a part of the lexical stock of a given language, internally coherent and strictly delineated from other "fields" with which it is in contact. How such "fields", e.g., of joy, garments, weather, etc., are formed – that depends on the spirit of the language concerned. In this way "semantic fields" make up a picture of the world and a scale of values in a given language. That evidently idealistic conception, permeated by the Hegelian idea of "the spirit of the nation", is strikingly correlated with those philosophical theories of language which from the positions of conventionalism make this or that "perspective of the world" depend on "the choice of language".

The method of investigating meanings by building "semantic fields" has been applied to concrete language by the school of Trier, Weisgerber and Porzig. As a matter of information, I shall mention here another, experimental, method of studying the meanings of expressions, which has been developed in the United States by Osgood and his collaborators[83]. The central idea of

[83] Ch. E. Osgood, G. J. Suci & O. H. Tannenbaum, *The Measurement of Meaning*, Urbana 1957.

that method consists in analysing meanings by a "semantic differential": meanings are established not on the strength of abstract lexical operations, but on the basis of experimental research as to how a given word is understood, and how it is being actually used by those who speak the language in question. That method too, although not based on the conception of the "semantic field", starts from the assumption that context influences meaning.

The linguists distinguish still other categories of linguistic meanings. They speak of etymological meaning, as distinct from actual meaning, which is important for the study of the history of language; further, they speak of emotional meaning as distinct from communicative meaning, the issue here being whether emotional elements belong to the verbal signs, or not, etc.

Finally, the largest and the most important section of the linguistic study of meanings covers investigations concerning changes in meanings and the regularities to which they are subjected. These matters are of great significance for the entire study of language as a whole, since they reveal its historical and social nature. They are, however, considerably specialized, and the reader is therefore referred to works devoted to those problems. My intention has been only to give general information on matters which may have a wider theoretical significance.

CHAPTER FOUR

THE COMMUNICATIVE FUNCTION OF LANGUAGE

"Für die Philosophen ist es eine der schwierigsten Aufgaben, aus der Welt des Gedankens in die wirkliche Welt herabzusteigen. Die unmittelbare Wirklichkeit des Gedankens ist die *Sprache*. Wie die Philosophen das Denken verselbständigt haben, so mussten sie die Sprache zu einem eignen Reich verselbständigen. Dies ist das Geheimnis der philosophischen Sprache, worin die Gedanken als Worte einen eignen Inhalt haben. Das Problem, aus der Welt der Gedanken in die wirkliche Welt herabzusteigen, verwandelt sich in das Problem, aus der Sprache ins Leben herabzusteigen ... Die Philosophen hätten ihre Sprache nur in die gewöhnliche Sprache, aus der sie abstrahiert ist, aufzulösen, um sie als die verdrehte Sprache der wirklichen Welt zu erkennen und einzusehen, dass weder die Gedanken noch die Sprache für sich ein eignes Reich bilden, dass sie nur *Äusserungen* des wirklichen Lebens sind".

(K. Marx, F. Engels: *Die deutsche Ideologie*)

THE communication process and the related sign-situation, i.e., the situation in which material objects and processes become signs in the social process of semiosis, have served us as the starting point and the basis of the analysis of such semantic categories as sign and meaning. But such analysis shows that in order to understand not only the communication process but also what sign and meaning are, it is necessary to refer to language by means of which we communicate with one another on the social plane and within which material objects and processes may, under definite circumstances, function as signs, that is, acquire definite meanings. That is why language and speech are raised to the rôle of fundamental categories in all semantic research. Moreover, the linguist, the logician, the psychologist, the anthropologist, etc., likewise refers to language and speech. Unfortunately they are not always in agreement in matters pertaining to those categories. They often make declarations which not only differ one from another, but are incompatible one with another; that arises from the multiplicity of aspects of the phenomenon under investigation, to the diversity of interests of the various disciplines concerned, and to differences in standpoints (mainly philosophical, although very few people in this connection call a spade a spade) concerning the problems of language. It is very important, therefore, to analyse the communicative function of language precisely from the point of view of its philosophical implications.

1. LANGUAGE AND "LANGUAGES"

I have to begin by making plain what I mean by "language" and by "speech". Otherwise I should risk serious misunderstandings which might considerably diminish the value of further analysis. I mean here neither an all-round analysis of those phenomena to which these terms are being applied as names, nor the analysis of the many points of view represented in the literature of the subject. I merely want to impart as much precision to the terms "language" and "speech" as will make it possible to discuss freely the cognitive and the communicative function of language.

We are interested here above all in the phonic language, which by reason of some of its properties is language *par excellence* and lies at the root of all other communication systems in civilized societies. That is why, in view of its functions and universality, it is understood as language *tout court*, if no other qualifications are added to indicate that some other special language is meant in a given particular case.

We know from the foregoing consideration concerning the signs that various factors come into play in the analysis of language; the aspects of that analysis may also be different, and as a result the definitions of language may vary. Some authors lay stress on the phonetic, and others on the semantic, aspect of language. The view-points on language differ as between the grammarian, the literary historian, the lexicographer, the sociologist, and the psychologist, and last but not least the man-in-the-street who is no specialist in any of the social sciences. Every one of them can, and often does, give his own, partial definition of language. These partial definitions are often pertinent and correct. Yet Mario Pei[1] is right in stating that precisely because of the pertinence and correctness of *all* those partial definitions, language as a phenomenon is something more than each of such definitions implies. Both the phonic and the semantic aspect, both the grammatical forms and categories and the function of the intermediary in the human process of communication, taken separately, are necessary, but not sufficient, conditions for the emergence of language processes.

In his book on the origin of language, Révész[2] lists its various definitions. The list is made somewhat at random, but it enables a certain typology: some authors emphasize the sign aspect of language and its arbitrary nature, others, in connection with its sign nature stress the expressive function of language, others, its denotative function, still others adopt psychologist, intentionalist, or behaviourist standpoints[3]. An exhaustive definition

[1] M. Pei, *The Story of Language*, London 1957.

[2] G. Révész, *The Origins and Prehistory of Language*, London 1956.

[3] Here is a footnote from Révész, op. cit., pp. 126–127, which includes selected definitions of language as given by the various authors:

EBBINGHAUS: Language is a system of conventional signs that can be voluntarily produced at any time. CROCE: Language is articulated, limited sound organized for the purpose of expression. DITTRICH: Language is the totality of expressive abilities of individual human beings and animals capable of being understood by at least one other individual. EISLER: Language is any expression of experiences by a creature with a soul. B. ERDMANN: Language is not a kind of communication of ideas but a kind of thinking: stated or formulated thinking. Language is a tool, and in fact a tool or organ of thinking that is unique to us as human beings. FROBES: Language is an ordered sequence of words by which a speaker expresses his thoughts with the intention of making them known to a hearer. J. HARRIS: Words are the symbols of ideas both general and particular: of the general, primarily, es-

would be cumbersome and overloaded, and its value more than doubtful. The definition ought to bring out not all aspects of the problem, but its aspects from some distinct point of view, the most important aspects and those connected with objective requirements of research. One of such aspects – in my opinion of extreme importance – is the social aspect of language as an

---

sentially and immediately; of the particular, only secondarily, accidentally and mediately. HEGEL: Language is the act of theoretical intelligence in its true sense, for it is its outward expression. JESPERSEN: Language is human activity which has the aim of communicating ideas and emotions. JODL: Verbal language is the ability of man to fashion, by means of combined tones and sounds based on a limited numbers of elements, the total stock of his perceptions and conceptions in this natural tone material in such a way that this psychological process is clear and comprehensible to others to its least detail. KAINZ: Language is a structure of signs, with the help of which the representation of ideas and facts may be effected, so that things that are not present, even things that are completely imperceptible to the senses, may be represented. DE LAGUNA: Speech is the great medium through which human co-operation is brought about. MARTY: Language is any intentional utterance of sounds as a sign of a psychic state. PILLSBURY-MEADER: Language is a means or instrument for the communication of thought, including ideas and emotions. DE SAUSSURE: Language is a system of signs expressive of ideas. SCHUCHARDT. The essence of language lies in communication. SAPIR: Language is a purely human and non-instinctive method of communicating ideas, emotions and desires by means of a system of voluntarily produced symbols.

To this I should like to add a number of other definitions which, in my opinion, are more important than many of those quoted by Révész:

CARNAP: A language, as e.g. English, is a system of activities or, rather, of habits, i.e., dispositions to certain activities, serving mainly for the purposes of communication and of co-ordination of activities among the members of a group. GARDINER: As a first approximation let us define speech as the use, between man and man, of articulate sound-signs for the communication of their wishes and their views about things. MORRIS: A language in the full semiotical sense of the term is any intersubjective set of sign vehicles whose usage is determined by syntactical, semantical, and pragmatical rules. SZOBER: We shall call phonic language the set of sounds used for the purpose of establishing communication with one's milieu or reproduced in one's mind for the purpose of clearly realizing one's own thought.

instrument by means of which men acquire knowledge about reality and communicate one to another the information thus acquired and the related emotional, aesthetic, volitional, etc., experiences. If we adopt such a starting point and such an aspect of research, we can attempt a general definition of the categories in which we are interested.

By language *tout court* I mean, as already indicated, the phonic language. And in conformity with the requirements formulated above, the phonic language is defined as *a system of verbal signs which serve to formulate thoughts in the process of reflecting objective reality by subjective cognition, and to communicate socially those thoughts about reality, as also the related emotional, aesthetic, volitional, etc. experiences.*

This definition does not cover a number of aspects of language phenomena which certainly are important from this or that point of view, but it high-lights such aspects as are, in my opinion, of primary importance in the study of language problems.

The first point is that the phonic language is a *system* of verbal signs, i.e. articulated sounds subject to grammatical, syntactical and semantic rules of *a given* language. Hence why an articulated sound becomes a sign, that is, has meaning, only and exclusively *within* a given language system.

Secondly, the suggested definition emphasizes the connection between language and thinking, and thereby the functions of language in the process of *reflecting* objective reality in the subjective cognition of that reality understood in the broadest sense of the term – that is, it covers both the material world and the world of man's psychic experiences, which in the last analysis are reducible to a function of that material world. This places the conception of language on a materialist foundation and dissociates it from all conventionalist theories, which endeavour to transform the rules that govern the verbal signs in a given language system into autonomous and arbitrary rules.

Thirdly, the definition stresses the communicative function of language in the sense of a social transmission of the results of both the cognitive process and subjective emotional, volitional, etc., experiences.

The distinction between "language" and "speech" rests on easily observable facts. The theoretical aspect of the issue has been raised in contemporary literature only by de Saussure, although in the terminological sense all the languages (I refer here to our cultural circle and its traditions), beginning with the distinction between γλῶσσα and λόγος in Greek and *lingua* and *sermo* in Latin, accept the difference between "language" as a system of linguistic facts and "speech" as the name of a type of action. Following de Saussure, that theoretical distinction has been adopted in all contemporary linguistics. Gardiner distinguishes between speech as an activity with clearly utilitarian ends in view, and language as a precise knowledge pertaining to communication by means of verbal signs[4]. The differentiation has been adopted in the Marxist literature of the subject, linguistic, psychological, etc. In his *Psychology* (in Russian) S. L. Rubinshtein defines speech as language functioning in the context of individual consciousness, and compares the difference between speech and language to the difference between individual and social consciousness.

The definition of the phonic language I have suggested above can easily be extended (with certain modifications) to cover other "languages". The human process of communication takes place not only by means of the phonic language, but also through other means of communication, either auxiliary or substitutive in relation to the phonic language. In my opinion, it is unnecessary pedantry to reserve the term "language" for the phonic language, as has been suggested by e.g., Leonard Bloomfield. As regards the term "speech", our direct linguistic intuition induces us rather to reserve it for the action of communication by means of the phonic language, and to use it in other cases only by way of a metaphor (e.g., when we say that the features

[4] A. Gardiner, *The Theory of Speech and Language*, Oxford 1951, p. 62.

of one's face tell us something, etc.). By contrast, the term "language" is used to denote various systems of communication, and in this case linguistic intuition enables us to speak equally of the phonic language and the language of gestures, symbols, colours, etc. The point is not to strive for some pedantic univocality of the term "language" unattainable in practice, but to distinguish the various meanings of that term according to a given context, and to realize precisely the differences between such meanings.

Consequently, as in the case of the phonic language, we may say that by language we mean *every system of signs of a definite type which serves the purpose of human communication* (including the communication of both the contents of acts of cognition and of emotional, etc., experiences) *and which in certain cases may serve to formulate thoughts in the process of cognition* (that is, in the process of reflection of objective reality in its subjective cognition). Two elements require explanation here: (1) the nature of the preference for the system of verbal signs as compared with other systems of signs; and (2) the nature of the difference between those two classes of systems as concerning their rôle in thought processes. As we shall see, these two issues are interrelated.

First of all it must be said that if articulated sounds and verbal signs have come to form the foundation of the system of the phonic language, which has thus risen to the status of the "natural" language, this has been due to the *particular usefulness* of that language in the thought and communication processes, and not to the fact that *only* the verbal signs can perform that function. The best proof that the latter is not the case is to be found in the fact that certain people who are physically handicapped use other systems of signs; for instance, the deaf-mutes use a language of gestures, and the blind, a tactile language. The fact that in both cases we have to do with a language learned especially for the purpose, and taken over from those who use the phonic language and *translate* the categories of the latter into a language of gestures or touch, does not alter the fact that other systems of signs are in a position to replace verbal signs (we have to do there with situations in which verbal signs are inaccessible to the persons concerned) in both the thought and the communication process. Nevertheless, verbal signs are superior to other signs in the possession of such practical values as the ease and scope with, and in, which they reach the hearer, their not being dependent on light (indispensable in the case of all the visual signs) nor on direct contact (indispensable in the case of all the tactile signs), and, finally, immense possibilities for forming combinations and differentiation in shades, etc.

These properties have raised the phonic language in human history to the rôle of *the natural* language the signs of which have become "transparent to meaning." We think in terms of that language and we are unable to think otherwise, because from our earliest childhood society inculcates in us the ability to think in terms of language. *Every* other system of signs is thus either auxiliary in relation to the phonic language (e.g., facial and other gestures which accompany speech, etc.) or is a specific substitute for that language, a translation of it into another system of signs (all the codes, etc.); *every* such system must then in turn be translated into terms of the phonic language. That is why these other languages are usually means of communication under definite circumstances, but not an instrument of thought. *Theoretically*, the latter alternative is possible too, and therefore the definition states that in certain cases those other languages (e.g., languages of gestures, touch, etc.) *may* serve to formulate thoughts in the process of cognition. *In reality*, this is observed only in connection with those disabilities which make it impossible for the persons affected to adopt the phonic language in the course of the social educational process. In ordinary cases, that process accounts for the fact that we are unable to free ourselves from the habit of thinking in terms of (phonic) language. Even in the case of brain injuries causing aphasia, thinking in terms of verbal signs does not disappear completely.

Thus other languages may, and actually do, appear, alongside the phonic language which, in view of the way it is being assimilated by man in the process of social education, we correctly treat as the natural language. Some of such languages, namely those which are auxiliary to the phonic language (facial and other gestures, etc.) are no less "natural" than the phonic language. All others are clearly artificial, and even arbitrary, as are all the codes or systems of mathematical, logical, etc., signs. Those systems, usually called "deductive languages", merit a few remarks.

Let us begin with the statement of the linguist L. Bloomfield, which will facilitate further discussion.

"Our numeral digits illustrate the advantage of a well arranged written symbolism. Simple discourses which move entirely in this domain can be carried out by means of a calculating machine. Short of this extreme case, we may cite cable codes, where the written forms are revised in the direction of brevity; or, again, systems of notation such as are used in symbolic logic, where a stock of symbols is so devised as to yield extremely simple rules of discourse. The construction of a calculating machine or the rules of arrangement and substitution in a system of logistics require great care end present great interest: it is decidedly advantageous to study them for their own sake and without reference to the linguistic end points of the sequences in which they operate. Nevertheless, if they are to operate, they must be so planned that, starting with speech-forms, they yield speech-forms in the end. No serious use would be made of a calculating machine, or of a code, or of a system of logistics, which failed to deliver a linguistically significant end result. By way of contrast, the reader may find it not without value to consider such non-linguistic systems as musical notation, say for the piano, or, again, the moves of a game of chess. Persons unaccustomed to the consideration of language are prone to the error of overlooking the linguistic character of notational or mechanical subsidiaries of language and viewing them as independent systems; at the same time, they may resort to the metaphor of calling these systems 'languages'. This metaphor is dangerous, since it may lead to the notion that such systems can liberate us from uncertainties or difficulties which inhere in the working of language"[5].

This quotation shows that L. Bloomfield – an eminent authority on linguistics, to whom neo-positivists eagerly refer – simply refuses the name of "language" to the various deductive calculi and systems. The point is interesting in that for many a mathematician and logician these calculi and systems are precisely languages *par excellence*, whereas the so-called natural (phonic) language is treated by them rather laconically because of the ambiguity and lack of precision of its expressions.

These may seem to be extremely radical formulations, but only because I have drawn conclusions from what implicitly results from certain opinions actually to be met with. But this is an inessential point, since we are not quarrelling either about words or about the honour and the moral authority of this or that language. What is at stake here is a much more important point, philosophical in nature, which may in no case be disregarded: the understanding of the relation between the formalized languages and the natural language, the understanding of their *derivative* nature in relation to the linguistic hinterland in the form of the natural language on which, as to origin and interpretation, they are based.

We shall not be concerned here with the ambiguity of the expressions belonging to the natural language and to their lack of precision, or with the contrasting properties of the formalized languages. This issue will be raised again later on. But here I should like to point out that that ambiguity, which is a shortcoming of the natural language from the point of view of certain research procedures, is at the same time its forte from the point

[5] L. Bloomfield, "Linguistic Aspect of Science", in *International Encyclopedia of Unified Science*, Vol. 1, Pt. 1, University of Chicago Press, 1955, pp. 228–229.

of view of the communication process: its great flexibility enables it to rise to the occasion when it has to serve as a means of expression in the social process of communication.

The point now under discussion is very simple, but also very important. As mentioned in Part I, at the stage when the phonic language already exists, all other languages, in particular such products of high spiritual culture as the formalized calculi and the deductive systems, sometimes called formalized *languages*, can, and do, develop only on the basis of the natural (phonic) language as specific translations and interpretations of such.

In imparting precision to such terms as "language", "speech" and "languages" we have come to face certain factual problems which indicate the path of further analysis. These are above all the two great issues in the theory of languages which have been covered by the definition of language suggested above, and now require further discussion:

(1) the relation between thinking in terms of language, and reality;

(2) the relation between thinking in terms of language, and the communication process.

2. LANGUAGE AND REALITY

Is the language in which we think something concerning reality when we learn what that reality is like, is the language by which we inform others about what we think about that reality with which we become acquainted, somehow connected with that reality? Or is it a product of an arbitrary process? An answer to this question is indispensible for the solution of any issue concerning sign, meaning, communication, etc. Every theory or philosophy of language is concerned *explicite* or *implicite* with the relationship between language and reality.

Two extreme standpoints are to be found in the literature of the subject in this connection. One of them starts from conventionalist assumptions and maintains that language is a product of an *arbitrary process*, and its rules are made in the same way as the rules of any game. The other standpoint is that language is an *image* of reality or that the structure of language resembles the structure of reality referred to in that language, and that this is why language can inform us about that reality. In my opinion, both these standpoints are erroneous and hamper a proper understanding of the rôle of language and its mechanism.

The concept of language as a game of chess was common among the neo-positivists. It has been held by Hempel, Ajdukiewicz, Carnap, Ayer, and others. There were, of course, differences between the standpoints of the various philosophers and logicians, but the essential points of that concept were common to all of them. It was the conviction that language, like logic (cf. Carnap's notorious "principle of tolerance"), can be constructed in an arbitrary manner by adopting *ad libitum* such or other assumptions, rules, etc., as in the case of devising a game. While rejecting such suggestions (just because language is one of those elements of culture which are most resistant to all arbitrariness and novelty), it is worth while to analyse what was their origin. Personally, I am convinced that the decisive rôle was played by an analogy with deductive systems and by the confusion of natural languages with formalized languages. In the case of a formalized language one can and may in fact behave in an arbitrary way, choose axioms, transformation rules, etc., at will. But the error consists in a mechanical transfer of what is valid for the "languages" of deductive theories on to an analysis of natural languages. This is an error, first of all, because they perform different functions and have different mechanism of their own. And now to the principal arguments for such a point of view. First, every game presupposes a knowledge of its rules, which are formulated in a phonic language. The dependence of a game on language is unindirectional. Should we then choose to treat language as a game, and verbal signs as counters handled in conformity with the rules of that game, we should arrive at a vicious circle in reasoning: how could we formulate and understand the rules of such a game?

Secondly, and closely connected with the argument cited above, language, in contra-distinction to a game, which is played merely for its own sake, has a communicative function, and verbal signs, as contrasted with counters in a game, refer to objects that are not words — they point "outside themselves" and that is why they are signs[6].

The error appears when that conception is confronted with the definition of the sign. Every sign, of course, functions as such only in a given sign-situation and it related to the system of a given language and to the reality about which it communicates something. Consequently, phonic language, which is a system of definite (verbal) signs is also connected with such a relativization and may be treated as a product of an arbitrary process only if it becomes a play of intellect and ceases to be a language in the proper sense of the term, that is, when it ceases to perform the fundamental functions of language in the process of cognition and communication.

Equally erroneous is the opposing conception, which treats language as an image of the reality referred to in that language. This is a vulgarized theory of the reflection of reality by language; being vulgarized, it can be refuted easily. As an example, one might quote the standpoint adopted by Wittgenstein in his *Tractatus*, or at least a certain interpretation of that standpoint, according to which the structure of a statement would be such as is the structure of the reality concerned. It seems sufficient to retort (as Max Black, Ryle, Ayer, and others have already done)[7] that in practice the sentence "the structure of a statement

[6] This argumentation against interpreting language as a game is drawn from *The Field Theory of Meaning* by Andrew Paul Ushenko, Ann Arbor 1958, pp. 14–15.

[7] Cf. e.g., M. Black, "Wittgenstein's 'Tractatus'", in M. Black, *Language and Philosophy*, New York 1949, pp. 152–165, and J. O. Urmson, *Philosophical Analysis*, Oxford 1956, pp. 141–145.

is the same as the structure of reality" has no comprehensible meaning. That is so because reality does not consist of any elements or parts to correspond to the elements or parts of sentences uttered.

Language is not an arbitrary game in which verbal signs serve as counters, nor is it a picture, or a direct mapping, of the structure of reality. Thus we may not detach language from reality and from its reflection in the human mind, and we may not treat language expressions as a pictorial *analogon* of reality. How then is that relation to be interpreted?

There is a very fine formulation by Marx:

"Speech is as old as consciousness, speech *is* a practical, real consciousness which exists both for other people and for myself. And speech comes to being, like consciousness, only from the need, the necessity of contact with other people"[8].

The interpretation of language as an *organon*, an instrument that serves communication purposes (an interpretation which is in conformity with the starting point of our analysis of the issues of the sign, meaning, and language) has been known in the literature of the subject, especially written from the linguistic point of view, since the time of Aristotle[9]. We are not interested here in the origin of language, or in the issue as to whether the nature of language as an *organon* requires a purposive or a causal interpretation. Our focal issue is that of the relation between language on the one hand, and the thought process and the reality referred to in language, on the other.

Let us begin with the relation between language and thinking.

An aspect of that issue was raised in the preceding chapter in the discussion of the relation between the verbal sign and notion. A defence was made there of the thesis that the meaning

---

[8] K. Marx, F. Engels, *Die deutsche Ideologie*, in *Werke*, Vol. 3, Berlin 1958, p. 30.

[9] By way of example I again refer to Révész, op. cit., pp. 97 ff.

of a verbal sign and notion are coincident. Can that thesis also be defended when it comes to the relation between language and thinking? In my opinion, yes. True, elements of sensory perception do appear in the thought process (not only as a genetic foundation of thinking in terms of ideas, but also as elements which accompany that process), but the same can be said as regards experiencing the content of linguistic processes. On the other hand, the thesis concerning non-linguistic thinking is based on an essential misunderstanding. The fact that the psychological analysis of thought processes reveals in them representations of various types which *accompany* thinking in terms of ideas (i.e., thinking by means of verbal signs), and the claim that that representational aspect of thinking is *independent* of linguistic processes, are two different things. The claim referring to the possibility of some form of non-linguistic thinking (as far as people are concerned, who are able to make use of the phonic language) can be supported only by those who believe in cognition without the intermediary of signs, who believe in some *direct* cognition or perception. I agree with Russell[10] that only a mystic can assert anything of that kind. In science, and in the light of its criteria, such an opinion is untenable.

More frequently, a more cautious view is to be encountered in the literature of the subject. It is stated, for example, that thinking and language do not fully coincide, but form an indivisible whole consisting of two distinct elements. For instance, Révész says that there is no speech process without thinking, and *vice versa*, thought cannot exist without language. Nevertheless, he holds that thinking embraces certain non-linguistic elements, and consequently that the conception of thought and language as a single indivisible function is untenable. This opinion, of course, is based on the assumption that the process of thinking

---

[10] In *An Inquiry into Meaning and Truth*, London 1951, p. 341, Bertrand Russell is right in calling mystics such thinkers as Bergson and Wittgenstein, who maintain that there is knowledge that is uncommunicable by words, and use words just to convey that idea.

includes certain elements that cannot be expressed in speech. Here again, we must point out, to declare that certain moods, emotional states, etc., connected with the process of thinking, are *difficult to express*; and to maintain that there exist certain thought processes or some emotional states, etc., connected with the former, which are essentially *inexpressible* and *incommunicable* – are two different things. Such an attitude is as difficult to adopt as that which Révész rejects together with the assertion about the basic dualism of language and thinking.

But the principal issue, which is of particular interest from the philosophical point of view, is connected with the relation between language and reality referred to in speech. That principal issue, however, is not separated from the foregoing; on the contrary, it can be solved only in connection with that foregoing issue. The first point to be explained is as to *which* relation we have in mind here: the relation between reality and language treated in abstraction from thinking, or the relation between reality and language treated jointly with thinking. What depends on a proper interpretation of that problem is not only the point from which we see the issue now under consideration, but also the possibility of solving that issue. When we treat language as a product separated from thinking, or when we interpret the process of thinking in the nominalist spirit and treat its products as *flatus vocis* (these are but two different formulations of a standpoint essentially the same), then we assume that language is of an arbitrary nature and thereby we deny that there should be any other relation between language and reality except the relation of *denotation* of certain objects by certain verbal signs on the principle of convention. The mutual relationship between language and reality comes to light only when, having understood the *unity* of language and thinking, we speak of a relation between reality and not merely language, but thought-language. The proper issue, however, is not the relation between reality and language "in itself", but the relation between reality and the human *process of cognition*, which anyhow takes place in a linguistic form (in the form of a system of verbal signs). As indicated above, the understanding of that point is decisive for the trend of the solution of the issue involved. There is no language "in itself", but, as facts prove, one *can* in research approach the problem exclusively from the point of view of the phonic aspect of language, the aspect of the material vehicles of meaning. In such a case, even if we recognize the historical and social foundations of the origin of language, we must conclude that there is no essential connection between a given sound and the nature of the thing to which that phonic sign refers, so that we must recognize, at least in a certain sense, the arbitrary nature of the verbal signs. If we stop at that, then the only road left for us is that which leads to conventionalism, to the conception of language as a game of chess, a conception which completely obliterates just that which should be the object of research.

And now let us approach the issue from a different angle. We are concerned not with language "in itself", but with the homogeneous function of thought-language or thinking in terms of language, which is characteristic of the cognitive process in the human stage of its development, that is in a stage of the development of abstraction, which is specific to human beings. In such an interpretation, the issue of the relation of the cognitive process (which is a linguistic process) to reality, appears in full light. Here the problem cannot be dismissed with a conventionalist explanation of language as play. Here we have to give an explicit answer to the question: what is the relation between our (linguistic) cognition and the object of that cognition, i.e. reality? The answer reveals all the philosophical implications of this or that standpoint. In such an interpretation one may deny the connection between thought-language and reality, one may deny the relation of reflection of reality by language, one may claim (as does e.g., Cassirer) that language creates reality, etc. But this is tantamount to one's philosophical declaration, and makes it imperative to choose one's philosophical standpoint. And that is a great deal, for in philosophical discussions the issue is more often to make one's standpoint known than to achieve universal agreement, which is practically impossible. And there would certainly be far fewer followers of the conventionalist solutions of the problems of language and its relation to reality if we could strip to the very end the falsehood of positivist declarations about rising above the traditional controversies in philosophy, if we could show the philosophical implications of conventionalism, and force those concerned to declare themselves either in favour of or against such implications. In the history of philosophy there have been few people who had boldness enough consciously to preach solipsism; and there are not many now who would *openly* preach subjective idealism (if not for other reasons, then because they would fear to lose scientific prestige in extra-philosophical circles).

The issue of the relation between thought-language and reality can also be formulated thus: Does the analysis of language enable us to understand some regularities in the extra-linguistic world, and may we consequently treat language autonomously, in abstraction from extra-linguistic facts? Such a formulation seems to be a happier one in that it approaches the same issue in a more concrete manner, less "philosophically", so to speak.

Two answers can be given to that question. One denies any relationship between language and extra-verbal reality, in the sense that language is shaped after the model of that reality (the denial being justified in various ways); the other admits the existence of such a relation (also resorting to various motivations).

The denial of the existence of relations between language and extra-verbal reality – in the sense of the possibility of finding in language information about the real world – is based, as has been mentioned above, on various arguments.

First of all, there is a conviction about a possibility of some direct cognition, supposed to be the true cognition. According to both Bergson's intuitionism and Husserl's theses, "true" cognition is a direct act and is non-linguistic. This is typical irrationalism with a mystical tinge, which discredits linguistic cognition and opposes to it some other mode of cognition: a mystical intuition of the object, intuition which in a single act makes it possible "truly" to grasp that object and to understand it. This denies relations between language (which is said to distort the picture of reality) and reality, in the sense of a reflection of that reality by language.

A similar approach is characteristic of those (although the starting point is different) who – like Humboldt in the past or Leo Weisgerber now – believe that language expresses "the spirit of the nation" which shapes the vision of the world in different manners according to the various linguistic systems. This refers to a relation with reality, but such a relation that is a denial of the thesis that language, together with human cognition, is shaped under the influence of that reality which is the object of cognition: it is claimed that language shapes rather than reflects, reality.

Finally, other approaches to the denial of a connection between language and reality lead through different variations of neo-nominalism which would have us believe that not only it is possible to study linguistic facts as autonomous phenomena, but also that only such an analysis is legitimate. So-called logical atomism, in the form at one time represented by Bertrand Russell, used to break up reality into facts-atoms which language cannot study without an appropriate apparatus and which it consequently distorts. The denial of such a connection was also reached – by way of somewhat divergent though similar paths – by neo-positivism, which perfected the thesis concerning the autonomy of language as the only object of philosophical analysis. This was the peak of semantic philosophy. It is characteristic that Russell, whose views are constantly evolving, is now criticizing neo-positivism for denying the connection between language and reality, a denial which is an expression of a specific agnosticism. This criticism is quoted here because I think it to be especially valuable, since it comes from the man who was one of the co-founders of the trend he now criticizes.

"I propose to consider whether anything, and, if so, what, can be inferred from the structure of language as to the structure of the world. There has been a tendency, especially among logical positivists, to treat language as an independent realm, which can be studied without regard to non-linguistic occurrences. To some extent, and in a limited field, this separation of language from other facts is possible; the detached study of logical syntax has undoubtedly yielded valuable results. But I think it is easy to exaggerate what can be achieved by syntax alone. There is, I think, a discoverable relation between the structure of sentences and the structure of the occurrences to which sentences refer. I do not think the structure of non-verbal facts is wholly unknowable, and I believe that, with sufficient caution, the properties of language may help us to understand the structure of the world"[11].

As already indicated, the interpretation of the relation between language and reality on the level of thought-language makes it imperative to adopt a definite philosophical standpoint. The controversy around that issue must be based on general philosophical foundations and is in fact the controversy about the relation between the process of cognition and reality.

I must declare that I see a possibility of solving the problem we are here concerned with only in the light of the theory of reflection, in the specific sense of the term, as imparted to it by Marxist philosophy.

In view of existing distortions of, and misunderstandings, in non-Marxist circles, concerning the theory of reflection, in particular in view of the erroneous identification of the Marxist theory of reflection with a theory of the same name as held by mechanistic materialists, the present analysis should be supplemented with an exposition of the fundamental theses of the

---

[11] B. Russell, *An Inquiry into Meaning and Truth*, p. 341.

Marxist theory of reflection. This, however, I shall not embark on here, limiting myself to warning possible critics against such misunderstandings.

The theory of reflection rejects both the extreme solutions: that which interprets language as a purely conventional product, uninfluenced by extra-linguistic factors, and that which in the structure of language sees a picture of the structure of reality.

The conception of language as a game, language as a product of an arbitrary convention, is refuted by practical experience which in transforming reality resorts to information obtained precisely through the intermediary of language, said not to be connected with reality. It is refuted by science, especially by linguistics, which proves that language develops under the influence of changes in real conditions existing in objective reality. It is refuted by the philosophical generalization of theory and practice in the form of the interpretation of cognition as a subjective reflection of objective reality. Taking all this into account, I defend the thesis that language inseparably connected with thinking, and performing together with thinking one and the same function on which the specific nature of human cognition is based, is formed in the process of human experience and is itself an empirical fact, and not a product of an arbitrary convention. This means that thought-language gives a specific reflection of reality, and that its development is caused by the development of reality itself and by the development of human understanding of that reality both in theory and in practice.

Is the reflection of reality by thought-language to be understood to imply that we have to do with some picture of reality in the structure of language? It has been stated above that the theory of reflection as applied to linguistic functions may not be identified with any vulgar theory of representation or a theory of the pictorial nature of that function. Such a vulgarized conception is based on a complete misunderstanding of the specific nature of the verbal signs as compared with other categories of signs, already discussed above in connection with the analysis of sign and meaning. The specific nature of the verbal sign consists above all in its breaking away from a pictorial function, so that it is in a position to perform special functions in the process of abstraction and to become "transparent to meaning". The reflection of reality in language does not consist in the relations between parts of the sentence corresponding to relations between some elements of reality. Division of reality into elements is something artificial, usually in itself a product of abstraction. Moreover, division of a sentence into parts differs according to the various linguistic systems, which fact prevents neither the cognition of reality nor the communication process concerned with such cognition (although, as will be seen later, certain complications may arise on this point). The reflection of reality in language, the "modelling" of language by reality, also does not consist in language being an "image" of reality in the sense of directly mapping that reality by the *form* of linguistic expressions (their sounds). One cannot reasonably deny the thesis concerning the arbitrary nature of the language signs, understood so that there is no necessary link between the sounds of words and the things, relations, actions, etc., to which those words refer, unless one also disregards the historical and social conditioning of the origin of the various expressions[12]. Thus the theory of reflection does not require renunciation of the thesis concerning the existence of conventional elements in language (who could reasonably deny that?); it requires only that language should not be *reduced* to a product of convention, dissociated from reality and consequently from the essential functions of human communication, that is, functions which lie at the root of language. Language and the signs of language perform their functions – of reflecting reality, of conveying information about that reality, etc. – not by any pictorial similarity to reality or by being an

[12] A different idea, namely that of the so-called *Lautbilder*, is represented e.g. by Eugen Lerch: "Vom Wesen des sprachlichen Zeichens", in *Acta Linguistica*, 1939, Vol. 1, No. 3, and Emile Benveniste: "Nature du signe linguistique", in *Acta Linguistica*, 1939, Vol. 1, No. 1.

analogon of the structure of that reality, but by way of their semantic aspect which coincides with what is called the content of the thought process. How all this occurs, can be explained (as indicated above) only by such specialized disciplines as physiology, psychology, etc. It will suffice here to state the specific nature of the verbal signs and explain where to look for more detailed information.

But the theory of reflection is not confined to the rejection of conventionalism and to stating that language, shaped under the influence of cognition of extra-linguistic objective reality, gives a *reflection* of that reality in a definite sense of the word. That theory also takes into account the dialectics of the relation between thought-language and the cognition of reality; and in turn that dialectics (confirmed beyond all doubt by linguistics, anthropology, etc.) consists in that thought-language, shaped as a reflection of reality in the process of human cognition, is also (mainly owing to the educational process which conveys through language the accumulated experience of the past generations) an *organon*, an instrument which shapes the manner of perceiving and comprehending that reality. This dialectics is of remarkable significance in understanding the proper relation between thought-language and extra-linguistic reality. That is why it will now be analysed in greater detail.

Let it be borne in mind that the subject matter of our analysis is not the relation between language and thinking, and *vice versa,* but the relation between thought-language and the process of human cognition. The results of research obtained by such disciplines as developmental psychology, psychopathology and cultural anthropology may shed some light on that issue. Each of these disciplines clarifies some aspect of the cognitive functions and of the dialectics of the mutual relations between thought-language and the process of acquiring knowledge about reality. The problems of developmental psychology of the child will be disregarded here, since that discipline gives pride of place to the influence of the social process of education, and thus shifts the stress to problems that differ from those we are principally concerned with. On the other hand, the issues of psychopathology and cultural anthropology may, in my opinion, play an important rôle in advancing the analysis of the problems which interest us here.

As regards psychopathology, we shall be interested mainly in the cases of *aphasia*, i.e., the loss of capacity for linguistic thinking in this or that form, following injuries to the brain[13]. These researches are principally connected with the name of Head and now have an ample literature devoted to them. Of course, the details are the domain of the specialists, and the philosopher can only study certain general results of research.

First of all, it must be realized that aphasia does not eliminate the function of thinking, but rather modifies it; neither, in principle, does it put an end to linguistic functions, although these, too, undergo a modification. These modifications are of special theoretical interest, since they reveal the inter-relationship as between thought-language and the cognitive process. The extreme forms of aphasia (verbal and semantic) consist, in the former case, in that the patient thinks and understands what he is told but has lost the ability to form words, and in the latter he utters words, but deprived of their semantic function, i.e., he utters sounds or sequences of sounds, but not words, not verbal signs *sensu stricto*. Theoretically most interesting, however, are the intermediate cases (syntactic and, in particular, nominal aphasia) when the patient retains the ability to speak and think at least in part, but in a modified form. Observation of such conditions enables us to gain a deeper insight into the mechanism of the dialectics of the elements which determine the process of cognition.

---

[13] H. Head in his *Aphasia and Kindred Discorders of Speech*, New York 1926, Vols. 1 & 2, differentiates between verbal *aphasia* (disfunction in word-formation), *syntactic* aphasia (disfunction in combining words into grammatically correct whole), *nominal* aphasia (disfunction in using words as general names), and *semantic* aphasia (disfunction in associating words with their corresponding meanings).

In the case of nominal aphasia, the patient uses words which are generic names, but he uses them in quite a different way, not as general names but as words connected with a given, concrete situation, which in the patient's mind is associated with a given word. The experts explain that by the fact that following an injury of the brain the patient has lost the ability to interpret reality in an abstract manner. In the cognitive process of normal persons, and in their behaviour resulting therefrom, their mind is "set" both to concrete facts connected with sensory perception of reality and to generic properties of objects and the process of abstract cognition; in certain cases, an injury to the brain results in the loss of the latter ability. In losing the ability to perceive properties of objects *in abstracto*, and to acquire an abstract cognition of those objects, the patient ceases to use words as generic names since he ceases to understand them as such; he loses the ability to use them in an abstract manner, but he does not completely lose the ability to use words in a given context. This is what Kurt Goldstein, one of the experts on aphasia, says on that subject:

"What we have said about the relation of language to the concrete attitude would make it comprehensible that the patient deprived of the abstract attitude would evince a lack of language. But does this explain why he is impeded particularly in naming objects? The elucidation of this phenomenon obtains from an analysis of the normal individual's behaviour in naming, which reveals that real naming takes place in the abstract attitude. When we name an object such as a table, we do not mean a special table with all its accidental properties but the table in general. The word is used as representative of the category table ... The fact that naming becomes impossible if the abstract attitude is lost reveals particularly the nature of naming. It is a confirmation of our assumption. The patient, we can say, cannot use words in naming because he cannot assume the abstract attitude. Since the patient faces the world with a particular attitude to which speech is not relevant, or which we could accompany only with individual words, the nominal words do not occur to him. He cannot even understand what we mean by naming because that presupposes the abstract attitude, which he cannot assume. That finds indirect confirmation in the fact that the patient can find words in connection with objects if he has such words which fit the concrete situation. The patient who cannot apply the word 'red' to different nuances of red, easily produces words such as 'strawberry red' and 'sky blue', etc., in relation to corresponding colors. He can do it because he has such individual words at his command ... The paramount importance of the kind of language which appears in naming becomes evident through other characteristic modifications of that language of the patients which also are comprehensible. They are the result of the impairment of the power of abstraction and are parallel with modifications in the behaviour of patients in general"[14].

Goldstein says that the language of the patient who suffers from nominal aphasia is transformed into a specific automaton which reacts to definite, concrete situations. Hence the limited use of such parts of speech as conjunctions, articles, adverbs, etc., which require a high level of abstraction[15]. The words that normally function as general are used by the patients as names of concrete objects or events. This is so because of the association of the word used with a concrete situation, without understanding by the patients — as proved by experiments — of the general character of words. This applies, for instance, to such a word as "thing". Goldstein even claims that the uttering of words by patients suffering from aphasia does not mean using a language, the signs of which have definite meanings.

Another interesting fact to which Goldstein refers is the loss of ability to understand metaphors, proverbs, etc., which is also connected with the loss of the capacity for abstract comprehension of verbal signs.

---

[14] K. Goldstein, "The Nature of Language", in *Language. An Inquiry into Its Meaning and Function* (ed. R. N. Anshen), New York 1957, pp. 23–24.

[15] Ibid., p. 25.

Goldstein's conclusion is as follows:

"If one considers their (the patients' – A. S.) condition from the aspect of the world in which the patients live, one can say that their world is correspondingly changed. What appear to us as objects in an organized world are for them complex sense experiences of an individual singular character which can be reacted to in a definite way but which are not connected with each other in a systematic unit. One can say that they have no 'world'. The change manifests itself in the above-mentioned modifications in the patients' language and in the loss of the world, and this indicates that they are *deprived of the essential characteristics of men* ... The words of the patients have lost their symbolic function and with that the ability to work as mediating agent between sense experiences and the world in which man alone can be man. The change in the patient's personality, which excludes him from the normal human community, brings the essential significance of the symbolic power to the fore and with that the significance of the symbolic character of language"[16].

What conclusions can be drawn from researches on aphasia appropriate to the issue of the mutual relations between thought-language and the process of cognition?

First of all, definite language-and-thought functions are consequences of definite cognitive abilities, abilities to perform analysis and synthesis of the data supplied by sensory perception. This is quite clear from the point of view of the physiology of the brain, and is a fact of remarkable significance not only as stressing the physiological foundations of thought processes, but also as emphasizing the unity of the language-and-thought functions. For the impairment of certain linguistic abilities, this or that form of aphasia obviously results in the impairment of corresponding abilities to think. The study of aphasia provides *scientific* evidence of the fact that abstract thinking in

---

[16] Ibid., pp. 28–29. Note that the author uses a specific terminology: the word "symbol" means here what we call "the verbal sign".

terms of concepts is impossible without language. This is a point of extreme importance, which fully accounts for a philosophical – strictly, epistemological – interest in researches on aphasia.

But our interest lies mainly in the issue of the unity of the language-and-thought functions. The study of aphasia shows that there is no abstract thinking without language. Are we, then, not justified in accepting the hypothesis that whenever we do not have to do with any impairment of the physiological functions of the brain, it is only the lack of language which causes the lack of abstract thinking? That hypothesis, so important for the confirmation of the thesis on the unity of language-and-thought functions, can be verified either by means of data supplied by developmental psychology, or by analysis of the known cases of some disability which has made it impossible to teach a child a phonic language. This is no longer a domain of physiopathology, since the brain is functioning normally, but the cases under investigation are similar in so far as in both groups of cases (although for different reasons) one of the functions of the process of cognition has been eliminated for a long time. That is why the case of Hellen Keller, deaf-mute and blind since her birth and taught to use a special language and writing, is of particular interest.

Helen Keller describes in her memoirs how she "discovered" language and verbal signs and how that discovery has influenced her thought processes:

"We walked down the path to the well-house, attracted by the fragrance of the honeysuckle with which it was covered. Someone was drawing water and my teacher placed my hand under the spout. As the cool stream gushed over my hand she spelled into the other the word *water*; first slowly, then rapidly. I stood still, my whole attention fixed upon the motion of her fingers. Suddenly I felt a misty consciousness as of something forgotten – a thrill of returning thought; and somehow the mystery of language was revealed to me. I knew then that w-a-t-e-r meant the wonderful cool something that was flowing over my hand. That living word awakened my soul, gave it light, hope, joy, set it free. There were barriers still, it is true, but barriers that in time could be swept away.

"I left the well-house eager to learn. Everything had a name, and each name gave birth to a new thought. As we returned to the house every object which I touched seemed to quiver with life. That was because I saw everything with the strange, new sight that had come to me"[17].

There are some important conclusions to be drawn here.

First, thinking in the strict sense of the term is inseparable from language and the ability to speak. Helen Keller puts it plainly when she reflects on how she passed from cognitive processes without the use of language to thinking in terms of language.

"She (the teacher – A. S.) brought me my hat, and I knew I was going out into the warm sunshine. This thought, *if a wordless sensation may be called a thought*, made me hop and skip with pleasure"[18].

Secondly, in certain definite situations a non-phonic language may exist – for instance, as in the case in question, a tactile language. Another point is that it is merely a translation from a phonic language.

Thirdly, from the passage cited it follows what is the rôle of the verbal signs as a means of making abstractions and arriving at abstract cognition in terms of concepts.

Exceptionally strong light is shed on that issue, so important for the dialectics of the cognitive process, by the data supplied by cultural anthropology. This refers above all to researches on language systems of primitive peoples and connections between those systems and ways of thinking.

The problem which we face (and it is a problem, in my opinion, of primary importance) can be formulated thus: are there any data testifying to the fact that the way of life and practical experi-

---

[17] H. Keller, *The Story of My Life*, 1936, pp. 23–24, quoted after S. K. Langer, *Philosophy in a New Key*, Cambridge (Mass.) 1957, pp. 62–63.

[18] Ibid. (italics – A. S.).

ence influence the way of thinking (i.e., the system of thought-language), and *vice versa,* that the historically developed system of thought-language influences the whole of man's practical experience and, consequently, his cognitive processes as well? There can be no doubt that this is an issue of immense importance for philosophy in general, and for epistemology in particular. There can also be no doubt that all actual research that can shed light on that issue must be eagerly welcomed by the philosopher interested in the problem of language, and especially by the Marxist philosopher in view of his predilection to approach epistemological issues from the point of view of historical and sociological analysis. That is why, even if the anthropological data so far at our disposal are too scanty to allow any final and sweeping generalizations (and I may anticipate further discussion by stating that this is the case), it is not possible to reject *a priori* or treat disparagingly the hypotheses based on such data.

At one time, Lévy-Bruhl formulated a hypothesis, based on the study of the psychology of primitive peoples (including the study of their languages), on the existence of pre-logical thinking and, consequently, a-logical thinking. That hypothesis, based chiefly on beliefs of primitive peoples (the problem of so-called participation), beliefs which seem to violate the principle of logical consistency, was not only poorly substantiated, but also largely arbitary. By now, it has been almost universally rejected. Marxist critics, when correctly attacking its weak points, raised, among other things, the objection that that theory helped the colonial powers to justify ideologically conquests of peoples supposed to be on so low a level that they even could not think logically. And that objection was undoubtedly correct. But to state facts confirmed by research and to interpret them in this or that way are two different things. Justified fear of a wrong interpretation has in many instances led to an incorrect denial of facts and to the rejection of issues resulting therefrom. And the hypothesis of Lévy-Bruhl included many things that were interesting and encouraged further investigations. First of all – this had been known before but was particularly stressed in the works of Lévy-Bruhl – the level of abstraction in the thinking of primitive peoples differs from that in the thinking of what are known as civilized peoples, and this difference finds reflection in respective language systems. That point cannot be denied or disregarded, since, first, it requires a careful investigation, and secondly, it is of considerable theoretical (and philosophical) significance.

The problem of connections between language and thinking and strictly speaking connections between thought-language and cognitive processes, has been more broadly and differently formulated in what is termed the Sapir-Whorf hypothesis.

Whereas the ideas of Lévy-Bruhl have at one time and another been much discussed in Marxist literature, the theory of Sapir and Whorf has been mentioned by Marxist authors only in exceptional cases[19]. Yet in the West that theory already has a comprehensive literature. Factual data are still not sufficient enough to permit a definite appraisal of that theory, but it certainly should not be passed over in silence[20].

Lévy-Bruhl based his hypothesis concerning a pre-logical type of thinking in primitive peoples not only on the analysis of such phenomena as what is known as participation, but also on concretism in thinking, a lack of general names, peculiar

---

[19] One of the exceptions is O. C. Ахманова who in her work *Очерки по общей и русской лексикологии* [Note on General and Russian Lexicology], Москва 1957, has devoted a few pages to report on the Sapir-Whorf hypothesis. Yet her criticism goes so far (which, in my opinion, is wrong) that it practically amounts to a complete rejection of that hypothesis.

[20] E.g., Paul Henle in his "Language, Thought and Culture", which is the first chapter of a comprehensive collective work under the same title (ed. Paul Henle, Ann Arbor 1958), says on the Whorf hypothesis: "Only after many more studies of this sort would it be possible even to suggest which features of a grammar might in general be expected to correlate with a culture. This is not, of course, to condemn the investigations which have been made, but merely to point out that they stand at the beginning of a vast inquiry. More data are required before it is even possible to formulate specific hypotheses; but this is often the case at the start of a new science" (op. cit., p. 24).

systems of counting, etc.; all this was supposed to prove that primitive thinking was "different", and at the same time of a lower order. Now, his hypothesis has been destroyed by anthropological (and linguistic) researches. The Sapir-Whorf hypothesis has nothing to do with Lévy-Bruhl's, as can be proved by a statement made by Sapir, who openly disagrees with Lévy-Bruhl:

"The lowliest South African Bushman speaks in the forms of a rich symbolic system that is in essence perfectly comparable to the speech of the cultivated Frenchman. It goes without saying that the more abstract concepts are not nearly so plentifully represented in the language of the savage, nor is there the rich terminology and the finer definition of nuances that reflect the higher culture. Yet the sort of linguistic development that parallels the historic growth of culture and which, in its later stages, we associate with literature is, at best, but a superficial thing. The fundamental groundwork of language – the development of a clearcut phonetic system, the specific association of speech elements with concepts, and the delicate provision for the formal expression of all manner of relations – all this meets us rigidly perfected and systematized in every language known to us. *Many primitive languages have a formal richness, a latent luxuriance of expression, that eclipses anything known to the languages of modern civilization*"[21].

The idea that languages of primitive peoples are not only not inferior to languages of civilized peoples but even in some respects superior to them is to be found in Whorf's works as well. Thus the concept differs from that of Lévy-Bruhl. Both are connected only by the common method of studying thought processes through the intermediary of linguistic phenomena.

The basic idea of the Sapir-Whorf hypothesis can be found earlier in the works of F. Boas, who as early as 1911 wrote in the introduction to the *Handbook of American Indian Languages*:

---

[21] E. Sapir, *Language. An Introduction to the Study of Speech,* New York 1921, p. 22 (italics – A. S.).

"It seems, however, that a theoretical study of Indian languages is not less important than a practical knowledge of them; that the purely linguistic inquiry is part and parcel of a thorough investigation of the psychology of the peoples of the world" (p. 63).

"... Language seems to be one of the most instructive fields of inquiry in an investigation of the formation of the fundamental ethnic ideas. The great advantage that linguistics offers in this respect is the fact that, on the whole, the categories which are formed always remain unconscious, and that for this reason the processes which lead to their formation can be followed without the misleading and disturbing factors of secondary explanation, which are so common in ethnology, so much so that they generally obscure the real history of the development of ideas entirely" (pp. 70-71)[22].

That idea was developed by E. Sapir in 1929 in his paper "The Status of Linguistics as a Science":

"Language is a guide to 'social reality'. Though language is not ordinarily thought of as of essential interest to the students of social science, it powerfully conditions all our thinking about social problems and processes. Human beings do not live in the objective world alone, nor alone in the world of social activity as ordinarily understood, but are very much at the mercy of the particular language which has become the medium of expression for their society. It is quite an illusion to imagine that one adjusts to reality essentially without the use of language and that language is merely an incidental means of solving specific problems of communication or reflection. The fact of the matter is that the 'real world' is to a large extent unconsciously built upon the language habits of the group. No two languages are ever sufficiently similar to be considered as representing the same social reality. The worlds in which different societies live are distinct

---

[22] Quoted after H. Hoijer, "The Sapir-Whorf Hypothesis", in *Language in Culture* (ed. H. Hoijer), University of Chicago Press. 1955, pp. 92–93.

worlds, not merely the same world with different labels attached ... We see and hear and otherwise experience very largely as we do because the language habits of our community predispose certain choices of interpretation"[23].

And in his essay on "Conceptual Categories of Primitive Languages" Sapir adds:

"The relation between language and experience is often misunderstood. Language is not merely a more or less systematic inventory of the various items of experience which seem relevant to the individual, as is so often naively assumed, but is also a self-contained, creative symbolic organization, which not only refers to experience largely acquired without its help but actually defines experience for us by reason of its formal completeness and because of our unconscious projection of its implicit expectations into the field of experience"[24].

Sapir's basic idea can be summarized thus: language is an active factor in shaping our image of the world, which image consequently varies according to the system of language which we use.

That idea has been assimilated by Benjamin Lee Whorf who has made it the foundation of his researches on the languages of American Indian tribes, in particular that of the Hopi. Whorf asks himself the question: how does the differentiation of systems of language influence the differentiation of our images of the world? This leads to another important issue: what accounts for the differentiation of language systems, and in particular, what is the rôle in that respect of the social milieu in which people who use different languages live?

The first issue has been analysed by Whorf in the light of the data supplied by the Hopi language (the Sapir-Whorf hypothesis was further illuminated by the study of other American Indian languages, e.g., Hoijer's researches on the Navajo

---

[23] *Language*, 1929, Vol. 5 (quoted after E. Sapir, *Culture, Language and Personality*, Berkeley 1957, pp. 68–69).

[24] *Science*, 1931 (quoted after Henle, op. cit., p. 1.).

language). Both Whorf and other scholars seen to confirm Sapir's thesis concerning an active rôle of language in shaping our picture of the world, which, if interpreted in a moderate way, should not give rise to objections of a philosophical nature. When formulating his thesis, Sapir outlined a programme of researches which were expected to confirm it. He intended a comparison between Indo-European languages on the one hand and American Indian and African on the other. That programme has been implemented by Whorf, whose conclusion is that the differences between the various Indo-European languages are so slight as compared with those between any Indo-European language and the Hopi language, that the former may be treated as a homogeneous group, which he has called SAE (Standard Average European). Now, when comparing the SAE group with the Hopi language, Whorf has advanced the following problem: what is the relation between the given system of language, on the one hand, and perception, organization of experience and behaviour patterns, on the other?

"That portion of the whole investigation here to be reported may be summed up in two questions: (1) Are our own concepts of 'time', 'space' and 'matter' given in substantially the same forms of experience to all men, or are they in part conditioned by the structure of particular languages? (2) Are there traceable affinities between (a) cultural and behavioral norms, and (b) large-scale linguistic patterns?"[25]

As a result of his researches, Whorf comes to the conclusion that the language system influences the way in which we perceive, experience and behave. The system of the Hopi language conditions the perception of reality as *events*, and not as things interpreted statically, and also conditions a specific interpretation of time: in the Hopi language there is no general category of "time" (in this connection Whorf draws a certain analogy with Einstein's theory of relativity).

[25] B. L. Whorf, "The Relation of Habitual Thought and Behavior to Language", in B. L. Whorf, *Language, Thought and Reality*, 1957, p. 138.

"At the same time, the Hopi language is capable of accounting for and describing correctly, in a pragmatic or operational sense, all observable phenomena of the universe. Hence, I find it gratuitous to assume that Hopi thinking contains any such notion as the supposed intuitively felt flowing of 'time', or that the intuition of a Hopi gives him this as one of his data. Just as it is possible to have any number of geometries other than the Euclidean which give an equally perfect account of space configurations, so it is possible to have descriptions of the universe, all equally valid, that do not contain our familiar contrasts of time and space. The relativity viewpoint of modern physics is one such view, conceived in mathematical terms, and the Hopi *Weltanschauung* is another and quite different one, nonmathematical and linguistic"[26].

In connection with his hypothesis, Whorf formulates a number of detailed principles, two of which stand out.

One of them is the principle of *linguistic relativism*, in conformity with which people perceive reality in this or that way according to the categories of thought imposed on them by language. He says:

"This fact is very significant for modern science, for it means that no individual is free to describe nature with absolute impartiality but is constrained to certain modes of interpretation even while he thinks himself most free. The person most nearly free in such respects would be a linguist familiar with very many widely different linguistic systems. As yet no linguist is in any such position. We are thus introduced to a new principle of relativity, which holds that all observers are not led by the same physical evidence to the same picture of the universe, unless their linguistic backgrounds are similar, or can in some way be calibrated"[27].

---

26 B. L. Whorf, "An American Indian Model of the Universe", in B. L. Whorf, *Language, Thought and Reality*, p. 58.

27 B. L. Whorf, "Science and Linguistics", in B. L. Whorf, *Language, Thought and Reality*, p. 214.

The second is the principle of the *objective necessity of the linguistic system*, which holds that the mode of thinking and perceiving reality, imposed by a given language system, does not depend on the consciousness of the individual.

"Actually, thinking is most mysterious, and by far the greatest light upon it that we have is thrown by the study of language. This study shows that the forms of a person's thoughts are controlled by inexorable laws of pattern of which he is unconscious. These patterns are unperceived, intricate systematizations of his own language – shown readily enough by a candid comparison and contrast with other languages, especially those of a different linguistic family. This thinking itself is in a language – in English, in Sanskrit, in Chinese. And every language is a vast pattern-system, different from others, in which are culturally ordained the forms and categories by which the personality not only communicates, but also analyzes nature, notices or neglects types of relationships and phenomena, channels his reasoning, and builds the house of his consciousness"[28].

All this is but one aspect of the problem. Should we confine ourselves to it alone, there would be a danger of subjective and conventionalist interpretations. But Whorf's hypothesis leads to other consequences as well, namely those which pertain to the influence of environment upon language. Thus we obtain a specific dialectic of relations between environment and language, which gives us effective protection against relativism and conventionalism.

This is how Whorf explains the differences between the Hopi language and the SAE group:

"In Hopi history, could we read it, we should find a different type of language and a different set of cultural and environmental influence working together. A peaceful agricultural society isolated by geographic features and nomad enemies in a land of

---

28 B. L. Whorf, "Language, Mind and Reality", in B. L. Whorf, *Language, Thought and Reality*, p. 252.

scanty rainfall, arid agriculture that could be made successful only by the utmost perseverance (hence the value of persistence and repetition), necessity for collaboration (hence emphasis on the psychology of teamwork and on mental factors in general), corn and rain as primary criteria of value, need of extensive *preparations* and precautions to assure crops in the poor soil and precarious climate, keen realization of dependence upon nature favoring prayer and a religious attitude toward the forces of nature, especially prayer and religion directed toward the ever-needed blessing, rain — these things interacted with Hopi linguistic patterns to mold them, to be molded again by them, and so little by little to shape the Hopi world-outlook"[29].

That quite materialist interpretation of the specific mental features reflected in the Hopi language, finds its concretization in the various forms of the influence of environment upon language, in particular upon vocabulary. It is by different living conditions and the resulting needs that Whorf explains the fact that the Eskimo, for instance, have very many terms for the various kinds of snow, which we call by one and the same term, and which the Aztecs called by the same term as ice and cold. In this he follows Sapir who in the same way explained the large number and the concrete character of the words used to denote the various marine creatures in the Nootka language, plants and topographical features in languages of desert peoples, etc. Similar explanations are resorted to when it comes to the lack of words denoting certain colours in the language of Navajo Indians, and, on the other hand, the various terms used by them to denote the various shades of black, which have no special names of their own in our language. Whorf, like other contemporary scholars, explains the concrete character of languages of primitive peoples not by a lower mental level in those peoples, but by different living conditions. From all this it follows clearly that in emphasizing the influence of language on human perception

[29] B. L. Whorf, "The Relation of Habitual Thought and Behavior to Language", in B. L. Whorf, *Language, Thought and Reality*, pp. 157–158.

Whorf does not claim that cognition is somehow unilaterally conditioned by language, but also notices the other aspect of the issue, namely the fact that language is shaped by reality, by the conditions of material existence of a given society.

These comments on the Sapir-Whorf hypothesis are an endeavour to present its principal ideas. I think that worth doing in view of the philosophical significance of those ideas and the fact that they are little known in Poland.

It is also interesting to note a coincidence between Whorf's principal ideas and the results of researches conducted quite independently by other scholars. In particular, I should like to draw attention here to the studies by Malinowski concerning the Trobriand people, and above all his splendid work, "The Problem of Meaning in Primitive Languages".

In the light of what has been said here on the relation between language and reality, it is worth returning to the issue of the conventionalist concept of language as an arbitrary system of rules, the concept of language as play.

Psychological, psychopathological, and anthropological researches force us to reject that concept as being at variance with facts; those facts show that language is connected with reality by the relation of reflection, understood in the special sense of the term, although at the same time language plays an active rôle in moulding our cognition and our image of the world. Reality shapes language, which in turn shapes our image of reality. What then is the origin of radically conventionalist conceptions which separate language from reality, and consequently transform it into the sole object of philosophical analysis?

Two main causes may be mentioned here:

(1) The correct desire to emphasize the active rôle of language in the process of cognition and in shaping our image of the world. This is the rational core of those conceptions which — e.g., Ajdukiewicz's radical conventionalism — stress the rôle of the varying conceptual apparatus in producing varying perspectives of the world.

(2) The incorrect transition from that thesis to the assertion concerning the arbitrary nature of the choice of this or that conceptual system, and consequently of this or that image of the world. There is here a confusion of natural languages with formalized "languages" (referred to above), and also a desire to escape from the ambiguity of every-day language to an artificial "ideal language" (a point to be discussed later on).

As regards the claim that language should be analysed and that language should be made the only subject matter of philosophical analysis, we may draw the following conclusions from the foregoing investigations:

Contrary to the common conventionalist opinion, the analysis of language is neither an autonomous nor a sufficient task.

It is not autonomous since the conception of language as a play, of language as an arbitrary product, is in complete contradiction with facts, which testify to intricate relationships between language and reality, and to the shaping of thought-language in the process of reflecting reality in human consciousness. Through the study of language as an integral social phenomenon we desire, in the last analysis, to learn something about reality. For while we reject the idea of the structure of language as an *analogon* of the structure of reality, we support the thesis concerning a specific reflection of reality by thought-language. Thus the analysis of language leads to (1) understanding of the cognitive process, and (2) acquiring knowledge about certain aspects of objective reality, including social reality.

The analysis of language is also not sufficient from the point of view of acquiring knowledge about reality. Language is not the only object of analysis in general, and philosophical analysis in particular. Indeed, it is an important object of research, and that not only because of the danger of paradoxes and antinomies, but chiefly because through the intermediary of language analysis we may arrive at other epistemological results. It is an object of particular importance for philosophical investigations, since philosophy offers generalizations of the research results of the various disciplines, and the study of the peculiar aspect of the cognitive process may be regarded as philosophy's own and fairly independent field of interest. Thus language problems take a front seat not because — as the neo-positivists would have had it — the clarification of meanings of expressions is *the only* task of philosophy, but because the clarification of meanings of expressions *also* is a task of philosophy, and a very important task at that.

In other words, in the achievements of the individual disciplines, as mentioned above, I see the confirmation of the thesis, frequently advanced, concerning the necessity strictly to distinguish between the two aspects of what is called the method of semantic analysis. One aspect is connected with a moderate interpretation of the requirement that such an analysis be made, and in the form imparted to it, for instance, by Kotarbiński it is fully acceptable: it becomes then the self-evident directive for understanding precisely *what* is being said, and *about what*, i.e., the directive of exact and precise formulation of statements. The other aspect is connected with an extreme interpretation of that requirement and implies the whole subjective content of semantic philosophy. Reference is made then to semantic analysis, but what it actually means is that the study and the explaining of meanings of expressions is *the only* task of philosophy, since language is the only object of that analysis, and everything else comprises pseudo-problems resulting from a faulty use of language (as Carnap puts it: from using it in the material, and not in the formal, manner). Such an interpretation of the method of semantic analysis differs radically from the former, moderate interpretation and for essential reasons (since it implies a subjective solution of basic philosophical problems) is not acceptable to an adherent of materialist philosophy. Moreover, it seems that such an interpretation must be unacceptable to any one who values a sober and scientific appraisal of facts above metaphysical speculations in philosophy, even if accompanied by anti-metaphysical declarations.

3. LANGUAGE AND EFFECTIVE COMMUNICATION

Distinguishing in language its communicative function, which consists in conveying thought contents, and the function of formulating thoughts, which consists in that we always think in some language (some authors are of the opinion that this is actually one and the same function, since speechless thinking is interpreted as a dialogue with oneself), we shall now concentrate attention on a special aspect of the communicative function. We shall be interested in *effective* communication, that is, communication which results in an actual *understanding* between at least two persons, one of whom uses a certain language in order to convey to the other his thoughts or emotions, and that other person upon perceiving the given signs of that language *understands* them in the same way as his interlocutor thinks and accepts them as such. From the social point of view, it is extremely important to know the causes of success and failure in the process of human communication, i.e., to know what assists and what hampers that process.

The *understanding* of signs, the understanding of language, is the basis of communication. In order to understand a sign we must perceive it and at the same time experience a psychic act, either such as in the case of phonic speech when the verbal sign is "transparent to meaning", or such as in the case of all other signs, which in some way or another are translated into a phonic language. In the latter case, we have to do with a complicated psychic process which includes association, inference, etc. These, however, are matters of interest mainly to the psychologist and the domain of psychological research. They are disregarded here, together with the whole complex of accompanying issues (understanding as an act, understanding as a disposition, etc). We shall bring out only one aspect, which will lead us to the proper subject matter of our study: the distinction between the understanding of the sign and the understanding of the intention of the user of the sign.

Let us consider an example, borrowed from Martinak: the little son of the station master, who has often watched his father, goes to the railway track, waves the red flag and thus stops the oncoming train. The engine driver has understood the sign, but he has not understood the intention of its user. For the child did not wave the flag in order to stop the train, since he did not even realize the consequences of that act.

This is a trivial example, which shows that conventional signs, confirmed by tradition, have, from the social point of view, objective meanings which need not coincide with the intentions of the people who use those signs without knowing the convention in question. Every performance of certain actions with which someone, without our knowledge, has connected a certain conventional meaning, may serve as an example.

The distinction between the understanding of the sign and the understanding of the intention of the user of the sign ceases to be trivial when one comes to analyse the difference between understanding certain ambiguous or vague terms and understanding the intention of the author of those terms. We have here to do with a vast range of possible misunderstandings, from the simplest, in which we do not know whether the man who says "*brak yest mukh*" is using the Polish or the Russian language, a difference which completely changes the meaning of the sentence (the example is taken from Kotarbiński and means in Polish "there are no flies" or "flies are lacking", and "marriage is eating flies" in Russian), to the more complicated, in which ambiguous words and homonyms appear in the text formulated in a given language, which may result in a wrong interpretation of the speaker's intentions. Another cause of misunderstanding may be vague expressions which, in view of the lack of exact definitions, admit of various interpretations.

A more complicated problem consists in distinguishing between the understanding of meanings of expressions and the recognition of convictions connected with those expressions. In other words, we have here to do with a distinction between communication in the sense of conveying *meanings* of expressions and communication in the sense of conveying *convictions*. If, in contradistinction to misunderstandings, we agree that *communication* is a process of producing signs by one party and of perceiving those signs by the other party, accompanied by *the same understanding* of those signs by both parties, then *effective communication* consists in such a process provided, moreover, that the same understanding of the signs is accompanied by *the same convictions*. When two men who have lost their way in a forest discuss which way they should go in order to find their way, and when finally one of them says "We must now turn to the right, because according to the map that is the only way to reach N", then the comment "Now they understand one another" (or, more strictly, though more artificially in English: "Now communication is established between them") may be taken either in the sense that they both interpret in the same way the meaning of the statement that they have to turn to the right (for there might be no understanding between them if one of them had a poor knowledge of his companion's language), or that they have agreed as to the choice of their way. In conformity with the terminology suggested, that second case is called effective communication. In order to establish effective communication it is necessary first to establish communication in the sense of an identical understanding of meanings of expressions.

Among the obstacles which render human communication difficult, i.e., which cause certain expressions to be understood in different ways by the communicating parties, the principal ones (if it is assumed that the parties concerned know well the language they are using) are: *ambiguity* and *vagueness* of expressions and *linguistic hypostases*. The method of precising the meanings of expressions, which is sometimes called semantic analysis, is intended to remove such shortcomings in human speech. If the requirement to resort to semantic analysis does not go beyond those limits, i.e., if it is confined to the requirement of making the meanings of expressions more precise, then it may not only not provoke objections but, on the contrary — let it be stated once more—it must command the support of every philosophical trend which aspires to being scientific. Let us then briefly examine what is the concrete purpose of that requirement (any profound analysis of the problem of vague expressions and linguistic hypostates would require a separate study).

A clear distinction must be made between ambiguous and vague expressions, although the issues involved are related. This distinction is of practical importance from the point of view of the applicability of the method of semantic analysis, since ambiguity can be removed by means of that method, whereas the vagueness of expressions is of an objective nature and cannot be completely eliminated.

The ambiguity of expressions essentially appears in two forms: a trivial case is represented by what are known as *homonyms*, where one and the same phonic form stands for quite different meanings (although the history of the given language may sometimes indicate connexions and transition stages between such meanings). *Polysemy*, which consists in that the meaning of a word varies according to the context, being different but similar in every case, is much more complicated from the point of view of the requirements of semantic analysis. We have to do with homonymy in the case of such a word as "last", which may mean a shoemaker's device, a measure of weight, "the latest and final", and "to continue in time"; and we have to do with polysemy when there is a feeling of affinity of meanings, as in the case of "to move", which may mean "to change one's own position or place", "to impart motion to an external object", "to evoke another's feelings" ("to make the feelings of another move"). Of course, there is no clear-cut demarcation line between homonymy and polysemy; but these two forms of ambiguity of words may be eliminated (thereby removing the danger of misunderstandings) by precising their meanings through placing them in contexts or by stating explicitly in which of its possible meanings the given word is being actually used.

Things bear a different aspect when it comes to the vagueness of words. That issue, extremely interesting from the philosophical point of view and discussed by many authors, has now a comprehensive literature and has stimulated many fertile ideas[30]. Max Black differentiaties between general and vague words and describes that difference thus:

"The finite area of this field of application of the word is a sign of its *generality*, while its vagueness is indicated by the finite area and lack of specification of its boundary"[31].

Black practically repeats the formulation of Marty, who wrote:

"What we mean by vagueness is the phenomenon that the *field of application of certain names is not strictly outlined*"[32].

Marty referred to names only, whereas Black rightly extends the problem to cover words in general. The point is that a vague word is such a general word with no strictly outlined field of application. Such words always have some "boundary" area concerning which it can never be stated with certainty that a given word is, or is not, applicable to it. Marty's examples are: "about a hundred", "sweetish", "greenish", "big", "small", "quickly", "slowly", etc.

If we disregard scientific terms, the meanings of which are established by convention, vagueness is a property of practically all words. That property is a reflection of the relative character of all classification which takes the form of general names or, more broadly, of general words. Things and phenomena that

---

30 The problem of vague words was studied by Peirce (cf. W. B. Gallie, *Peirce and Pragmatism*, Edinburgh 1952, pp. 173–180). Penetrating remarks on the subject are to be found in *Untersuchungen zur Grundlegung der allgemeinen Grammatik und Sprachphilosophie* by Anton Marty (Vol. 1, Halle a. S. 1908, pp. 52 ff.). Bertrand Russell has devoted to that problem his well-known study "Vagueness" (*Australasian Journal of Philosophy*, Vol. 1, 1923), and Max Black, a work under the same title ("Vagueness").

31 M. Black, "Vagueness", in M. Black, *Language and Philosophy*, p. 31.

32 Marty, op. cit., p. 52.

belong to objective reality are much richer and much more many-sided than can be rendered by any classification, and by the words which express such a classification. In objective reality, there are transitions between the classes of things and of phenomena, represented by words, and these transitions, these "boundary phenomena", account for the fact which we call the vagueness of words. Such is the meaning of the statement that the vagueness of words is an *objective* phenomenon. Black resorts to a different argumentation:

"Vagueness is clearly an objective feature of the series to which the vague symbol is applied"[33].

That is why the only way to avoid vagueness of words is a convention which strictly outlines the boundaries of the field to which a given word refers (although no such strictly outlined boundaries exist in reality). Science often resorts to precising terms by way of an arbitrary convention. For instance, we may adopt, for certain purposes, the convention that water flowing in its natural bed not wider than *n* metres shall be called a "rivulet", and if the bed be wider than *n* metres, then it shall be called a "river", etc. Can that be useful in practice? Of course, the importance of such definitions, which in principle are quite arbitrary, cannot be doubted. But, as has been said above, reality does not divide itself into such "sharply" outlined compartments, and therefore it can be said that a complete elimination of the vagueness of words would make our language a great deal poorer. This is not a declaration against precision in making statements, and against the endeavour to eliminate the vagueness of words and the resulting misunderstandings, but it does draw attention to the objective limits of such a procedure. It is only against this background that we can fully understand the failure of the conception of an "ideal" language.

Philosophical longings for an "ideal" language arise out of age-old complaints about the imperfection and unreliability

---

[33] M. Black, "Vagueness", p. 42.

of language, sources of many mistakes in human cognition. This, too, gave rise to radical tendencies (from Plato to Bergson) to oppose unreliable linguistic cognition to "true" non-linguistic cognition. Other thinkers, like Descartes in his *Meditations*, Bacon in *Novum Organum*, or Berkeley in his *Treatise*, sadly point to language as a source of error and illusions, and tell us to be cautious in using language as an instrument in the process of cognition. Still others, who adopt the thesis concerning an analogy between the structure of language and the structure of reality, see the danger of a "bad" language in the fact that verbalism projects upon reality and accounts for its faulty interpretation, and that we wrongly take properties of words to be properties of things (e.g., Russell in "Vagueness"); on the other hand, they see the benefits of a "good" language mainly in that through becoming acquainted with such a language we become acquainted with reality. Such convictions have given birth to the opinion that the building of an "ideal" language would be a way out from all philosophical difficulties. It is self-evident why the adherents of that opinion were mainly logicians, and especially experts in mathematical logic. Those people who were used to handling mathematical and logical symbols and to construct formalized systems and "languages" succumbed most easily of all to the temptation to make an ideal, perfect language which would make it possible to remove all those imperfections of speech which are sources of errors in cognition. The most outstanding representatives of that tendency were Russell and Wittgenstein. It was they who had worked out a theory which held that through the study of grammar, and especially of syntax, of language, one can study reality, and thus laid the theoretical foundations of the neo-positivist doctrine — so fashionable at a later stage — concerning the analysis of the logical syntax of language as *the sole* task of philosophy. Russell and Wittgenstein also developed the conception that the building of an ideal language, with a perfect logical syntax, might lead to the elimination of nonsense. That doctrine, too, was adopted and made popular by neo-positivism[34].

[34] In 1903 Bertrand Russell wrote in *The Principles of Mathematics*: "The study of grammar, in my opinion, is capable of throwing far more light on philosophical questions than is commonly supposed by philosophers" (p. 42). Many years later, in 1940, in the book *An Inquiry into Meaning and Truth* he repeats, though more carefully: "For my part, I believe that, partly by means of the study of syntax, we can arrive at considerable knowledge concerning the structure of the world" (p. 347). This conception is dealt with by Wittgenstein. Russell states in his "Foreword" to Wittgenstein's *Tractatus*: "The essential business of language is to assert or deny facts. Given the syntax of a language, the meaning of a sentence is determinate as soon as the meaning of the component words is known. In order that a certain sentence should assert a certain fact there must, however the language may be constructed, be something in common between the structure of the sentence and the structure of the fact" (p. 8).

Wittgenstein affirms firmly this thesis: "2.18 What every picture, of whatever form, must have in common with reality in order to be able to represent it at all – rightly or falsely – is the logical form, that is, the form of reality."

On the need of constructing an ideal language and on its functions Wittgenstein wrote as follows: "3.323 In the language of everyday life it very often happens that the same word signifies in two diferent ways – and therefore belongs to two different symbols – or that two words, which signify in different ways, are apparently applied in the same way in the proposition ... 3.324 Thus there easily arise most fundamental confusions (of which the whole of philosophy is full). 3.325 In order to avoid these errors, we must employ a symbolism which excludes them, by not applying the same sign in different symbols and by not applying signs in the same way which signify in different ways. A symbolism, that is to say, which obeys the rules of *logical* grammar – of logical syntax. (The logical symbolism of Frege and Russell is such a language, which, however, does still not exclude all errors)."

Russell agrees with this Wittgenstein's conception and writes in his "Foreword": "A logically perfect language has rules of syntax which prevent nonsense, and has single symbols which always have a definite and unique meaning. Mr Wittgenstein is concerned with the conditions for a logically perfect language – not that any language is logically perfect, or that we believe ourselves capable, here and now, of constructing a logically perfect language, but that the whole function of language is to have meaning, and it only fulfils this function in proportion as it approaches to the ideal language which we postulate" (p. 8).

The conception of an ideal language became bankrupt principally because of its inseverable connection with the assertion that the structure of language is a reflection of the structure of reality. Thus, a perfect language would have to possess a perfect structure which would faultlessly reflect the structure of reality. But here is the basic error in that conception, a vicious circle in reasoning. The structure of reality becomes knowable, according to that conception, through the structure of language, but to be able to build an ideal language one would have to know in advance what is the structure of that reality[35].

But that is not the most important point. Another aspect of the problem is of interest here: the uselessness of the conception of an ideal language (even if we abandon the thesis devoted to the analogy between the structure of language and that of reality) from the point of view of the communicative function of language. It may seem paradoxical that communication requires the vagueness of words. But should we completely eliminate, by a convention, the vagueness of words then, as has already been said above, we should so impoverish our language and so restrict its communicative and expressive function, that the result would defeat the purpose: human communication would take place with difficulty, since the instrument by means of which we communicate with one another would have been injured.

In connection with these remarks which, I repeat, may sound like a paradox, I should like to quote some of Max Black's conclusions concerning Wittgensteins *Tractatus*:

"It is certain that language is a great deal more complex than the accounts supplied by any of the authors mentioned in this essay would suggest. The defect in their answers is not in the character of their method but in the fact that their fragmentary and approximative conclusions are presented as if they were complete analyses"[36].

---

35 I. M. Copi, "Artificial Languages", in *Language, Thought and Culture* ed. P. Henle.

36 M. Black, "Wittgenstein's 'Tractatus' ", p. 165.

Renunciation of an ideal language and of absolute precision of statements does not, however, mean a renunciation of striving for a maximum possible precision. We may not absolutely eliminate the vagueness of words because that is an objective property. But we may restrict it, and even totally eliminate it for certain purposes, by making use of appropriate conventions. We are in a position – and that is the most important point – to eliminate the ambiguity of words by interpreting them in their contexts, by adopting definitions that impart precision to terms, etc. We are also able to reduce, or even completely to eliminate, the danger of misunderstandings due to linguistic hypostases.

This is an old and comparatively simple issue, and yet it has bothered philosophers for so long. This has been so probably because this issue is coupled with the great controversies about the world-outlook, and its solution depends on the standpoint adopted in those controversies.

There is a very fine statement by J. S. Mill:

"The tendency has always been strong to believe that whatever receives a name must be an entity or being, having an independent existence of its own; and if no real entity answering to the name could be found, men did not for that reason suppose that none existed, but imagined that it was something particuliarly abstruse and mysterious, too high to be an object of sense"[37].

We have here to do with an old issue which bears the traditional name of the controversy around the universals. But it is by no means an obsolete problem, belonging only to the Middle Ages. Far less is it, as some authors claim, a purely linguistic issue. It is connected with an important ontological issue, which is also involved in the contemporary fundamental philosophical controversy between materialism and idealism,

---

[37] Quoted after C. K. Ogden & I. A. Richards, *The Meaning of Meaning*, London 1953, p. XXIV.

and which appears in connection with the various controversies about the problems and subject matters of the various particular disciplines. The Platonism of Cantor and Russell, reism originated by Franz Brentano toward the end of his life (*Von den Gegenständen des Denkens*, 1915; *Über das Sein im uneigentlichen Sinne*, 1917) and independently from Brentano developed by Kotarbiński, are eloquent illustrations of that statement. That the issue is not a purely linguistic one, is realized even by scientists who are somewhat remote from materialism, as for instance by Willard van Orman Quine, the author of one of the finest works published since World War II on the notion of existence and linguistic hypostases:

"It is no wonder, then, that ontological controversy should end in controversy over language. But we must not jump to the conclusion that what there is depends on words. Translatability of a question into semantical terms is no indication that the question is linguistic. To see Naples is to bear a name which, when prefixed to the words 'see Naples', yields a true sentence; still there is nothing linguistic about seeing Naples"[38].

The controversy over the interpretation of the words "is" and "exists" is only seemingly a linguistic controversy, a controversy over words. To put it as cautiously as possible, we may say once more that the requirement of semantic analysis, which makes us remember that the existence of a word (this principally applies to names) does not imply the existence of a corresponding object in the direct sense of the word "exists" (that is in such a sense in which we say that a house, a table, or any other object exists — is a correct requirement. The point is not to eliminate general words and to devise a special language for that purpose, but to eliminate hypostases, i.e., the danger of concluding erroneously that if a general name exists then a corresponding "general object" exists as well. To escape the danger of idealistic

---

[38] W. v. O. Quine, *From a Logical Point of View*, Cambridge (Mass.), 1953.

metaphysics in our thinking, a special notation is used in formalized lan guages (a symbol is used to mark whether the object referred to actually exists). If such a notation is not used, one has to bear in mind the danger of hypostases in the interpretation of statements. This is not a method of universal validity, but it generally proves effective.

As stated above, communication (in the sense of the same understanding of the sense of a statement by both parties) is a necessary, but not a sufficient, condition of effective communication. For an effective communication it is necessary not only that a given statement should be understood in the same way by both parties, but also that those parties concerned should share the convictions connected with that statement. This, however, is a socio-psychological issue rather than a linguistic one. Nevertheless, it must be borne in mind that that problem — so important from the social point of view — is closely connected with semantics in the broad sense of the term and forms its component part.

In this field, too, classical philosophical literature has a praiseworthy tradition to its credit. Francis Bacon's crusade in his *Novum Organum* against *idola*, in particular *idola specus*, *idola fori* and *idola theatri*, is a very fine example of a philosopher's interest in the issues of sociotechnics, an example of his understanding of the important function of social psychology (*idola specus*), to a certain extent of the sociology of knowledge (*idola theatri*), and of semantic analysis as well (*idola fori*), in the struggle against superstitions and in the striving for better possibilities of effective communication between men.

What is reasonable and worth continuation in so-called general semantics consists precisely in certain sociotechnical ideas intended to remove, or at least to reduce, obstacles hindering effective communication. The necessity, emphasized by the adherents of that school, to make people assimilate the principles of concrete thinking (appending of indices to general names in order to stress the individual nature of every object which is a designatum of a general name; taking into account the time of events and the changes resulting from the flow of time and changes in external conditions; the use of "etc." to indicate that a description is never exhaustive) and the principles of antiverbalism (the statement that a name is not the thing it denotes; the use of quotation marks to stress the general and vague character of words; the use of the hyphen to indicate that words often separate things which should not be separated from one another etc.) is connected with certain definite sociotechnics.

The important point is that while we reject the erroneous and often fantastic theoretical substantiation of those principles we should not lose sight of their rational content. And most important is it to realize the *practical significance* of semantic researches. Marxist philosophers, who always lay stress on the links connecting theory with practice, greatly abhor "abstractionism". As often happens, fear is not a good adviser, and hence they often eye with suspicion the various disciplines and researches which seem abstract, though in fact they are most closely connected with practice. Such is the case of semantics.

We are now witnessing its rehabilitation. Not only in linguistics, where the development of semantic researches has never faced major difficulties, but also in logic. For it has turned out that the study of logical syntax and metalanguage have very practical applications in the construction of translating machines, mechanical memory devices, etc. It is also worth while to draw attention tó another field of applications of semantics, unfortunately neglected in socialist countries, which is a *scientific theory of propaganda.* The situation is quite paradoxical: a field of social activity which is so closely connected with social and class struggle has been neglected by Marxist science for wrongly interpreted doctrinal reasons. All that has been discussed in this book and is connected with our knowledge of effective communication and with improving that communication, belongs to the theoretical foundations of the science of mass propaganda, a science which in capitalist countries already has a vast literature (at least as far as some aspects of the problem are concerned) and which in our countries is practically non-existent.

That issue, too, can only be indicated here, since it requires a separate study, quite different in nature from the present book. But the actual purpose of the present book consists precisely in pointing to certain research problems, in order to stimulate a more detailed and broader investigation of them in future.

BIBLIOGRAPHY

This list includes the works actually used. Further bibliographical reference can be found in the items marked with an asterisk

Абаев В. И., "Н. Я. Марр (1864—1934). К 25-летию со дня смерти" [N. Marr (1864–1934). On the 25th Anniversary of Death]. In: *Вопросы языкознания*, 1960, № 1, pp. 90–99.

Абаев В. И., "Понятие идеосемантики" [The Concept of Ideosemantics]. In: *Язык и мышление,* т. 11, Москва 1948.

Ajdukiewicz K., "Empiryczny fundament poznania" [The Empirical Foundation of Cognition]. In: *Sprawozdania Poznańskiego Towarzystwa Przyjaciół Nauk*, 1936, nr 1, pp. 27–31.

Ajdukiewicz K., "Epistemologia a semiotyka" [Epistemology and Semiotics]. In: *Przegląd Filozoficzny*, R. 44, 1948, z. 4, pp. 336–347.

Ajdukiewicz K., "Logika a doświadczenie" [Logic and Experience]. In: *Przegląd Filozoficzny*, R. 43, 1947, z. 1–4, pp. 1–21.

Ajdukiewicz K., "On the Notion of Existence". In: *Studia Philosophica*, 1949–1950, Vol. 4, pp. 7–22.

Ajdukiewicz K., *O znaczeniu wyrażeń* [On the Meaning of Expressions]. Odbitka z [reprint from]: *Księga Pamiątkowa Polskiego Towarzystwa Filozoficznego we Lwowie*, Lwów 1931, Książnica-Atlas.

Ajdukiewicz K., "Problemat transcendentalnego idealizmu w sformułowaniu semantycznym" [The Problem of Transcendental Idealism in a Semantic Formulation]. In: *Przegląd Filozoficzny*, R. 40, 1937, z. 3, pp. 271-287.

Ajdukiewicz K., "Sprache und Sinn". In: *Erkenntnis*, 1934, B. 4, pp. 100–138.

Ajdukiewicz K., "Das Weltbild und die Begriffsapparatur". In: *Erkenntnis*, 1934, B. 4, pp. 259–287.

Ajdukiewicz K., "Die wissenschaftliche Weltperspektive". In: *Erkenntnis*, 1935, B. 5, pp. 22–30.

Ajdukiewicz K., "W sprawie artykułu prof. A. Schaffa o moich poglądach filozoficznych" [Concerning the Paper by Prof. A. Schaff On My Philosophical Views]. In: *Myśl Filozoficzna*, 1953, nr 2 (8), pp. 292–334.

Ajdukiewicz K., "W sprawie 'uniwersaliów'" [Concerning 'Universals']. In: *Przegląd Filozoficzny*, R. 37, 1934, z. 3, pp. 219–234.

Ajdukiewicz K., *Język i poznanie*, T. I, *Wybór pism z lat 1920-1939* [Language and Cognition, Vol. I, Selected Works 1920-1939]. Warszawa 1960, PWN.

Ахманова О. С., *Фонология* [Phonology] Москва 1954, Изд. Моск. Унив.

Ахманова О. С., *Очерки по общей и русской лексикологии* [Notes on General and Russian Lexicology]. Москва 1957, Учпедгиз.

Ахманова О. С., *О психолингвистике* [Psycholinguistics]. Москва 1957, Изд. Моск. Унив.

Albrecht E., *Beiträge zur Erkenntnistheorie und das Verhältnis von Sprache und Denken.* Halle (Saale) 1959, M. Niemeyer.

Albrecht E., *Die Beziehungen von Erkenntnistheorie. Logik und Sprache.* Halle (Saale) 1956, M. Niemeyer.

Алексеев М. Н., Колшанский Г. В. "О соотношении логических и грамматических категорий" [On the Relationship between Logical and Grammatical Categories]. In: *Вопросы языкознания,* 1955, № 5, p. 3–19.

Ammer K., *Einführung in die Sprachwissenschaft.* B. 1, Halle (Saale) 1958, M. Niemeyer.

Андреев, И. Д., *Основы теории познания* [Principles of Epistemology] 1959, Изд. АН СССР.

Apostel L., Mandelbrot B., Morf A., *Logique, langage et théorie de l'information.* Third volume of: *Études d'épistémologie génétique*, Paris 1957, Presses Univ. de France.

Асмус В. Ф., "Критика буржуазных идеалистических учений логики эпохи империализма" [A Criticism of Idealistic Bourgeois Theories of Logic in the Period of Imperialism]. In: *Вопросы логики,* Москва 1955, Изд. АН СССР, pp. 192—284.

Atti del XII Congresso Internationale di Filosofia, Vol. 1, Firenze 1958, Sansoni Editore.

Augustine St., *Confessions.* Trans. by F. J. Sheed, London 1943, Sheed & Ward.

Auscombe G. E. M., *An Introduction to Wittgenstein's 'Tractatus'*. London 1959, Hutchinson Univ. Library.

Ayer A. J., *The Foundations of Empirical Knowledge.* London 1947, The Macmillan Co.

Ayer A. J., *Language, Truth and Logic.* London 1948, Victor Gollancz.

Ayer A. J., "Meaning and Intentionality". In: *Atti del XII Congresso* ..., Vol. I, pp. 139–155.

Ayer A. J., *The Problem of Knowledge.* London 1956, The Macmillan Co.

Babcock C. M., *The Harper Handbook of Communication Skills.* New York 1957, Harper & Brothers.

Bautro E., *Idea lingwistyki i semantyki prawniczej* [The Concept of Legal Linguistics and Semantics], Lwów 1935 (Druk "Alfa").

Belevitch V. *Langage des machines et langage humain.* Bruxelles 1956, Office de Publicité.

Benjamin A. C., "Outlines of an Empirical Theory of Meaning". In: *Philosophy of Science*, July 1936, Vol. 3, No. 3, pp. 250–266.

Benveniste E., "Communication animale et langage humain". In: *Diogène*, 1952, No. 1, pp. 1–7.

Benveniste E., "Nature du signe linguistique". In: *Acta Linguistica*, 1939, Vol. 1, Fasc. 1, pp. 23–29.

Bergmann G., *The Metaphysics of Logical Positivism.* New York 1954, Longmans, Green & Co.

Bergson H., *La pensée et le mouvant* (Chap. VI: "Introduction à la méthaphysique"). Paris 1955, Presses Univ. de France.

Beth E. W., "Semantics as a Theory of Reference". In: *Philosophy in the Mid-Century.* A Survey, Vol. 1, ed. by R. Klibansky, Firenze 1958, La Nuova Italia Editrice, pp. 62–100.

Black M., *Critical Thinking. An Introduction to Logic and Scientific Method.* New York 1952, Prentice-Hall.

Black M., *Language and Philosophy. Studies in Method.* New York 1949, Cornell Univ. Press.

Black M., "Russell's Philosophy of Language". In: *The Philosophy of Bertrand Russell*, ed. by P. A. Schlipp, New York 1951, Tudor Publ. Co., pp. 227–255.

Black M., "The Semiotic of Charles Morris". In: M. Black, *Language and Philosophy.*

Black M., "Vagueness". In: M. Black, *Language and Philosophy.*

Black M., "Wittgensteins 'Tractatus'". In: M. Black *Language and Philosophy.*

Bloomfield L., *Language.* London 1957, George Allen & Unwin.

Bloomfield L., "Linguistic Aspects of Science". In: *International Encyclopedia of Unified Science*, Vol. 1, Pt. 1, Chicago 1955, Univ. of Chicago Press, pp. 215-277.

Boas F., *Kultur und Rasse.* Leipzig 1914, Verlag von Voit und Co.

Boas F., *Race, Language and Culture.* New York 1949, The Macmillan Co.

Boas F., "Symbols and History". In: (Ed. R. N. Anshen) *Language …*, pp. 102-121.

Bocheński J. M., *Contemporary European Philosophy.* Berkeley and Los Angeles 1956, Univ. of California Press.

Bodmer F., *The Loom of Language.* London 1943, George Allen & Unwin.

Богуславский В. М., "Слово и понятие" [Word and Notion]. In: (ред. Д. П. Горский) *Мышление и язык,* pp. 213—275.

Bourgeand W., Brocker W., Lehmann J., "De la nature du signe". In: *Acta Linguistica*, 1942-1943, Vol. III, Fasc. 1, pp. 24-30.

Bréal M., *Essai de sémantique. Science des significations.* Paris 1904, Librairie Hachette et Cie.

Brentano F., *Psychologie vom empirischen Standpunkt.* B. 1 – Leipzig 1924, B. 2 – Leipzig 1925, Verlag von Felix Meiner.

Brentano F., "Über das Sein im uneigentlichen Sinne, abstrakte Namen und Verstandesdinge" (1917). In: F. Brentano *Psychologie ...*, B. 2.

Brentano F., "Von den Gegenständen des Denkens". In: F. Brentano *Psychologie ...*, B. 2.

Brentano F., *Wahrheit und Evidenz ...* eingeleitet von Oskar Kraus. Leipzig 1930, Verlag von Felix Meiner.

Bridgman P. W., *The Logic of Modern Physics.* New York 1949, The Macmillan Co.

British Philosophy in the Mid-Century. A Cambridge Symposium, ed. by C. A. Mace, London 1957, George Allen & Unwin.

Brown R. W., *Words and Things.* Glencoe (Illinois) 1958, The Free Press.

Brunot F., *La pensée et la langue.* Paris 1953, Masson et Cie.

Брутян Г. А. "Идеалистическая сущность семантической философии" [The Idealistic Essence of Semantic Philosophy]. In: Современный субъективный идеализм, Москва 1957, Госполитиздат, pp. 287-338.

Брутян Г. А., *Теория познания общей семантики* [The Epistemology of General Semantics]. Ереван 1959, Изд. АН Армянской ССР.

Bühler K., *Sprachtheorie. Die Darstellungsfunktion der Sprache.* Jena 1934, Gustav Fischer.

Bühler K., "Die Symbolik der Sprache" In: *Kant-Studien*, B. 33, Berlin 1928.

Булаховский А. Л., *Введение в языкознание* [Introduction to Linguistics] ч. II, Москва 1953.

Buyssons E., "La nature du signe linguistique". In: *Acta Linguistica*, 1941, Vol. II, Fasc. 2, pp. 83–86.

Carnap R., "Die alte und neue Logik". *Erkenntnis*, 1930–1931, B. 1, p. 12–26.

Carnap R., "Empiricism, Semantics and Ontology". In: *Revue Internationale de Philosophie*, 1950, No. 11. Reprinted in: (Ed. L. Linsky) *Semantics ...*, p. 207–228.

Carnap R., "Foundations of Logic and Mathematics". In: *International Encyclopedia ...* Vol. 1, Pt. 1, pp. 139–214.

Carnap R., *Introduction to Semantics.* Cambridge (Mass.) 1948, Harvard Univ. Press.

Carnap R., "Logical Foundations of the Unity of Science". *International Encyclopedia ...* Vol. 1, Pt. 1, pp. 42–62.

Carnap R., *The Logical Syntax of Language.** London 1937, Kegan Paul Co.

Carnap R., *Der logische Aufbau der Welt.* Berlin 1928.

Carnap R., *Meaning and Necessity*, Chicago 1947. Univ. of Chicago Press.

Carnap R., "Die physikalische Sprache als Universalsprache der Wissenschaft". In: *Erkenntnis*, 1931, B. 2, pp. 432–465.

Carnap R., "Psychologie in physikalischer Sprache". In: *Erkenntnis*, 1932–1933, B. 3, pp. 107–142.

Carnap R., *Symbolische Logik*. Wien 1954, Springer Verlag.

Carnap R., "Testability and Meaning". In: *Philosophy of Science*, 1936, Vol. 3, No. 4, pp. 419–471, and 1937, Vol. 4, No. 4, pp. 1–40.

Carnap R., "Überwindung der Metaphysik durch logische Analyse der Sprache". In: *Erkenntnis*, 1931, B. 2, pp. 219–241.

Carroll J. B., *The Study of Language*.* Cambridge (Mass.) 1955, Harvard Univ. Press.

Casares J., *Introducción a la lexicografia moderna*. Madrid 1950.

Cassirer E., *An Essay on Man. An Introduction to a Philosophy of Human Culture*. New York 1954, Doubleday Anchor Books.

Cassirer E., *Language and Myth* [without date], Dover Publ. Inc.

Cassirer E., *The Philosophy of Symbolic Forms*. Vol. 1: Language. New Haven 1953, Yale Univ. Press.

Chang Tung-sun, "A Chinese Philosopher's Theory of Knowledge". In: (Ed. S. I. Hayakawa) *Our Language and Our World*, pp. 299-324.

Chase St., *Guides to Straight Thinking*. New York 1956, Harper & Brothers.

Chase St., *The Power of Words*.* New York 1954, Harcourt, Brace & Co.

Chase St., *The Tyranny of Words*.* New York 1938, Harcourt, Brace & Co.

Cherry C., *On Human Communication*.* New York 1957, John Wiley & Sons.

Чикобава А. С. *Проблема языка как предмета языкознания* [Language as Object of Linguistics] Москва 1959, Госучпедгиз.

Чикобава А. С., *Введение в языкознание* [Introduction to Linguistics], Москва 1953, Госучпедгиз.

Chomsky N., *Syntactic Structures*. The Hague 1957, Mouton & Co.

Chwistek L., "Antynomie logiki formalnej" [Antinomies in Formal Logic]. In: *Przegląd Filozoficzny*, R. 24, 1921, z. 314, pp. 164-171.

Chwistek L., *Granice nauki. Zarys logiki i metodologii nauk ścisłych* [The Limits of Science. An Outline of the Logic and Methodology of the Exact Sciences]. Lwów-Warszawa [1935], Książnica-Atlas.

Chwistek L., "The Theory of Constructive Types". Pt. 1. In: *Rocznik Polsk. Tow. Matem.*, T. 2, Kraków 1923, pp. 9-47.

Cohen M., *Le langage. Structure et évolution*. Paris 1949/50, Editions Sociales.

Cohen M., *Pour une sociologie du langage*. Paris 1956, Ed. Albin Michel.

Cohen M., "Structure sociale et structure linguistique". In: *Diogène*, 1956, No. 15, pp. 46–57.

Copi I. M., "Artificial Languages". In: (Ed. P. Henle) *Language, Thought and Culture,* pp. 96–120.

Cornforth M., *Science Versus Idealism in Defence of Philosophy Against Positivism and Pragmatism.* London 1955, Lawrence and Wishart.

Czeżowski T., *Logika. Podręcznik dla studiujących nauki filozoficzne.* [Logic. A Textbook for the Students of Philosophy]. Warszawa 1949, PZWS.

Darmesteter A., *La vie des mots étudiée dans leurs significations.* Paris [without date], Librairie Ch. Delagrave.

Dąmbska I., "Z semantyki zdań warunkowych" [The Semantics of Conditional Sentences]. In: *Przegląd Filozoficzny,* R. 41, 1938, z. 3, pp. 241–267.

Дегтерева Т. А. "Развитие методов и общей проблематики в советском языкознании" [The Development of Methods and Problems in Soviet Linguistics]. In: *Принципы научного анализа языка* [Principles of a Scientific Analysis of Language], Москва 1959, Изд. В. П. Щ., pp. 3–44.

Delacroix H., *Le langage et la pensée.* Paris 1924, Librairie Felix Alcan.

Dettering R., "What Phonetic Writing Did to Meaning". In: (Ed. S. I. Hayakawa) *Our Language and Our World,* pp. 325–342.

Державин Н. С. "Слово — сигнал и слово — символ в процессе глоттогонии" [Word as Signal and Word as Symbol in the Process of Glottogony] In: *Языкознание и материализм,* вып. II, Москва 1931, Гос. Соц. Экон. Изд. pp. 174–192.

Dewey J., *Experience and Nature.* London 1929, George Allen & Unwin.

Doroszewski W., "Czynnik społeczny i indywidualny w rozwoju znaczeniowym wyrazów" [Social and Individual Factors in the Semantic Evolution of Words]. In: *Symbolae Grammaticae in honorem Ioannis Rozwadowski.* Vol. 1. Cracoviae 1927, pp. 19–35.

Doroszewski W., "Le structuralisme linguistique et les études de géographie dialectale". Reprint from *Proceedings of the VIII International Congress of Linguists.*

Doroszewski W., "Uwagi o semantyce. Z dyskusji logiczno-semantycznej" [Notes on Semantics. A Discussion of Logic and Semantics]. In: *Myśl Filozoficzna* 1955, nr. 3 (17), pp. 83–94.

Doroszewski W., *Z zagadnień leksykografii polskiej* [Issues of Polish Lexicography]. Warszawa 1954, PIW.

Ducasse C. J., "Symbols, Signs and Signals". In: *The Journal of Symbolic Logic,* June 1939, Vol. 4, No. 2, pp. 41–52.

Engels F., *Dialectic of Nature.* Transl. and ed. by C. Dutt, London 1940, Lawrence and Wishart. Chapt. IX: "The Part Played by Labour in the Transition from Ape to Man".

Engels F., *Herr Eugen Dühring's Revolution in Science* (*Anti-Dühring*), London 1940, Lawrence and Wishart.

Erdmann K. O., *Die Bedeutung der Wortes.* Leipzig 1910, Eduard Avenarius.

Estrich R. M., Sperber H., *Three Keys to Language.* 1952, Rinehart and Co.

Feibleman J. K., *Inside the Great Mirror. A critical examination of the philosophy of Russell, Wittgenstein and their followers.* The Hague 1958, Martinus Nijhoff.

Фессалоницкий С. А. "Обзор литературы по вопросам связи языка и мышления" [A Review of Literature on the Relationship between Language and Thinking]. *Вопросы языкознания*, 1953, № 3, pp. 121–130.

"Filosofia e Simbolismo" – *Archivio di Filosofia* (Organo dell' Istituto di Studi Filosofici). Roma 1956, Fratelli Bocca Editori.

Forest A., "La communication". In: *Atti del XII Congresso* ..., Vol. 1, pp. pp. 157-172.

Frank Ph., *Modern Science and Its Philosophy.* Cambridge 1950, Harvard Univ. Press.

"Frege on Russell's Paradox". In: *Translations from Philosophical Writings of Gottlob Frege.* Oxford 1952, Basil Blackwell.

Frege G., "On Sense and Reference". In: *Translations* ...

Fries Ch. C., *The Structure of English.* London 1957, Longmans, Green & Co.

Frisch K. v., Benveniste E., "Lettres à la Rédaction". In: *Diogène* 1954, No. 7, pp. 129–132.

Fritz Ch. A., Jr, *Bertrand Russell's Construction of the External World.* London 1952, Routledge & Kegan Paul.

Gaertner H., *Gramatyka współczesnego języka polskiego* [A Grammar of Contemporary Polish Language]. Part 2. Lwów 1933, Książnica-Atlas.

Gätschenberger R., *Symbola. Anfangsgründe einer Erkenntnistheorie.* Karlsruhe i. B. 1920, G. Braun.

Gätschenberger R., *Zeichen, die Fundamente des Wissens.* Stuttgart 1932, Frommann.

Галкина-Федорук Е. М., "О форме и содержании в языке" [Form and Content in Language] In: [ред. А. П. Горский] *Мышление и язык* [Thinking and Language], pp. 352-407.

Галкина-Федорук Е. М., "Основные вопросы языкознания в трудах Ленина" [The Fundamental Issues of Linguistics in the Works of V. Lenin] *Иностранный язык в школе,* 1951, № 1, pp. 3–12.

Галкина-Федорук Е. М., *Слово и понятие* [Word and Notion] Москва 1956, Учпедгиз.

Галкина-Федорук Е. М., "Слово и понятие в свете учения классиков марксизма-ленинизма" [Word and Notion in the Light of Works of Classics of Marxism-Leninism] *Вестник Московского Университета,* Серия Общ. Наук, вып. 4, сентябрь 1951, № 9, pp. 105–125.

Галкина-Федорук Е. М. "Современный русский язык" [Contemporary Russian Language] *Лексика,* Москва 1954, Изд. Моск. Ун–та.

Галкина-Федорук Е. М. *Суждение и предложение* [Proposition and Sentence] Москва 1956, Изд. Моск. Ун-та.

Галкина-Федорук Е. М. "Знаковость в языке с точки зрения марксистского языкознания" [Sign-Function in Language from the Point of View of Marxist Linguistics] *Иностранный язык в школе,* 1952, № 2, pp. 3–11.

Gallie W. B., *Peirce and Pragmatism.* Edinburgh 1952, The Pelican Series.

Gamillscheg E., *Französische Bedeutungslehre.* Tübingen 1951, M. Niemeyer.

Gardiner A., *The Theory of Speech and Language.* Oxford 1951, The Clarendon Press.

Gawroński A., *Szkice językoznawcze* [Essays on Linguistics]. Warszawa 1928, Gebethner i Wolff.

Gleason H. A., Jr, *An Introduction to Descriptive Linguistics.* New York 1955.

Goldstein K., *Language and Language Disturbances.* New York 1948, Grune & Stratton.

Goldstein K., "The Nature of Language". In: [Ed. R. N. Anshen] *Language* ..., pp. 18-40.

Goodman N., "On Likeness of Meaning". In: [Ed. L. Linsky] *Semantics* ..., pp. 65–74.

Горский Д. П., "Извращение неопозитивизмом вопросов логики" [The Distortion of the Issues of Logic by Neo-Positivists]. In: *Современный субъективный идеализм* [Contemporary Subjective Idealism], pp. 219–286.

Горский Д. П., "К вопросу об образовании и развитии понятий" [On the Formation and Evolution of Concepts]. *Вопросы философии,* 1952, № 4, pp. 64–77.

Горский Д. П., "О роли языка в познании" [On the Rôle of Language in Cognition]. In: *Вопросы философии* 1953, № 2, pp. 75–92.

Горский Д. П., "Роль языка в познании" [The Rôle of Language in Cognition]. In: [ред. А. П. Горский] *Мышление и язык* [Thinking and Language], pp. 73-116.

Granet M., "L'expression de la pensée en chinois". In: *Journal de Psychologie* 1928, No. 8, pp. 617-656.

Greenberg J. H., *Essays in Linguistics.* Chicago 1957, Univ. of Chicago Press.

Greenwood D., *Truth and Meaning* [Foreword by H. L. Searles]. New York 1957, Philosophical Library.

Greniewski H., *Elementy logiki formalnej* [Elements of Formal Logic]. Warszawa 1955, PWN.

Gusdorf G., *La parole.* Paris 1956, Presses Univ. de France.

Hamann R., *Das Symbol.* Gräfenhainichen 1902, Wilhelm Hecker.

Hamburg C. H., *Symbol and Reality. Studies in the Philosophy of Ernst Cassirer.* The Hague 1956, Martinus Nijhoff.

Hampshire St., "The Interpretation of Language: Words and Concepts". In: [Ed. C. A. Mace] *British Philosophy ...*, pp. 267-279.

Hampshire St., *Thought and Action.* London 1959, Chatto & Windus.

Hare R. M., *The Language of Morals.* Oxford 1952, The Clarendon Press.

Hartmann P., *Sprache und Erkenntnis zur Konstitution des explizierenden Bestimmens.* Heidelberg 1958, Carl Winter.

Hayakawa S. I., *Language in Thought and Action**. New York 1949, Harcourt, Brace & Co.

Hayakawa S. I., "Semantics, General Semantics and Related Disciplines". In: [Ed. S. I. Hayakawa] *Language, Meaning and Maturity*, pp. 19–37.

Hayakawa S. I., "What Is Meant by Aristotelian Structure of Language?" In: [Ed. S. I. Hayakawa] *Language, Meaning and Maturity*, pp. 217–224.

Head H., *Aphasia and Kindred Disorders of Speech.* Vols. 1 and 2. New York 1926, The Macmillan Co.

Helmholtz H., v., "Die Tatsachen in der Wahrnehmung". In: H. v. Helmholtz' *Vorträge und Reden.* B. 2. Braunschweig 1903, Fr. Vieweg und Sohn.

Hempel C. G., "Le problème de la vérité". In: *Theoria* (A Swedish Journal of Philosophy and Psychology), 1937, Vol. 3, Parts 2 and 3, pp. 206-246.

Hempel C. G., "On the Logical Positivists' Theory of Truth". *Analysis*, 1935, Vol. 2, No. 4.

Hempel C. G., "Problems and Changes in the Empiricist Criterion of Meaning", In: [Ed. L. Linsky] *Semantics ...*, pp. 161-185.

Herdan G., *Language as Choice and Chance.* Groningen 1956, P. Noordhoff.

Herder J. G., *Über den Ursprung der Sprache.* Berlin 1959, Akademie-Verlag.

Hetper W., "Rola schematów niezależnych w budowie systemu semantyki" [The Rôle of Independent Schemes in Building a System of Semantics]. *Archiwum Tow. Nauk. we Lwowie*, dz. 3, t. 9, z. 5, Lwów 1938, pp. 253–264.

Hodges H. A., *Languages. Standpoints and Attitudes.* London 1953, Oxford Univ. Press.

Hofstätter P. R., *Vom Leben des Wortes.* Wien 1949, Universitätsverlag.

Hoijer H., "The Sapir-Whorf Hypothesis". In: [Ed. H. Hoijer] *Language in Culture*, pp. 92–105.

Holloway J., *Language and Intelligence.* London 1955, The Macmillan Co.

Humboldt W., v., *Über das vergleichende Sprachstudium.* Verlag von Felix Meiner in Leipzig, Taschenausgaben der "Philosophischen Bibliothek", H. 17.

Huppé B. F., Kaminsky J., *Logic and Language*, New York 1956, A. A. Knopf.

Husserl E., *Ideen zu einer reinen Phänomenologie und phänomenologischen Philosophie.* Halle a. S., M. Niemeyer.

Husserl E., *Logische Untersuchungen.* B. 1. und 2. Halle 1913-1921, M. Niemeyer.

Ingarden R., *Das literarische Kunstwerk.* Halle 1931, M. Niemeyer.

Ingarden R., *O dziele literackim* [The Literary Work]. Warszawa 1960, PWN.

Jakobson R., "Linguistic Glosses to Goldstein's 'Wortbegriff' ". 1959, *Journal of Individual Psychology*, Vol. 15, pp. 62–65.

Jakobson R., "On Linguistic Aspects of Translation". In: *On Translation* [Ed. Reuben A. Brower]. Cambridge (Mass.) 1959, Harvard Univ. Press, pp. 232–239.

Jakobson R., *Poetyka w świetle językoznawstwa* [Poetics in the Light of Linguistics]. Wrocław 1960, Ossolineum.

Jakobson R., Halle M. *Fundamentals of Language.* The Hague 1956, Mouton & Co.

Jaspers K., *Philosophie.* B. 2: *Existenzerhellung.* Berlin 1932, Verlag von Julius Springer.

Jespersen O., *Language, Its Nature, Development and Origin.* London 1954, George Allen & Unwin.

Jespersen O., *The Philosophy of Grammar.* London 1955, George Allen & Unwin.

Joergensen J., "The Development of Logical Empiricism". In: *International Encyclopedia of Unified Science*, Vol. 2, No. 9, Univ. of Chicago Press 1951.

Johnson E. S., *Theory and Practice of the Social Studies.* New York 1956, The Macmillan Co.

Johnson W., *People in Quandaries.* The Semantics of Personal Adjustment.* New York 1946, Harper & Brothers.

Juret A., *Les idées et les mots.* Paris 1960, Librairie Philosophique.

Kaufmann F., *Methodology of the Social Sciences.* London 1958, Thames & Hudson.

Kemeny J. G., "A New Approach to Semantics". Part 1. In: *The Journal of Symbolic Logic*, March 1956, Vol. 21, No. 1, pp. 1–27.

Kemeny J. G., "Models of Logical Systems". In: *The Journal of Symbolic Logic*, March 1948, Vol. 13, No. 1, pp. 16–30.

Keyes K. S., Jr., *How to Develop Your Thinking Ability*. New York 1950, McGraw Hill Book Co.

Klemensiewicz Z., *Język polski* [Polish Language]. Lwów-Warszawa 1937, Książnica-Atlas.

Kokoszyńska M., "Logiczna składnia języka, semantyka i logika wiedzy" [The Logical Syntax of Language, Semantics, and the Logic of Knowledge]. In: *Przegląd Filozoficzny*, R. 39, 1936, z. 1, pp. 38–49.

Колщанский Г. В., "В чем различие знаковых систем" [Differences Between Sign Systems]. In: *Вопросы философии*, 1960, pp. 126–134.

Kołakowski L., "Filozofia nieinterwencji" [The Philosophy of Non-intervention]. In: *Myśl Filozoficzna*, 1953, nr 2 (8), pp. 335–373.

Korzybski A., *Manhood of Humanity. The Science and Art of Human Engineering*. New York 1923, E. P. Dutton & Co.

Korzybski A., *Science and Sanity. An Introduction to Non-Aristotelian Systems and General Semantics*. Lancaster (Penn.) 1941.

Kotarbińska J., "Pojęcie znaku" [The Concept of Sign]. In: *Studia Logica*, 1957, vol. 6, pp. 57–133.

Kotarbiński T., *Elementy teorii poznania, logiki formalnej i metodologii nauk* [Elements of Epistemology, Formal Logic and the Methodology of Sciences]. Lwów 1929, Zakł. Nar. im. Ossolińskich.

Kotarbiński T., *Przegląd problematyki logiczno-semantycznej* [A Review of Issues of Logical Semantics]. Odbitka z [reprint from:] *Sprawozdania z czynności i posiedzeń Łódzk. Tow. Nauk.* za I półr. 1947, R. 2, nr 1 (3), Łódź 1947.

Kotarbiński T., *W sprawie pojęcia prawdy* [On the Concept of Truth]. Odbitka [Reprint] z 37 rocznika *Przeglądu Filozoficznego*, Warszawa 1934.

Ковтун Л. С., "О значении слова" [The Meaning of Words]. In: *Вопросы языкознания*, 1955, № 5, pp. 65–77.

Kraft V., *Der Wiener Kreis. Der Ursprung des Neopositivismus*. Wien 1950, Springer Verlag.

Kronasser H., *Handbuch der Semasiologie*. Heidelberg 1952, Carl Winter.

Курилович Е. Р. "Заметки о значении слова" [Notes on the Meaning of Words]. In: *Вопросы языкознания*, 1955, № 3, pp. 73–81.

Kuryłowicz J., "Les structures fondamentales de la langue". In: *Esquisses Linguistiques*, Wrocław-Kraków 1960, Ossolineum.

Kuryłowicz J., "Linguistique et théorie du signe". In: *Esquisses Linguistiques*, Wrocław-Kraków 1960, Ossolineum.

Kuryłowicz J., "Podstawy psychologiczne semantyki" [The Psychological Foundation of Semantics]. In: *Przegląd Filozoficzny*, R. 30, 1927, z. 4, pp. 319–322.

Kuryłowicz J., "Struktura morfemu" [The Structure of Morpheme]. In: *Esquisses Linguistiques*, Wrocław-Kraków 1960, Ossolineum.

Langer S. K., *Feeling and Form. A Theory of Art*. London 1953, Routledge & Kegan Paul.

Langer S. K., "On Cassirer's Theory of Language and Myth". In: *The Philosophy of Ernst Cassirer*. Ed. by P. A. Schlipp. New York 1958, Tudor Publ. Co., pp. 379–400.

Langer S. K., *Philosophy in a New Key*. A Study in the Symbolism of Reason, Rite and Art*. Cambridge (Mass.) 1957, Harvard Univ. Press.

Language: An Enquiry into Its Meaning and Function. Planned and edited by R. N. Anshen, New York 1957, Harper & Brothers.

Language in Culture. Ed. by H. Hoijer, Chicago (Illinois) 1955, Univ. of Chicago Press.

Language, Meaning and Maturity. Selections from *ETC: A Review of General Semantics 1943-1953*. Ed. by S. I. Hayakawa, New York 1954, Harper & Brothers.

Language, Thought and Culture. Ed. by P. Henle, Ann Arbor 1958, Univ. of Michigan Press.

The Language of Wisdom and Folly. Ed. by I. J. Lee, New York 1949, Harper & Brothers.

Lee I. J., *How to Talk with People*. New York 1952, Harper & Brothers.

Lee I. J., *Language Habits in Human Affairs*. New York 1941, Harper & Brothers.

Lenin V. I., *Materialism and empiriocriticism. Critical comments on a reactionary philosophy*. Moscow 1947, Foreign Languages Publishing House.

Ленин В. И., *Философские тетради* [Philosophical Notebooks]. Ленинград 1947, Гос. Издат. Полит. Лит.

Леонтьев А. Н., Леонтьев А. А., "О двояком аспекте языковых явлений" [The Double Aspect of Linguistic Phenomena]. In: *Философские науки*, 1959, № 2, pp. 116–125.

Lerch E., "Vom Wesen des sprachlichen Zeichens. Zeichen oder Symbol?" In: *Acta Linguistica*, 1939, vol. 1, fasc. 3, pp. 145–161.

Le Roy E., "Science et Philosophie". Extrait de la *Revue de Métaphysique et de Morale*, Paris, Juillet 1899.

Le Roy E., "Sur quelques objections adressées à la nouvelle philosophie". In: *Revue de Métaphysique et de Morale*, 1901, pp. 292–327 and 407–432.

Le Roy E., "Un positivisme nouveau". In: *Revue de Métaphysique et de Morale*, 1901, pp. 138–153.

Leśniewski St., "Grundzüge eines neuen Systems der Grundlagen der Mathematik". In: *Fundamenta Mathematicae*, 1929, t. 14, pp. 1–81.

Leśniewski St., "O podstawach ontologii" [The Foundations of Ontology]. In: *Sprawozdania z posiedzeń Tow. Nauk. Warsz.*, Wydz. 3, R. 23, z. 4–6, Warszawa 1930, pp. 111–132.

Левиковская К. А., *Лексикология немецкого языка* [The Lexicology of the German Language]. Москва 1956, Госучпедгиз.

Lévi-Strauss C., *Anthropologie structurale.* Paris 1958, Librairie Plon.

Lévy-Bruhl L., *Les fonctions mentales dans les sociétés inférieures.* Paris 1912, Librairie Félix Alcan.

Lewis C. I., *Mind and the World-Order.* New York 1929, Charles Scribner's Sons.

Lewis C. I., "The Modes of Meaning". In: [Ed. L. Linsky] *Semantics* ..., pp. 49–63.

Logic and Language. First and second series. Ed. by A. G. N. Flew, Oxford 1955, Basil Blackwell.

Логические исследования. Сборник статей [Logical Researches. Collected Papers]. Москва 1959, Изд. АН СССР.

Longabaugh Th., *General Semantics. An Introduction.* New York 1957, Vantage Press.

Лонтев Т. П., "О природе значения языкового знака" [The Nature of the Meaning of Language Sign]. In: *Вопросы философии*, 1960, № 7, pp. 127–135.

Lundberg G. A., Schrag C. C., Larsen O. N., *Sociology.* New York 1954, Harper & Brothers.

Лурия А. Р., "Роль слова в формировании временных связей у человека" [The Rôle of Words in the Formulation of Temporal Relations by Man]. In: *Вопросы психологии*, 1955, № 1, pp. 73–86.

Лурия А. Р. *Травматическя афазия* [Traumatic Aphasia], Москва 1947.

Łoś J., "The Algebraic Treatment of the Methodology of Elementary Deductive Systems". In: *Studia Logica*, 1955, vol. 2, pp. 151–211.

Łoś J., "On the Extending of Models". (I). In: *Fundamenta Mathematicae*, 1955, t. 42, pp. 38–54.

Łoś J., *Gramatyka polska* [A Grammar of the Polish Language]. Part II: *Słowotwórstwo* [Word-Formation]. Lwów 1925, Zakł. Nar. im. Ossolińskich.

Łoś J., "Zakres wyrazu i pojęcia" [The Extension of Word and of Notion]. *Język Polski*, R. 12, 1927, nr 3, pp. 73–75.

Łuszczewska-Romahnowa S., "Wieloznaczność a język polski" [Ambiguity and the Polish Language], In: *Kwartalnik Filozoficzny*, 1948, t. 17, pp. 47–58.

Malinowski B., "The Problem of Meaning in Primitive Languages. Supplement". In: C. K. Ogden, I. A. Richards *The Meaning of Meaning*, pp. 296-336.

Marhenke P., "The Criterion of Significance". In: [Ed. L. Linsky] *Semantics ...*, pp. 137–159.

Maritain J., "Language and the Theory of Sign". In: [Ed. R. N. Anshen] *Language ...*, pp. 86–101.

Marx K., Engels F., *Die deutsche Ideologie. Werke*, B. 3. Berlin 1958, Dietz Verlag.

Marks K., Engels F., *Die Heilige Familie, oder Kritik der kritischen Kritik. Gegen Bruno Bauer und Konsorten.* Leipzig 1953.

Marx K., "Theses on Feuerbach". In: F. Engels, *Ludwig Feuerbach and the End of Classical German Philosophy.* Moscow 1949, Foreign Languages Publishing House.

Marouzeau J., *La linguistique ou science du langage.* Paris 1950, Librairie Orientaliste Paul Geuthner.

Marouzeau J., *Notre langue.* Paris 1955, Librairie Delagrave.

Марр Н. Я., "Этапы развития яфетической теории" [The Stages of Development of the Japhetic Theory]. In: Н. Я. Марр. *Избранные работы*, Т. I., Ленинград 1933, Изд. ГАИМК. In particular the following works have been utilized: "Индоевропейские языки Средиземноморья" [The Indo-European Languages of the Mediterranean Region] "Основные достижения яфетической теории" [The Basic Achievements of the Japhetic Theory]; "К происхождению языков" [On the Origin of Languages]; "Яфетические языки" [The Japhetic Languages].

Марр Н. Я., *Яфетическая теория* [The Japhetic Theory]. Баку 1928, Азгиз.

Марр Н. Я., *Язык и мышление* [Language and Thinking]. Москва 1931, Госсоцэкгиз.

Марр Н. Я. Язык и современность [Language and Contemporaneity]. Ленинград 1932, Изд. ГАИМК.

Martin R. M., *Truth and Denotation. A Study in Semantical Theory.* London 1958, Routledge & Kegan Paul.

Martinak E., *Psychologische Untersuchungen zur Bedeutungslehre.* Leipzig 1901, Verlag von J. A. Barth.

Marty A., *Untersuchungen zur Grundlegung der allgemeinen Grammatik und Sprachphilosophie.* B. 1. Halle a. S. 1908, M. Niemeyer.

Maruszewski M., "Uwagi o badaniach psychologicznych nad specyfiką ludzkiego działania" [Remarks on Psychological Researches on the Specific Traits of Human Action]. In: *Z problematyki psychologii i teorii poznania* [Problems of Psychology and Epistemology], Warszawa 1958, PWN, pp. 101–200.

Mauthner F., *Beiträge zu einer Kritik der Sprache.* B. 1: *Zur Sprache und zur Psychologie.* B. 2: *Zur Sprachwissenschaft.* B. 3: *Zur Grammatik und Logik.* Leipzig 1923, Verlag von Felix Meiner.

Mead G. H., *Mind, Self and Society*. Chicago (Illinois) 1955, Univ. of Chicago Press.

"The Meaning of " 'Meaning' ". A Symposium by F. C. S. Schiller, B. Russell and H. H. Joachim". In: *Mind*, October 1920, No. 116, pp. 385–414.

Meillet A. "Comment les mots changent de sens". In: A. Meillet, *Linguistique historique el linguistique générale*. T. 1. Paris 1948, Eduard Champion, pp. 230–271.

Meinong A., *Über Annahmen*. Leipzig 1910, Verlag von J. A. Barth.

Meredith G. P., "Semantics in Relation to Psychology". In: *Archivum Linguisticum*, 1956, Vol. 8, Fasc. 1, pp. 1–12.

Мещанинов И. И., *Новое учение о языке* [A New Theory of Language] Ленинград 1936.

Мещанинов И. И., *Общее языкознание* [General Linguistics]. Ленинград 1940, Учпедгиз.

Milewski T., *Zarys językoznawstwa ogólnego*. [An Outline of General Linguistics], Part 1: "Teoria językoznawstwa" [The Theory of Linguistics] Lublin-Kraków 1947.

Mill J. St., *Système de logique déductive et inductive*. T. 1 et 2. Paris 1866, Libr. Philos. de Lagrange.

Miller G. A., *Language and Communication*.* New York-Toronto-London 1951, McGraw Hill Book Co.

Mises R. v., *Positivism. A Study in Human Understanding*. Cambridge (Mass.) 1951, Harvard Univ. Press.

Moore, G. E., *Philosophical Papers*. London 1959, George Allen & Unwin.

Moore G. E., "Russell's 'Theory of Descriptions' ". In: *The Philosophy of Bertrand Russell*. Ed. by P. A. Schlipp. New York 1951, Tudor Publ. Co., pp. 175–225.

Morris Ch. W., "Foundations of the Theory of Signs". In: *International Encyclopedia of Unified Science*. Vol. 1, No. 2, Chicago (Illinois) 1938, Univ. of Chicago Press.

Morris Ch. W., *Logical Positivism, Pragmatism and Scientific Empiricism*. Paris 1937, Hermann et Cie.

Morris Ch. W., *The Open Self*. New York [without date], Prentice-Hall.

Morris Ch. W., *Signs, Language and Behavior*.* New York 1946, Prentice-Hall.

Mostowski A., *Logika matematyczna. Kurs Uniwersytecki* [Mathematical Logic. A University Course]. Warszawa-Wrocław 1948.

Mostowski A., "On Models of Axiomatic Systems". *Fundamenta Mathematicae*, 1952, t. 39, pp. 133–158.

Mounin G., "Communication linguistique humaine et communication non-linguistique animale". *Les Temps Modernes*, Avril-Mai 1960, No. 169–170, pp. 1684–1700.

Мшвенирадзе В. В., "О философской сущности 'семантической концепции истины'", [The Philosophical Essence of the 'Semantic Concept of Truth'], In: *Логические исследования* [Logical Researches], pp. 48–68.

Мышление и язык [Thinking and Language]. Ред. Д. П. Горский, Москва 1953, Госполитиздат.

Nagel E., *Logic Without Metaphysics*. Glencoe (Illinois) 1956, The Free Press.

Нарский И. С., "Философская сущность неопозитивизма" [The Philosophical Essence of Neo-Positivism]. In: *Современный субъективный идеализм* [Contemporary Subjective Idealism], pp. 140–218.

Nauka Pawłowa a filozoficzne zagadnienia psychologii. Zbiór artykułów. [The Pavlovian Theory and the Philosophical Problems of Psychology. Collected Papers]. Warszawa 1954, PWN.

Nehring A., "The Problem of the Linguistic Sign". In: *Acta Linguistica*, vol. VI, fasc. 1, Copenhague 1950.

Neurath O., "Soziologie im Physikalismus". In: *Erkenntnis*, 1931, B. 2, pp. 393–431.

Nyrop K., *Das Leben der Wörter*. Leipzig 1903, Eduard Avenarius.

Ogden C. K., Richards I. A., *The Meaning of Meaning*. London 1953, Routledge & Kegan Paul.

Osgood Ch. E., Suci G. J., Tannenbaum P. H., *The Measurement of Meaning*. Urbana 1957, Univ. of Illinois Press.

Ossowska M., "Słowa i myśli" [Words and Thoughts]. Odbitka [Reprint] z 34 rocznika *Przeglądu Filozoficznego*, Warszawa 1931.

Ossowska M., "Stosunek logiki i gramatyki" [The Relationship between Logic and Grammar]. Odbitka [Reprint] z *Kwartalnika Filozoficznego*, Kraków 1929.

Ossowska-Niedźwiecka M., "Semantyka profesora St. Szobera" [The Semantics of Professor S. Szober]. *Przegląd Filozofiiczny*, R. 28, 1925, z. 4, pp. 258–272.

Ossowski St., "Analiza pojęcia znaku" [An Analysis of the Concept of the Sign]. Odbitka [Reprint] z *Przeglądu Filozoficznego*, 1926, z. 1–2, Warszawa 1926.

Our Language and Our World. Selections from *ETC: A Review of General Semantics*, 1953–1958, New York 1959, Harper & Brothers.

Öhman S., *Wortinhalt and Weltbild*. Stockholm 1951.

Панфилов В. З. "К вопросу о соотношении языка и мышления" [Concerning the Relationship between Language and Thinking]. In: [ред. Д. П. Горский] *Мышление и язык* [Thinking and Language], pp. 117–165.

Pap A., *Semantics and Necessary Truth. An Inquiry into the Foundations of Analytic Philosophy*. New Haven 1958, Yale Univ. Press.

Partrige E., *The World of Words*. London 1954, Hamish Hamilton.

Paul H., *Prinzipien der Sprachgeschichte*. Halle 1886, M. Niemeyer.

Paulhan Fr., "Qu'est-ce que c'est le sens des mots?" *Journal de Psychologie*, 1928, No. 4–5, pp. 289–329.

Pei M., *The Story of Language*. London 1957, George Allen & Unwin.

Peirce Ch. S. "How to Make Our Ideas Clear". In: *Values in a Universe of Change. Selected Writings of Charles S. Peirce*. Stanford (California) 1958, Stanford Univ. Press.

Peirce Ch. S. "Issues of Pragmatism". In: *Values in a Universe of Change*.

Peirce Ch. S., "Logic as Semiotic: The Theory of Signs". In: *Philosophical Writings of Peirce*. Selected and edited with an introduction by Justus Buchler. New York 1955, Dover Publ., pp. 98–119.

Peirce Ch. S., "What Pragmatism Is". In: *Values in a Universe of Change*.

Perelman Ch., "Logique, langage et communication". In: *Atti del XII Congresso* ..., vol. 1, pp. 123–135.

Philosophy and Analysis. Ed. by M. MacDonald, Oxford 1954, Basil Blackwell.

Piaget J., *La formation du symbole chez l'enfant*. Neuchâtel 1959, Delachaux et Niestlé.

Piaget J., *Introduction a l'épistémologie génétique*. T. 1: "La pensée mathématique". T. 2: "La pensée physique". T, 3: "La pensée biologique ..., psychologique et ... sociologique". Paris 1950, Presses Univ. de France.

Picard M., *Der Mensch und das Wort*. Erlenbach-Zürich 1955, Eugen Reutsch Verlag.

Pichon E., "Sur le signe linguistique". In: *Acta Linguistica*, 1940–41, vol. II, fasc. 1, pp. 51–52.

Platon, "Kratylos". In: *Platons Ausgewählte Werke*, B. 3, München 1918, Georg Müller Verlag.

Poincaré H., *Science et Hypothèse*, Paris 1935, Flammarion.

Poincaré H., *Science et Méthode*. Paris 1908, Flammarion.

Poincaré H., *La Valeur de la Science*. Paris 1935, Flammarion.

Попов П. С., "Понятие слова в свете марксистского учения о непосредственной связи языка и мышления". [The Concept of Word in the Light of the Marxist Theory of a Direct Relation between Language and Thinking]. In: *Вестник Московского Университета*, Серия Общественных Наук, 1954, апрель, вып. 2, № 4, pp. 69–84.

Попов П. С., "Значение слова и понятие" [Word-Meaning and Notion]. In: *Вопросы языкознания*, 1956, № 6, pp. 33–47.

Porzig W., *Das Wunder der Sprache*. Bern 1957, Francke Verlag.

Потебня А., *Мысль и язык* [Thought and Language]. Харьков 1913.

Poznański E., "Operacjonalizm po trzydziestu latach" [Operationism Thirty Years Later]. In: *Fragmenty filozoficzne. Seria druga. Księga Pamiątkowa ku uczczeniu ... T. Kotarbińskiego* [Fragmenta Philosophica. Part

Two. Memorial Publication Presented ... to T. Kotarbiński]. Warszawa 1959, PWN, pp. 178-218.

“Проблема соотношения языка и мышления” (обзор статей, поступивших в редакцию) [The Issue of the Relationship between Language and Thinking (A Review of Articles Received by the Editors)]. In: *Вопросы языкознания*, 1958, № 5, pp. 105–111.

Протасения П. Ф., “О так называемом языке жестов” [On the so-called Language of Gestures]. *Белорусский Гос. Университет им. Ленина. Научные труды по философии* [Lenin Byelorussian State University Philosophical Papers], вып. 1, Минск 1956, pp. 106–131.

Протопопов В. П., Рушкевич Е. А., *Исследование расстройств абстрактного мышления у психически больных и их физиологическая характеристика* [The Study of Disturbances in Abstract Thinking in Mental Patients and Their Physiological Characteristics]. Киев 1956, Госмедиздат УССР.

Quine W. van O., *From a Logical Point of View.** Cambridge (Mass.) 1953, Harvard Univ. Press.

Quine W. van O., “Meaning and Translation.” In: *On Translation*, pp. 148–172.

Quine W. van O., *Word and Object.* The Technology Press of the MIT, 1960.

Quinton A., “Linguistic Analysis*.” In: *Philosophy in the Mid-Century*, Vol. 2, pp. 146–202.

Рамишвили Д. И., “Неприемлемость теории первичности языка жестов с точки зрения психологических закономерностей речи” [On the Inacceptability of the Theory of the Priority of a Language of Gestures from the Point of View of Psychological Regularities of Speech]. In: *Известия Акад. Педагогических Наук РСФСР. Вопросы Психологии Мышления и Речи*, вып. 81, Москва 1956.

Ramsey F. P., *The Foundations of Mathematics and Other Logical Essays.* New York 1931, Harcourt, Brace & Co.

Rapoport A., *Operational Philosophy. Integrating Knowledge and Action.* New York 1953, Harper & Brothers.

Rapoport A., *Science and the Goals of Man. A Study in Semantic Orientation.* New York 1950, Harper & Brothers.

Rapoport A., “What is Semantics?” In: (Ed. S. I. Hayakawa) *Language, Meaning and Maturity*, pp. 3–18.

Rasiowa H., “Algebraic Models of Axiomatic Theories”. In: *Fundamenta Mathematicae*, 1955, t. 41, pp. 291–310.

Read A. W., “An Account of the Word ‘Semantics’ ”, In: *Word*, August 1948, Vol. 4, No. 2, pp. 78–97.

Reichenbach H., *Elements of Symbolic Logic.* New York 1947, The Macmillan Co.

Reichenbach H., *Experience and Prediction.* Chicago (Illinois) 1938, Univ. of Chicago Press.

Reichenbach H., *The Rise of Scientific Philosophy.* 1956, Univ. of California Press.

Révész G., *The Origins and Prehistory of Language.** Transl. J. Butler. London 1956, Longmans, Green & Co.

Révész G., "Thinking and Speaking". (A symposium). In: *Acta Psychologica*, 1954, Vol. X, No. 1–2.

Révész G., "Thought and Language", In: *Archivum Linguisticum*, 1950, Vol. 2, Fasc. 2, pp. 122–131.

Ревзин И. И., "Структуральная лингвистика, семантика и проблемы изучения слова" [Structural Linguistics, Semantics, and Issues of the Study of Words]. In *Вопросы языкознания* 1957, № 2, pp. 31—41.

Резников Л. О., "Гносеологические основы связи мышления и языка" (Gnoselogical Principles of the Relation between Thinking and Language]. In: *Ученые записки Ленингр. Ун-та* (Dissertations Published by Leningrad University], № 248, *Диалектический материализм.* Изд. Ленингр. Ун-та, 1958, pp. 136—163.

Резников Л. О., *Понятие и слово* [Notion and Word]. Ленинград 1958, Изд. Ленингр. Ун-та.

Richards I. A., *The Philosophy of Rhetoric.* New York 1950, Oxford Univ. Press.

Richards I. A., *Practical Criticism.* London 1935.

Richards I. A., *Principles of Literary Criticism.* London 1955, Routledge & Kegan Paul.

Roback A. A., *Destiny and Motivation in Language.* Cambridge (Mass.) 1954, Sci-Art Publishers.

Rothstein J., *Communication, Organization and Science.* Indian Hills (Colorado) 1958, The Falcon's Wing Press.

Rozwadowski J., *O zjawiskach i rozwoju języka* [Linguistic Phenomena and Language Development]. Kraków 1950, Gebethner.

Rozwadowski J., "Semantyka a gramatyka" [Semantics and Grammar]. In: *Wybór Pism* [Selected Works], t. III, pp. 138–160. Warszawa 1960, PWN.

Rozwadowski J., *Semazjologia, czyli nauka o rozwoju znaczeń wyrazów. Jej stan obecny, zasady i zadania* (Semasiology, or the Science of the Evolution of Meanings of Words. Its Present State, Principles and Tasks]. Lwów 1903, Tow. Filologiczne.

Rozwadowski J., "Słowotwórstwo i znaczenie wyrazów." (Word-Formation and the Meaning of Words]. In: *Wybór Pism* [Selected Works], Vol. III, pp. 21–95. Warszawa 1960. PWN.

Рубинштейн С. Л., *Бытие и сознание* (Existence and Consciousness]. Москва 1957, Изд. АН СССР.

Рубинштейн С. Л., „К вопросу о языке, речи и мышлении" (Concerning Language, Speech and Thinking]. In: *Вопросы языкознания*, 1957, № 2, pp. 42–48.

Рубинштей С. Л., *Основы общей психологии* (Гл. XI: "Речь") [Principles of General Psychology, (Chap. XI: "Speech")], Москва 1946, Госучпедгиз.

Рубинштей С. Л., *Принципы и пути развития психологии* [Psychology, Its Principles and Evolutions]. Москва 1959, Изд. АН СССР.

Rudek W., "W sprawie 'Uwag o semantyce' prof. W. Doroszewskiego" (Concerning Professor W. Doroszewski's "Notes on Semantics"] In: *Myśl Filozoficzna*, 1957, No. 1 (27), pp. 195–219.

Ruesch J., Kees W., *Nonverbal Communication*. Berkeley 1956, Univ. of California Press.

Russell B., *The Analysis of Mind*. London 1921, George Allen & Unwin.

Russell B., *Human Knowledge. Its Scope and Limits*. London 1948, George Allen & Unwin.

Russell B., *An Inquiry into Meaning and Truth*. London 1951, George Allen & Unwin.

Russell B., "On Denoting". In: B. Russell *Logic and Knowledge. Essays 1901–1950*. London 1956, George Allen & Unwin.

Russell B., "On Propositions: What They Are and How They Mean". In: B. Russell *Logic and Knowledge*.

Russell B., "The Philosophy of Logical Atomism". In: B. Russell *Logic and Knowledge*.

Russell B., *The Principles of Mathematics*. London 1937, George Allen & Unwin.

Russell B., "Vagueness". *Australasian Journal of Philosophy*, 1923, 1.

Russell B., "The Semantic Aspect of Aphasia". In: *Archivum Linguisticum*, 1956, Vol. 8, Fasc. 1, pp. 20–22.

Russell B., Whitehead A. N., *Einführung in die mathematische Logik*. Berlin 1932, Drei Masken Verlag.

Ryle G., "The Theory of Meaning". In: Ed. G. A. Mace *British Philosophy*..., pp. 237–264.

Sapir E., *Culture, Language and Personality. Selected Essays*. Berkeley 1957. Univ. of California Press.

Sapir E., *Language. An Introduction to the Study of Speech*. New York 1921, Harcourt, Brace & Co.

Saussure F. de, *Cours de linguistique générale*. Paris 1949, Payot.

Schaff A., *Poglądy filozoficzne Kazimierza Ajdukiewicza* (The Philosophical Views of Kazimierz Ajdukiewicz]. Warszawa 1952, KiW.

Schaff A., *Pojęcie i słowo. Próba analizy marksistowskiej* (An Attempt of a Marxist Analysis of Notion and Word]. Łódź 1946, "Książka".

Schaff A., "W sprawie oceny poglądów filozoficznych K. Ajdukiewicza" [Concerning the Evaluation of the Philosophical Views of K. Ajdukiewicz]. *Myśl Filozoficzna* 1953, nr. 3 (9), pp. 201–223.

Schaff A., *Z zagadnień marksistowskiej teorii prawdy* [Issues of the Marxist Theory of Truth]. Warszawa 1951, KiW.

Schlanck M. "Mechanism and Historical Materialism in Semantic Studies". In: *Science and Society*, 1947, Vol. XI, No. 2.

Schlanck M., "The Social Basis of Linguistics." In: *Science and Society*, 1936, Vol. 1, pp. 18–44.

Schlick M., *Allgemeine Erkenntnislehre*. Berlin 1918.

Schlick M., "Form and Content. An Introduction to Philosophical Thinking". In: M. Schlick *Gesammelte Aufsätze 1926–1936*. Wien 1938, Gerald und Co.

Schlick M. "Meaning and Verification." In: M. Schlick *Gesammelte Aufsätze 1926–1936*.

Schlick M., "Über das Fundament der Erkenntnis." In: M. Schlick *Gesammelte Aufsätze 1926–1936*.

Schlick M., "Die Wende der Philosophie". In: *Erkenntnis*, 1930-1931, B. 1, pp. 4-11.

Schmidt W., *Deutsche Sprachkunde*. Berlin 1959, Volk und Wissen Volkseigener Verlag.

Schuchardt-Brevier. *Ein Vademekum der allgemeinen Sprachwissenschaft*. Halle 1922, M. Niemeyer.

Sechehaye A., Bally Ch., Frei H., "Pour l'arbitraire du signe". In: *Acta Linguistica*, 1941, Vol. II, Fasc. 3, pp. 165–169.

Semantica — Archivio di Filosofia (Organo dell Istituto di Studi Filosofici). Roma 1955, Fratelli Bocca Editori.

Semantics and the Philosophy of Language. [Ed. by L. Linsky], Urbana 1952, Univ. of Illinois Press.

Серебренников В. А., "К проблеме связи явлений языка с историей общества" [On the Relation between Linguistic Phenomena and Social History]. In: *Вопросы языкознания*, 1953, 1.

Шаумян С. К., "Лингвистические проблемы кибернетики и структурная лингвистика" [Linguistic Issues of Cybernetics and Structural Linguistics]. In: *Вопросы философии*, 1960, № 9.

Шемякин Ф. Н., „Теория Леви-Брюля на службе империалистической реакции" [Lévy-Bruhl's Theory in the Service of Imperialist Reaction]. In: *Философские записки*. Вып. 5.

Шенгельс Е. И., "О грамматических значениях в плане содержания" [Grammatical Meanings from the Point of View of Content]. In: *Принципы научного анализа языка*, Москва 1959, Изд. ВПШ pp. 45–63.

Шор Р., *Язык и общество* [Language and Society]. Москва 1926, Изд. Работник Просвещения.

Шорохова Е. В., *Материалистическое учение И. П. Павлова о сигнальных системах* [Pavlov's Materialistic Theory of Systems of Signals]. Москва 1955, Изд. АН СССР.

Смирницкий А. И., *Объективность существования языка* [The Objective Existence of Language]. Москва 1954, Изд. Моск. Унив.

Смирницкий А. И. "Значение слова" [The Meaning of Words]. In: *Вопросы языкознания*, 1955, № 2, pp. 79–89.

Smith B. L., Lasswell H. D., Casey R. D., *Propaganda, Communication and Public Opinion.* Princeton 1946, Princeton Univ. Press.

Sondel B., *The Humanity of Words. A Primer of Semantics.* New York 1957. The World Publ. Co.

Спиркин А. Г. "Происхождение языка и его роль в формировании мышления" [Language: Its Origin and Function in the Formation of Thinking]. In: *Мышление и язык*, ред. А. П. Гурский, pp. 3-72.

Сталин И., *Марксизм и вопросы языкознания* [Marxism and the Problems of Linguistics]. Москва 1950, Госполитиздат.

Stebbing L. S., *A Modern Introduction to Logic.* London 1945, Methuen & Co.

Stegmüller W., *Das Wahrheitsproblem und die Idee der Semantik.* Wien 1957, Springer Verlag.

Stern G., *Meaning and Change of Meaning.* Göteborg 1931, Elanders boktryckei aktiebolag.

Stevenson Ch. L., *Ethics and Language.* New Haven 1948, Yale Univ. Press.

Stopa R., *Narodziny myśli i mowy ludzkiej* [The Birth of Human Thought and Speech]. Kraków 1948, Książnica Powszechna.

Straus E., *Vom Sinn der Sinne. Ein Beitrag zur Grundlegung der Psychologie.* Berlin 1956, Springer Verlag.

Strawson P. F., *Introduction to Logical Theory.* London 1952, Methuen & Co.

Studies in the Philosophy of Charles Sanders Peirce. Ed. by Ph. P. Wiener and Fr. H. Young, Cambridge (Mass.) 1952, Harvard Univ. Press.

Sturtevant E. H. *An Introduction to Linguistic Science.* New Haven 1950, Yale Univ. Press.

Suszko R., "Logika formalna a niektóre zagadnienia teorii poznania" [Formal Logic and Certain Issues of Epistemology]. In: *Myśl Filozoficzna*, 1957, nr. 2 (28), pp. 27–56 and nr. 3 (29), pp. 34–67.

Suszko R., "Syntactic Structure and Semantical Reference". In: *Studia Logica*, 1958, Vol. 8, pp. 213–244.

Symbols and Society. Ed. by L. Bryson, L. Finkelstein, H. Hoagland, R. M. Mac-Iver. New York 1955, Harper & Brothers.

Szober St., *Wybór pism* [Selected Works]. Warszawa 1959, PWN.

Szober St., *Zarys językoznawstwa ogólnego* [An Outline of General Linguistics]. Z. 1., Warszawa 1924, Wyd. Tow. Miłośników Języka Polskiego.

Tarski A., *Logic, Semantics, Metamathematics.* Oxford 1956, Clarendon Press.

Tarski A., "O pojęciu wynikania logicznego" [The Concept of Logical Consequence]. In: *Przegląd Filozoficzny,* R. 39, 1936, z. 1, pp. 58–68.

Tarski A., "O ugruntowaniu naukowej semantyki" [Laying Foundations for Scientific Semantics]. In: *Przegląd Filozoficzny,* R. 39, 1936, z. 1, pp. 50-57.

Tarski A., *Pojęcie prawdy w językach nauk dedukcyjnych* [The Concept of Truth in Formalized Languages]. Warszawa 1933, Nakł. Tow. Nauk. Warsz.

Tarski A., "The Semantic Conception of Truth and the Foundations of Semantics". In: *Philosophy and Phenomenological Research,* 4 (1944). Reprinted in: [Ed. L. Linsky] *Semantics* ..., pp. 11–47.

Thompson M., *The Pragmatic Philosophy of Ch. S. Peirce.* Chicago 1953, Univ. of Chicago Press.

Травничек Фр., "Некоторые замечания о значении слова и понятий" [Some Remarks on the Meaning of Word and of Notion]. In: *Вопросы языкознания,* 1956, № 1, pp. 74–76.

Trier J., *Der deutsche Wortschatz im Sinnbezirk des Verstandes. Die Geschichte eines sprachlichen Feldes.* Heidelberg 1931, Carl Winters Universitätsbuchhandlung.

Troubetzkoy N. S., *Principes de phonologie.* Paris 1957, Libr. C. Klincksieck.

Ullman St., "The Concept of Meaning in Linguistics". In: *Archivum Linguisticum,* 1956, Vol. 8, Fasc. 1, pp. 12–20.

Ullman St., *The Principles of Semantics. A Linguistic Approach to Meaning.** Oxford 1957, Basil Blackwell.

Ullman St., "Word-form and Word-meaning". In: *Archivum Linguisticum,* 1949, Vol. I, Fasc. 2, pp. 126–139.

Urban W. M., "Cassirer's Philosophy of Language". In: *The Philosophy of Ernst Cassirer.* Ed. by P. A. Schlipp. New York 1958, Tudor Publ. Co., pp. 401–441.

Urban W. M., *Language and Reality.* London 1951, George Allen & Unwin.

Urmson J. O., *Philosophical Analysis. Its Development Between the Two World Wars.* Oxford 1956, At the Clarendon Press.

Ushenko A. P., *The Field Theory of Meaning.* Ann Arbor 1958, Univ. of Michigan Press.

Vendryes J. *Le langage. Introduction linguistique a l'histoire.* Paris 1921.

Виноградов В. В., „Основные типы лексических значений слов" [Fundamental Types of Lexical Meanings of Words]. In: *Вопросы языкознания,* 1953, № 5, pp. 3–29.

Виноградов В. В., "Свободная дискуссия в 'Правде' по вопросам языкознания и ее значение для дальнейшего развития советской науки о языке". [A Free Discussion in "Pravda" on Linguistic Problems and Its Significance for the Promotion of Soviet Studies of Language]. In: *Вопросы языкознания в свете трудов И. В. Сталина* [Problems of Linguistics in the Light of the Works of J. Stalin] 1950, Изд. Моск. Ун-та, pp. 5–31.

Волков А. Г., Хабаров И. А., "К вопросу о природе языкового знака" [Concerning the Nature of the Language Sign]. In: *Вопросы философии*, 1959, № 11, pp. 79–90.

Волошинов В. Н., *Марксизм и философия языка* (*Основные проблемы социологического метода в науке о языке*) [Marxism and the Philosophy of Language (Basic Problems of the Sociological Method in Linguistics)]. Ленинград 1930.

Vossler K., *Geist und Kultur in der Sprache.* Heidelberg 1925, Carl Winters Universitätsbuchhandlung.

Востриков А. В., "Классики марксизма-ленинизма о связи языка и мышления" [The Classics of Marxism-Leninism on the Relation between Language and Thinking]. In: *Вопросы философии,* 1952, № 3, pp. 47–64.

Выготский Л. С. *Мышление и речь. Психологические исследования* [Thinking and Speech. Psychological Researches]. Москва 1934, Госсоцэкгиз.

Wallon H. *De l'acte à la pensée. Essai de psychologie comparée.* Paris 1942, Flammarion.

Walpole H., *Semantics. The Nature of Words and Their Meanings.* New York 1941, W. W. Norton & Co.

Weinberg H. L., *Levels of Knowing and Existence. Studies in General Semantics.* New York 1959, Harper & Brothers.

Weinberg J. R., *An Examination of Logical Positivism,* London 1936, Kegan Paul.

Weisgerber J. L., *Das Gesetz der Sprache.** Heidelberg 1951, Quelle und Mayer.

Weisgerber J. L., *Die Muttersprache im Aufbau unserer Kultur.** Düsseldorf 1957, Pädagogischer Verlag Schwann.

Weisgerber J. L., *Die Sprache unter den Kräften des menschlichen Daseins.* Düsseldorf 1954, Pädagogischer Verlag Schwann.

Weisgerber J. L., *Vom Weltbild der deutschen Sprache.** Halbband 1 und 2. Düsseldorf 1953–1954, Pädagogischer Verlag Schwann.

Welby V., *What is Meaning? Studies in the Development of Significance.* London 1903, The Macmillan Co.

Wells R., "Philosophy of Language". In: *Philosophy in the Mid-Century,* Vol. 2, pp. 139–145.

Wendt P. R., "The Language of Pictures". In: [Ed. S. I. Hayakawa] *Our Language and Our World*, pp. 247–255.

Whatmough J.,*Language.A Modern Synthesis*. London 1956, Secker & Warburg.

Whatmough J., *Language. A Modern Synthesis.*) 1957, The Mentor Series.

Whitehead A. N., *Symbolism. Its Meaning and Effect*. Cambridge (Mass). 1958. At the Univ. Press.

Whitehead A. N., Russell B., *Principia Mathematica.* Vol. 1. Cambridge 1925, Cambridge Univ. Press.

Whorf B. L., "An American Indian Model of the Universe". In: B. L. Whorf, *Language, Thought and Reality.*

Whorf B. L., "Language, Mind and Reality". In: B. L. Whorf, *Language, Thought and Reality.*

Whorf B. L., *Language, Thought and Reality. Selected Writings.* 1957. Massachussetts Institute of Technology.

Whorf B. L., "The Relation of Habitual Thought and Behavior to Language". In: B. L. Whorf *Language, Thought and Reality.*

Whorf B. L., "Science and Linguistics". In: B. L. Whorf *Language, Thought and Reality.*

Wiener N., *The Human Use of Human Beings. Cybernetics and Society.* New York 1956, Doubleday & Co.

Wilson J., *Language and the Pursuit of Truth.* Cambridge 1956, Cambridge Univ. Press.

Wilson M. L., *The Concept of Language.* University of Toronto Press 1959.

*Wissenschaftliche Weltauffassung. Der Wiener Kreis**. Wien 1929, Artur Wolf.

Wittgenstein L., *Philosophical Investigations.* Oxford 1953, Basil Blackwell.

Wittgenstein L., *Tractatus Logico-Philosophicus.* London 1933, Kegan Paul, Trench, Trubner & Co.

Wundt W., *Vőlkerpsychologie.* B. 1 und 2: *Die Sprache.* Leipzig 1911-1912, W. Engelmann.

Zawadowski L., "Rzeczywisty i pozorny wpływ kontekstu na znaczenie" [The Real and the Apparent Influence of Context upon Meaning]. In: *Sprawozdania Wrocl. Tow. Nauk.* [Transactions of the Wrocław Scientific Society], 4, 1949, dod. 2, Wrocław 1951.

Жинкин Н. И. *Механизмы речи* [The Mechanisms of Speech]. 1958, Изд. Акад. Педагогических Наук.

Звегинцев В. А., *Эстетический идеализм в языкознании. К. Фосслер и его школа* [Aesthetical Idealism in Linguistics. K. Vossler and His School]. Москва 1956, Изд. Моск. Ун-та.

Звегинцев В. А., *Проблема знаковости языка* [The Issue of the Sign-nature of Language]. Москва 1956, Изд. Моск. Ун-та.

Звегинцев В.А. *Семасиология* [Semasiology]. Москва 1957, Изд. Моск. Ун-та.

INDEX OF NAMES